eMarketing eXcellence

eMarketing eXcellence
The Heart of eBusiness

Second edition

PR Smith and Dave Chaffey

ELSEVIER
BUTTERWORTH
HEINEMANN

AMSTERDAM • BOSTON • HEIDELBERG • LONDON • NEW YORK • OXFORD
PARIS • SAN DIEGO • SAN FRANCISCO • SINGAPORE • SYDNEY • TOKYO

Elsevier Butterworth-Heinemann
Linacre House, Jordan Hill, Oxford OX2 8DP
30 Corporate Drive, Burlington, MA 01803

First published 2002
Reprinted 2003 (twice)
Second edition published 2005

British Library Cataloguing in Publication Data
A catalogue record for this book is available from the British Library

Library of Congress Control Number: 2005924567
A catalogue record for this book is available from the Library of Congress

ISBN 0 7506 6359 6

For information on all Elsevier Butterworth-Heinemann
publications visit our website at http://www.books.elsevier.com

Working together to grow
libraries in developing countries

www.elsevier.com | www.bookaid.org | www.sabre.org

ELSEVIER   BOOK AID International   Sabre Foundation

Typeset by Charon Tec Pvt. Ltd, Chennai, India
www.charontec.com
Printed and bound in Great Britain

Contents

Preface

Why eMarketing eXcellence?

E-marketing impacts all aspects of marketing from strategy and planning through the marketing mix, marketing communications, buyer behaviour to marketing research. *eMarketing eXcellence* highlights the most significant opportunities and defines the new marketing approaches needed.

E-marketing impacts all organizations. *eMarketing eXcellence* shows how to assess the extent of the impact and then develop and resource an effective plan.

E-marketing does not exist in a vacuum. Planning must ensure that e-marketing integrates with the marketing objectives and the corporate aims of moving towards e-business. *eMarketing eXcellence* shows how to develop a plan that achieves this integration.

The e-marketing imperative is further indicated by success stories from leading adopters of e-marketing such as Alliance and Leicester, BMW, Diageo, ING Direct, Siebel and TUI who have found e-marketing to be effective and are substantially increasing their online marketing expenditure to double-digit percentages of total marketing communications spend.

How is eMarketing eXcellence structured?

eMarketing eXcellence has been developed for efficient learning. It is structured around ten self-contained chapters, each of which supports learning through a clear structure based on sections with clear learning outcomes, summaries and self-test questions. The E-marketing Insight boxes give varied perspectives from practitioners and academics while the E-marketing Excellence boxes give examples of best practice.

Chapter 1 Introduction to e-marketing

This chapter introduces e-marketing and its benefits and risks. It describes the difference between e-commerce, e-business and e-marketing; the dangers of sloppy e-marketing; how to present a business case for going online and the benefits – Sell, Serve, Save, Speak and Sizzle.

Chapter 2 ReMix

The digital world affects every aspect of business, every aspect of marketing and every aspect of the marketing mix. Some argue that physical distribution, selling and pricing absorb the

biggest impact. In fact all the elements of the mix are affected by this new world. This chapter shows you exactly how.

Chapter 3 E-models

The business world is changing faster than ever before. Old approaches and models are being turned on their head. The white heat of change causes many business people to wake up sweating in the middle of the night and check the locks on their old business models. To no avail. The wired and unwired world has moved on overnight turning old models over and paving the way for a host of new business models.

Chapter 4 E-customers

This chapter looks inside the online customer's mind. We explore customers' issues, worries, fears and phobias as well as other motivators for going online … and how marketers can respond to these behaviours. We also look at on-site behaviour, the online buying process, web analytics and the many influencing variables. We finish with a look to the future, your future and how to keep an eye on the e-customer.

Chapter 5 E-tools

This is where the online world begins to get really interesting. Once we move beyond the PC and into the wireless world of pervasive technology, a whole new vision appears. Always on, everywhere, easy to use, integrated marketing will exploit these new tools.

Chapter 6 Site design

This chapter will make you think about web sites a little differently. As you read through the chapter, we urge you to draw deep on your web site experiences and the key design components you observe. We illustrate best practice in design such as persona/scenario analysis of customer journeys, usability, accessibility and information architecture.

Chapter 7 Traffic building

Having a great web site is absolutely no use if no one uses it. This chapter shows you how to build traffic – how to acquire visitors to your site. The more experienced e-marketer reading this will find some refreshing reminders and new information sources while the less experienced should take careful note of the mix of traffic generating techniques including search engine marketing, online PR, online partnerships, interactive advertising, opt-in e-mail and viral marketing.

Chapter 8 E-CRM

Online customer relationship management is packed with fundamental commonsense principles. Surprisingly, many companies do not adhere to them. Serving and nurturing customers into lifetime customers makes sense as existing customers are, on average, five times more profitable. At the heart of this is permission marketing based on a good database – the marketer's memory bank, which if used correctly, creates arguably the most valuable asset in any company.

Chapter 9 E-business

Why did the dotcom disasters occur? Clicks-and-mortar companies generally outperform pureplay Internet companies. Why didn't these new e-businesses survive? Where did they go wrong? The answer is that they weren't e-businesses. They weren't even businesses since many were ignorant of business essentials such as the need to integrate front-office systems with back-office systems, keeping close to customers, delivering real added value, etc. This chapter clarifies what is meant by e-business, a much abused concept.

Chapter 10 E-planning

E-marketing is fundamentally the discipline of marketing set in the context of the e-business e-environment. So, not surprisingly, the successful e-marketing plan will be based on traditional marketing disciplines and planning techniques, but only if these are then adapted for the new media environment and then mixed with new techniques adopted for the purpose. This chapter shows you how to do this, based on the well-established principles of SOSTAC® and the 3M resources.

Who is this book for?

Marketing and business professionals

This book has been developed to support a range of professionals involved with e-marketing.

- *Marketing managers* responsible for defining an e-marketing strategy, implementing strategy or maintaining the company web site alongside traditional marketing activities.
- *E-marketing specialists* such as new media managers, e-marketing managers and e-commerce managers responsible for directing, integrating and implementing their organizations' e-marketing.
- *Senior managers and directors* seeking to identify the right e-business and e-marketing approaches to support their organizations' strategy.
- *Information systems managers* also involved in developing and implementing e-marketing and e-commerce strategies.
- *Technical project managers* or *web masters* who may understand the technical details of building a site, but want to enhance their knowledge of e-marketing.

Students

This book has been created as the core text for the CIM e-marketing professional development award. As such, *eMarketing eXcellence* will support the following students in their studies:

- *Professionals studying for the CIM E-marketing award.* The book provides comprehensive coverage of the syllabus for this award and is the core text.

- *Postgraduate students on specialist masters degrees in electronic commerce, electronic business or e-marketing and generic programmes in Marketing Management, MBA, Certificate in Management or Diploma in Management Studies* which involve modules or electives for e-business and e-marketing.
- *Undergraduates on business programmes* which include marketing modules on the use of digital marketing. This may include specialist degrees such as electronic business, electronic commerce, Internet marketing and marketing or general business degrees such as business studies, business administration and business management.
- *Postgraduate and undergraduate project students* who select this topic for final year projects/ dissertations – this book is an excellent source of resources for these students.
- *Undergraduates completing work placement* involved with different aspects of e-marketing such as managing an intranet or company web site.

What does the book offer to lecturers teaching these courses?

This book is intended to be a comprehensive guide to all aspects of deploying e-marketing within an organization. It builds on existing theories and concepts and questions the validity of these models in the light of the differences between the Internet and other media, and references the emerging body of literature specific to e-business, e-commerce and e-marketing. Lecturers will find this book has a good range of case study examples to support their teaching. Web links given in the text and at the end of each chapter highlight key information sources for particular topics.

Learning features

A range of features have been incorporated into *eMarketing eXcellence* to help the reader get the most out of it. They have been designed to assist understanding, reinforce learning and help readers find information easily. The features are described in the order you will find them.

At the start of each chapter:

- *Overview:* a short introduction to the relevance of the chapter and what you will learn.
- *Overall learning outcome:* a list describing what readers can learn through reading the chapter and completing the self-test.
- *Chapter topics:* chapter contents and the learning objectives for each section.

In each chapter:

- *E-marketing Excellence boxes:* real-world examples of best practice approaches referred to in the text.
- *E-marketing Insight boxes:* quotes, opinions and frameworks from industry practitioners and academics.

- *Definitions:* key e-marketing terms are highlighted in bold and the glossary contains succinct definitions.
- *Web links:* where appropriate, web addresses are given for further information, particularly those to update information.
- *Section summaries:* intended as revision aids and to summarize the main learning points from the section.

At the end of each chapter:

- *Summary:* also intended as revision aids and to summarize the main learning points from the chapter.
- *References:* these are references to books, articles or papers referred to within the chapter.
- *Further reading:* supplementary texts or papers on the main themes of the chapter. Where appropriate a brief commentary is provided on recommended supplementary reading on the main themes of the chapters.
- *Web links:* these are significant sites that provide further information on the concepts and topics of the chapter. All web site references within the chapter, for example company sites, are not repeated here. The web site address prefix 'http://' is omitted for clarity except where the address does not start with 'www'.
- *Self-test questions:* short questions which will test understanding of terms and concepts described in the chapter and help relate them to your organization.

At the end of the book:

- *Glossary:* a list of all definitions of key terms and phrases used within the main text.
- *Index:* all key words and abbreviations referred to in the main text.

Preface to the second edition

The e-marketing world has moved on since we wrote the first edition of this book (2001/2). Many of the forecasts that we made have proved true – most of the dotcoms did die; more customers continue to flock online; all businesses need to integrate 'e' into their businesses. Many won't survive without it. Nothing too surprising there, you might say. What is surprising is that there are still many many examples of sloppy e-marketing. Some of this sloppy marketing stems from a lack of integration of 'e' into other business processes. This is possibly because many marketers overestimated the short-term tactical impact of the Internet and currently underestimate its medium to longer term strategic impact.

Many of the permission-based approaches to e-marketing we recommended in the first edition have now become legal requirements due to European and US laws such as the European Community Electronic Communications Directive and the US 'CAN-SPAM' laws. E-marketers also now have to make sure their web sites are accessible to be compliant with the Disability and Discrimination Act.

Techniques for improving site design have become more refined, and we also reference these in the second edition. We look at how usability studies and persona/scenario analysis and a planned information architecture can be used to develop customer-centric sites. Traffic building too has changed with search engine optimization remaining an important technique, but with greatly increased importance of pay per click search engine marketing and affiliate marketing for e-retailers.

Despite the constant changing nature of markets, the fundamental principle remains the same – stick close to customers. Talk to them. Listen to them. Understand them better than they understand themselves. Become customer experts. Be crystal clear about the target markets, who they are, how you access them, why you are going after them. How you compare to competition both in reality and in customers' perceptions. Then develop credibility before raising visibility. After that, strong and clear value propositions help to win customers' and prospects' permission (permission marketing). Use e-marketing analysis techniques such as surveys, audience data and web analytics to refine your online offering. You can then refine your proposition and develop relations (relationship marketing) through effective, usable web sites and timely reminders – whether by opt-in email, text messages, direct mail or even telephone (permission allowing).

Many readers will be moving from their first e-plan onto the next generation of e-plans. We hope this book helps to move you along the evolutionary path towards e-plans that really help to boost performance in an integrated way. Although the benefits of e-marketing span right across an organization's functions (customer feedback, customer service, product enhancement, sales, finance/payment, delivery, administration and marketing), we tend to link it strongly to marketing communications plans. The reality is that any e-marketing plan needs to be a part of a marketing communications plan and it also should be part of a broader marketing plan. Needless to say the e-plan should fit in with the overall business plan. Enjoy the read and let us know what you think.

Paul (www.prsmith.org) and Dave (www.davechaffey.com)

Acknowledgements

Our thanks to our many friends and colleagues who have helped us in many ways. In particular, Paul Smith would like to thank Alison Bowditch, Martin Burke, Lou Burrows, Peter Hurst, Jan Klin, Mike Langford, Martin Lindstrom, Gerry McGovern, Paul O'Sullivan, Steve Saunders and John Twomey. Dave Chaffey would like to thank the following for e-inspiration: Bryan Eisenberg, Ashley Friedlein, Jim Novo, Jim Sterne and John Woods.

All web site screenshots included in this book are examples of best practice. We thank all companies who have agreed to have their sites included and offer our apologies to those it has not been possible to contact.

Finally thanks to the Smith clan: Beverley, Aran, Cian and Lily and the Chaffey clan: Sal, Zoe and Sarah.

Chapter

1

Introduction to
e-marketing

'Execution is the missing key between aspirations and results'.

Bossiddy and Charan, 2004

This chapter introduces e-marketing and its benefits and risks. It describes the difference between e-commerce, e-business and e-marketing; the dangers of sloppy e-marketing; how to present a business case for going online and the benefits – Sell, Serve, Save, Speak and Sizzle.

OVERALL LEARNING OUTCOME

By the end of this chapter you will be able to:

- Describe the development of the electronic marketspace
- Outline an approach to developing an e-marketing plan
- Describe the key benefits of e-marketing.

CHAPTER TOPIC	LEARNING OBJECTIVE
1.1 Introduction	Outline the benefits and risks of e-marketing
1.2 The wired-up world	Outline the characteristics of the new marketspace
1.3 B2C, B2B, C2B and C2C	Identify different forms of collaboration between marketplace members
1.4 E-definitions	Describe the difference between e-commerce, e-business and e-marketing
1.5 Sloppy e-marketing	Avoid basic e-marketing mistakes
1.6 Objectives	Outline the five basic e-marketing objectives
1.7 Objective – Sell	Define objectives for selling to the customer online
1.8 Objective – Serve	Define objectives for serving the customer online
1.9 Objective – Speak	Define objectives for speaking to the customer online
1.10 Objective – Save	Define objectives for saving online
1.11 Objective – Sizzle	Define objectives for enhancing the brand online
1.12 Introduction to e-strategy	Outline approaches to achieving e-marketing objectives
1.13 Tactics, action and control	Outline e-marketing tactics, actions and control

1.1 Introduction

This chapter introduces you to the world of **e-marketing**; its background and its benefits. It explores the current e-marketing situation, e-marketing definitions as well as examples of good and bad e-marketing. The chapter also reviews the purpose, objectives, reasons or benefits of going online. Finally, a strategic perspective is suggested that can be used before engaging in any of the more tactical e-tools.

The chapter is structured using a simple *aide-mémoire*, called **SOSTAC®**. Although SOSTAC® is used by thousands of professionals to produce all kinds of plans (marketing plans, corporate plans, advertising plans and e-marketing plans), we won't look at building an e-marketing plan until Chapter 10. Instead we'll use SOSTAC® at this stage to provide a structure to this introductory chapter.

INTRODUCING SOSTAC® PLANNING FOR E-MARKETING

SOSTAC® stands for Situation, Objectives and Strategy, Tactics, Action and Control (Figure 1.1). It is described in more detail in Smith (1998, 2001) and Smith *et al.* (1999, 2004) who note that each stage is not discrete, but there is some overlap during each stage of planning – previous stages may be revisited and refined, as indicated by the reverse arrows in Figure 1.1. The planning stages are:

- **Situation Analysis** means 'where are we now?' (In the context of this chapter, this includes definition of 'e' terms, growth in users and change in the marketplace as well as examples of good and bad e-marketing).
- **Objectives** means 'where do we want to be?' Why bother going on-line, what are the benefits, what is the purpose of going to all of this effort? We describe five main objectives, reasons or benefits of going online.
- **Strategy** means 'how do we get there?' Strategy summarizes how to fulfil the objectives. What stage of 'e'volution and level of database integration is required, what segments and

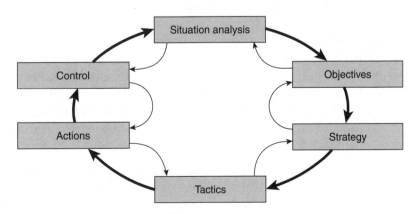

Figure 1.1   SOSTAC® planning framework

positioning should drive the overall marketing mix and which e-tools should be selected? Getting your e-strategy right is crucial. As Kenichi Ohmae says (Ohmae, 1999), 'there's no point rowing harder if you're rowing in the wrong direction'.

- **Tactics** reviews the tactical e-tools and the details of the marketing mix; we won't address them in any detail in this introductory chapter.
- **Actions** refers to action plans and project management skills – essential skills we won't go into in this chapter.
- **Control** looks at how you know if your e-efforts are working, and what improvements can be made – again, we won't delve in too deeply in this chapter.

As mentioned, we are going to use SOSTAC® not to build a plan but to give a structure to this chapter. Later on, in Chapter 10, we will show how any e-marketing plan needs to be a part of a marketing communications plan and how it should also fit into a broader marketing plan. For now, we will use SOSTAC® as a structure for this introductory chapter.

SECTION SUMMARY 1.1

Introduction to e-marketing

The SOSTAC® planning framework is used to structure this chapter. SOSTAC® is:

- **Situation** – where are we now?
- **Objectives** – where do we want to be?
- **Strategy** – how do we get there?
- **Tactics** – which tactical tools do we use to implement strategy?
- **Actions** – which action plans are required to implement strategy?
- **Control** – how do we manage the strategy process?

1.2 Situation – the wired-up world

Let's consider the current situation of e-marketing – where the marketplace migrates into the **electronic marketspace**. How significant is this change? The Internet is continuing to grow rapidly and seamlessly across borders and into an online world already inhabited by almost a billion customers. Given its scale and the benefits it offers to these customers and businesses, it is a big part of the future of all businesses. The Internet is far more than 'just another channel to market' – a misguided phrase that is heard surprisingly frequently. We will explain this later under the 5 Benefits (or 5 Ss).

Despite the vast number of people (and businesses) buying online, don't you think it's a little weird when you consider that millions, billions and even trillions of dollars, pounds and euros pass seamlessly through wires interconnecting lots of devices all around the world? Perhaps even weirder when you consider a lot of it will be wireless. Some say it's 'surreal' others say it's 'sublime' and others again say 'ridiculous' when you consider that the direction of many of these millions, billions and trillions will be determined by **robots**, **info-bots**, **shopping-bots**, automated **portals** and **infomediaries**. The future Weird Wired World may sound like a wonder of convenience when our washing machines negotiate the best price and choose the best utility supplier for any particular wash – courtesy of embedded chips complete with Internet access. Or is it introducing unnecessary complexity for which demand is limited?

THE CONNECTED WORLD

And it's not just washing machines, but rather anything and everything can be wired up, or connected, to the Internet. The old world way of accessing the Internet was via the PC. What are the up-and-coming ways of accessing the Internet? **Interactive digital TV**, interactive radio, interactive kiosks, mobile phones, palm tops, planes, trains and automobiles all access the Internet. The **convergence** of these new digital access devices is described in more detail in Chapter 5. In fact the average luxury car today has more computing power in it than the rocket that landed on the moon. Cars can also be 'connected' so that they can alert roadside repair companies to your location before you actually break down. Just about anything can be wired up, courtesy of the powerful combination of computer chips and cordless or wireless technology such as **WAP** technology (Wireless Application Protocol) and **Bluetooth** as used by mobile phones and other hand-held devices. Everything can be wired up – even Barbie dolls. In fact, MIT (Massachusetts Institute of Technology) Director, Nicholas Negroponte forecasts that by 2010 'there will be more wired up Barbie dolls than Americans'.

FORECASTS

In the UK, where consumers spend more time online than watching TV, 50 000 home users are now switching to broadband each week. With 27 million people online in the UK in 2004 and 1 billion projected to be online globally during 2005, it is easy to see the long-term importance of e-marketing. Anyone wanting to survive in the hyper competitive global marketplace (some call the 'digital networked economy') must develop their e-marketing now. There is no real choice for most businesses as this global digital networked economy brings with it new, previously unseen and unheard of, competitors right into local businesses' back yard. In Europe alone, large audiences flock online to eBay (65 m), Amazon (47 m), Yahoo Shopping (17 m) and Wal-Mart (12 m). Many of these competitors simply didn't exist ten years ago. We cannot imagine what the next ten years may bring. The Interactive Media in Retail (www.imrg.org) trade body suggest that by 2009 a quarter of all the UK's shopping will be online with a further 20 per cent of purchases influenced by online research. One thing is for sure – it is highly unlikely that your organization will survive if it doesn't adapt to the rapidly changing online marketplace.

Compilations of global numbers of Internet users (Figure 1.2) show a dramatic growth. They also show the importance of mobile media. There are significantly more mobile subscribers than Internet users and the rate of growth is larger. Notice that the penetration per

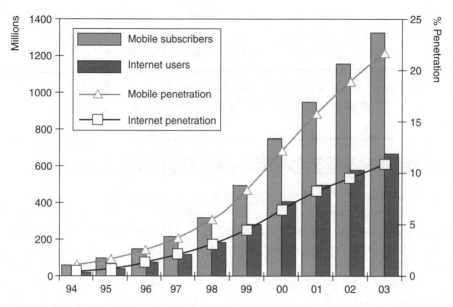

Figure 1.2 Worldwide trends in number of Internet users and mobile subscribers (vertical axis) and penetration per 100 adults. (*Source:* ITU, 2004)

100 adult population is still relatively low since use of these media is much lower in developing countries – what is sometimes called the 'digital divide'.

Forecasts, however, suggest that over the next few years the growth in the number of new Internet users amongst individuals and companies accessing via PC will decline. Is this the end of Internet growth? No – growth will continue as mobile **3G** Internet devices increase both the number of users and, more importantly, their frequency and duration of use. On top of this they will spend more as they enjoy more convenience, discover better deals and slowly worry less about fraud. They will increase their 'share of wallet', or share of spending towards online spending. They may also spend longer online. Already Americans spend more time online but visit fewer sites than Europeans. The process of consolidation – where people visit fewer sites to satisfy their wide ranging needs – has started in America and is following in Europe. So now is the time to ensure your e-marketing is good enough to catch the new adopters before they select their chosen few sites.

E-MARKETING INSIGHT

B2B access in developed countries

In most developed countries, more than three-quarters of businesses have Internet access, regardless of size (Figure 1.3). Over 95% of medium sized companies and over 99% of large companies are connected. Micro businesses are less connected, and in some countries – particularly France and the UK – they are 'clicking off'.

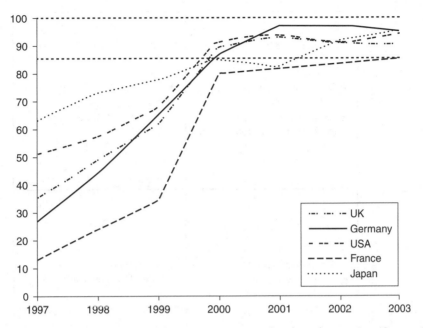

Figure 1.3   Percentage of businesses with Internet access in developed countries. (*Source:* DTI, 2003)

The wired-up world

More customers are spending an increasing part of their lives in the virtual world. They are using automated tools to find the products that best meet their needs. Marketers need to respond to customers' needs in this new wired-up world.

1.3 Situation – B2C, B2B, C2B and C2C

The options for digital communications between a business and its customers are summarized in Figure 1.4. Surprisingly, the bulk of Internet business both now and in the foreseeable future comes from business-to-business or industrial and commercial markets known as **B2B** (business-to-business) and not consumer markets known as business-to-consumer (**B2C**) markets (like cars and cola).

B2B AND B2C

This is where the bulk of online business occurs. Most estimates suggest that B2B companies will reap ten times more revenue than their B2C counterparts. Once upon a time marketing used to learn from the **FMCG** manufacturers like Guinness, Coca-Cola and Heinz, while

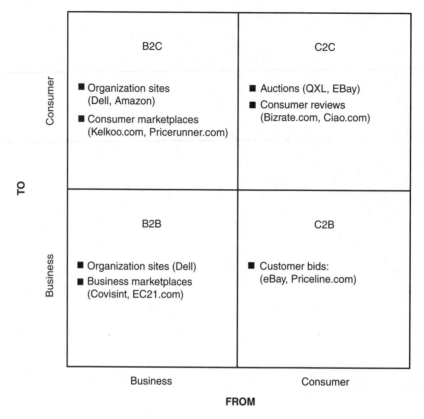

Figure 1.4 Options for online communications between an organization and its customers

industrial marketing, or B2B marketing, was considered by some to be less exciting. This is now no longer the case.

In the online world, B2B is already much bigger than B2C. Several years ago General Electric made the decision to procure $1 billion worth of purchases online in year one, followed by $3 billion in year two, followed by total procurement online. Cisco systems announced many years ago that they will no longer do business with suppliers who can't take orders over the web. Major organizations, such as government councils, are also moving online, e.g. from 2005 the British Government's Local District Councils only procure their goods and services online.

Several years ago Ford and General Motors combined forces through the **B2B marketplace** Covisint (www.covisint.net) and moved their then $300 and $500 billion dollar supply chains online. So the B2B e-world is already vast and there is much more to come. Already large-scale trading is occurring.

C2B

Whether B2C or B2B, don't forget **C2B**. Customer-to-business models play a significant role in successful e-marketing businesses whether B2B or B2C. Customers and communities evolve around the business, influence and eventually drive the business. C2B models are explored in Chapter 3 on new models.

Back to B2B, today B2B leads the world of e-marketing and e-business. We can learn a lot from them. But first let's clarify the terminology or jargon of e-business, e-marketing and e-commerce.

TYPES OF ONLINE PRESENCE

When assessing the relevance and potential of e-marketing for a business, remember that different business types offer different opportunities and challenges. Chaffey *et al.* (2003) identify four main types of online presence:

1 **Transactional e-commerce site**. E-retailers provide products available for purchase online. The main business contribution is through sale of these products. The sites also support the business by providing information for consumers who prefer to purchase products offline.

   Visit these examples: an end-product manufacturer such as Vauxhall (www.vauxhall.co.uk) or online retailers such as Amazon (www.amazon.com).

2 **Services-oriented relationship building web site**. Provides information to stimulate purchase and build relationships. Products are not typically available for purchase online. Information is provided through the web site along with e-newsletters to inform purchase decisions. The main business contribution is through encouraging offline sales and generating enquires or leads from potential customers. Such sites also help by adding value for existing customers by providing them with information of interest to them.

   Visit these examples: a B2B example is management consultants such as Pricewaterhouse-Coopers (www.pwcglobal.com) and Accenture (www.accenture.com). A B2C example is the UK portal for energy supplier British Gas (www.house.co.uk). Most car manufacturer sites may be services-oriented rather than transactional.

3 **Brand-building site**. Provide an experience to support the brand. Products are not typically available for online purchase, although merchandise may be. The main focus is to support the brand by developing an online experience of the brand. They are typical for low-value, high-volume fast moving consumer goods (FMCG brands).

   Visit these examples: Tango (www.tango.com), Guinness (www.guinness.com).

4 **Portal or media site**. These **intermediaries** provide information or news about a range of topics. Portal refers to a gateway to information with a range of services such as a search engine, directory, news, shopping comparison, etc. This is information both on the site and links through other sites. These are the three different types of **destination sites** described above. Portals have a diversity of options for generating revenue including advertising, commission-based sales and sale of customer data (lists).

   Visit these examples: Yahoo! (www.yahoo.com) (B2C) and FT.com (www.ft.com) or Silicon (www.silicon.com) (B2B).

Note that these are not clear-cut categories of Internet sites since some businesses may have sites which have a transactional, services-oriented, brand-building and media component depending upon the range of products they offer. Virgin (www.virgin.com) is an example of one such company.

E-MARKETING EXCELLENCE

Argos and RS Components exploit new markets

When catalogue retailer Argos (www.argos.co.uk) launched its web site, it found that sales were not limited to its core B2C market. Around 10 per cent of the site's customers were B2B – the web provided a more convenient purchase point than the previous retail chain. It has since changed its product offering to accommodate this new segment. Conversely B2B company RS Components found a significant proportion of sales were B2C, so reaching new customers via its online presence.

E-MARKETING EXCELLENCE

The C2B service of Priceline (www.priceline.co.uk)

An example of a completely new commercial mechanism that has been made possible through the web is provided by Priceline.com Europe Ltd (Figure 1.5), a licensee of Priceline.com Incorporated. This travel site is characterized by its unique and proprietary 'Name Your Own Price™' buying service. Here, users enter the price they wish to pay for airline tickets, hotel rooms or car hire together with their credit card details. If Priceline can match the user's price and other terms with inventory available from its participating suppliers, the deal will go ahead. This business model has been successful in the US where Priceline.com Incorporated, a NASDAQ listed company (PCLN), had a user base in 2000 of more than 5 million. In the UK, Priceline Europe has three core services: airline tickets, hotels and car hire.

SECTION SUMMARY 1.3

B2C, B2B, C2B and C2C

E-marketing involves collaboration between different parties that can be characterized by four main interactions:

- B2C – business-to-consumer (B2C e-tail is arguably the most talked about)
- B2B – business-to-business (less talked about, but with the most transactions)
- C2C – customer-to-customer interactions (best known as consumer auctions, but can also be achieved as B2C and B2B communities)
- C2B – customer-to-business (novel buying models where customers approach the business on their own terms).

Figure 1.5 Priceline.com Europe web site (www.priceline.co.uk)

 1.4 Situation – e-definitions

There are many terms with the e-prefix and many different interpretations. Within any organization, developing a common understanding for terms such as e-commerce, e-business and e-marketing, and how they interrelate, is important to enable development of a consistent, coherent strategy.

E-commerce is primarily about selling online or the ability to transact online. This includes e-tailing, online banking and shopping – which involve transactions where buyers actually buy and shoppers actually shop. Some suggest that e-commerce is any online transaction such as a responding to an enquiry or an online catalogue search.

E-commerce itself does not include the marketing nor the back office administration processes that are required to actually run a business. It has been said that 'the days of e-commerce are numbered as companies realise the advantages of e-business'. (David Siegel). **E-business** has a broader perspective. It involves the automation of all the business processes in the value chain – from procurement or purchasing of raw materials, to production, to stock holding, distribution and logistics, to sales and marketing, after sales, invoicing, debt collection and more. **E-business** creates the ability to run a business online. This includes e-marketing and e-commerce.

E-marketing is at the heart of e-business … getting closer to customers and understanding them better, adding value to products, widening distribution channels and boosting sales and after sales service. As with mainstream marketing, e-marketing is a way of thinking, a way of putting the customer at the heart of all online activities, e.g. getting different user groups to test your web site on different browsers in different settings on different connections.

Figure 1.6 summarizes the definition of e-marketing, e-commerce and e-business. It considers three of the possible alternative relationships between e-marketing, e-commerce and e-business. Which do you think is most appropriate? We would suggest (c) is most appropriate although often the terms are used interchangeably.

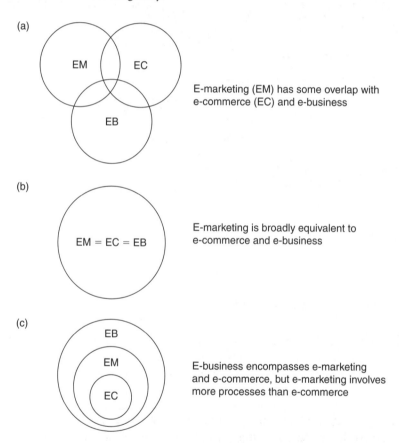

Figure 1.6   Three alternative relationships between e-marketing, e-commerce and e-business

E-MARKETING – THE DYNAMIC DIALOGUE

Simply put, e-marketing is marketing online whether via web sites, banner ads, opt-in e-mail, interactive kiosks, interactive TV, mobiles or m-commerce. It involves getting close to customers, understanding them better and maintaining a dialogue with them. It is broader than e-commerce since it is not limited to transactions between an organization and its stakeholders, but includes all processes related to marketing.

This dynamic dialogue is at the heart of good marketing. E-marketing builds on the database (of customers and prospects) and creates a constant flow of communications between customers and suppliers and between customers themselves. Dynamic means what it says. Dynamic does not mean static web pages. It's a two-way flow of communications – an ongoing discussion between customer and supplier. Remember that e-marketing also involves using electronic communications to manage the internal marketing process and better understand customers including marketing research and analysis.

David Siegel says:

> *'e-marketing is not about building a web site, but building a web business ... harmonising the power of customers'. Siegel (2000)*

E-marketing can help create a business which is customer led ... where the customer participates – through a constant dialogue, a dynamic dialogue, expressing interests, requesting products and services, suggesting improvements, giving feedback ... where ultimately, the customer drives the business.

THE CUSTOMER-LED BUSINESS

Now we can leave B2B and B2C models and see where e-marketing creates a new dynamic C2B model. A customer-to-business (C2B) model is one in which customers drive the business, freely communicate and are involved with new product suggestions, pricing, design and service. The customers help to shape the future of the business.

Although some different business models and marketing models are emerging, the same basic marketing principles apply whether online or offline:

- get close to customers, listen to them
- involve them
- serve them
- add value
- find the best ones
- nurture them into lifelong customers and replicate them
- and of course test, test, test, measure and improve.

To help define e-marketing in more detail, let's look at what marketing is. The UK Chartered Institute of Marketing define marketing as:

> *'The management process responsible for identifying, anticipating and satisfying customer needs profitably'.*

What does e-marketing involve?

Now let's consider how e-marketing can fulfil the definition of marketing, if, properly implemented. Let's break up the definition into manageable chunks:

E-marketing can identify, anticipate and satisfy customer needs efficiently.

Taking a web site as a major part of e-marketing, consider how a web site can fulfil the definition of marketing (identify, anticipate and satisfy customer needs profitably). It can:

- *Identify* needs from customer comments, enquiries, requests and complaints solicited via the web site's e-mail facility, bulletin boards, chat rooms and of course, sales patterns (seeing what's selling and what's not), and observing new customer groupings identified by data-mining through customer data, sales and interests (recorded using **web analytics** which reveals insights into interests determined by pages visited). Even **online surveys** asking how to improve the site or requesting suggestions for product improvements or new products identify current and sometimes future customer needs. Finally there is a proliferation of online secondary sources of research, many of which provide free in-depth insights into customer needs.

- *Anticipate* customer needs by asking customers questions and engaging them in a dynamic dialogue built on trust. And of course a little bit of what Amazon call **collaborative filtering** helps Amazon to identify and anticipate what customers might like given that buyers of similar books have similar interests. Customers often welcome suggested books from Amazon. And today's sophisticated profiling techniques allow many companies to do their own **data mining** to discover and anticipate buyers' needs, like Tesco's feta cheese, beer and nappy sales. This is old technology. More recent sophisticated **profiling** technology allows some companies to analyse your interests without even knowing your name – courtesy of the **cookie** – a bit of code sent to your PC (with your permission) when you visit certain sites. So without knowing your name, it knows your interests. It recognizes your PC and records which types of sites (interests) you have. So when you visit a web site and an unusually relevant banner ad drops down, this is no coincidence – cookies have anticipated your desires and needs.

- *Satisfy* needs with prompt responses, punctual deliveries, order status updates, helpful reminders, after sales services and added value services combine with the dynamic dialogue. The dialogue maintains permission to continue communicating and then adds value by delivering useful content in the right context (right time and right amount).

- *Efficiently* means in an automated way (or partially automated) … an efficient, yet hopefully not impersonal, way (i.e. it allows tailor-made technology to increase the marketer's memory as the relationship effectively blossoms during the customer's life – increasing **lifetime value**). 'Efficiently' probably should mean efficiently and effectively as otherwise it could alienate the vast armies of not-for-profit marketers.

And if the web site is integrated with customer relationship management (**CRM**) systems and **mass customization** then the relationship deepens and needs are completely satisfied in a very efficient automated two-way process. This, also, of course provides some protection from the inevitable onslaught of competition.

E-MARKETING INSIGHT

The IDM defines digital marketing

You will often hear e-marketing and digital marketing used interchangeably. Practitioners often refer to e-marketing or Internet marketing. But digital marketing is often referred to by some agencies and trade publications such as *New Media Age* (www.nma.co.uk) and *Revolution* (www.revolutionmagazine.com). The IDM (www.theidm.com) has created qualifications in digital marketing ratified by its Digital Marketing Council who have defined digital marketing as follows. You will see the similarity with our definition of e-marketing.

Digital marketing is:

Applying …	Digital technologies which form online channels to market … (web, e-mail, databases, plus mobile/wireless and digital TV)
to …	Contribute to marketing activities aimed at achieving profitable acquisition and retention of customers … (within a multi-channel buying process and customer lifecycle)
through …	Recognizing the strategic importance of digital technologies and developing a planned approach to improve customer knowledge (of their profiles, behaviour, value and loyalty drivers), then delivering integrated targeted communications and online services that match their individual needs.

The first part of the definition illustrates the range of access platforms and communication tools that form the online channels which e-marketers use to build and develop relationships with customers. The second part of the definition shows that it should not be the technology that drives e-marketing, but the business returns from gaining new customers and maintaining relationships with existing customers. It also emphasizes how e-marketing does not occur in isolation, but is most effective when it is integrated with other communications channels such as phone, direct mail or face-to-face. Online channels should also be used to support the whole buying process from pre-sale to sale to post-sale and further development of customer relationships. The final part of the definition summarizes approaches to customer-centric e-marketing. It shows how it should be based on knowledge of customer needs developed by researching their characteristics, behaviour, what they value, what keeps them loyal and then delivering tailored web and e-mail communications.

e-definitions

E-commerce generally refers to paid-for transactions, whether B2C or B2B, but others include all communications between customers and business. E-business is broader, including e-commerce, and is a means to optimize all business processes that are part of the internal and external value chain. E-marketing is best considered as how e-tools such as web sites, CRM systems and databases can be used to get closer to customers – to be able to identify, anticipate and satisfy their needs efficiently and effectively.

1.5 Situation – sloppy e-marketing

Identifying, anticipating and satisfying customer needs is all simple common sense. Yet common sense is not common. Sloppy e-marketing has become commonplace … broken sites, delayed deliveries, impersonal responses, non-responses.

Whether it's unclear objectives, lack of strategy or simply lousy execution, good e-marketing is relatively rare.

Take Toys R Us online. Many years ago they were allegedly sued for late fulfilment at Christmas. Several families who purchased online were disappointed by the non-arrival of Christmas presents. They sued. The site lost sales, irritated customers and damaged the brand.

Many other web sites damage the brand when they don't respond. They invite e-mails through the web site, but then do not respond quickly. Many top company web sites in the USA don't respond within four days. In a medium where quick response is expected, eager customers are ignored and insulted. The brand gets damaged by its own web site. It's the same in Germany, the supposed bastion of efficiency. Many top companies don't reply quickly to incoming e-mails and in some cases they never reply at all.

Other sites frustrate customers with poor navigation. Research shows very high attrition rates of customers successfully completing purchases due to different causes of sloppy e-marketing (Figure 1.7). The web sites of 80 per cent of Britain's top 50 retailers perform inconsistently with slow response times, timeouts and errors (Leyden, 2004). Despite online sales outgrowing offline sales in many sectors, separate research reveals that 40 per cent of the UK's top retailers spend too little on maintaining and developing their online operations (Armitt, 2004). It is no surprise then that other research findings revealed that only 37 per cent of customers are satisfied with their e-tailers' service (Hill, 2004). Mainstream (offline) marketing is not much better with 50 per cent of the FTSE 1000 unable to profile their customers and 50 per cent of CRM projects failing (Mazur, 2004). We are swimming in a sea of sloppy marketing and e-marketing. It is not surprising that Bossiddy and Charan (2004) suggest that 'execution is the missing key between aspirations and results'. Budgeting for the delicate balance of resources required to run an online operation is a science not yet fully understood. It consists of the 3Ms – men (men and women – the human resource), money (budgets) and minutes (time scales and time horizons for production, delivery, service, etc.). At a very basic level, how many of us train staff in using our own web site? How many humans are required to deal with incoming e-mail enquiries and

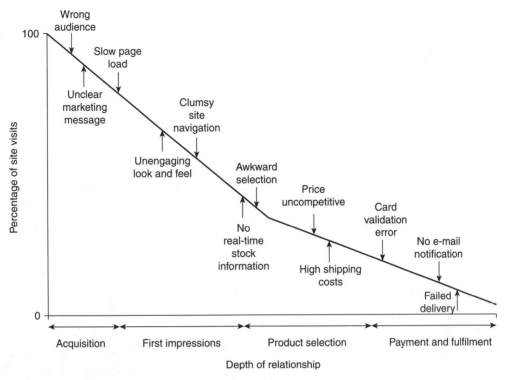

Figure 1.7 E-marketing sloppiness causes high attrition rates

outgoing telephone calls triggered by 'call-back' facility on the web site? Or can it be automated and personalized? Or do staff have to learn the administrative procedures integrated with the web site? How much money should be invested in stock (remember Toys R Us) and delivery systems? How much time is allowed to notify customers of deliveries? How much time to set up a project and integrate with the existing (legacy) database systems, etc.?

What kind of budget ratio should be allocated between creating a web site, servicing it and generating traffic? This is discussed in Section 7.10.

In a speech way back in April 2000, Gartner Group CEO Michael Fleisher predicted that 95 to 98 per cent of dotcom companies would fail in the next two years.

In what many saw as an inflammatory speech, he mentioned that the majority of dotcom company owners are hollow, shallow and motivated by greed and jealousy! He was right. Clever technology is not enough. Customers do not want bits of technology, they want complete solutions.

Very few tough questions were asked like: 'Does the product fit with changing customer needs? Do customers understand the benefits? Does the brand have relevant and distinctive values?'

Another shocking quote, this time from former Yahoo VP, direct marketing, Seth Godin:

> *'Nearly 30 million corporate web sites have been built over the last two years and more than $2b have been invested in cyberspace marketing. And it's all been wasted'.*

He was right too. Good e-marketing does not require rocket science, just common sense. But common sense is not common. Good e-marketing is not common. Neither, for that matter, is good marketing.

For example, can you believe that many advertisements and sales promotions damage the brand (remember Hoover)? Many, in fact, most, brands don't survive the test of time. These once successful, much loved, high profile brands die. Why? Markets change and move away and static brands get left behind.

Chapter 3 on changing e-models shows why many of the old world models, business models, marketing models, distribution models, pricing models, advertising models do not fit the new world of e-marketing. New models are required and the e-models chapter invites you to create some new models and examine other new emerging models. Whether marketing offline or online, do not forget the basics of good business – carefully thought-through ideas, attention to detail and excellent execution can be the difference between success and failure.

SECTION SUMMARY 1.5

Sloppy e-marketing

There are many examples of poor e-marketing. This may result from unclear objectives, lack of strategy or simply lousy execution. Marketers should assess and minimize the risks before embarking on e-marketing.

1.6 Objectives

One reason why many new businesses, and in particular new e-businesses, go horribly wrong is often because objectives are not clearly agreed and companies keen to get on with it jump straight to tactical e-tools (such as web sites and banner ads) without first agreeing clearly defined objectives and razor sharp strategies.

The following sections on objectives cover the purpose or reasons why businesses go online. They examine the kind of clear objectives and goals that will drive good e-marketing.

So before making the change to e-marketing first be clear: Why you want to go online? What are the objectives? What advantages and benefits are expected?

You must be clear why you're getting into e-marketing. What are the objectives? Apart from competitive paranoia? What are the benefits? There are five broad benefits, reasons or objectives of e-marketing:

- Grow sales (through wider distribution, promotion and sales)
- Add value (give customers extra benefits online)
- Get closer to customers (by tracking them, asking them questions, creating a dialogue, learning about them)

- Save costs (of service, sales transactions and administration, print and post)
- Extend the brand online. Reinforce brand values in a totally new medium.

There is a section on each of these 'objectives'.

All these e-marketing objectives can be summarized as the 5 Ss – Sell, Serve, Speak, Save and Sizzle. These are covered in the next five sections. Once you have defined (and quantified) 'where you are going' (your objectives), you can then decide 'how to get there' – Strategy. First consider objectives.

SECTION SUMMARY 1.6

Objectives

Organizations need to be clear about the objectives of e-marketing, so that the appropriate resources can be directed at achieving these objectives. A useful framework for developing objectives is the 5 Ss of Sell, Serve, Speak, Save and Sizzle.

1.7 Objective – Sell – using the Internet as a sales tool

Just about anything can be sold online from books to bikes, jobs to jets, turbines to toys and chemicals to kidneys. A young boy recently tried to auction one of his kidneys on eBay. Bidders were waiting but fortunately the deal was scrapped when the online auction house realized what was happening. Therein lies one of the many cyber challenges – regulating what is reasonable and proper to sell. Although just about anything can be sold online, the Internet impacts some industries more than others, particularly education, entertainment and advisory services – many of which can be digitized and delivered down the line.

But even this is changing, as cyber sales rocket across industry sectors and types. We all know that companies like Dell and IBM sell millions of dollars of PCs online every day. In parallel, more and more industrial buying is shifting online. General Electric buy billions of dollars worth of raw materials only online. Ford and GM are merging their buying power to buy online. Companies must be able to sell or transact online to meet these customers' new online needs. A key objective to set is the **direct online revenue contribution** for different products and different markets. This defines the proportion of sales transactions completed online. For example, a bank might try to achieve 15 per cent of its insurance sales online in the UK.

But remember that many other products and services are partly bought online. Shoppers browse online collecting information, prices and special offers before visiting stores and showrooms or picking up the phone to negotiate better deals. So **mixed-mode selling** is a must! Organizations have to be able to both sell online and offline. Therefore it is essential to accommodate those that want to buy online and those that want to just browse. Already BMW find approximately half of their test drives are generated from their web site, although a much smaller number of customers would want to purchase online. 'Clicks and mortar' organizations offer customers re-assurance of a real presence (building/mortar) along with the easy accessibility of the net. So another objective to set is the **indirect online revenue contribution** – the proportion of sales that are influenced by digital communications. A similar objective is the **reach** of the web site within its target audience.

So why not take it to the next level and offer the web visitor who wants a real test-drive delivery of the vehicle for the weekend? Assuming the visitor is screened and fits the ideal profile and suitable insurance is taken out, wouldn't this close the sales cycle and accelerate mixed mode selling?

Companies like Kozmo.com delivered pizzas and videos to homes in selected cities within one hour. The potential for online sales just grows. Unless, of course, there are many millions who still enjoy shopping, queuing, parking, paying and sitting in traffic instead of enjoying parks, picnics, families, music, reading …

The real crunch may come when businesses realize the power of the Internet's potential for distribution – extending the availability of many products and services without physically having to display a product. Take London's Millennium Eye. The service could be extended and distributed to a much wider audience than London's immediate tourist market. Anyone around the world could log on to a live web cam (camera) and take the 30-minute virtual ride to enjoy stunning views at night or by day. This service could be revenue generating whilst promoting tourism simultaneously. Equally, the Louvre, the Pyramids and many more attractions can now extend their distribution of both the point of purchase (i.e. buying a ticket) and the point of consumption (enjoy the view from your home). Sales and distribution opportunities abound.

So online sales will continue to grow. But there are other additional benefits, or objectives for e-marketing including serving, speaking, saving and sizzling. You can explore each of these at your leisure.

SELLING WHAT TO WHOM

There is a tendency, when setting online sales objectives, to use a low-risk approach of selling existing products into existing markets. This is the market penetration approach shown in Figure 1.8, which you may recognize as the Ansoff matrix – used by marketers for over 40 years to determine strategic priorities. We will see in later chapters that objectives should also be set for selling new digital products into new markets as appropriate.

E-MARKETING EXCELLENCE

EasyJet Sell

EasyJet was founded by Stelios Haji-Ioannou, the son of a Greek shipping tycoon who reputedly used to 'hate the Internet'. In the mid-1990s Haji-Ioannou reportedly denounced the Internet as something 'for nerds', and swore that it wouldn't do anything for his business. However, he decided to experiment with a prototype site, and sat up and took notice when sales started to flow from the site. Based on early successes, easyJet decided to invest in the new channel and proactively convert customers to using it. To help achieve this they set an initial target of 30 per cent of seats by the year 2000. By August 2000, the site accounted for 38 per cent of ticket sales and by 2001 over 90 per cent of seats. In 2005, phone sales are down to just single digit percentages, but are significant enough for the phone channel to be retained. Of course, this success is based on the relative ease of converting direct phone-sale customers to online customers.

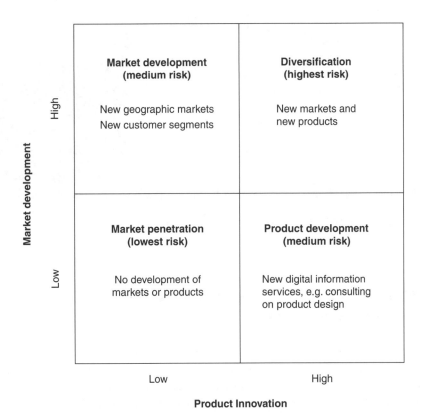

Figure 1.8   Online opportunities for product and market innovation

Objective – Sales

The clearest benefit of e-marketing is the capability to sell from an online presence. Although this may not be practical for all products, an online presence is still important in supporting the buying decision leading to sales through traditional channels. An online presence also offers opportunities to sell into new markets and reach particular segments.

Figure 1.9   EasyJet site from 2001 showing incentive for online booking

1.8   Objective – Serve – using the Internet as a customer-service tool

Another e-marketing objective is serving or adding value. How can a web site help customers, improve their experience or add value to their experience? Take newspapers. Newspapers can allow readers to create their own newspapers through personalization. They are no longer constrained by publication times, but can be accessed at any time. Their readers can set up alerts to notify them by e-mail as soon as an event breaks.

Another example: for customers who like their wines, the Marks & Spencer web site tests their visitors' knowledge of labels and grapes. And if, having chosen a wine, you're unsure of what to eat, Ragu's web site offers free recipes (and encourages visitors to send the recipe to a friend).

If, after dinner you're not sure which toothpaste to use, visit the Mentadent web site where visitors can get sample toothpaste and free oral care advice. Visitors can even e-mail questions to a resident dentist.

And if life gets really interesting you might join a virtual club of fun seekers who not only give their permission but actually welcome e-mails from specific airlines informing them of last minute unsold seats on airline trips for the weekend. Or wouldn't it be nice if the 07.06 train to London is late or, worse still, cancelled, and someone texts you or calls you? This may save you a lot of time and frustration. Time is an increasingly scarce and valuable commodity. Some technology allows you to shift time, e.g. TiVo type technology allows TV viewers to watch what they want when they want and not be subject to the limitations of a TV schedule.

SERVING THE B2B AUDIENCE

All these examples are B2C. Examples of excellent added value, online, can also be found in B2B markets. Companies like Fedex, GE, and Dell add value through their web sites all the time. They also build switching costs as customers become more and more locked into their excellent services.

Take GE Power Systems – they have created a web based tool called a 'turbine optimizer' which enables operators of any GE turbine to measure their machine's efficiency by comparing its performance against any similar turbines anywhere in the world. The tool then shows the operator how to improve the turbine's performance (and how much money the improvement is worth). It then helps the turbine operator to schedule a service call to make the improvement happen. This used to take weeks, in the online world it takes seconds.

Dell adds value by integrating its web help system into a customer's own Enterprise Resource Planning system (ERP). This means that when a customer orders online from Dell this triggers both Dell's system and the customer's own system simultaneously, which in turn updates both systems as to orders, approvals, budgets, stock, etc. This also makes switching suppliers more difficult.

Intel add value by sharing relevant information with their customers. They track their stocks (inventories) second by second and make this information available to their customers. Customers return the favour with information about their own stocks.

Fedex go one step further and give customers a free PC loaded with software that tracks the customer's packages around the world. The PC can be used for non-Fedex purposes as well. While adding value it also creates switching costs, because should the customer ever want to switch to another supplier they have to return the PC.

Real added value leaves customers tingling. Take the London Eye. It could add real value to the customer experience by offering to record the customer's experience (and comments) via a web cam installed in each capsule. It could be delivered to the customer's PC, TV or mobile phone instantaneously.

A web site's main purpose is to help customers (and other stakeholders such as suppliers and distributors). The big question to ask is: 'How can my web site help my customers? How can I add extra value?' The search for new ways to add value is continuous.

Added value, extra service, call it what you want, it becomes part of the product or service. Web sites can become part of a product or service. Do you agree?

E-MARKETING INSIGHT

Patricia Seybold on adding value to B2B services

Seybold (1999) defines eight success factors to achieve e-marketing. Two of these refer to adding value and they still ring true today. She says:

- *'Let customers help themselves'*. This 'customer self-service' can be enquiring about delivery of a product or obtaining after-sales support.
- *'Help customers do their jobs'*. Give information about best practice to help professionals complete their day-to-day work.

E-MARKETING EXCELLENCE

EasyJet Serve

When easyJet customers have a query, the easyJet contact strategy is to minimize voice calls through providing carefully structured Frequently Asked Questions (FAQ) and e-mail forms.

SECTION SUMMARY 1.8

Objective – Serve

A web presence can be used to add value for customers at different stages of the buying process, whether pre-sales, during the sale or post sales support.

Objective – Speak – using the Internet as a communications tool

1.9

A web site can be used as a new communications channel to increase awareness, build brand, shape customer opinion and communicate special offers. The box 'EasyJet Speak – using the web as a PR tool' illustrates some approaches. As well as speaking to customers, the Internet provides a tool to listen to customers – to get closer to them. In the last 100 years marketers have got worse at knowing customers. We've become separated and distanced by middlemen, distributors, agents, retailers, advertising agencies and market research agencies. The world of e-marketing opens up the opportunity to get close to customers again ... to speak to them and to listen to them in ways that were not previously possible.

E-marketers can enjoy direct access to customers, their attitudes, their interests and their buying patterns through chat rooms, questionnaires, web logs and databases.

Chat rooms offer a new approach to focus groups (small groups of customers who discuss your product, pack, advertisements, etc.). Although they are not classified formally as focus groups, they do have many similarities. MTV, the music channel, claim they have 'year long focus groups' where customers discuss their products freely (bands, videos, DJs). This is invaluable information. Chat rooms can be moderated by a facilitator (just like face-to-face focus groups) or unguided (or un-moderated) in a free flowing manner.

Questionnaires, on the other hand, are more structured and guide the respondent through specific questions. Online questionnaires can annoy web visitors, since they take time. The e-marketer either keeps them short (and builds the questions across pages) or wins permission to ask for the respondent's time and information by rewarding them with a suitable incentive. Do not put a pop-up or lengthy questionnaire on your opening page as it will drive traffic away from your site.

Having said that, open questions, like 'how can we help you?' or the opportunity to key in what you're looking for (into an onsite search engine) helps customers and simultaneously allows the e-marketer to see what is of interest to the visitor. It also reveals how customers may categorize things differently. This is invaluable information.

Web analytics also present the opportunity of seeing what are the most popular pages (i.e. what's of interest to customers) and how long they spend on specific pages. Web logs, or web stats, also track customers as they search on site so that the e-marketer can see how visitors' minds work – how they search and how they process information (how they move from page to page). Comparing enquiries (visitors) to sales (customers) reveals conversion ratios. How good are you at converting an enquiry into a sale or a sample? This ratio is important and should be watched carefully. High traffic (visitors) and low sales gives a low **conversion ratio** and suggests the web site needs to be improved. Whereas low traffic and high sales give a high conversion ratio which suggests the web site design is fine but perhaps more resources need to be spent on generating traffic.

Web logs, chat rooms and questionnaires can work together. For example, the web log can reveal items or pages that are not popular. The chat room facilitator can ask 'why?' and a questionnaire can later check to see if the chat room reasons are valid with a wider audience.

And of course the database behind the web site is a warehouse full of valuable information about customers and their patterns of purchasing, responses to promotions and much more. **Data mining** the **data warehouse** can reveal intriguing insights into buyer behaviour. Did you know that a significant number of frozen food buyers also have motor bikes? And the majority of nappy (diaper) buyers after 6 p.m. are male? What do you do with this data? Well one supermarket placed beer beside nappies and beer sales increased.

Combine the database with **collaborative filtering** (or rules such as 'if buy product "A" then likely to want product "C" ') and the e-marketer has a very powerful weapon ... the dynamic dialogue.

Speaking to customers, monitoring their purchases, suggesting other relevant products and all in a helpful, non-intrusive manner. If your local delicatessen remembers your name and asks if you'd like to try some particular paté because they remember you bought a particular type of cheese last time, then you welcome this dialogue. The same applies here except this can be automated. This helps to create a dynamic dialogue with the customer.

> ### E-MARKETING EXCELLENCE
>
> **EasyJet Speak – using the web as a PR tool**
>
> EasyJet are active in using the web as a PR tool, some examples:
>
> - EasyJet jets were emblazoned with oversize 'www.easyJet.com' logos
> - EasyJet ran a competition to guess the losses of rival airline GO and received 65 000 entrants and also enhanced press coverage
> - Owner Stelios Haji-Ioannou has a personal views page, 'message from Stelios'
> - Standard press releases pages are regularly updated.

SECTION SUMMARY 1.9

Objective – Speak

One of the many benefits of e-marketing is getting close to customers again. Speaking to them. You can explore the other benefits (selling, serving, saving and sizzling) now or later.

1.10 Objective – Save – using the Internet for cost-reduction

Another e-marketing objective is 'saving'. Saving money, time and effort. Savings emerge in customer service, transactional costs, and of course, print and distribution.

Good systems help customers to service themselves. This obviously saves money, and if done in a simple, speedy and efficient manner, increases customer satisfaction.

When Fedex estimated they save between $2–5 when they service customers via the web site rather than over the phone. This saves many millions of dollars per annum. Similarly, Dell showed they saved between $5 and $10 per customer which adds up to many millions. Cisco save hundreds of millions of dollars every year now through their web-based customer services.

Other estimates suggest that transactional costs have huge savings when completed on line. For example, the cost of an over-the-counter transaction in a bank is over $1 compared to 1 cent when completed online.

In addition to efficiency gains of e-systems, many businesses negotiate better deals online (from suppliers anywhere in the world). These businesses can also enjoy new economies of scale from the bigger purchasing power emerging from the new online purchasing alliances like GM and Ford, mentioned in Section 1.7.

Other savings are found in print and distribution. Annual reports, sales literature, user manuals and much more can be stored and distributed electronically – saving storage space, paper, trees, fuel (transport) and of course, money and time.

Some companies find other savings by using the Internet for cheaper phone calls. Other companies find savings by soliciting cost-saving ideas from their employees, customers and even general visitors to their web sites.

Other companies find their web operations not only save money but generate extra revenues through banner advertising. Busy sites attract traffic. Advertisers need audiences, so some sites allow advertisers to advertise on their web sites, for a price.

E-MARKETING EXCELLENCE

EasyJet save on call-centre expansion

The Internet is important to easyJet since it helps to reduce running costs, important for a company where each passenger generates a small profit. Part of the decision to increase the use of the Internet for sales was to save on the building of a £10 million contact centre which would have been necessary to sustain sales growth if the Internet was not used as a sales channel.

As an example, a 1999 sales promotion offered 50 000 seats to readers of *The Times*. The scalability of the Internet helped deal with demand since everyone was directed to the web site rather than the company needing to employ an extra 250 telephone operators.

SECTION SUMMARY 1.10

Objective – Save

So e-marketing saves money in many different ways. Of all the benefits of e-marketing (selling, serving, speaking, sizzling and saving), saving is the one that will help to present any business case as the financial fraternity relate to savings very quickly. The other benefits of e-marketing (selling, serving, speaking and sizzling) will strengthen your business case.

1.11 Objective – Sizzle – using the Internet as a brand-building tool

The Internet offers new opportunities to build and strengthen the brand. To add some 'sizzle' to the brand. To add extra value (or 'added value'), extend the experience and enhance the image. Ask yourself 'what experience could a web site deliver that would be truly unique and representative of the brand?' A newspaper that allows you to build your own newspaper and have it delivered electronically, or a car manufacturer that allows you to build your own car, or a camera company that allows you to learn how to use its cameras by simulating taking photographs with different settings and allowing you to compare and contrast the results (and also gives you tips on how to maintain your camera and protect your films and photos, and invites you to send your best photos in to a competition). A travel company that gives you a 'virtual friend' – after you tell them what your interests are (via an online questionnaire) the 'friend' suggests ideas for things you would like to do in the cities you choose to explore. Cosmetic companies offer online games, screensavers, viral e-mails, video clips and soundtracks to enhance the online brand experience. See the Tango e-marketing insight box in Section 2.7. This extra sizzle can enhance the brand in away that can only be done online.

Brands are important as they build trust, recognition, and, believe it or not, relationships between the buyer and the supplier. Sometimes brand imagery is the only real differentiator between products.

The brand is affected by both reality and perception: the *reality* of the actual experience enjoyed (or suffered) when using the brand, the *perception*, or image, associated with the particular product. In addition to the real experience, these perceptions are built through: advertising, sales promotions, direct mails, editorial exposure (PR), exhibitions, telesales, packaging, point-of-sale, web sites and the most potent communications tool, word-of-mouth.

All of these communications tools work both online and offline. For example, banner ads, incentives, offers and promotions. E-mail campaigns (**opt-in e-mail** campaigns) are also increasing.

And since many consider the Internet to be a new publishing medium, editorial opportunities abound. From chat rooms to bulletin boards, to newsletters, to e-zines there is a host of new PR/editorial opportunities. There are also virtual exhibitions and call-back technology (a button on a web site which allows the web site visitor to request a telephone call from the company).

And packaging and point-of-sale are still required in the online world as some sites recreate the shopping mall experience. As the visitor selects stores and aisles, packaging and point-of-sale skills are still required.

These all contribute to the brand. As does the experience – the quality of the experience, both online and offline. Remember sloppy web sites damage the brand. Slow e-mail responses damage the brand. Non-responses can kill it.

There is no doubt that e-marketing can help to build the brand. Many analysts see e-marketing as a way to build both the brand image and the overall company value. Yet another benefit of e-marketing. You can see the other benefits or objectives of e-marketing – adding value, getting closer to customers, selling and saving – whenever you need to build your business case.

E-MARKETING EXCELLENCE

Oasis Sizzle

Several years ago, the pop band Oasis launched a free CD attached to *The Sunday Times* newspaper who advertised the fantastic sales promotion heavily. The CD contained older tracks that could be played on a CD player plus four new tracks from the new album. These were encrypted so they could only be played four times on a PC and the user is automatically directed to HMV.co.uk to buy the album. The CD also contained an interview with the band, the video for the album's single, The Hindu Times, and links to the Oasis web site www.oasisnet.com with HMV donating 50p to the communications agency, Spero's favourite charity, Big Time Cultural Bank.

SECTION SUMMARY 1.11

Objective – Sizzle

Objectives should also consider how to enhance a brand by adding value online. This can include adding to the experience of the brand through interactive facilities. Protecting the brand through achieving trust about security and confidentiality is also important.

1.12 Introduction to e-strategy

Strategy summarizes how you achieve your objectives. Strategy is influenced by both the prioritization of objectives (sell, serve, speak, save and sizzle) and of course, the amount of resources available.

E-strategy guides the choice of target markets, positioning and propositions which in turn guide the optimum marketing mix, sequence of e-tools (such as web sites, opt-in e-mail, e-sponsorship, viral marketing), service level and evolutionary stage. The evolutionary stages of e-marketing are indicated in the box: 'Evolutionary stage models and e-strategy'. Chapter 9 illustrates similar evolutionary stage models for e-business.

E-strategy also affects the traditional marketing mix as the **product** can be extended on line, the **place** of purchase can be expanded, not to mention web **price** transparency, online **promotions** and the **people** who service the web site enquires, the automated **processes** and the importance of having a professional presence or **physical evidence**. The remix required for e-marketing is examined in Chapter 2.

One essential part of e-strategy is the development of the dynamic dialogue and the eventual full use of the integrated database potential. Regardless of how the customer comes into contact, he or she must be dealt with as a recognizable individual with unique preferences. The fully integrated database is essential so that the customer's name, address, previous orders are recalled and used appropriately. This requires careful planning as described in Chapter 8.

So the components of e-strategy include:

- Crystal clear objectives (what you want to achieve online)
- Target markets, positioning and propositions
- Optimum mix of tactical e-tools (web site, banner ads, etc.)
- Evolutionary stage (what stage you want to be at)
- Online marketing mix (particularly service levels)
- Dynamic dialogue (ongoing with the customer)
- Integrated database (recognize and remember each customer whether via web or telephone).

Strategy is crucial. As Kenichi Ohmae observed (Ohmae, 1999):

> *'There is no point rowing harder if you are rowing in the wrong direction'.*

This is just a brief glimpse at e-strategy. It is examined in more depth in Chapter 10.

E-MARKETING INSIGHT

Evolutionary stage models and e-strategy

Quelch and Klein (1996) developed a five-stage model referring to the development of sell-side e-commerce. For existing companies their stages are:

1 Image and product information
2 Information collection
3 Customer support and service
4 Internal support and service
5 Transactions.

Chaffey *et al.* (2003) suggest there are six choices for a company deciding on which marketing services to offer via an online presence:

- Level 0. No web site or presence on web.
- Level 1. Basic web presence. Company places an entry in a web site listing company names such as www.yell.co.uk to make people searching the web aware of the existence of the company or its products. There is no web site at this stage.
- Level 2. Simple static informational web site. Contains basic company and product information sometimes referred to as 'brochureware'.
- Level 3. Simple interactive site. Users are able to search the site and make queries to retrieve information such as product availability and pricing. Queries by e-mail may also be supported.
- Level 4. Interactive site supporting transactions with users. The functions offered will vary according to company. They will be usually limited to online buying. Other functions might include an interactive customer service helpdesk which is linked into direct marketing objectives.
- Level 5. Fully interactive site supporting the whole buying process. Provides relationship marketing with individual customers and facilitating the full range of marketing exchanges.

Discussion of relevant stages and their sequence can be used by any company to help define their e-strategy.

SECTION SUMMARY 1.12

Introduction to e-strategy

E-strategy defines a company's approach to achieving its e-marketing objectives. It should include the range of tactical e-tools and a revised marketing mix.

1.13 Tactics, actions and control

Tactics are the details of strategy. Tactical e-tools include the web site, opt-in e-mail, banner ads, virtual exhibitions and sponsorship. Tactics require an understanding of what each e-tool can and cannot do. Tactics may also involve where and how each tool is physically used, whether with a kiosk, interactive TV, mobile or alternatives (such as microwave).

Each one is a mini project requiring careful planning, good project management skills combined with tactical 'nous' and creativity. Action, or implementation, also requires an appreciation of what can go wrong from cyber libel to viruses, to mail bombs, hackers and hijackers to cyber squatting and much more ... contingency planning is required. What happens when the server goes down or a virus comes to town? What happens if one of the e-tools is not working, or is not generating enough enquiries? Something has to be changed.

But how do you know if it's going well? Performance is measured against the detailed targets. Time has to be made for a regular review of what's working and what's not. Good marketers have control over their destinies. They do not leave it to chance and hope for the best. They reduce risk by finding what works and what doesn't – so that e-tactics, or even the e-strategy can be changed if necessary.

Real marketers also want to constantly improve. Which tools are giving the best return on investment? Why? Other control mechanisms include measuring number of hits, number of unique visitors, number of conversions (visitors that purchase/subscribe), churn rate (number of people who ask to be taken off the subscription list or database).

Some companies ask managers to present 'Learnings' alongside their actual performance. Learnings mean anything they have learned from the marketplace during the last period. This forces a culture of constant improvement.

Finally, control also includes **competitive intelligence** – monitoring your competitors – what they're doing; what they're repeating; what works for them; what they're stopping.

Good marketers also have contingency plans or practise risk management. What happens if plan 'A' doesn't work? Or worse still, what happens if competition cut prices? Or worse still, what happens if the server goes down and your network crashes? Do you have a second server? Good marketers think things through.

So to conclude: e-marketing will continue to grow despite the vast array of sloppy sites and services. Winners will address these issues. Winners will plan strategically for both the evolutionary stages and the specific e-marketing objectives: sell, serve, speak, save and sizzle.

SECTION SUMMARY 1.13

Tactics, action and control

Tactics are the details of strategy. Tactical e-tools include the web site, opt-in e-mail, banner ads, virtual exhibitions and sponsorship. Actions include project planning and implementation while control involves assessing the results against objectives.

CHAPTER SUMMARY

1 SOSTAC® is a planning framework suitable for e-marketing and can be used for developing all types of plans, including e-marketing plans. It stands for Situation, Objectives and Strategy, Tactics, Action and Control.

2 The wired-up world connects businesses to consumers using an ever-increasing range of devices from PCs to phones to TVs to fridges and cars.

3 E-marketers need to assess the particular relevance of B2C, B2B, C2B and C2C marketing to their organization.

4 E-marketing and e-commerce are a subset of e-business that involve the automation of all business processes. E-marketing can assist in all elements of marketing – providing new techniques to identify, anticipate and satisfy customer needs efficiently.

5 Sloppy e-marketing can arise from poorly defined objectives, lack of strategy or poor execution. Risk assessment can minimize the risks of this occurring.

6 Clear objectives are required for e-marketing in order that resources can be directed at achieving these objectives and we can measure whether our targets are achieved.

7 The first of the 5 S objectives is 'Sell'. Using the Internet as an additional sales channel to reach new and existing customers.

8 The second of the 5 S objectives is 'Serve'. Using the Internet for customer service and adding value. Value can be added using a range of techniques including 24/7 access to support information and online tools.

9 The third of the 5 S objectives is 'Speak'. Using the Internet as a communications tool for inbound and outbound communications integrated with other media.

10 The fourth of the 5 S objectives is 'Save'. Using the Internet to increase efficiency and so reduce costs.

11 The fifth of the 5 S objectives is 'Sizzle'. Using the Internet as a brand building tool, by increasing brand awareness and enabling interaction with the brand.

12 E-strategy entails defining approaches to achieve e-marketing objectives using a range of tactical e-tools and a revised marketing mix.

13 Tactics are the details of strategy. Tactical e-tools include the web site, opt-in e-mail, banner ads, virtual exhibitions and sponsorship.

References

Armitt, C. (2004) High Street Bandits don't take entailing seriously. *New Media Age*, 15 October.

Bossiddy, L. and Charan, R. (2004) *Execution – the discipline of getting things done*. Crown Business.

Chaffey, D., Mayer, R., Johnston, K. and Ellis-Chadwick, F. (2003) *Internet Marketing: Strategy, implementation and practice*. Financial Times/Prentice Hall, Harlow, 2nd edition.

DTI (2003) *Business In The Information Age – International Benchmarking Study 2003*. Department of Trade and Industry. Based on 6000 phone interviews across businesses of all sizes in eight countries. Available from www2.bah.com/dti2003.

Hill, S. (2004) Etailers offer poor customer service. *New Media Age*, 2 September.

ITU (2004) Internet Reports 2004. International Telecommunications Union (www.itu.int).

Leyden, J. (2004) Wobbly Shopping Carts Blight UK e-Commerce. *The Register*, 4 June.

Marden, E. (1997) *The Laws of Choice. Predicting customer behaviour*. Free Press, New York.

Mazur, L. (2004) Poor Profiling. *Marketing Business*, February.

Ohmae, K. (1999) *The Borderless World: Power and Strategy in the Interlinked Economy*. Harper Business, New York.

Quelch, J. and Klein, L. (1996) The Internet and international marketing. *Sloan Management Review*. Spring, 61–75.

Seybold, P. (1999) *Customers.com*. Century Business Books, Random House, London.

Siegel, D. (2000) *Futurize Your Enterprise. Business Strategy in the age of the e-customer*. John Wiley, New York.

Smith, P.R. (2003) Great Answers to tough marketing questions. Kogan Page, 2nd edition.

Smith, P.R. and Taylor, S. (2004) *Marketing Communications: an integrated approach*. Kogan Page, London, 4th edition.

Smith, P.R., Pulford, A. and Berry, C. (1999) *Strategic Marketing Communications*. Kogan Page.

Further reading

Chaffey, D. (2004) *E-Business and E-Commerce Management: Strategy, implementation and practice*. Financial Times/Prentice Hall, Harlow, 2nd edition. Chapter 8 introduces the concept of e-marketing and its relationship with e-commerce and e-business.

DTI (2003) *Business In The Information Age – International Benchmarking Study 2003*. Department of Trade and Industry. Available from www2.bah.com/dti2003.

Web links

ClickZ (www.clickz.com) has articles and statistics on a wide range of e-topics.

E-consultancy (www.e-consultancy.com). Detailed insights and events about e-marketing best practice.

The Interactive Media in Retail (www.imrg.org). Trade body for e-retailers reporting on growth and practice within UK and European e-commerce.

International Telecommunications Union (ITU) (www.itu.int/ti/industryoverview/index.htm). Choose Internet indicators. This presents data on Internet and PC penetration in over 200 countries.

Marketing Online (www.marketing-online.co.uk) is a source for links to web sites concerned with Internet marketing strategy, implementation and practice. Produced by Dave Chaffey.

Marketing Sherpa (www.marketingsherpa.com) Case studies and news about e-marketing.

New Media Age (www.nma.co.uk) A UK digital marketing trade weekly.

New Media Knowledge (www.nmk.co.uk) Articles and events about new media developments.

Net Imperative (www.netimperative.co.uk) Updates and reports on the UK new media landscape.

Revolution magazine (www.revolutionmagazine.com) keep up-to-date on e-marketing best practice for the range of new media with the UK trade monthly for digital marketing.

Trend Spotting (www.trendspotting.com) identifies trends that are happening out there.

UK Netmarketing (www.chinwag.com). The premier e-mail discussion list for insiders in the UK e-marketing industry.

Self-test

1 Summarize each element of the SOSTAC® framework.

2 Describe how customers and companies are becoming interconnected.

3 Assess the potential for B2C, B2B, C2B and C2C interactions via your online presence.

4 Devise a diagram outlining the difference between e-business, e-marketing and e-commerce.

5 List your experiences of sloppy e-marketing.

6 Describe the need for objectives and the characteristics of suitable objectives.

7 Outline 'Sell' e-marketing objectives for your organization.

8 Outline 'Serve' e-marketing objectives for your organization.

9 Outline 'Speak' e-marketing objectives for your organization.

10 Outline 'Save' e-marketing objectives for your organization.

11 Outline 'Sizzle' e-marketing objectives for your organization.

12 Summarize e-strategies to achieve the objectives you have described in Questions 7 to 11.

13 Summarize the main tactical e-tools used by your organization.

Chapter

2

ReMix

'A marketer is like a chef in a kitchen ... a mixer of ingredients'.

Frederick Bartels, 1963

The digital world affects every aspect of business, every aspect of marketing and every aspect of the marketing mix. Some argue that physical distribution, selling and pricing absorb the biggest impact. In fact all the elements of the mix are affected by this new world. This chapter shows you exactly how.

By the end of this chapter you will be able to:

- Understand the online implications of each element of the marketing mix
- Extend each element of the mix into the online world
- Begin to plan each element of the mix in the online world.

CHAPTER TOPIC		LEARNING OBJECTIVE
2.1	Introduction	Identify the different elements of the marketing mix and where they fit into the e-marketing plan.
2.2	What is the marketing mix?	Appreciate the many different approaches to the marketing mix.
2.3	Beyond the mix	Identify the marketing skills required to take you beyond the mix.
2.4	Product	Assess the full potential of extending any product online.
2.5	Price	Review your pricing and consider some dynamic pricing models.
2.6	Place	Identify the online distribution issues and challenges.
2.7	Promotion	Discuss the problems and opportunities of the online communications mix.
2.8	People	Analyse why online service requires a delicate balance of people and automation.
2.9	Processes	List the components of process and understand the need to integrate them into a system.
2.10	Physical evidence	Identify the digital components that give 'evidence' to customers and check that your web site has them.
2.11	An extra 'P', partnerships	So much of marketing today is based on strategic partnerships, marketing marriages and alliances that we have added this 'P' in as a vital ingredient in today's marketing mix.

2.1 Introduction to ReMix

The **marketing mix** is a well-established conceptual framework that helps marketers to plan their approach to each market. At worst, it provides a checklist of decisions which marketers must make. At best, marketers integrate, or mix, these decisions together and allocate their resources accordingly. In this chapter we examine how the mix applies today. Online developments affect every aspect of business, every aspect of marketing and every aspect of the marketing mix. So do we have to throw out the old marketing mix concept or can it still be applied? Is a radical remix needed?

There is a raging debate amongst marketers about which mix is the most appropriate regardless of online or offline. Some feel that the traditional version of the mix simply misses the mark. There are others who feel it is a useful starting point. Some argue that physical distribution, selling and pricing absorb the biggest impact from the Internet. In fact all the elements of the mix are affected by the online world.

Although an extra element of the mix is suggested at the end of the chapter, this chapter does not seek to create a new mix but examines how the old mix is radically changed by the fast changing digital environment. Figure 2.1 summarizes the main elements of the marketing

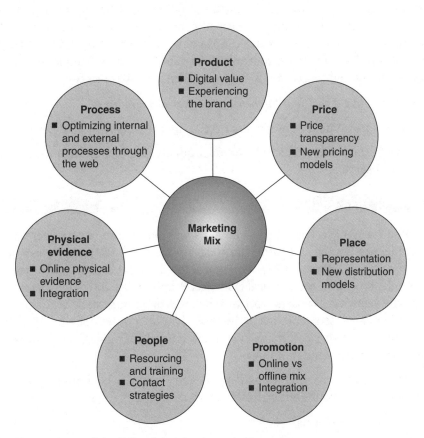

Figure 2.1 Keys aspects of the 7 Ps of the classic marketing mix

mix and key issues of how the mix is changed in the digital environments that are explored in this chapter.

The overall balance of the marketing mix is strategic and the details of the mix are tactical. For example, deciding whether to heavily discount prices and raising a high profile in a broad array of down-market web sites and communities is strategic. The tactical details would list the sites and communities and relevant prices in detail.

SECTION SUMMARY 2.1

Introduction to the marketing mix

The marketing mix is a well-established conceptual framework that helps marketers to structure their approach to each market. It should be re-examined and reapplied for the online world.

2.2 What is the marketing mix?

The **marketing mix** rose to prominence in the early 1960s, although it was first referred to in 1949 at an American Marketing Association conference. Around the start of the 1960s, Canadian Jerome McCarthy (McCarthy, 1960) coined the term the '4 Ps': **product, price, place, promotion.** The four Ps are controllable variables which, when planned and carefully mixed together in the right way, satisfy customers. In 1963 Bartels said:

> *'A marketer is like a chef in a kitchen …. a mixer of ingredients'.*

So what are the ingredients that marketers need to mix together to satisfy customer needs?

Some of the controllable factors include: product quality, product availability, product image, product price and service.

EXTENDING THE MIX

Since that time many have argued that the **4 Ps** worked for products rather than services. American academics Booms and Bitner then developed the **7 Ps**, sometimes known as the service mix (Booms and Bitner, 1981). They considered the extra Ps crucial in the delivery of services – people, processes and physical evidence. People create and deliver a service – if they aren't happy the service falls apart. Processes are even more important as the process of production is not behind closed doors (as in the case of products) but open for all to see. Finally, when buying intangible services, many customers rely on cues given from physical evidence (such as uniforms, badges and buildings).

Some feel that for interactive marketing Peppers and Rogers' **5 Is** should replace the 7 Ps in the information age. Do your online efforts support:

- *Identification* – customer specifics
- *Individualization* – tailored for lifetime purchases

- *Interaction* – dialogue to learn about customers' needs
- *Integration* – of knowledge of customers into all parts of the company
- *Integrity* – develop trust through non-intrusive marketing such as **permission marketing**?

The 5 Is do not supplant the 7 Ps but rather are complementary to them since the 5 Is define the process needed, whereas the 7 Ps are the variables that the marketer controls.

Another explanation of the mix emerged when Frenchman Albert Frey suggested that the mix of marketing variables could be categorized into two groups:

- The offering (product, packaging, service and brand) and
- The methods/tools (distribution channels, personal selling, advertising and sales promotion).

MIXING THE MIX

Regardless of the approach to the mix, the same principle applies – stick close to customers; use marketing research to learn what they need and supply it better than competition by mixing the right mix.

Marketers mix the mix in different ways, sometimes with astonishing degrees of success. The mix can be mixed in different ways to satisfy different segments.

Online shopping comparison site Bizrate (www.bizrate.com) rates e-tailers by a broad range of variables: 'ease of ordering; product selection; product info; price; web site quality; on-time delivery; product representation; customer support; privacy policies and shipping and handling'. Shop Spy (Figure 2.2, www.shopspy.co.uk) rates e-tailer categories based on navigation, range of goods, ease of ordering, payment and delivery and returns policy after benchmarking the site and acting as a **mystery shopper**.

The trick is knowing which variables are most important for the ideal customer. You need to know what your targeted 'ideal' customers base their decisions on: is it best price, best quality, best delivery, service, best image, best environment?

Not only can research help to answer the question, but today's dynamic customer communities can give useful guidance. In fact Section 2.4 on 'product' mentions the **'prosumers'** who help car companies to design the perfect car for them – the customer is involved in defining the mix.

What price and quality level is right? Knowing where and when the customer wants to buy. Knowing how to catch their attention and present it in the right way.

Sometimes tough decisions mean chopping and changing the mix. For example, faster and wider distribution might mean more money spent on stocks and delivery vehicles and less money spent on advertising. The permutations are vast.

Figure 2.2 ShopSpy comparison site rates e-tailers out of 100

SECTION SUMMARY 2.2

What is the marketing mix?

Marketing touches every part of the corporation. One way of structuring, or categorizing, the set of decision variables is through the marketing mix. There are several different approaches including the 4 Ps and 7 Ps. These have to be re-evaluated for the new media. The 7 Ps which are explored in this chapter are:

- Product
- Price
- Place

- Promotion
- People
- Physical evidence
- Processes.

2.3 Beyond the mix

The previous section showed that there are many different approaches to the marketing mix such as the 4 Ps, 5 Is and 7 Ps. On top of all of this, today's marketers need skills that go beyond the basic mix. By the end of this section you will know what skills you need. Although the mix provides a useful framework for marketers, other factors also need to be considered. Decisions on the mix are not made until marketing strategy first determines **target markets** and required **brand positionings**.

Marketers also need to know how to manage alliances (partnerships and marketing marriages), databases and how to build customer relationships that give lifetime value.

Everything today is about relationships. The choice of mix should help to grow relationships:

- Relationship marketing means keeping customers happy for life.
- Strategic alliances and partnerships are all about relationships.
- Supply chain management is increasingly built on relationships – sharing data and systems and budgets.
- If the trends towards **consolidation** (customers choosing fewer suppliers) and **commoditization** (competition producing similar products) continue, then much business will be won and lost depending on the relationship between buyer and supplier.

Marketers have to understand relationships and how to make them work – whether online and offline – with customers and suppliers.

As we will see in Chapter 8 on e-customer relations management, relationships blossom when important things are, first, remembered (like your name and preferences) and, second, acted upon (such as your birthday or wedding anniversary). As organizations become accessible 24/7/365 through a wide range of devices and people, an integrated database can help remember names, needs, events and a lot more (in both B2C and B2B markets).

> ### E-MARKETING INSIGHT
>
> **Segmentation and positioning according to Professor Peter Doyle**
>
> Doyle on segmentation – Segmentation is the key to marketing. If there is one golden rule for upcoming marketers then it is segmentation. Why? For two reasons. First people are heterogeneous. Different customers want different things. So to satisfy customers you have to provide different solutions for different customers. The second reason is that people are prepared to pay different prices.

> Doyle on positioning – Positioning is central to marketing strategy. Positioning refers to how a brand is perceived in the minds of a target group of customers. Positioning is the encapsulation of two key concepts. The first is the target market – what is your choice of segment? Second – what will make the customer prefer your product to competitors'? How can we achieve a differential advantage? (*Source:* Multimedia Marketing Consortium, 2000a).

SECTION SUMMARY 2.3

Beyond the mix

Before choosing the marketing mix, marketing strategy first determines target markets and required brand positionings. Then excellent marketers think beyond the short term mix and think 'long term'. This means choosing a mix that nurtures 'lifetime customers'. Ask how each marketing mix decision affects my customer relations. Relationship marketing permeates all the decisions marketing managers have to make about the mix. Excellent marketers have database skills, partnership skills and relationship skills built into all their decisions regarding the marketing mix ... whether 4 Ps, 5 Ps or 7 Ps.

2.4 Product

By the end of this section you will understand online value propositions, be able to assess the potential of extending your product online and spot opportunities for other products online. You will also be able to begin to assess your overall business as a result of the online opportunity.

> *'Destroy your business.com'*

That's what Jack Welsh, ex CEO of General Electric, told his managers. The implication being rethink your product before the online competition does it for you. In fact Jack used to say that the new CEO would have to go further – and recreate GE all over again.

The online world offers a host of new opportunities and prompts these product-related questions:

- What benefits do you deliver to your customers?
- Can they be delivered online?
- What other benefits might your customers like?
- Can these benefits be delivered online?
- What is your business? Can it be delivered online?

DIGITAL PRODUCTS

Ghosh (1998) suggested companies should consider how to modify product and add **digital value** to customers. These are huge questions that can reshape your whole business.

E-MARKETING INSIGHT

Digital value

Ghosh talks about developing new products or adding digital value to customers. He urges companies to ask:

1 Can I afford additional information on or transaction services to my existing customer base?

2 Can I address the needs of new customer segments by repackaging my current information assets or by creating new business propositions using the Internet?

3 Can I use my ability to attract customers to generate new sources of revenue such as advertising or sales of complementary products?

4 Will my current business be significantly harmed by other companies providing some of the value I currently offer?

He suggests you need to analyse each feature of your product or service and ask how can each of these features be improved or adapted online.

These changes can be substantial – one such example is Hughes Christenson, an oil drilling tool company who discovered they had a much more lucrative online oil drilling advisory service.

There is no doubt that every product or service can find some added value online. Even for soft drinks such as Pepsi and Tango there is a shift from physical interactions to non-physical brand experiences.

So it's not just digitizable products and digitizable services that extend themselves into the online world, but any products from any business.

Obviously the entertainment, education and advice services are ideal, but surprisingly so are complex industrial products (witness the GE turbine optimizer referred to in Chapter 1). In fact the more complex the product, the more online opportunity since there is a need to educate, train, test, install and service – most of which can be integrated online. Figure 2.3 shows how the online presence can be used to communicate the options for a complex product selection. The site visitor selects their requirements and suitable models are indicated.

Even less complex but high involvement consumer purchases such as cars can be aided online through 'mixed mode' purchasing.

Remember to keep asking 'what information do my ideal target customers seek?' 'How can I excel at giving them this online?' Communities of customers can be tapped into to help answer this question. This is the idea of the **prosumer** – the proactive consumer who participates in the design of products/services.

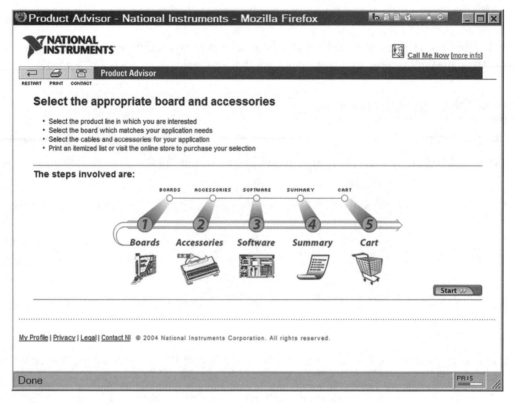

Figure 2.3 National Instruments Product Advisor (www.ni.com)

E-MARKETING INSIGHT

Alvin Toffler and the prosumer

The prosumer concept was introduced in 1980 by futurist Alvin Toffler in his book *The Third Wave*. According to Toffler, the future would once again combine production with consumption. In *The Third Wave*, Toffler saw a world where interconnected users would collaboratively 'create' products. Note that he foresaw this over 10 years before the web was invented!

Alternative notions of the prosumer, all of which are applicable to e-marketing, are catalogued at Logophilia WordSpy (www.logophilia.com/WordSpy):

1 A consumer who is an amateur in a particular field, but who is knowledgeable enough to require equipment that has some professional features ('professional' + 'consumer').

2 A person who helps to design or customize the products they purchase ('producer' + 'consumer').

3 A person who creates goods for their own use and also possibly to sell ('producing' + 'consumer').

4 A person who takes steps to correct difficulties with consumer companies or markets and to anticipate future problems ('proactive' + 'consumer').

An example of the prosumer idea is illustrated by BMW, who, prior to the launch of a new model set up an interactive web site where users could design their own dream roadster. The information was stored automatically in a database and as BMW had previously collected data on its most loyal customers, the database could give a very accurate indication of which combinations were the most sought after and should therefore be put into production.

THE EXTENDED PRODUCT

Online opportunities for enhancing product value can also be identified. Ask 'how can I move beyond the core product?' The different elements of **extended product** can be highlighted or delivered online. What other products and services would a customer really value? Which of these services can be produced cost effectively and better than competitors?

The extended product also includes incorporating tools to help users during their use of the product. A good example of this is the tools Citroën provides for fleet car managers (Figure 2.4).

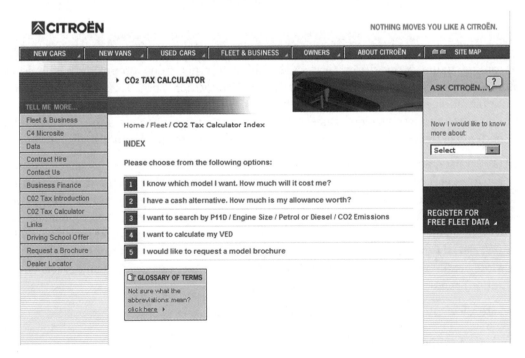

Figure 2.4 Citroën CO_2 tax calculator tool (www.citroen.co.uk)

The extended product contributes to perceptions of quality. Quality and credibility are inextricably linked. 'Develop credibility before raising visibility' makes sense, otherwise you end up making a lousy low-profile company into a lousy high-profile company. Credibility requires quality products and services – these can be demonstrated by:

- Endorsements
- Awards
- Testimonies
- Customer lists
- Customer comments
- Warranties
- Guarantees
- Money back offers.

Remember also – you need to analyse competition continuously. What is their core and extended product offering? That's the easy bit. Increasingly, the hard bit is knowing who your competition is, as boundaries and categories collapse. Witness Yahoo offering electricity and Virgin offering telephone services; it seems there are no boundaries, just shares of wallet based on relationship marketing. This means that once a supplier wins a customer's trust it is possible that the customer will consolidate the number of suppliers and start to buy a wider range of products and services from the same supplier. If the relationship is right the share of wallet can grow. This brings us back to the online value proposition – what exactly is being offered to the customer? Can you summarize your company's OVP?

ONLINE VALUE PROPOSITION

The **online value proposition** (previously called Internet value proposition) should be different to the offline proposition. Ideally, the proposition should exploit some of the unique advantages of being online which include: immediacy, interactivity and depth of content, faster, more convenient, easier, as well as cheaper to buy online, faster to buy online and better experience online, new experiences online, more resources/information online ...

The OVP must somehow reinforce core brand values and clearly summarize what a customer can get from you online that they cannot get elsewhere (including competitors and offline offers). This is quite a task and requires very careful consideration of customer needs, competitive offering, company strengths and resources available. Many sites, in fact most sites, do not achieve this. Observe competitors' sites and their offerings, can you distinguish between them? A cleverly created advertising strap line appearing on a web site can summarize the offering. More detailed pages in offline communications or on the web site (e.g. under the 'About Us' option) can describe the proposition more fully.

Here are a few OVPs that appear to match the strap lines:

- Kelkoo – Compare. Buy. Save. – www.kelkoo.com
- Autotrader – The biggest and best car site on the planet – www.autotrader.com

- Boosey and Hawkes – a world of music – www.boosey.com
- MUtv – The television channel dedicated to Manchester United – www.mutv.com
- EasyJet – the web's favourite airline (which suggests cheapest tickets) – www.easyjet.com.

Interestingly, Amazon use the line 'Top Seller' instead of their previous 'Earth's biggest selection at competitive prices' – www.amazon.com

Web guru Jakob Nielsen has an interesting exercise which assesses whether a web site communicates effectively during the first ten seconds:

Guideline 1

1 Collect the taglines from your own site and your three strongest competitors.

2 Print them in a bulleted list without identifying the company names.

3 Ask yourself whether you can tell which company does what.

4 More important, ask a handful of people outside your company the same question.

Guideline 2

1 Look at how you present the company in the main copy on the home page.

2 Rewrite the text to say exactly the opposite.

3 Would any company ever say that?

4 If not, you're not saying much with your copy, either.

The OVP is more than the sum of features, benefits and prices; it should encompass the complete experience of selecting, buying and using the product or service. The traditional categories of the different elements of the marketing mix are beginning to blur as proposition merges with product experience. About time too as all of the mix must be seamlessly integrated.

SECTION SUMMARY 2.4

Product

Find the ideal product that you can deliver, can afford, are good at, can protect and go for it! The online world allows you to create a whole range of new versions, variations and even new products and services. Finally, play to your strengths and exploit your distinctive competitive advantage by having a strong and clear OVP.

2.5 Price

Pricing and **price models** are being turned upside down by the Internet. Have you noticed? Imagine being paid one day and the next day having to pay for delivering the same service? AOL used to pay ABC News for content. Now ABC pays AOL to place its content on

AOL pages. It's happened in advertising also. Audiences used to pay for the media, now the media pay audiences to watch their ads through infomediaries such as AllAdvantage (www.alladvantage.com).

In this section you will see why you need to review your prices and your pricing models regularly as transparent and dynamic pricing impact all markets.

NEW PRICING APPROACHES

New **buying models** require new pricing approaches.

Name-your-price services such as Priceline (www.priceline.com), transparent pricing and global sourcing (particularly by giant procurement mergers like Ford and Chrysler) are forcing marketers radically to rethink their pricing strategies.

A growth in competition is caused partly by global suppliers and partly by globalized customers searching via the web, which puts further pressure on prices. Many online companies enjoy lower margins with more efficient web-enabled databases and processes. They also cut out the middleman and his margin. So they revel in the ultra-competitive nature of online global markets.

And there's more ... barter, countertrade, strategic alliances, technology transfer, licences, leasing as well as auctions, and reverse auctions where sellers compete to supply a buyer, counter auctions ... are all putting downward pressure on prices. On the other hand, web sites can track customer segments and their sensitivity to prices against their activity on the site, or past purchase habits recorded in host databases or stored in cookies held on the user's computer (with their permission), e.g. if a customer's history shows two visits to a particular product page, then an automatic online coupon might nudge the unsure customer to buy. In theory, marketers with well-managed databases can tailor prices to discrete segments at optimum prices.

PRICING UNDER PRESSURE

Pricing is under pressure through the continual trend towards **commoditization**. Something new is commoditized almost every day. Once buyers can (a) specify exactly what they want, and (b) identify suppliers, they can run **reverse auctions**. Qualified bidders undercut each other – for both business and consumer products. Colvin (2000) reported that through MedicineOnline.com elective procedures such as laser eye corrections or plastic surgery required by a particular customer are fought over by rival practices.

Price transparency is another factor. As prices are published on the web, buyer comparison of prices is more rapid than ever before. Storing prices digitally in databases potentially enables shopping bots and robot shoppers to find the best price. Price comparison sites have been around for five years now, e.g. www.screentrade.co.uk (insurance, Figure 2.5). This site was originally a neutral intermediary, but was purchased by Lloyds TSB which is an interesting **countermediation** strategy. This customer empowerment creates further downward pressure on prices. This is what happens when customers want to take control of the relationship rather than the other way around.

Figure 2.5 Screentrade insurance comparison site (www.screentrade.co.uk)

And it's not going to get any easier to sustain old prices. A prototype next generation e-commerce server from the University of Washington uses gaming strategies to decide when to bargain even harder during the negotiation of complex contracts.

Add to this online cost savings which can be passed to customers and you see further downward pressure. Take the car market, at launch several new online car retailers such as Virgin Cars (www.virgincars.com) and Jamjar (www.jamjar.com) promised 30 per cent savings.

Prices are complex; options for the price package include:

- Basic price
- Discounts
- Add-ons and extra products and services
- Guarantees and warranties
- Refund policies
- Order cancellation terms
- Revoke action buttons.

Ironically, the money-rich and time-poor customers in B2C markets may be much slower than buyers in B2B markets where transaction values are often higher, so savings are more significant. B2B marketplaces such as EC21 (Figure 2.6), known as exchanges or hubs, and auctions will grow in significance.

Figure 2.6 EC21 global B2B marketplace (www.ec21.com)

Much routine and repetitive buying will be carried out in these B2B exchanges. Major corporations are already buying through online exchanges and auctions.

Marketers (and buyers) will need new skills – defining the strengths and weaknesses of various exchanges and auctions.

Experienced business people know the impact of buying efficiencies. Martin Butler estimates that a 5% saving in procurement equals the same contribution as 30% increase in sales for many manufacturing companies (Butler, 2001).

Marginal costing may be required – for many digitized products the marginal cost is almost zero. Some companies (such as software vendors) are redefining their business and becoming service providers and give the product away at cost. They make their money on selling the add-ons and extras. A very different pricing model or just a traditional loss leader approach?

Some call it **second layer selling.** For example, companies sell end-of-term cars from corporate fleets, contract hire and leasing companies and car rental companies to affinity groups such as large employers. The cars themselves are sold at cost while the add-ons and extras make a profit – insurance, finance, recovery services.

One other consideration is moving from fixed prices to rental, and leasing prices. Cars, computers, flight simulators and now even music can be hired or leased.

E-MARKETING EXCELLENCE

GlaxoSmithKline reduces prices through reverse auctions

Healthcare company GlaxoSmithKline started using online reverse auctions way back in 2000 to drive down the price of its supplies. For example, it bought supplies of a basic solvent for a price 15 per cent lower than the day's spot price in the commodity market and Queree (2000) reported that on other purchases of highly specified solvents and chemicals, SmithKline Beecham is regularly beating its own historic pricing by between 7 and 25 per cent. She says: 'FreeMarkets, the company that manages the SmithKline Beecham auctions, quotes examples of savings achieved by other clients in these virtual marketplaces: 42 per cent on orders for printed circuit boards, 41 per cent on labels, 24 per cent on commercial machinings and so on'.

The reverse auction process starts with a particularly detailed Request for Proposals (RFP) from which suppliers ask to take part and then selected suppliers are invited to take part in the auction. Once the bidding starts, the participants see every bid, but not the names of the bidders. In the final stages of the auction, each last bid extends the bidding time by one more minute. One auction scheduled for two hours ran for four hours and twenty minutes and attracted more than 700 bids!

SECTION SUMMARY 2.5

Price

The Internet is changing pricing for ever. Prices are under pressure. Pricing structures and options are becoming more complex. It is crucial to get the pricing right in the short, medium and long term. Review new price structures in your markets driven by customers looking for lower prices available through a range of online tools including reverse auctions, customer unions, commoditization, cybermediaries, intermediaries, infomediaries and shopping bots.

2.6 Place

To understand the significance of place, consider which is the most successful **brand** in the soft drinks markets? The answer is Coca-Cola not Pepsi. It is readily available almost whenever and wherever customers could need it. Their excellent **distribution** gives them the edge.

This logic also transfers to the electronic marketspace. Esther Dyson says:

> *'You put coke machines in places where you think people might want to drink a coke. On the Internet you put Amazon buttons in places where there might be people inclined to buy books'.*

So, place involves the place of purchase, distribution and in some cases, consumption. Some products exploit all three aspects of place online, for example digitizable products such as software, media and entertainment.

But it's not just digitizable products and services – all products and services can extend themselves online by considering their online representation for place of purchase and distribution. Even perishable goods such as food and flowers are sold online as customers like the increased convenience and reduced cost of ordering online and often using delivery partners for offline fulfilment.

WHICH PLACE? REPRESENTATION

Berryman *et al.* (1998) highlighted the importance of place in e-commerce transactions when they identified the three different locations for online purchases shown in Figure 2.7. When many companies think about making their products available online, they tend to think only of selling direct from their web site (a). However, other alternatives for selling products are from a neutral marketplace (b) such as EC21 (www.ec21.com) and also through going direct to the customer (c) – an example of this is a business-to-business auction such as that described for GlaxoSmithKline in Section 2.5 where the supplier goes to the customer's site to bid. So companies need to consider the alternatives for online **representation**.

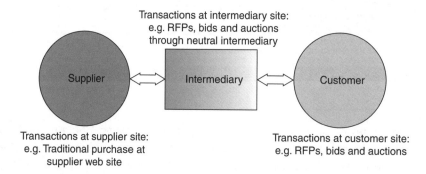

Figure 2.7 Alternative representation locations for online purchases

NEW DISTRIBUTION MODELS

So place is vital and an explosion of radically new ideas has occurred in the online world of distribution in the last five years. Here are a few:

- *Disintermediation* – This is removing the middleman to deal direct with customers instead of through agents, distributors and wholesalers. Note that this can create channel conflict as middlemen feel the squeeze. For example, Hewlett Packard sell a lot of equipment to hospitals. But, when hospitals started going directly to the HP site firstly for information and then secondly to place orders, it posed a big question: do we pay commission to the sales representative for this?

- *Reintermediation* – This is the emergence of new types of middlemen who are brokers, such as Bizrate, who unite buyers with sellers.
- *Infomediation* – A related concept where middlemen hold data or information to benefit customers and suppliers.
- *Channel confluence* – This has occurred where distribution channels start to offer the same deal to the end customer.
- *Peer-to-peer services* – Music swapping services such as Napster and Gnutella opened up an entirely new approach to music distribution with both supplier and middleman removed completely, providing a great threat, but also opportunity to the music industry.
- *Affiliation* – Affiliate programmes can turn customers into sales people. Many consider sales people as part of distribution. Others see them as part of the communications mix.

Excellent distribution requires a deep understanding of when and where customers want products and services. Partnership skills are also required as much distribution is externally sourced whether order fulfilment, warehousing, logistics or transport.

SECTION SUMMARY 2.6

Place

Distribution, or place, is crucial to the success of any enterprise. Assuming your organization has a reasonable product or service, online or offline the principle is the same: increase your representation and make it widely and readily available to target customers. Marketers today need to think of multi-channels for distribution to ensure they make their products and services easily available to as many ideal customers as possible.

2.7 Promotion

The Internet extends and integrates all ten online communications tools. This section summarizes the opportunities and the challenges of online communications that are explored in more detail in Chapter 7 on traffic building. First we consider the range of online promotion tools that are available. We then give guidelines as to how these tools can be best exploited.

ONLINE COMMUNICATIONS TOOLS

Online promotion is continuing to grow in importance and gaining an increasing share of marketers' budgets and efforts – whether a text message that changes behaviour immediately or key words that attract more enquiries or contextual banner ads that changes attitudes, or viral marketing that makes people talk about a brand. Online channels can do things that offline communications simply cannot, e.g. some web sites can promote, communicate and create a brand experience which is unique to the online users. Take the soft drink, Tango; it is renowned for its irreverence and fun approach. Tango.com brings the irreverence alive in a way that only the Internet can with games such as The Shocking Adventures of Nylon Neddie (see e-marketing insight box).

The complete promotional mix or communications mix – the ten communications tools (advertising, selling, sales promotion, PR, sponsorship, direct mail, exhibitions, merchandising, packaging, and word-of-mouth) – can be used to communicate or promote in the online or offline world. They can all be extended online in new and dynamic ways. Think about their online equivalents. Table 2.1 summarizes the online equivalents of these established communications tools.

Table 2.1   Online executions of different communications tools

Promotional mix	Online executions
1 Advertising	Interactive ads, pay per click keyword advertising
2 Selling	Virtual sales staff, affiliate marketing, web rings, links
3 Sales promotion	Incentives, rewards, online loyalty schemes
4 PR	Online editorial, e-zines, newsletters, discussion groups, virals
5 Sponsorship	Sponsoring an online event, site or service
6 Direct mail	Opt-in e-mail and web response
7 Exhibitions	Virtual exhibitions
8 Merchandising	Shopping malls, e-tailing, the interface
9 Packaging	Real packaging is displayed online
10 Word-of-mouth	Viral, affiliate marketing, e-mail a friend, web rings, links

Although web sites can be considered a separate communications tool, they are best thought of as an integrator of all ten tools shown in Table 2.1.

GUIDELINES FOR EFFECTIVE PROMOTION

The online promotional challenges marketers need to respond to can be summarized by the six key issues of mix, integration, creativity, interaction, globalization and resourcing.

1. Mix

E-marketers need to mix the **promotional mix**. This involves deciding on the optimum mix for different online promotional tools. Think about whether you use the full range of promotional tools in Table 2.1 and whether you are using the most cost effective techniques for acquiring your target customers.

Tango online

'*Clever, interactive, cool and wild*' is how the judges described the tango.tv web site, which was redeveloped by Grand Union. The purpose of this redevelopment was to make the site a central part of Tango's marketing activity. It had previously been used to post content, including viral games and TV ads, and to collect customer data.

Objective

Tango is renowned for its quirky TV ads and wanted to use the web site to build interactivity and participation around these, and create more enduring brand awareness among its target audience of teenage boys and girls.

Strategy

Grand Union developed three core campaigns for Tango to encourage kids to get involved online, including a game titled. The Shocking Adventures of Nylon Neddie, which centred on a character who builds up static electricity by rubbing his nylon-clad thighs. This added interactivity to the TV ads as they corresponded to each level of the game. Tango also used the site to extend the reach of its 'The Big Drench' promotional roadshow, which ran in cities across the UK, and featured several games, including Drench Roulette, in which players had to stand underneath a 30 ft-tall apple-shaped installation filled with water. An online 'soak-'em-up' game gave teenagers who couldn't make it to the events a chance to get involved and win prizes.

Results

Tango said that the investment in the site helped the brand grow 15.5% in terms of volume (litres) and 17% in terms of value last year. This corresponded to an increase in sales representing a growth in value of £5.7 m. The judges commented that the site fits very well with both the Tango strategy and audience, and were impressed with the integration of the web site into the campaigns as a whole. (*Source:* New Media Awards 2004, www.nma.co.uk/awards04).

2. Integration

Both online and offline communications must be integrated. All communications should support the overall positioning and **online value proposition** which the e-marketing strategy defines.

A single consistent message and a single integrated database are needed – which recognizes and remembers customers' names and needs regardless of which access devices are being used (TV, telephone, PC or hand-held device).

Online integration is difficult enough. Online and offline integration requires even more management skills.

E-MARKETING INSIGHT

Ten golden rules of IMC

1 Get management support for IMC (integrated marketing communications) by ensuring they understand its benefits to the organization.

2 Integrate at different levels by putting IMC on the agenda of different meetings; horizontally between managers in different functions such as distribution and production and ensure that PR, advertising and sales are integrating their efforts.

3 Maintain common visual standards for logos, typefaces and colours.

4 Focus on a clear marketing communications strategy. Have clear communications objectives. Have clear positioning statements. Link core values into every communication.

5 Start with a zero budget – build a new communications plan by specifying the resources needed and prioritizing communications activity accordingly.

6 Think customers first. Identify the stages before, during and after each purchase and develop a sequence of communications activities that help the customers through each stage.

7 Build relationships and brand values. All communications should strengthen customer relationships. Ask how each communication tool enables you to do this. Customer retention is as important as customer acquisition.

8 Develop a good marketing information system which defines who needs what information when. IMC defines, collects and shares vital information.

9 Share artwork and other media. Consider how advertising imagery can be used across mail shots, new releases and the web site.

10 Be prepared to change it all. Constantly search for the best communications mix.

---

3. Creativity

Today's marketer can exploit the vast untapped creative opportunities presented by the Internet. The only limitation is your imagination. Imagine sponsoring a virtual experience.

Or sending opt-in e-mails that make customers sit up and take notice.
Or developing the ultimate virtual exhibition.
Or ... moving into virtual immersion ...

Of course creativity must fit the overall communications strategy – communications impact is most powerful in the new context.

4. Interaction

Next comes the extra layer of creativity – interaction. This enhances the experience and deepens the communications impact (and can also collect customer data). This is where the online opportunity can really create some 'sizzle'.

5. Globalization

Then of course there are the added complications of a global audience. Web sites open your window to the world. When global audiences look in (to your site) they may not like what they see. See the e-marketing excellence box for some examples of the cultural and business practices that need to be considered for the Japanese market.

E-MARKETING EXCELLENCE

Adjusting the offering for the Japanese market

These are the many issues Clifford (2000) reported that Priceline (www.priceline.com) should be considering for a different culture:

1 Web site design – Japanese read from right to left.
2 Profit margins – Japanese negotiate fiercely. They do thorough research. Priceline may not get as good margins in this market.
3 No cancellations policy – Contracts in Japan 'are not perceived as final agreements. Traditionally, if either party has remorse there are renegotiations'.
4 One-hour acceptance or rejection of bids – Japanese don't like to make snap decisions.
5 Bargain hunting – Bargaining and price hunting is not talked about. Talking about haggling is tacky.
6 Customer service – 'At times you need to pretend that you are sure that your Japanese friend or colleague has understood you, even if you know this is not the case. This is important for maintaining a good relationship'.
7 Giveaways – 'In Japan, avoid giving gifts with an even number of components, such as an even number of flowers in a bouquet. Four is an especially inauspicious number; never give four of anything'.

6. Resourcing

The online communications opportunity is infinite. However resources to design and maintain the content, interactions and the database are not infinite. Resources are also needed to service customer enquiries whether online or offline.

Even ensuring consistent use of the brand requires time, energy and money.

Finally, remember all communications are wasted if the rest of the mix is wrong, for example a poorly targeted product.

SECTION SUMMARY 2.7

Promotion

All ten communications tools should be reviewed for how they can be extended and enriched online. Online communications challenges include: mix, integration, creativity, globalization and resourcing. Take advantage of the characteristics of the new media through promotion that is: dynamic, carefully targeted, highly relevant and helps build and ongoing relationships based on the permission and trust of the customer.

2.8 People

In services marketing, people, or staff, are considered a crucial element of the marketing mix. As more products add online services to enhance their offerings 'people' become more and more important. By the end of this section you will understand how service needs a balance of people and automation and what the key management challenges are.

WHY ARE PEOPLE IMPORTANT?

Think about why so many clicks and mortar companies outperform pure dotcoms. As well as experience of the marketplace, people (and process) are key – real people, real buildings and established integrated systems that deliver goods and services. People are important since everyone in your organization is an ambassador and a sales person for your company.

Given that everyone represents the company, you can see the importance of having happy staff.

Happy Staff = Happy Customers = Happy Shareholders

The challenge, of course, is to recruit the right people, train them and reward or motivate them appropriately. This is a real issue as the MGCC *Benchmarking Report* (2004) reveals that call centres' service is getting worse, in fact deteriorating over a four-year period. As Professor Merlin Stone (personal communication) says: 'we are sitting on a customer service time bomb'. This is in a turbulent environment where customer expectations are rising and often times satisfying these rising expectations is not enough to keep customers loyal. However, we ignore customer service at our peril.

DELIVERING ONLINE SERVICE

Remember the 90:10 ratio? Some suggest that web sites should adopt the 90:10 ratio as the value or service to sales pitch ratio. This implies that the bulk, 90 per cent, of your web site should be designed to service customers.

In the online world much service can be automated. How well does your site make use of the following?

- **Autoresponders**. These automatically generate a response when a company e-mails an organization, or submits an online form.
- **E-mail notification**. Automatically generated by a company's systems to update customers on the status of their order: for example, order received, item now in stock, order dispatched.
- **Call-back facility**. Customers fill in their phone number on a form and specify a convenient time to be contacted. Dialling from a representative in the call centre occurs automatically at the appointed time and the company pays, which is popular.
- **Frequently asked questions (FAQs)**. For these, the art is in compiling and categorizing the questions so customers can easily find (a) the question and (b) a helpful answer.
- **On-site search engines**. These help customers find what they're looking for quickly and are popular when available. Some companies have improved conversion to sale greatly by improving the clarity of the results the search engines return. Site maps are a related feature.
- **Real-time live chat**. A customer support operator in a call centre can type responses to a site visitor's questions. For example a widely deployed technology such as LivePerson (www.liveperson.com).
- **Co-browsing**. Here the customer's screen can be viewed by the call-centre operator in combination with callback or chat.
- **Virtual assistants**. These come in varying degrees of sophistication and usually help to guide the customer through a maze of choices.

IS AUTOMATION ALWAYS BEST? INBOUND CONTACT STRATEGIES

The concept of '**customer self-service**' or 'web self-service' is prevalent in e-marketing. Customer self-service enables the customer to obtain the information they need faster and saves the business money. However, we need to pause and ask whether all customers want to conduct all their interactions online.

Think of buying an air ticket via the web. This is fine if you have a particular flight in mind, and it is available. If it is not, our experience is that it is quicker to talk to a customer representative who is knowledgeable of the alternatives available.

Some online customer segments just want to browse, others want to find specific information and others again want to buy or get customer support. Of the segment that wants to buy, a sub-segment want to buy off-line and need personal contact either via phone, letter, or personal visit. Alternatively they cannot find the information they need online in the **FAQ** or via the online search engine. At this point the customer will want to contact the company by e-mail or phone. Inbound contact strategies aim to control the volume and medium of enquiries and responses. Responses may be by **autoresponder**, e-mail, phone or real time chat with sales staff as shown in Figure 2.8.

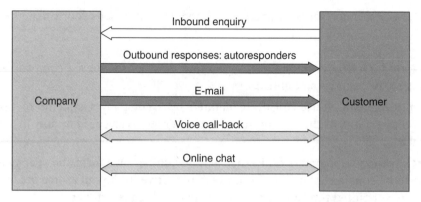

Figure 2.8   Customer contact alternatives for an inbound e-mail enquiry

Many companies such as the Nationwide bank (www.nationwide.co.uk) use an **inbound contact strategy** of customer choice or '**customer preferred channel**'. But the easyJet e-marketing excellence box in Section 1.7 shows that you can give customers a choice, but steer them towards using the web as a contact tool.

A key figure for measuring the effectiveness of your inbound contact strategy is the average number of contacts to resolve an issue. Remember that many questions will not be answered by the first e-mail. Companies need to decide whether the best strategy is to switch the customer to phone or online chat to resolve the issue rather than bouncing multiple e-mails between customer and contact centre. Two-way interactions such as voice, online chat and co-browsing (where the customer's screen can be viewed by the call-centre operator) will be more effective in resolving an issue immediately.

KEEPING CONTENT FRESH

Many organizations now have many thousands of web pages, often across separate web sites and different technology platforms. To keep the content fresh, up-to-date and relevant to the customer has significant management and resource implications. We will see in Section 6.7 how **Content management systems (CMSs)** are essential to the consistency and management of any large site since it will enable **content owners** in different parts of the organization to update the content they are responsible for. They also provide workflow facilities which can automatically prompt a content owner to update content and use e-mail to remind other staff to review and authorize publication. But having the right technology is only part of the story. Managers of content owners must have strategies to keep content fresh. These may include:

1 *Regular update dates* such as start of month for some content types like news or promotions.
2 *Triggers for publication.* Every new press release or product or price change must go on site.
3 *Ownership of content in job description.* The quality of content, including freshness, is part of staff performance appraisal (this is a 'stick' approach).
4 *Explaining benefits of content update to content owners.* Showing that updates will save the content owner time, e.g. in explaining things on the phone or by helping them sell more (this is a carrot approach).

5 *Using the CMS to set content expiry dates*. For certain content types, expiry dates can be set and an e-mail alert sent to the content owner.

6 *Publish dates of when pages on site last updated*. Some organizations use a chart to show which pages are updated least frequently to shame staff into taking ownership!

7 *Real-time content delivery* taking articles or items from a database, so partially automating the update process (the database still needs to be updated).

TRAINING AND RESOURCING

Of course staff need to be trained and motivated whether they man the web site, the telephones, the field sales, the reception. What happens if a web transaction fails and the customer calls the centre? Can call centre staff access the web database to complete the transaction, or do they have to collect all the details again? A seamless, integrated contact database is required.

A key resourcing issue is whether to identify specific staff to handle contacts from different channels or empowering staff to answer questions from a variety of channels. Current thinking suggests the latter approach is best since this increases the variety of work and results in more knowledgeable staff who can better answer customers' queries.

It is worth investing in continual staff training as well as in online tools. Benchmark research from Harvard (Kotter and Heskett, 1992) revealed that companies who invest in all three key stakeholders (employees, customers and shareholders) outperform those that invest in only two or less (say customers and shareholders).

A final point is that although some consider the Internet 'marginalizes the role of direct customer contact', it is also used to recruit quality staff. Most potential recruits these days check out the web site as a matter of course. If they don't they're probably not management material!

SECTION SUMMARY 2.8

People

People/staff are important. People are the differentiating factor that has helped many 'clicks and mortar' companies outperform the virtual companies. In fact, service – before, during and after a sale – is required if repeat business is to be enjoyed. Contact strategies should be developed that give customers choice of contact, but minimize costly interactions with staff. Automated services help but people are also required. It is a delicate balancing act but bear them both in mind when integrating online and offline marketing activities. Recruitment, training and motivation are required. And remember, happy staff = happy customers = happy shareholders. Beware of the customer service time bomb.

2.9 Physical evidence

The aim of this section is to highlight the different aspects of physical evidence a web site can display and check your web site has them.

WHAT IS ONLINE PHYSICAL EVIDENCE?

When buying intangible services, customers look for physical evidence to reassure them. In the offline world this includes buildings, uniforms, logos and more. In the online world the evidence is digital – primarily through web sites but also through e-mail.

In the online world, customers look for other cues and clues to reassure themselves about the organization. So firstly, a reassuring sense of order is required. This means web sites should be designed with a consistent look and feel that customers feel comfortable with, as explained in Chapter 6 Site design. But on site reassurance can extend far beyond this, particularly for an e-tailer, by using:

- Guarantees
- Refund policies
- Privacy policies
- Security icons
- Trade body memberships
- Awards
- Customer lists
- Customer endorsements
- Independent reviews
- News clippings.

Physical evidence should help integrate the online and offline world. Many white goods retailers such as the Carphone Warehouse (www.carphonewarehouse.com) use coupons printed out online which can be redeemed for a discount at a store. This helps conversion-to-sale rates and also tracks how the online presence is impacting offline sales.

Remember that physical evidence emerges in the offline world – if goods and services are delivered offline then the normal physical evidence is required, i.e. professional packaging, paperwork, delivery vehicles and uniforms can all reinforce the right message.

Equally they can damage the brand if they are not managed. Imagine a scruffy delivery person in a filthy broken-down van belching fumes stopping outside your home or office. The offline evidence would damage the online evidence. So, both need to be managed carefully.

SECTION SUMMARY 2.9

Physical evidence

Customers look for cues and clues for reassurance. Web sites can provide these in the form of high quality site design and reassurance through guarantees, refund policies, privacy policies, security icons, trade body memberships, awards, customer lists, customer endorsements, independent reviews, news clippings. Encourage web site visitors to print coupons or white papers as physical evidence to keep your company at the front of their minds.

Offline activities can provide them in the form of professional looking buildings, delivery vans and uniforms. Evidence, whether physical or digital needs to be managed constantly.

2.10 Process

Process refers to the internal and sometimes external processes, transactions and internal communications that are required to run a business. Excellent execution of these is vital. By the end of this section you will be able to identify the components of process and understand how they need to be integrated into a database.

THE IMPORTANCE OF PROCESS

'Execution, execution, execution' is the new mantra, said Booze Allen and Hamilton (2003). 'Execution is the missing link between aspirations and results', say Larry Bossiddy and Ram Charan (2004). Excellent processes are where e-commerce ends and e-business begins. Un-integrated e-commerce sites create problems as witnessed by US online toy stores whose web sites and associated processes did not link into an information system explaining to customers when stocks were unavailable.

Traditional offline services have processes continually on view with the manufacturing process for goods behind closed doors. Online services and their process of production are not as visible since much of the processes operate in systems unseen by the customer. Some of the process, or system, is on view, like menus, form filling, shopping baskets, follow-up e-mails and of course the interactions on web sites. It is on this part of the process and its outputs that customers will judge service.

It seems that many companies have not yet learnt how to optimize these processes – 80 per cent of potential buyers exit before they make their purchase. This suggests ordering is too complicated or confusing, or the system simply doesn't work smoothly.

OPTIMIZING INTERNAL PROCESSES

To understand the importance of process, consider a simple online enquiry and subsequent online sale of a book. How should the system work? Think about which events or actions need to take place for the order to be fulfilled and for the customer to be satisfied.

These are some of the events that need to happen, and they must be backed up by an efficient, seamless process:

- Customer wants to check availability – Does the site show number in stock and when next available if out of stock (see Dabs.com (www.dabs.com) for good practice).
- Product specification or price is changed – Is the change seamlessly reflected in web site and price lists or catalogues?
- Customer places order – Is the site updated to indicate changed number in stock? Is the customer notified by e-mail that their order has been processed? Is the finance system updated to include the new order within the month's revenue?

- Customer makes e-mail enquiry – Can the system cope when a wave of telephone calls and e-mails hit and respond promptly and accurately?
- Produce dispatched – Is the customer notified of this event by e-mail? Can they track their order if required?

Optimization involves minimizing the people involved with responding to each event and providing them with the right information to serve the customer. Minimizing human resources can occur through redesigning the processes and/or automating them through technology. The problem is that many sites simply do not have efficient systems in place. They lack the logistical and fulfilment infrastructure required to trade online.

Processes continue beyond the sale with feedback, upselling, cross selling, product development and improvement built in as part of the processes.

The front end, customer interface – whether on a web site, interactive TV screen, mobile phone screen or even a telephone sales person – must integrate with the back end systems which are out of sight in the back offices and warehouse. This is easier said than done. Some 50 per cent of the FTSE 1000 companies still do not have a robust and single view of their customers (Mazur, 2004).

A well managed process integrates into the business processes and systems which, in turn, shave costs and slash inventories. Some companies take orders and payment immediately and ask third party suppliers to supply directly. So stock (and working capital required to fund stock) is reduced to zero. In fact, because the company receives payment from the customer and doesn't pay the supplier for 30 or 60 days, the company generates surplus cash. This creates negative working capital because instead of having to fund stock with working capital the supply process is so tight it generates its own funds.

E-MARKETING INSIGHT

Wobbly Shopping Carts Blight UK e-commerce

UK e-commerce sites are slapping customers in the face, rather than shaking them by the hand. Turning consumers away once they have made a decision to buy is commercial suicide.

- 20% of shopping carts did not function for 12 hours a month or more
- 75% failed the standard service level availability of 99.9% uptime
- 80% performed inconsistently with widely varying response times, time-outs and errors – leaving customers at best wondering what to do next and at worst, unable to complete their purchases.

(*Source:* Leyden, 2004)

OPTIMIZING EXTERNAL PROCESSES

Reviewing processes and systems can help radically to redesign supply and distribution chains, and in the process, compete much more effectively.

For many organizations, Jack Welsh's internal slogan 'Destroy Your Business.com' (before the dotcoms do) makes a lot of sense just from the process side alone. Reinvent the business process so it's faster, lighter on resources and, most importantly, makes the customer happy.

Classic marketing empathizes with the customer – what kind of problems, priorities, and procedures do they need? What will delight them? Then build the process that caters for the many diverse types of customers out there.

How value chains need to be revised is another aspect of process that is considered in Chapter 9, E-business.

SECTION SUMMARY 2.10

Process

Good processes and systems can create competitive advantage. There's lots of poor processes that kill sales and damage the brand. Processes can have a huge impact on your organization.

2.11 An extra 'P', partnerships

Perhaps there is a new P in the mix, 'partnerships' or marketing marriages or alliances. With almost two thirds (64%) of the UK top 1000 companies confirming they have staff dedicated to partnership marketing (Craggs, 2002) it is not surprising, a few years later, to find award-winning e-marketing campaigns revealing a common pattern – partnerships. Although increasingly important in the offline world of marketing, clever partnerships are also emerging as keys that open the doors to vast new markets. Hence the emergence of alliance managers. Here are a few examples:

Ford Galaxy teamed up with Tesco and AOL to gain access to a million new online customers within its target audience of 30–44-year-old women with children. Ford also wanted to be associated with brands that have already improved its target audience's lives.

MUtv (the TV channel devoted to Manchester United) partnered with Sky and Century Radio in an attempt to develop its product so it could create an exciting proposition which quickly attracted 379 000 unique users in 98 countries. Combine this with MORI's estimated MUFC global fan base of 70 million and you can see the potential.

In the online world, many e-retailers now have staff dedicated to managing online partnerships, particularly for **affiliate marketing,** which is covered in Chapter 7.

Partnerships

We cannot do everything ourselves. Partnerships can help enormously but they require skilled management.

1 The marketing mix must be re-examined for the online world since there are many new opportunities to vary the mix to take advantage of the characteristics of digital media.

2 The main elements of the traditional marketing mix are product, price, place, promotion, people, processes and physical evidence. Alternative models such as the 5 Is of identification, individualization, interaction, integration, integrity have been developed in recognition of the potential of one-to-one/relationship marketing online.

3 Relationship building and service quality is vital with the trends towards consolidation and commoditization. Building relationships and increasing loyalty is required to increase profitability.

4 **Product.** Products can be extended online by offering new information-based services and interaction with the brand to create new brand experiences.

5 **Price.** Reduction in market prices is caused by online price transparency through purchasing methods such as reverse auction, price comparison and shopping bots. B2B exchanges and hubs will become significant for routine purchase of commoditized products. Marketers will continually have to monitor prices to remain competitive.

6 **Place.** Changes in the place of promotion, purchase, distribution and usage of products are considered when specifying the place element of mix. Disintermediation and reintermediation are major marketplace changes which must be responded to.

7 **Promotion.** Online options for all elements of the promotional mix from advertising, selling, sales promotion, PR, sponsorship, direct mail, exhibitions, merchandising, packaging to word-of-mouth should all be reviewed for the promotion part of the mix. Key issues in devising the promotional mix are integration, creativity, globalization and resourcing.

8 **People.** People are a significant contributor to the mix since service quality is a key differentiator online or offline. Organizations need to decide on the best balance of automated online customer service and traditional human service to provide customers with service quality and choice while at the same time minimizing service costs.

9 **Physical evidence.** The quality of the site is the physical evidence online, so it is important to reassure customers buying intangible services through a site that meets acceptable standards of speed and ease of use. This can be supplemented by certification by independent organizations.

10 **Process.** All processes impact customers in terms of product and service quality. In the online context it is particularly important to revise processes by integrating front and back office systems to provide efficient response to customer support requests and fulfilment.

11 **Partnerships.** Marketing marriages and alliances can be potent but need experienced management.

References

Bartels, F. (1963) *The History of Marketing Thought*. Richard D. Irwin, Homewood, Illinois.

Berryman, K., Harrington, L., Layton-Rodin, D. and Rerolle, V. (1998) Electronic commerce: three emerging strategies. *The Mckinsey Quarterly*, No 1, 152–9.

Booms, B.H. and Bitner, M.J. (1981) Marketing strategies and organizational structures for service firms, in *Marketing of Services*, eds J. Donnelly and W. George, pp. 477–51, American Marketing Association, Chicago.

Booze, Allen & Hamilton (2003) The four bases of organisational DNA. *Strategy & Business*, Winter Issue, 33.

Bossiddy, L. and Charan, R. (2004) Execution – the discipline of getting things done. Crown Business.

Butler, M. (2001) Techno Business. *Winning Business*, January, p. 75.

Clifford, L. (2000) Shatner will fly in Japan; Priceline may not. An interview with Japanese business expert Terri Morrison (co-author *Kiss or Blow – How to do business in 60 countries*). *Fortune*, 2 October.

Colvin, G. (2000) Value Driven, You Might Get Your Next Face Lift Online. *Fortune*, 29 May.

Craggs, J. (2002) Partnership Marketing Professionals and their Presence in Top British Companies. *CRM Community News*.

Dyson, E. (1999) www.medialifemagazine.com/newspapers/archives/jan00/news20104.html. 31 December.

Ghosh, S. (1998) Making Business Sense of the Internet. *Harvard Business Review*, March–April, pp. 126–35.

Kotter, J. and Heskett, J. (1992) *Corporate Culture and Performance*. Free Press, New York.

Leyden, J. (2004) Wobbly Shopping Carts Blight UK e-Commerce. TheRegister.co.uk, 4 June.

Mazur, L. (2004) Poor Profiling. *Marketing Business*, February.

McCarthy, J. (1960) *Basic marketing: a managerial approach*. Richard D. Irwin, Homewood, Illinois.

McMillan, S. (2001) *Next Generation eBusiness*. IBM UK.

MGCC (2004) *Benchmarking Report 2004*. Merchant's Global Contact Centre.

Multimedia Marketing Consortium (2000a) Interactive Marketing. *CD 10 Integrated Marketing Communications*. www.multimediamarketing.com. London.

Multimedia Marketing Consortium (2000b) Interactive Marketing. *CD2 Segmentation, Positioning and the Marketing Mix*. www.multimediamarketing.com. London.

Nielsen, J. (2001) Tagline blues: what's the site about. 22 July. www.useit.com.

Peppers, D. and Rogers, M. (1997) *One to One Future*. Doubleday, New York, 2nd edition.

Queree, A. (2000) *Financial Times* Technology supplement. 1 March.
Toffler, A. (1980) *The Third Wave*. Bantam Books, New York.

 ## Further reading

Bickerton, P., Bickerton, M. and Pardesi, U. (2000) *CyberMarketing*. Butterworth-Heinemann, Oxford. Chartered Institute of Marketing series, 2nd edition. Chapter 6 Exploiting your global niche – the best marketing mix.

Chaffey, D., Mayer, R., Johnston, K. and Ellis-Chadwick, F. (2003) *Internet Marketing: Strategy, Implementation and Practice*. Financial Times/Prentice Hall, Harlow, Essex, 2nd edition. See Chapter 5 The Internet and the marketing mix.

Cumming, T. (2001) *Little e, big commerce*. Virgin Business Guides, London. Chapter 6 Set marketing strategies and targets.

Smith, P.R. and Taylor, J. (2004) *Marketing Communications: an integrated approach*. Kogan Page. London, 4th edition. Chapter 1 Marketing and the integrated communications mix.

 ## Self-test

1 For each element of the marketing mix (7 Ps) list two differences introduced by the digital world.

2 How appropriate are the 5 Is of identification, individualization, interaction, integration and integrity as a replacement for the marketing mix?

3 What is the principal way in which product can be varied through an online presence?

4 Summarize in one sentence how an online presence can be used to enhance brands.

5 Explain the reasons for price transparency and marketing responses to this phenomenon.

6 Describe the relevance of disintermediation and reintermediation to your organization and actions that have been/should be taken.

7 Summarize online applications of advertising, PR, direct selling and word-of-mouth promotional mix tools.

8 Recommend a channel contact strategy for inbound communications to your organization.

9 How does the concept of physical evidence relate to your organization's web site?

10 Assess how your online presence contributes to the main business processes and to what extent they have been streamlined by the move online.

Chapter 3

E-models

'The rapid growth of first multi-channel, then digital, then personal video recorders and soon higher-speed broadband are simply the pre-tremors of the real volcanic eruption that technology is about to unleash. At the risk of being overdramatic I would say that most traditional television broadcasters are today standing about the equivalent of one mile from Mount St Helens. When it blows, frankly, that is too close and then it will be too late to run'.

Ofcom chairman Lord Currie's address to the
Royal Television Society quoted in ZDNet (2005).

OVERVIEW

The business world is changing faster than ever before. Old approaches and models are being turned on their head. The white heat of change causes many business people to wake up sweating in the middle of the night and check the locks on their old business models. To no avail. The wired and unwired world has moved on overnight turning old models over and paving the way for a host of new business models.

OVERALL LEARNING OUTCOME

By the end of this chapter you will:

- Understand why many of the old models are redundant.
- Appreciate the many new business models that are emerging.
- Select which models are appropriate for your business.

CHAPTER TOPIC	LEARNING OBJECTIVE
3.1 Introduction	Outline the changes to existing models, and new models
3.2 New models required	Describe the drivers of new models and action required in response
3.3 E-business models – value chains	Outline changes and responses to value chain models
3.4 E-business models – production models	Understand and respond to implications of changes to production models
3.5 E-business models – procurement	Assess the implications of e-procurement from both buyer and seller perspectives
3.6 E-business models – distribution models	Analyse the relevance of new distribution models
3.7 Communications models	Describe differences in communications models and how they can be exploited
3.8 Customer buying models	Summarize changes to buying models and assess their implications
3.9 Customer information processing	Assess differences in customer information processing that occur online
3.10 Loyalty models	Assess the relevance of new loyalty models

3.1 Introduction to e-models

Whether business models, revenue models, procurement models, distribution models or buying models, old models are being replaced by new and revised models. This chapter explores some of the changes to existing models and explores the novel models that are emerging to see how they relate to your business.

It is the fluid, flexible and agile businesses that embrace the new models enabled by technology and exploit the opportunities presented by the new economy.

Before exploring the different models, let's clarify what is a model. A model is anything that represents reality. It could be a model aeroplane, a map, a diagram, algebra or a formula. Here, we are particularly interested in descriptive models that describe a process – the current way in which a business operates in its dealings with customers, suppliers and distributors. This chapter does not address prescriptive models that forecast results and events.

There are many different implications of change in different types of models:

- **Value chains** and **distribution channels** are restructured as existing channel partners are bypassed and new channel partners and **value networks** are formed and reformed.
- Supermarkets become banks as radical changes to **business models** and **revenue models** are enacted.
- 'Markets become conversations' (Levine *et al.*, 2000), where dialogue between customers and employee and customer drive the relationships.
- Marketing becomes transparent as customers manage the relationship with companies rather than the other way around. Systems and control mechanisms are opened up to customers.
- Brand equity changes from being visually driven to interactively driven.
- Businesses can become what Charles Handy calls a 'box of contracts', as many functions are outsourced to form a **virtual business**.

In reviewing changes to models, a useful framework is to look at different members of the marketspace as shown in Figure 3.1. We can consider e-models from:

1 *A buy-side e-commerce perspective.* This includes new supply chain and procurement models.
2 *A sell-side e-commerce perspective.* This includes distribution models and customer-related models including communications models.
3 *An internal organization perspective.* This includes new models for restructuring internal business processes. This perspective is considered in Chapter 9, E-business.
4 *A value chain perspective.* This integrates across the three perspectives above and includes the emerging role of value networks.

CAUTION REQUIRED

Do you remember, in the introductory chapter, we highlighted the accuracy of the CEO of Gartner Group's gloomy forecast that 95–98 per cent of dotcoms would be dead in two years?

Well he also added that there would be a return to 'old economy concepts' such as market share, brand equity and operational integrity. Many of the dotcoms had no integrated business processes, no control mechanisms, no clear propositions, just bits of clever technology. In this chapter we are not advocating a radical change to models as essential for all companies – but a review of new alternative models is essential for many. In the future, successful businesses will have hybrid business models tailored to the online economy, but based on traditional economy concepts such as strong propositions carefully targeted at the right customer segments.

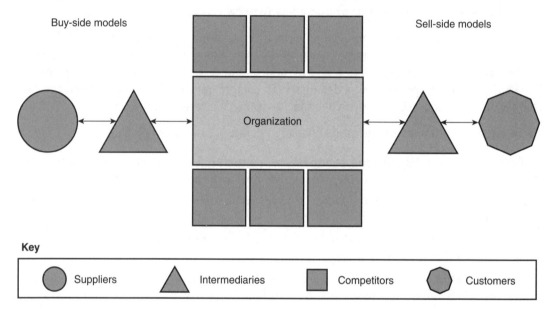

Figure 3.1   Different perspectives for model changes in an organization's marketplace

---

E-MARKETING INSIGHT

One perspective on model change

The Financial Times (Jackson, 2000) reported the three biggest shift in models as follows:

1 Turning customers into sales agents (Amazon affiliate links with their customer's web sites and member-get-member programmes).

2 Paying customers to use your product (paying customers to view adverts and trial products).

3 Free shares (some web businesses offer free shares for simply signing up and opening up an account).

It is apparent that this perspective on models is limited to sell-side e-commerce.

SECTION SUMMARY 3.1

Introduction to e-models

Models describe the process by which business is conducted between an organization, its customers, suppliers, distributors and other stakeholders. Managers constantly need to review how electronic communications change existing models and offer new models that may confer competitive advantage.

3.2 New models required

What happens when people stop watching TV and stop going to the shops? What happens when a significant proportion of the population, say 10 per cent, stop watching advertisements on TV and the web. They filter out banner ads and junk mail. They also only watch non-commercial TV (e.g. BBC3) or use TiVo technology to filter out the ads and watch the programmes only, when they want. They also stop shopping in shops because they realize they have better things to do plus better deals to get by going online instead?

COMMODITIZATION – THE DRIVER OF MANY NEW MODELS

All markets eventually tend towards **commoditization** as competition catches up, matches features, quality and prices. Assume that prices and quality are similar then what affects sales volume? We can construct a very simple model which shows that the advertising can differentiate the brands and that distribution can ensure competitive advantage. The model would look like this:

$$A + D = S \ldots \text{Advertising} + \text{Distribution} = \text{Sales}$$

But what if 'A + D' don't work for some segments any more? Should the business forget about this small, but growing, percentage of the market and let the market segment move away? Or can it devise new models to try to keep these customers? There is no single right answer here.

Through time, commoditization will further reduce the role of 'A + D'. Price driven shopping bots will be used to scour the web for best deals, brands will suffer as cheapest prices will be chosen every time. So success will be determined by **searchbots**. Are there any new models to deal with this? How can the brand be saved from the ravages of rational, price-driven, searchbots scouring the world for the best deal delivered locally?

How can retailers 'beat the bot'? How can a retailer make an impression on a bot driven shopper (a customer who uses shopping bots to find the best price)? There are no easy answers here. Creative solutions are required for the many new scenarios that are emerging. One option is to change the price positioning of a product and make sure it is competitively listed on every shop-bot. The other alternative followed by the Abbey bank is to remove yourselves from the shop-bot. Europeans like to save money through Internet shopping, and ii ingly, TV shopping (almost 50 shopping channels on European TV).

New models are required in response to these changes. But visualizing new models is difficult – we are constrained by the layers of caution and comfort in which we insulate ourselves. To escape the confines of these layers we need to think laterally. Think freely. Think of new models, new approaches, new ways to solve problems. As with any brainstorming, we will discard many options, selecting those that offer genuine improvements to business performance. The remainder of this chapter considers some of the many options for new models.

E-MARKETING INSIGHT

The impact of comparison sites

In October, 2000, *Revolution* reported a dispute between Abbey National and financial comparison site Moneysupermarket.com. This dispute highlights the positive and negative impact of online comparisons. The bank had reportedly requested that several comparison sites not list them. Simon Nixon, chief executive of Moneysupermarket.com, was reported as saying:

> *'We've all predicted the effect that the Internet will have by giving customers information and choice. If Abbey National is worried about unfavourable comparisons on mortgage rates, then the ball is fairly and squarely in their court'.*

SECTION SUMMARY 3.2

New models required

We need new models to respond to changes in the environment such as reduced TV watching and reduced trips to the shops and the increase in commoditization. We need to think creatively; consider new models; adapt old models; consider mixed mode models and let common sense prevail so that real models create real solutions to the new economy's opportunities.

3.3 E-business models – value chains

Michael Porter's (1980) now classic **value chain** model highlighted how value is added as raw materials are processed and developed into products, which eventually arrive at buyer markets (Figure 3.3). The difficulty with this model when considering online activities is the dominant imagery associated with the 'chain' part of the concept. This suggests a binding link between various components of the model. The Internet and the web have substantially weakened any such ties. The technology enables temporary collaborations and facilitates outsourcing of internal operations. Indeed the whole concept of a continuous chain where a company has sole use and control is not relevant in a highly networked environment. The emergent concept is of a highly fluid **value network** as shown in Figure 3.2. The old value

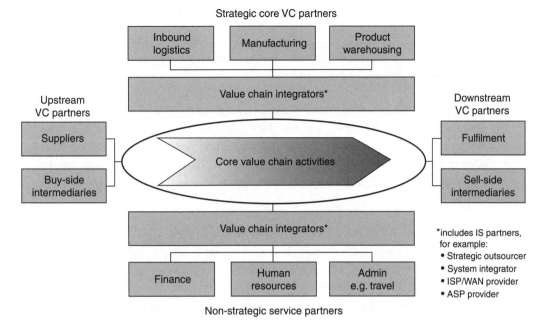

Figure 3.2 Elements of a value network

chain is being replaced with non-linear value networks which extend the business operations into trusted partner companies who fulfil any aspect of the old value chain. Plug and play companies pick off specific processes in today's value networks and offer their services to companies with weak elements in the value chain/network. As businesses move towards value networks they minimize physical infrastructure and non-critical assets to create 'zero gravity' (zero physical assets which tie them down). The difficult question raised in Chapter 1, 'what business are we in?' emerges again and again.

Value networks are different as they emphasize:

- The electronic interconnections between partners and the organization and directly between partners enable real-time information exchange between partners.
- The dynamic nature of the network. The network can be readily modified according to market conditions or in response to customer demands. New partners can readily be introduced into the network and others removed if they are not performing.

Different types of links can be formed between different types of partners. For example, integrated databases may be established with key suppliers, while e-mail links may suffice for less significant suppliers.

In the last millennium, businesses often aimed to own every part of what was known as the value chain (**vertical integration**). Today there has been a general move to **virtual integration** where businesses seem to be what Charles Handy once referred to as a 'box of contracts'. Such a business sub-contracts or outsources key services to businesses who are better at that

particular service. The business only retains those parts in which it has a core competency and a competitive advantage.

Speaking at the World Economic Forum in Davos, John Hagel assessed the future implications of outsourcing as follows (Kirkpatrick, 2001):

> *'Most organizations up to now have been an unnatural bundle of three very different kinds of businesses: finding and building customer relationships; creating and marketing products; and managing your infrastructure, from overseeing call centres to delivery systems. Companies are going to have to be world class in just one of these categories and rely on others who are themselves world class to provide the other two'.*

This is the incredible part. In the search for core competencies, some businesses find that their core strengths lie elsewhere outside their traditional business. Perhaps in a peripheral business or a secondary business. This, in turn, forces a business to consider the very nature of its business and ask difficult questions like 'what business are we in?' GE, Drill company has switched from manufacture and distribution of oil bits to information aligning themselves with core competencies that customers require. Another example illustrates how partnerships, strategic alliances and marketing marriages can be used to deliver a service. Consider BBC's web cast of golf's prestigious Ryder Cup. Here, various ISPs provided the backbone, Progressive Networks provided the technology and BBC the content.

It is worth noting, however that not everyone agrees with the 'outsourcing fiends', particularly when you outsource management of the customer relationship, in particular customer contacts. All the other outsourcing opportunities do, however, require good partnership skills.

E-MARKETING INSIGHT

Deise: value chains to value networks

Deise *et al.* (2000) describe value network management as:

> *'the process of effectively deciding what to outsource in a constraint-based, real-time environment based on fluctuation'.*

They go on to say that:

> *'in the value network world, companies will have to build businesses on three key principles'*:
>
> *1 Owning the customer relationship.*
>
> *2 Focusing on differentiating core competencies.*
>
> *3 Building the best value network to provide other competencies.*

E-MARKETING EXCELLENCE

Cisco outsource core competencies?

Cisco is well known as the manufacturer of hardware components such as routers that comprise Internet infrastructure. However, it was suggested at the World Economic Forum in Davos, that increasingly it is changing its role to become increasingly a software and services firm through outsourcing or partnering for manufacture and other value chain functions and focusing mainly on integration (Kirkpatrick, 2001). Cisco CEO John Chambers was reported as saying

> *'we're already much of the way there. About 70% of Cisco's hardware goes directly from the deeply interconnected partners who make the products to customers, without a Cisco employee's ever handling any goods'.*

Chambers emphasized that he continually re-evaluates what should be Cisco's primary business.

SECTION SUMMARY 3.3

E-business models – value chains

Value chains are being replaced by dynamic value networks. Asking 'what business are we in' helps to identify your core strengths. Identifying your core business can determine your future.

3.4 E-business models – production models

The old linear model of 'design and build, brand it, sell it' is being replaced by a more dynamic model. A model that involves customers more with the new product development process and suppliers more in the ordering process.

So instead of a linear production process with customers at the end of it, the new model actually has feedback and input from customers coming in much earlier, more frequently, in fact an integral part of the production process. Figure 3.3 shows how the Michael Porter style **value chain** in part (a) is being replaced by a customer driven value chain, part (b).

THE PROSUMER AND NEW PRODUCT DEVELOPMENT

The **prosumer** has arrived. Look around you and you'll see it happening. From TV to toys to cars and computers. Customers are increasingly involved in the production process.

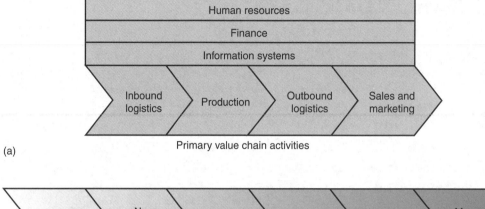

Secondary value chain activities

Human resources

Finance

Information systems

| Inbound logistics | Production | Outbound logistics | Sales and marketing |

Primary value chain activities

(a)

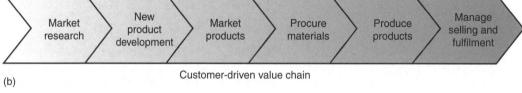

| Market research | New product development | Market products | Procure materials | Produce products | Manage selling and fulfilment |

Customer-driven value chain

(b)

Figure 3.3 New versus old value chain model

Chapter 5 has an interesting example of how MTV used text messages and the web to create a show based on the customers' votes. But look around you and observe 'people TV' in action. It uses real people/customers/audience type of people as the stars of the production (reduces costs). Audiences then take control and vote for who should stay or go. The web cam keeps running. The hits keep counting and the show goes on partly created and largely controlled by the customer.

Cars are no exception when it comes to the prosumer. Visitors can assemble and order their own car online. The customers fill in the order form and specification forms (not the sales rep). More interestingly, BMW actually had customers' online help to design and choose a final version.

We all know how clever Dell, IBM and many others are at integrating their production process right into their customers' own internal systems so that customers can order directly online what they need, when they need it. The box 'Barbie and the young prosumer' illustrates another example of using the web to involve the customer in NPD.

E-MARKETING EXCELLENCE

Barbie and the young prosumer

A few years ago girls' doll company Barbie.com realized that their efforts to design a website for 6–12-year-old girls were not working. They recruited a group of 6–12-year-old girls to redesign the site. Traffic doubled within a month and went on to double again after a few months. The average visit lasts for 26 minutes.

Today the site is called Everythinggirl.com and contains many friendly features including 'Make a wish list' which 'is easy and fun'. Click on 'Find more faves' and when they see something they really like they simply click on it to add it to their wish list. When finished visitors are invited to 'print your wish list, e-mail it to family and friends or save it for later' thereby giving the company some very useful feedback on its most (and least) popular products, raising the profile of the brand by word-of-mouth and influencing decision makers who buy the dolls.

CHANGES IN THE ROLE OF THE SUPPLIER IN PURCHASING

The roles of supplier and customer in the purchasing process have also changed.

> *'What's happening is a shift towards consumption in which the lines have blurred between producer and consumer or customer. The customer provides information as to what they want … the relationship of the customer to producer is radically changed and enhanced by the Internet'. Alvin Toffler quoted in Daly (2000)*

The box 'Shell Chemical radically changes its supply chain management' gives an example of this phenomenon of increased supplier participation in practice.

E-MARKETING EXCELLENCE

Shell Chemical radically changes its supply chain management

In the late 1990s Shell Chemical introduced a new Lotus Notes based system called SIMON (Shell Inventory Managed Order Network). This system transformed the way that Shell deals with its customers. IBM (2001) quotes a manager of the system:

> *'SIMON enables the transfer of responsibility for inventory management from customer to supplier. There is no need for a Shell Chemical customer to place an order. Through SIMON, we're able to proactively keep vital inventory on their shelves, so to speak. Customers pay only for what they consume. We are their sole-source supplier. It's a cutting-edge supplier/ customer business model – one that's built on a relationship of mutual trust and a belief that there are significant benefits to be realized on both sides'.*

SECTION SUMMARY 3.4

E-business model – production models

Customer participation creates ownership before the product or service is even produced. It's all commonsense marketing orientation – involving customers in the production process. Conversely, through sharing information on inventory, suppliers can become more involved in the procurement process.

3.5 E-business models – e-procurement

E-procurement has been one of the great drivers of online transactions in the B2B sector as it has been driven by cost-reduction efficiencies that can have a major impact on profitability. This makes e-procurement projects much easier to justify to financial directors.

For companies with a large number of purchases, reducing the cost per order can create major savings, as illustrated by the box on Cambridge Consultants' experience. Even in the last millennium, a Tranmit report (1999) provided some illustrations – typical medium to large companies issue between 1000 and 5000 requisitions a month and are spending between £600 000 and £3 million annually on the procurement process based on the £50 median cost per item. In exceptional cases, the numbers of requisitions was between 30 000 and 40 000 per month. In these cases, the annual cost of procurement could be between £18 million and £43 million!

E-procurement should be directed at improving performance for each of the 'five rights' of purchasing (Baily *et al.*, 1994) which are sourcing items:

1 At the right price.
2 Delivered at the right time.
3 Are of the right quality.
4 Of the right quantity.
5 From the right source – helps multi-sourcing and sourcing difficult-to-find materials.

In the introductory chapter we explained how major companies like GE had made a policy of total online procurement. Many others have since seen the significant savings that can be enjoyed. Internet driven price-transparency combined with giant procurement unions like Ford and Chrysler exploit the power of global sourcing to force prices down. For smaller businesses, customer unions force prices down.

Add in auctions and reverse auctions and prices tumble even further. As the trend towards commoditization continues, something new is commoditized almost every day. This means **reverse auctions** are easy to set up. Once buyers can (a) specify exactly what they want, and (b) identify suppliers, they can run reverse auctions for anything – from hydro electric dams to cosmetic surgery. Different companies use different terms, e.g. TradingPartners.com call it 'accelerated e-sourcing' and FreeMarkets.com call it 'spend management'. Over a five-year period, Volkswagen have saved $5.5 billion.

Don't forget the buyer's aid – shopping bots – robot shoppers that find the best price. Even complex purchases will be facilitated online by software using game strategies.

Moving beyond reduced prices, e-procurement reduces paperwork, meetings, errors and delivery times as fully integrated e-procurement between buyer and supplier links suppliers' and buyers' internal communications systems together.

Needless to say, multiple sources can be secured while sourcing globally.

Finally, e-procurement can help to source difficult-to-find materials. Changes in the supply chain and the value creation networks have created opportunities for new types of intermediaries, companies that provide specialist services to satisfy a shortfall in the market. This might be a hub that brings together specialist product suppliers, as in the agricultural markets in the USA, or it could involve innovative information processing services, which is common in the financial services sector.

E-MARKETING EXCELLENCE

Schlumberger benefits through e-procurement system

The oilfield services division of Schlumberger installed an e-procurement system in order to replace existing systems, some paper-based and some computer-based, with a single system that would speed up purchasing. The system has resulted in lower transaction costs for placing orders and also reduced cost of goods as the price of products has declined through greater competition and negotiation of lower prices for the electronic channel.

With the new system, employees act as purchasing agents, ordering directly via their desktop PCs. The system runs on the Schlumberger intranet and enables staff to access a simplified catalogue of office supplies and technical equipment. For example, one of the suppliers is OfficeDepot. Although OfficeDepot can post its entire catalogue at an electronic marketplace, employees at Schlumberger only see a subset of relevant products for which special prices have been negotiated. Once the items have been selected, the system automatically produces a requisition that is electronically routed to the person who will approve it, and it is then converted into a purchase order without intervention from purchasing staff.

Source: Based on a summary of a dialogue between Alain-Michel Diamant-Berger and Andrea Ovans (Ovans, 2000)

E-PROCUREMENT ACTIONS FOR B2B MARKETERS

Given the benefits of e-procurement, how should B2B marketers respond? Clearly they need to be proactive in explaining the benefits of e-procurement to their customers.

Relatively few businesses have integrated their systems with those of their suppliers (DTI, 2003) – overall, levels of integration are low, even among leading nations, with generally fewer than 20 per cent having their business systems integrated with suppliers (some countries like Japan and France have seen decreases in the proportion of business with linked ordering systems). Marketers need to communicate the benefits to the people who matter – the purchasing and production managers and financial directors at buying organizations who will see the benefits in terms of increased efficiencies and reduced costs, and the IT managers who will be involved in introducing such systems. RS Components, the supplier mentioned in the Cambridge Consultants box, arranges e-procurement briefings for these members of the buying unit and uses advocates such as Frances Pullen to explain the benefits.

Marketers should also consider the options the purchaser has for the *location* of purchasing. Purchasing direct from the supplier's web site is only one option. All these options need to be evaluated and then appropriate **representation** achieved. The purchasing company can purchase at these three locations identified by Berryman *et al.* (1998):

1 At a supplier's site (seller-controlled sell-side e-commerce)
2 Get your suppliers to go to your site (buyer-controlled at buy side)
3 Intermediary (a neutral marketplace).

Figure 3.4 summarizes the options and shows that marketers also need to decide whether to provide e-procurement options for all customers (one-to-many) or to select customers.

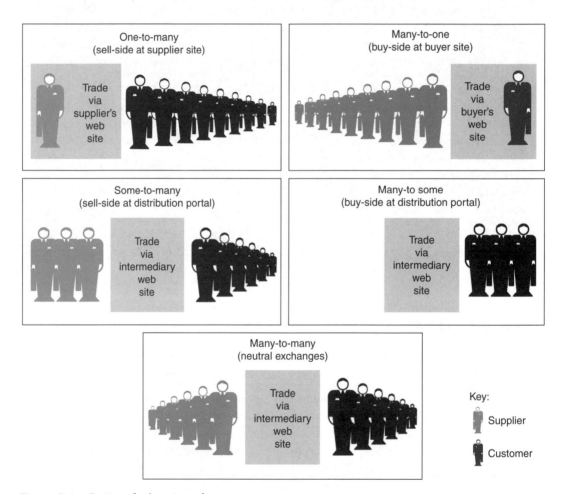

Figure 3.4   Options for location of e-procurement

Finally, remember that enabling e-procurement involves merging existing paper-based or electronic procurement systems with systems from intermediaries and/or customers, so the marketer will need to be conversant with the technical constraints that are imposed on e-procurement.

E-MARKETING INSIGHT

Purchasing manager Francis Pullen of Cambridge Consultants on e-procurement

Cambridge Consultants has a supplier base of nearly 4000 companies, with 20 new ones added each month. Rapid procurement is important. Francis Pullen says: 'We charge our clients by the hour, so if a product is faulty or late we have engineers waiting for new parts to arrive. This doesn't align with our fast time to market business proposition'.

Francis Pullen analysed the internal cost of raising an order. This took into account every step, from the engineer raising a paper requisition, through processing by purchasing, the cost of handling the delivery once it arrived, invoice matching and clearance and even the physical cost of a four-part purchase order form. The whole process involved between eight and ten people and cost the company anywhere from £60 to £120, depending on the complexity of the order, but even for a simple item like boxes of paperclips.

Through using e-procurement from one of its preferred suppliers (RS Components, www.rswww.com) low-value ordering has proved much more cost efficient (down to £10 per order). Invoice matching costs are also reduced, since the purchase card statement lists all purchases made each month.

Source: White paper, RS Components web site www.rswww.com

SECTION SUMMARY 3.5

E-business models – e-procurement

The digital environment provides opportunities to enhance the management of the buying function and reduce costs. The benefits of this mode of operation are that companies access a wider range of potential suppliers. Additionally, benefits can be derived from the streamlining of the physical side of the buying process; the cost incurred and time wasted while paper-based communications change hands. Marketers need to be active in communicating the benefits of e-procurement.

3.6 E-business models – distribution models

Arguably, distribution is the most important element of the marketing mix. It really does create a competitive edge. Chapter 2 explored this in more detail. By the end of this section you will understand how distribution models are changing. This includes concepts such as disintermediation, reintermediation, portals, hubs, metamarket switchboards, infomediaries, shopping bots, web links and affiliates.

DISINTERMEDIATION

In the old days it was simple. Manufacturers produced, distributors distributed and customers bought:

M————————W/S————————R————————C
Manufacturer   Wholesaler   Retailer   Customer

Then some retailers grew big enough to deal directly with the manufacturer:

M————————R————————C
Manufacturer   Retailer   Customer

Then some manufacturers realized the power of combining direct marketing with Internet technology and marketed their goods directly to the end customer. This is **disintermediation:**

M————————C
Manufacturer   Customer

Disintermediation means taking out the middleman and allows 'pirating the value chain'. In reality, many manufacturers had multi-channel policies doing some of all three.

M————————W/S————————R————————C
M————————————————————R————————C
M————————————————————————————————C

REINTERMEDIATION

Some major retail chains prefer to keep middlemen in the chain as they don't want to be tied up with paperwork, admin, storage and logistics. They can outsource this to a middleman... a kind of **reintermediation**.

Some companies either outsource the whole logistics side or form strategic alliances with specialist delivery companies who deliver anything including pizzas and videos within 30 minutes of an online order in selected cities and towns.

With the Internet came new forms of middlemen (reintermediates) such as: non-physical **portals**, **hubs**, **metamarket switchboards**, **infomediaries**, **shopping bots** and web links and **affiliates**.

AFFILIATES

One of the biggest model changes in the online world is of course the phenomenon of turning customers or third parties into sales agents or affiliates. Amazon's network of 900 000 affiliate links from their customers' web sites is a powerful network of virtual middlemen that creates a protectable competitive advantage. Affiliate marketing is considered more in Section 7.4.

The Internet also brought with it an opportunity to get closer to customers again. Marketing had previously been pulled away from customers, separated by distributors, ad agencies and market research companies. Internet technology now offers the opportunity to get close to customers, to speak to them individually and listen to them. In addition the technology facilitates a direct dialogue with end customers.

Of course it is essential that a database, a good CRM system and suitable resources are in place for one-to-one marketing to occur.

In the consumer sector, B2C, clicks and mortar organizations (or businesses with both online presence and also an offline physical presence such as a shop) outperformed the pure dotcoms.

Ideally you distribute your products and services wherever customers are, making it easy for them.

In the online world distribution can be extended by e-tools such as kiosks, interactive intelligent vending machines. These are explored in Chapter 5 on e-tools.

Finally radically new distribution models embrace C2C and P2P. Customer-to-customer or peer-to-peer systems such as Napster and Gnutella present new models, ideally suited to the online world. Although their legality has been challenged, they do open up some new ideas for distribution of ideas, messages and perhaps one day many products and services.

DISTRIBUTION CHANNEL ACTIONS FOR MARKETERS

Tactics must be developed for the phenomena of disintermediation and reintermediation including affiliates. The practicality of disintermediation should be reviewed, considering issues such as who to use for physical distribution of goods direct to customers and the risk of channel conflict with existing channel partners. Options for reintermediation should also be considered. Organizations need to review their representation across new intermediaries or decide whether to create rival intermediaries (**countermediation**).

E-MARKETING INSIGHT

Mayer and Norris on channel conflict

Mayer and Norris contend that channel conflict is never a reason not to move forward with electronic commerce plans. The key is to develop strategies that minimize the impact of channel conflict. They say:

> *'companies that do not own or closely control their non-electronic distribution channels risk damaging long-standing relationships and revenue streams. For example, when Compaq started allowing online sales of its computers at discount prices, traditional retailers threatened to stop selling its products. As a result, Compaq ceased selling through online discounters and was forced to re-evaluate its relationships with all distribution channels'.*

On the other hand:

> *'Companies that control their own channels risk cannibalizing off-line revenues with online revenues. This takes customers out of existing*

channels, decreasing the older channels' profitability. For example, as more consumers use online banking, commercial banks have been unable to justify maintaining as many physical branches'.

They suggest three scenarios for action:

1 Companies with easily transferable businesses and little control over their channels may face significant channel conflicts. Examples of industries facing significant channel conflict include insurance, music, airlines, computer manufacturers, appliances, furniture and securities trading. These businesses should *cooperate* with existing channels online as a way to avoid conflict.

2 Companies with easily transferable businesses, but high channel control, face moderate levels of channel conflict, most often related to cannibalization of existing channels. Industries in this area include many retail chains (i.e. office supplies, books, toys), cellular telephone providers and many franchise organizations. Companies in this category often *link* their existing channels with the online channels to enhance the benefit of having all channels together.

3 Companies with businesses that do not transfer to the Internet, and that have little control over channels, face minimal channel conflict. Industries in this category include real estate, repair shops, car manufacturers and hair salons. These companies' channels will likely view electronic commerce as a threat to their control of the customer relationship. Therefore, firms like this should *collaborate* with older channels.

Source: Based on Digitrends article by Andrew Mayer and Dawn Norris at: www.digitrends.net/ebiz/13644_8905.html 20 June 2000.

SECTION SUMMARY 3.6

Sell-side distribution models

Marketers need to review the implications of the phenomena of disintermediation ('cutting out the middleman') and reintermediation (the presence of new online intermediaries and marketplaces). Risks to be assessed in disintermediation include channel conflict and for reintermediation include increased commoditization of products and price competition.

3.7 Communications models

This section primarily explores how multi-stage communications models are moving into web-based community communications models. Brief reference is also made to other communications models including viral marketing, affiliate marketing and permission-based marketing.

In the last millennium, mass communications models were popular – and the simple model looked like this:

Then opinion leaders and opinion formers were identified as important elements in communications models. So they were targeted to help encourage word-of-mouth spread. Here the sender sends a message and some of it goes directly to the customer and some is picked up by opinion formers who subsequently pass the message on to customers.

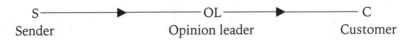

Add in some feedback and interaction and you've got conversations with the arrows also indicating flowbacks to the sender:

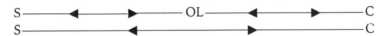

Think about who are the opinion formers and opinion leaders in your marketplace? Separate online from offline influencers. They may include business leaders, celebrity users, journalists, public speakers, consultants, professional bodies and awards, influential networks, accrediting bodies, chat room moderators, news groups, etc. Word of mouth works much more quickly online than offline.

Now comes the interesting bit. With the Internet came the easier facilitation of customer communities – where customers talk to each other (C2C) and back to the company (C2B).

The flow of communications eventually becomes like a web of communications between customers and opinion leaders – all built around the brand. The company facilitates these conversations. In doing so, it keeps close to customers as it can look and listen to what's being said. It can also communicate easily with the customers and ultimately develop strong relationships. Newsgroups, discussion rooms hosted by the brand, discuss the brand, its applications, problems, issues, ideas, improvements and a broader array of topics linked with some of the brand values. In a sense, a web of conversations is being spun around the brand (Figure 3.5).

Referrals are part of C2C and eventually C2B as the referred customer contacts the business. Viral marketing is an extension of this C2C or P2P model where customers pass the message on. This is accelerated word of mouth. Clever, creative messages with interesting ideas, amazing images, special offers, announcements and invitations are good for viral marketing. For more on viral marketing, see Section 7.7.

Affiliate marketing discussed in Section 3.6 also spreads awareness of a brand amongst a community of relevant customers, who in turn talk to each other and can spread ordinary or clever viral messages amongst their own communities.

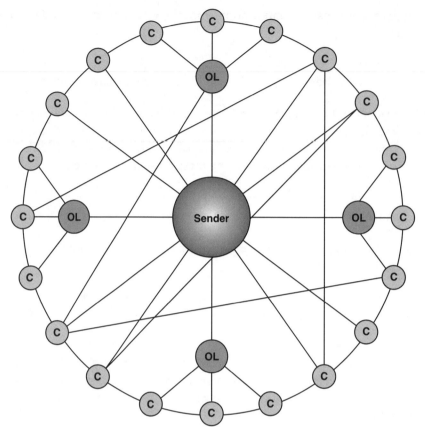

Figure 3.5 A web of conversations – accelerating word-of-mouth. C, customer; OL, opinion leader

Implicit in all of these communications models is **permission-based marketing**. In this time-compressed, information-cluttered world, customers resent unsolicited SPAM. Excellent e-marketers win permission to send future messages. Now the sender asks permission to send a message. If the customer agrees a message is finally sent. There is more on permission-based marketing in Section 8.2.

ADVERTISING

All the models are changing. None more so than advertising. Advertising agencies are confronted by another big shift in their communications models. They have to move from 'getting attention' to 'giving attention'. This presents new challenges to agencies used to winning attention and creating brand awareness. Now when visitors land on the brand's site, it is the brand who must pay attention.

Once audiences paid for the media which carried the ads, today many marketers pay the audience for consuming the media (e.g. web-browsing).

Chaffey *et al.* (2003) on communication models

Figure 3.6 illustrates the interaction between an organization (O) communicating a message (M) to customers (C) for a single-step flow of communication. It is apparent that for traditional mass-marketing in (a) a single message (M_1) is communicated to all customers (C_1 to C_5). With a web site with personalization facilities (b) there is a two-way interaction with each communication potentially unique. Note that many brochure-ware sites do not take full advantage of the Internet and merely use the web to replicate other media channels by delivering a uniform message.

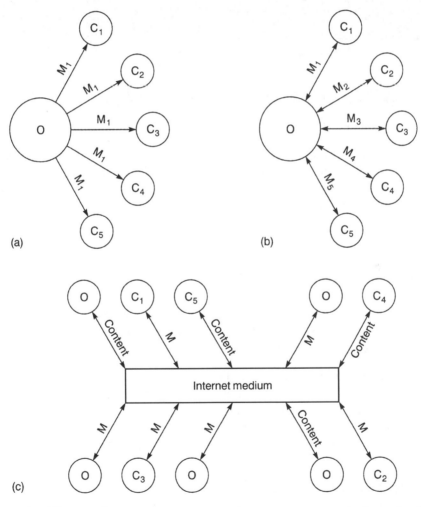

Figure 3.6   The differences between one-to-many and one-to-one communication using the Internet (organization (O), communicating a message (M) and customers (C)). (a) Traditional one-to-many mass marketing communication; (b) one-to-one Internet-based communication; (c) many-to-many communications via the Internet media

E-MARKETING INSIGHT

Has e-marketing communications gone full circle?

Medieval markets were busy with people talking to each other, shouting, cajoling, meeting, introducing, etc. Since then we've moved through many developments including one-to-one, relationship marketing, CRM, CMR and more. Today's information clutter combined with information fatigue syndrome, means traditional communications strategies are not working. This is exacerbated by filtering software, TiVo technology, media fragmentation and new privacy laws which mean that direct mail, telemarketing, mainstream advertising and even PR events are struggling to get through the clutter. Affiliate marketing, network marketing and P2P (peer-to-peer) marketing are re-emerging. Does this bring us all the way back to medieval marketing – talking to people on a one-to-one basis?

Source: Smith (2004)

SECTION SUMMARY 3.7

Web communication models

This section explored how multi-stage communications models are moving into web-based community communications models. Brief reference was also made to other communications models including viral marketing, affiliate marketing and permission-based marketing. New models bring new opportunities.

3.8 Customer buying models

What goes through a customer's mind moments before they purchase? What stages do they go through when making a purchase? To sell, you have to know how and why people buy. By the end of this section you will be able to select and draw a suitable buying model for online customers.

The choice of model obviously depends on the type of purchase and the type of buyer. We are going to consider an online consumer making a purchase. We will consider two different purchasing scenarios – one for a **high-involvement purchase** (e.g. a car or a PC) and one for a low-involvement routine purchase (e.g. a can of cola). Chapter 4 on e-customers considers these in much more detail. In this short section we'll outline the models in action.

HIGH-INVOLVEMENT PURCHASES

For a high-involvement purchase like a car, customers go through a rigorous buying process from: problem identification to information search to evaluation to decision-to-buy through to post purchase.

As we will see in Chapter 4, a good web site (and/or a good interactive advertisement on TV) helps buyers move through all, or most, of these stages in the buying process. Some buyers prefer to browse online and buy offline (or just test drive), while others prefer to test, browse and buy online.

The introductory chapter emphasized the importance of being able to offer this **mixed-mode** of online and offline sales. The integrated database and integrated communications should be able to identify prospects online and close sales offline even if it means delivering a test drive car to the door. Surprisingly, most businesses are still struggling to integrate their databases. Many businesses during the dotcom boom rushed to adopt e-commerce systems without integrating them fully with other systems, e.g. an order placed on a web site might have to be manually entered into a production or delivery schedule (DTI, 2003). It gets worse: 50 per cent of CRM projects fail (Gartner Group, 2004). So the database and its integration still present one of marketing's main challenges.

LOW-INVOLVEMENT PURCHASES

Obviously, not all purchases require this much effort. There are many, many low-involvement purchases that we make every day, which do not warrant this kind of effort. Despite being almost 100 years old, and criticized by some, the *AIDA* model of attention (awareness), interest, desire and action is still used by many professionals.

There are many buying models such as *ATR* or awareness, trial and reinforcement – generate awareness, facilitate an easy trial and then reinforce it with advertising from then on. There are many adaptations which web sites can use. Oracle's 'See Try Buy' function allows customers to research and then test Oracle products for free, then buy them online.

Finally, one of the most interesting developments for customer-buying models has to be **customer unions** or the **co-buying** approach, allowing customers to aggregate their demand to win better pricing deals, e.g. Let's Buy it.com.

E-MARKETING EXCELLENCE

Oracle applies the ATR model

An online example of the ATR model for a high involvement purchase is illustrated by the Oracle web microsite supporting its e-business suite (Figure 3.7). It uses the following approach, which occurs entirely online, if required:

- See (online seminars and webcasts explaining the benefits of the product)
- Try (online demonstrations of the suite)
- Buy (online purchase).

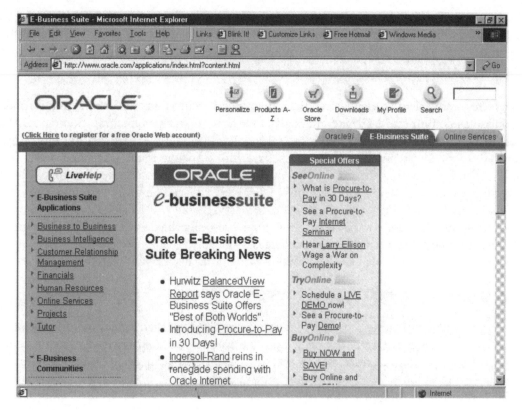

Figure 3.7 Oracle web site from 2001 illustrating 'See, Try, Buy' approach to ATR

SECTION SUMMARY 3.8

Customer buying models

Online marketers must check to see their online activities (web sites, wap sites, kiosks or other e-tools) accommodate all the stages of the buyer's buying process – whether linear problem solving, AIDA, ATR or others.

3.9 Customer information processing

This section is a short one and leads you into the next chapter on e-customers by raising more questions than answers about online information processing.

There are many models for information processing, some so complex that they render themselves relatively useless in terms of practical application. We are going to look briefly at two of the more practical information processing models – one for banner ads and one for web sites: Rossiter and Bellman (**banner ads**) and also Hofacker (web sites). Rossiter and Bellman

(1999) developed the ALEA model that describes the online advertising experience as a process whereby attention is gained, followed by learning. If the consumer's emotional responses to the ad content are positively or negatively reinforced, further attention may be paid to the ad and further learning may take place until the brand's attributes are accepted.

This ALEA model is a 'heterarchy' of possible responses and does not specify a definitive sequence except that (1) attention must precede learning and emotional responses, and (2) that learning and emotional responses must precede acceptance.

Rossiter and Bellman (1999) hypothesize that sustained attention is directly related to the evaluative intensity of the consumers' emotional response to a content node encountered during a visit to a web ad.

They also theorize that brand attitude will be directly affected by the appropriateness of the sequence of emotions encountered during a visit to an Internet advertisement and by the appropriateness of the final emotion experienced. Furthermore, they propose that consumers with a high-category need should tend to process the online ad linearly in a 'hierarchy of effects' sequence (a logical pattern of pages) while those with a low-category need should process fewer pages of the site in a random order.

A separate model, Hofacker's model (Hofacker, 2001, see Section 4.6 for more detail), has five stages of on-site information processing:

1 Exposure – is the message there long enough for a customer?
2 Attention – what grabs the attention – movement, colour …?
3 Comprehension and perception – how does the customer interpret the stimulus?
4 Yielding and acceptance – is the information accepted by the customer?
5 Retention – how well can the customer recall their experience?

Each stage acts as a hurdle, since if the site design or content is too difficult to process, the customer cannot progress to the next stage. The e-marketer fails.

SECTION SUMMARY 3.9

Customer information processing models

Understanding how customers process information helps marketers to communicate more clearly. We have looked at models by Rossiter and Bellman for banner ads and also Hofacker for web sites.

3.10 Loyalty models

Are you loyal to a brand online? Why – what makes you loyal? By the end of this section you will know the components of loyalty.

We know repeat business is on average, five times more profitable than new business. On the other hand, low loyalty has a high cost as constantly recruiting new customers is expensive.

You need to identify and target your ideal customers and then move them up the ladder of loyalty (Considine and Murray, 1981) so that they become loyal lifetime customers. In fact, move them on to becoming advocates spreading your message. So how do you develop loyalty and strong relations with customers? Quality product, quality service and quality sites are basic prerequisites. In fact satisfying customers should be replaced by delighting customers since many satisfied customers still defect. On top of this we are getting worse at customer service (Cerasale and Stone, 2004). After this comes privacy and security. Respect and protect your customers' privacy. Ensure and reassure them of security. Add value to the relationship and reinforce brand values at every opportunity. Integrate your products and services into your customers' systems. Extend the partnership and share systems – this provides a certain amount of 'lock-in' where customers avoid the disruption caused by changing suppliers.

Going back to 'added value', rewarding customers is one way of adding value to the relationship. There are a number of innovative approaches emerging to reward and encourage online customer loyalty. All involve the visitor being offered some form of reward for buying. Rewards may take a number of different forms, e.g. credits, click miles. Remember there's always room for creativity. Take the Coca-Cola auction. Coca-Cola has amalgamated the loyalty notion with the auction model. In the physical world the potential bidder collects Coke can ring pulls, which once registered can be used to bid for a range of products. Vouchers are another method – visitors to www.richersounds.co.uk can print a 'buy one, get one free' voucher and then visit the store to redeem it. This approach can be used to increase sales and enhance the value of a site by increasing and retaining the user-base.

It is important to explore ways to develop a loyal on-line customer base. Evidence suggests that site users return to their favourite group of sites, similar to their favourite store. Many emerging pure play companies are relying on the growth of their user base rather than the growth of loyalty among their existing user base. This has yet to be proven as a sound strategic approach as many companies following this approach have closed as funding has ceased to be available. Eventually, repeat business, lifetime loyalty and relationship marketing will separate the winners from the losers. Loyalty is so important it pops up in every chapter of this book, Section 4.7 giving further details.

E-MARKETING INSIGHT

The IDIC loyalty model

Peppers and Rogers (1998) have applied their work on building one-to-one relationships with the customer to the web. They suggest the IDIC approach as a framework for using the web effectively to form and build relationships. IDIC stands for:

1 *Customer identification.* This stresses the need to identify each customer on their first visit and subsequent visits. Common methods for identification are use of cookies or asking a customer to log on to a site.

2 *Customer differentiation.* This refers to building a profile to help segment customers. Characteristics for differentiating customers are described in Section 4.9.

3 *Customer interaction.* These are interactions provided on site such as customer service questions or creating a tailored product.

4 *Customer communications.* This refers to personalization or mass-customization of content or e-mails according to the segmentation achieved at the acquisition stage. Approaches for personalization are explained in Section 8.6.

SECTION SUMMARY 3.10

Loyalty

Quality product, quality service and quality sites are basic prerequisites to achieve online customer loyalty. Reward schemes can also be used to enhance loyalty.

CHAPTER SUMMARY

1 Models describe the process by which business is conducted between an organization, its customers, suppliers, distributors and other stakeholders. Managers need constantly to review how electronic communications change existing models and offer new opportunities.

2 New and revised models are required to respond to changes in industry structure and customer behaviour.

3 The value network rather than value chain concept is often more representative of business partnerships since it illustrates the transient nature of partnerships as the optimal partnership is formed for different events.

4 Production models indicate the importance of the prosumer in new product development. The relationship between B2B supplier and customer is also being revised through the ability to share information on production and inventory.

5 E-procurement offers major benefits in terms of efficiency. The right members of the buyer unit should be targeted online and offline to communicate these benefits.

6 Disintermediation, reintermediation and affiliate networks are significant changes to the distribution channel that should be carefully evaluated by marketers.

7 New media have enabled a change from many-to-one, to many-to-some and to one-to-one communication. Other new communications techniques are viral marketing, affiliate marketing and permission-based marketing.

8 E-marketing must accommodate the linear process for high involvement purchases, mixed-mode buying and traditional models such as AIDA and ATR.

9 Hofacker's customer information processing model of exposure–attention–comprehension and perception-yielding and acceptance and retention is a valuable method of enhancing the communications efficiency of a web site.

10 A quality product, service, web site are basic prerequisites to build customer loyalty.

References

Baily, P., Farmer, D., Jessop, D. and Jones, D. (1994) *Purchasing principles and management*. Pitman Publishing, London.

Berryman, K., Harrington, L., Layton-Rodin, D. and Rerolle, V. (1998) Electronic commerce: three emerging strategies. *The Mckinsey Quarterly*, No. 1, 152–9.

Cerasale, M. and Stone, M. (2004) *Business Solutions on Demand*. Kogan Page.

Chaffey, D., Mayer, R., Johnston, K. and Ellis-Chadwick, F. (2003) *Internet Marketing: Strategy, Implementation and Practice*. Prentice Hall/Financial Times, Harlow, 2nd edition.

Considine, R. and Murray, R. (1981) *The Great Brain Robbery*, The Great Brain Robbery, CA.

Daly, J. (2000) Interview with Alvin Toffler. *Business 2.0 Magazine*, September 15.

Deise, M., Nowikow, C., King, P., Wright, A. (2000) *Executive's guide to e-business. From tactics to strategy*. John Wiley and Sons, New York.

DTI (2003) Business in the Information Age – International Benchmarking Study. Available from http://www2.bah.com/dti2003.

Durlacher (2000) Trends in the UK new economy. *Durlacher Quarterly Internet Report*, November 2000, pp. 1–12.

Gartner Group (2004) CRM Marketing Business. February.

Hofacker, C. (2001) *Internet Marketing*. Wiley, New York, 3rd edition.

Hoffman, D.L. and Novak, T.P. (1996) Marketing in Hypermedia Computer-mediated environments: conceptual foundations. *Journal of Marketing*, 60 (July), pp. 50–68.

IBM (2001) IBM e-business web site case study.

Jackson, T. (2000) Marketing brainwave falls foul of rule book. *Financial Times*, 14 March, p. 19.

Kirkpatrick, D. (2001) Great Leap Forward: From Davos, Talk of Death. *Fortune*, March 5.

Levine, R., Locke, C., Searls, D. and Weinberger, D. (2000) *The Cluetrain Manifesto*. Perseus Books, Cambridge, MA.

Ovans, A. (2000) E-procurement at Schlumberger. *Harvard Business Review*. May–June, pp. 21–3.

Rossiter, J.R. and Bellman, S. (1999) A Proposed Model for Explaining and Measuring Web Advertising Effectiveness. *Journal of Current Issues and Research in Advertising*, Vol. 21, No. 11, pp. 13–31.

Smith, P. (2004) *Shape The Agenda*. Chartered Institute of Marketing, Jan. 2004 www.shapetheagenda.com.

Tranmit (1999) *Procurement Management Systems: a corporate black hole. A survey of technology trends and attitudes in British industry*. Published by Tranmit, UK. Survey conducted by Byline Research. Report available at www.rswww.com/purchasing .

ZDNet (2005) ISPs fear greater Net regulation. 27 January. www.zdnet.co.uk.

Further reading

Deise, M., Nowikow, C., King, P. and Wright, A. (2000) *Executive's guide to e-business. From tactics to strategy*. John Wiley and Sons, New York. Introductory chapters consider buy- and sell-side options and later chapters look at value chain transformation.
Fingar, P., Kumar, H. and Sharma, T. (2000) *Enterprise E-commerce*. Meghan-Kiffler Press, Tampa, FL. These authors present a model of the different actors in the e-marketplace that is the theme throughout this book.

Web links

ASCET Project (www.ascet.com). Excellent collection of articles coordinated by Accenture and Montgomery research.
Conspectus (www.conspectus.com). Industry studies on range of industry topics including procurement.
Institute of Logistics and Transport (www.ciltuk.org.uk). Overview of logistics, plus links to related sites.
See also links in Chapter 9, E-business.

Self-test

1 Summarize the scope of e-business models.
2 Explain the concept of commoditization.
3 Do you think value networks or the external value chain is a more useful model for defining e-marketing strategy?
4 Explain the relevance of the prosumer concept to the modern marketer.
5 Describe how the B2B marketer can use the concept of e-procurement to enhance sales to existing and new customers.
6 Describe marketing tactics to accommodate changes to the distribution channel for your organization.
7 Outline the changes from traditional mass communication to new communications models.
8 Which e-marketing tactics should be developed to accommodate different buying models?
9 Apply Hofacker's model of customer information processing to your organization's web site.
10 Outline models to help build customer loyalty.

Chapter **4**

E-customers

'That's what's so scary about customer retention in the online space. We've created this empowered, impatient customer who has a short attention span, a lot of choices, and a low barrier to switching'.

Laurie Windham, 2001

This chapter looks inside the online customer's mind. We explore customers' issues, worries, fears and phobias as well as other motivators for going online... and how marketers can respond to these behaviours. We also look at on-site behaviour, the online buying process and the many influencing variables. We finish with a look to the future, your future and how to keep an eye on the e-customer.

OVERALL LEARNING OUTCOME

By the end of this chapter you will:

- Understand online customers and their buying behaviour and how they differ to offline customers.
- Overcome the issues and concerns online customers have.
- Begin to move e-customers through their online mental stages.

CHAPTER TOPIC	LEARNING OBJECTIVE
4.1 Introduction	Identify customer expectations and how to satisfy them
4.2 Motivations	Evaluate and respond to the factors that encourage users to adopt and stay using the Internet
4.3 Expectations	Determine the facilities that customers require online
4.4 Fears and phobias	Evaluate and manage the fears and phobias that hinder online transactions
4.5 The online buying process	Support the buying process through traditional and digital channels
4.6 Online information processing	Recognize how visitors process information and how marketers can respond to this. Identify the online buying process
4.7 Relationships and loyalty	Understand online relationship marketing techniques to maintain customer relationships
4.8 Communities	Assess the suitability of techniques used to foster online communities and how to build active/lively online communities
4.9 Customer profiles	Describe the profile characteristics of online customers, both B2C and B2B
4.10 Researching the online customer	Assess the process, techniques and measures used to research and assess online marketing effectiveness
4.11 The post-PC customer	Paint a picture of the future and the new online customer's changing behaviour patterns

4.1 Introduction to e-customers

Understanding customers is fundamental to successful marketing. Good marketers know their target customers inside out and upside down. Understanding online customers (or the way customers behave when they are online) is even more important, as the geographic and cultural spread is often much wider. Online customers also have different attitudes to both acquiring information and buying online. On top of this, the same person may both think and behave differently online than offline. So overall e-marketers have to watch their online customers even more closely and support their behaviour.

IDEAL CUSTOMERS

Then comes the interesting bit – understanding your best customers. Who are your ideal customers? You have good and bad customers. Bad ones continually haggle about prices, pay late, constantly complain, grab all your promotions and leave you as soon as another company comes along. The ideal customers, on the other hand, are the ones that pay on time, give you as much notice as possible, share information, become partners giving you useful feedback. You know the ones – they are a pleasure to work with. But who are they? What makes them different? What do they really want? How can you help them even more? Are they online? Targeting, satisfying and keeping the ideal customer is crucial.

Ideal customers are worth more than you think. Pareto's 80:20 law suggests that 80% of your sales come from only 20% of your customers. Research suggests that your best 20% of customers generate 140% of your profits. This means that many of your other customers generate losses. A company's best customer could be worth 30 times the worst customer.

Who are your best customers? Are any of them online? Are all of them online? So we need to know our ideal customer's profile – who they are, where they are, what they want, what they spend, any distinguishing characteristics. How do we recognize them on a database? What questions should we ask them about themselves? We need to know them better than we know ourselves!

We need to understand their mindset, their attitudes and aspirations. We also need to know the barriers to buying online – their fears and phobias. We need to know where our proposition sits with their needs, their lives, their jobs – 'their worlds' – both online and offline.

We also need to know their purchasing process – the stages they move through and the information needs they have at each stage. We need to know their information processing stages – how they acquire information – how they learn about products and offers. How their perception screens out some offers and filters in others. We need to know how new media can cope with this.

In general, the online customer is different to the offline customer. The online customer has more power than ever before. Despite living in an information-cluttered and time-compressed world, the online customer is empowered like never before: more information, transparent prices, more rights. They also realize the value of their time and attention. Witness the rise of permission-based marketing and the demise of the effectiveness of intrusion-based marketing.

Remember, assumptions you might have about existing offline customers may not apply online. Even the same customer may display different characteristics online and offline.

Introduction to e-customers

This chapter explores online customers – who they are, why they go online, their expectations, their fears and phobias. We examine their online buying process as well as their internal mental processes right through to forming relationships and building communities. The chapter finishes with a look at the future – the 'post-PC customer' and shows you how to research the online customer.

4.2 Motivations

By the end of this section you will be able to discuss why customers go online. We will try to lift the lid on online customers' heads, look inside their minds and explore what drives them online. Finally we'll see how we can use this knowledge to get, and keep, more online customers.

Understanding customer motivations is not an option or a luxury. It's an absolute necessity for survival. If you don't know what customers want then how can you satisfy them? If you can't satisfy them, how can you keep them or even attract them in the first place? Without this deep understanding of your customers you're just shooting in the dark and hoping for the best. Not the way to run a business.

So we need to know why customers go online? What are their motives? What needs are being satisfied?

WHY DO CUSTOMERS VENTURE ONLINE?

Research presented in Figure 4.1 shows that socializing, catching up on news, shopping/browsing, being entertained and being educated are typical reasons people give for going online. So, socializing through e-mail and chat rooms is the killer application in the B2C markets. Billions of e-mails are sent every day and SMS (text) messages are catching up. Leveraging the strong desire to socialize should not be underestimated. It is one of Maslow's basic defined needs.

The second most popular activity is finding out about products, regardless of whether they are to be purchased online or offline, so we need to facilitate the process of mixed-mode buying – browsing online and buying offline.

Internet users are active, not passive; they enjoy their power and love to exercise it. Comparison shopping puts them in control. The empowered online customer has more knowledge than ever before from sharing information with others and from comparison sites or shop-bots. How well do you know the comparison sites for your products and services? Seek them out and monitor them continuously.

Surprisingly, not all online customers hate real physical shopping. They just like getting good deals and being in control (Windham, 2001). The convenience of online shopping may grow in

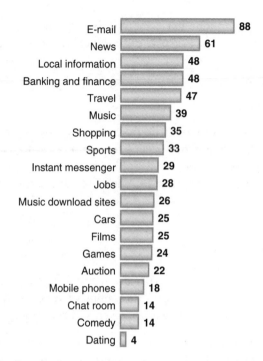

Figure 4.1 Popularity of online activities in Europe. Countries surveyed: 1000 respondents per country: UK, FR, DE, ES, IT (all 1000 respondents), BE, NL (500), DK, SE, NO (333). (*Source:* EIAA, 2004)

importance as time-compressed customers realize the time saving nature of online shopping. Time saving can satisfy several needs simultaneously as the time saved can be spent fulfilling a range of unfilled needs.

Incidentally, many products fail to sell in large volumes online since the products don't pass de Kare-Silver's 'electronic shopping test' (see box) which measures the likelihood of online retail purchases.

However, mixed-mode shopping (i.e. online browsing) suggests an Internet presence makes sense, as shown in Figure 4.2. This also shows the potential for growth of online browsing and buying and since this is a European average, the adoption is already much higher in some countries. The data shows that some products such as tickets, books and electrical goods have a much higher conversion rate of browsers to buyers. Of course, the Internet is still having an important role in the purchase decision for those who browse online and buy offline as part of mixed-mode buying.

It's simple: if customers can't find the right information about your products and service propositions, then you don't even make it into the 'considered set' of brands being considered by a potential customer.

The third most popular online activity is entertainment. After adult entertainment comes games, music and checking up on the latest news about the favourite band, sports team or celebrity.

Conversion (%)

Travel tickets	41 | 64	(64)
Holidays	29 | 64	(45)
Theatre/cinema tickets	35 | 49	(71)
Books	31 | 48	(65)
Electrical goods	20 | 40	(50)
Cars	8 | 38	(21)
Properties – renting/purchasing	6 | 36	(17)
Buying music	23 | 35	(66)
Mobile phones	9 | 33	(27)
Music downloads	13 | 32	(41)
Clothes	20 | 29	(69)
Insurance	10 | 28	(36)
Home furnishings	8 | 28	(29)
Financial products	9 | 28	(32)
Computer games	12 | 25	(48)
Furniture	7 | 22	(32)
Car accessories	8 | 21	(38)
Food/grocery shopping	9 | 20	(45)
Car hire	8 | 18	(44)

Figure 4.2 Percentage of Internet users browsing (light bar) and buying (dark bar) in Europe during 2004. Conversion percentages are the proportion of all who research the product online who buy online. (*Source:* EIAA, 2004)

It is no surprise that Yahoo! is the most popular site worldwide since it offers these key activities of socializing, product information, purchasing and entertainment through e-mail and chat, search engines and product guides, shopping, community and games.

For the B2B market, international benchmarking studies (DTI, 2003), suggest that the main drivers for adopting e-commerce are cost-efficiency and selling – tapping into the global market. B2B e-marketplaces deliver cost savings through global sourcing, auctions and bids as well as reducing supplier numbers, reducing inventories, access to wider/deeper products and services. Enlightened businesses are also using the Internet to get closer to customers, serve them better, build the brand and reach more customers.

E-MARKETING INSIGHT

Laurie Windham on online customer motivations

Windham (2001) noted that for US consumers:

'Around a third of web shoppers described themselves as comparison shoppers, much higher than traditional shoppers. Think, if customers feel they have executed the evaluation and decision phases successfully they can be more sure they have made the right decision and this will reduce post-purchase dissonance'.

'Only 1% of people who were web shoppers said that they hated going to the shops, while 10% of traditional purchasers said they hated going to the stores'.

RESPONDING TO CUSTOMER MOTIVATIONS

Once you know why people go online, you can apply a very simple marketing formula:

1 Find out why people buy and what are their aspirations and expectations. Then…

2 Reflect the reasons, aspirations and expectations in your communications. This way you give customers what they want instead of what you want.

Of course, you have to be able to deliver the promised benefits. Otherwise repeat sales die, bad word of mouth spreads and the online activities damage the brand. Don't promise what you cannot deliver.

Existing offline customers can be encouraged to go online before they are besieged by other, competitive, online offerings. Remember someone, somewhere, is analysing and targeting your market right now.

Tempt customers by offering channel choice and, something customers can't get elsewhere, the **online value proposition (OVP)** detailed in Chapter 6. Tell them how it works and how they can use it. Other motivators such as the social aspect can be used: For home users, and sometimes, for business users also, it is an important social tool enabling conversations with participants known and unknown, from near and far. Also useful member-get-member promotions amongst existing customers help members to help others with useful information about interesting offers. Word of mouth and referrals are a powerful tool. Remember, reassurance is vital since security is a major fear and phobia. Section 4.4 later in this chapter explores fears and phobias.

We suggest that you consider the 6Cs of customer motivation to help define the OVP (Chaffey, 2004):

1 **Content** – We know content is still king, online content should provide something that supports other channels. Often this means more detailed, in-depth information to support the buying process or product usage. As well as text-based content which is king for business-to-business there is also interactive content which is king for consumer sites and particularly brands. Remember that context is also king. Context provides the right information, personalized for the right segment using the right media to achieve relevance.

2 **Customization** – **Mass customization** of content delivers personalized content viewed as web site pages or e-mail alerts. This is commonly known as personalization or tailoring of content according to individuals or groups – see Siebel.com for a great example.

3 **Community** – Community, these days known as 'social networks'. Online channels such as the Internet are known as 'many-to-many' media meaning that your audiences can contribute to the content. For consumer retail, review sites such as Epinions (www.epinions.com) are important for informing customer perceptions of brands. Similarly in business markets some specialist communities have been set up. For example, e-consultancy (www.e-consultancy.com) has forums and reviews which discuss issues in the supply of e-business services.

4 **Convenience** – Convenience is the ability to select, purchase and in some cases use products, from your desktop at any time; the classic 24/7 availability of a service.

5 **Choice** – The web gives a wider choice of products and suppliers than traditional media. The success of online intermediaries such as Kelkoo (www.kelkoo.com) and Screentrade (www.screentrade.com) is evidence of this.

6 **Cost reduction** – The Internet is widely perceived as a relatively low-cost place of purchase. In the UK, Vauxhall have keyed into this perception by offering Vauxhall Internet Price (VIP), in other words lower prices than through dealer-based distribution. Similarly a key component of the easyJet OVP when it launched was single tickets that were £2.50 cheaper than phone bookings. This simple price differential together with the limited change in behaviour required from phone booking to online booking has been a key factor in the easyJet online ticketing channel effectively replacing all other booking modes.

E-MARKETING INSIGHT

De Kare-Silver's electronic shopping test

This assesses the consumer's propensity to purchase a retail product using the Internet. De Kare-Silver suggests factors that should be considered in the electronic shopping test:

1 *Product characteristics.* Does the product need to be physically tried, or touched before it is bought?

2 *Familiarity and confidence.* Considers the degree the consumer recognizes and trusts the product or brand.

3 *Consumer attributes.* These shape the buyer's behaviour – are they amenable to online purchases in terms of access to the technology, skills available and do they no longer wish to shop for a product in a traditional retail environment?

Typical results from the evaluation, where products are scored out of 50 for suitability for electronic commerce, are:

- Groceries (27/50)
- Mortgages (15/50)
- Travel (31/50)
- Books (38/50)

De Kare-Silver states that any product scoring over 20 has good potential, since the score for consumer attributes is likely to increase through time. Given this, he suggests companies will regularly need to review the score for their products.

SECTION SUMMARY 4.2

Motivations

B2C customers are motivated to go online for a range of reasons – social, shopping, entertainment. B2B customers are driven by cost savings, speed and selling. Enlightened companies realize there are other motivators such as enhanced customer relationships. In addition to delivering an excellent product or service, find what motivates your customers and then reflect it through your online and offline communications – a simple formula for success.

4.3 Expectations

By the end of this section you will begin to know how to manage customer expectations. This section reviews what customers expect when they visit a web site and how to deliver these expectations.

WHAT ARE THE ONLINE EXPECTATIONS?

Online customers have raised expectations. They expect higher standards in terms of service, convenience, speed of delivery, competitive prices and choice. They also want, if not expect, to be in control, secure and safe. The problem with raised expectations is that firstly, they are crushed more easily and secondly they can damage the brand if not fulfilled.

Online customers expect fast service and fast delivery. The Internet and everything associated with it suggests speed. If online businesses do not deliver speedily then online customers are disappointed, annoyed, angry and sometimes vociferous. Even if delivery takes the same time as the retail store, the online customers often expect a little more (whether price discount, wider choice or whatever). This is the problem with raised expectations.

Now consider a customer's expectations when buying a book online. Top of the list of online customer expectations is minimizing the time on site and delivering what is promised, but there are many other requirements (see box on customer expectations).

Online customers, quite reasonably, expect things to work – they expect to find what they want easily and buy what they want easily. The Internet is a quagmire for the destruction of both raised expectations and even ordinary expectations.

Sadly, it seems there are many exceptions to perfect service. Customer service is critical, research summarized in Figure 4.3 shows that poor customer service rather than price or features is the number one reason why customers don't remain loyal to a company.

So, the most significant expectations are customer service and we need to work hard to deliver this across the many interactions between company and customer before, during and after the buying process. Section 4.5 discusses the online buying process.

E-MARKETING EXCELLENCE

Customer expectations for an online retail purchase

Our expectations are informed by our peers and by past experience. So when we shop online we expect, or indeed demand, that the experience will be superior to traditional shopping. The list of requirements is long.

1 Easy to find what you're looking for by searching or browsing.
2 Site easy to use, pages fast to download with no bugs.
3 Price, product specification and availability information on site to be competitive and correct, but we probably prefer great customer services to great prices – this is what will keep us loyal.

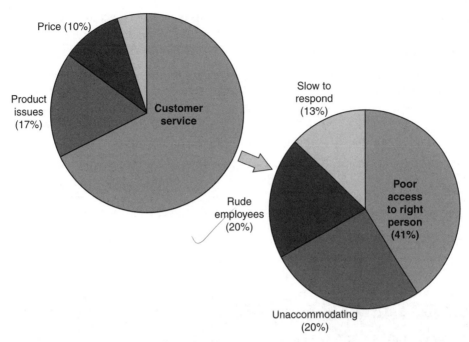

Figure 4.3 Summary of reasons why customers change supplier. (*Source:* Purdue University cross-sector study)

4 Specification of date, time and delivery to be possible.

5 E-mail notification when order placed and then dispatched.

6 Personal data remains personal and private and security is not compromised.

7 Verification for high-value orders.

8 Delivery on time.

9 Returns policy enabling straightforward return or replacement.

… and finally, quick online or offline answers to questions when the expectations above aren't met. This means traceability through databases, someone who knows your order status and can solve your problems.

MANAGING CUSTOMER EXPECTATIONS

Customers' expectations can be managed, met and exceeded. How do we do this? Here are three stages:

1 *Understanding expectations*. Managing the expectations of the demanding customer starts with understanding these expectations. Use customer research and site benchmarking to help

this. Use standard frameworks to establish the gap between expectation and delivery and prioritize to solve the worst shortcomings. Use scenarios to identify the customer expectations of using the services on your site.

2 *Setting and communicating the service promise.* Expectations can best be managed by entering into an informal or formal agreement as to what service the customer can expect through customer service guarantees or promises (see box). It is better to under-promise than over-promise. A book retailer that delivers the book in 2 days when 3 days were promised will earn the customer's loyalty better than the retailer who promises 1 day, but delivers in 2!

3 *Delivering the service promise.* Commitments must be delivered through on-site service, support from employees and physical fulfilment. If not, online credibility is destroyed and a customer may never return. Detailed techniques on delivering the service promise are given in the 'Service guarantees and promises' box.

E-MARKETING EXCELLENCE

Service guarantees and promises

These can be made for a range of aspects:

- Information accuracy (product specifications, price, availability and delivery times) must all be accurate. How many customers did the retailer who mistakenly offered television sets for sale at £2.99 lose when it informed customers who had placed orders that it would not honour the order?

- E-mail response. How long will the company take to respond for different sorts of enquiries?

- Security guarantees. What happens if security is compromised?

- Delivery guarantees. What happens if delivery is late?

- Return guarantees. What happens if the product is unsuitable?

- Price promises. If you are offering the best prices, this should not be an empty promise. If a company uses an *attack e-tailing* approach then frequent comparison with competitors' prices and real-time adjustment to match or better them is required. This approach is important on the Internet because of the transparency of pricing and availability information made possible through shopping comparison sites such as Pricerunner (www.pricerunner.com) and Kelkoo (www.kelkoo.com). As customers increasingly use these facilities then it is important that price positioning is favourable.

Service promises can also be formalized in a service level agreement (SLA). If a business purchases a hosting service from an Internet service provider, its obligations and what it will do if they are not met will be clearly laid out in a service level agreement.

Expectations

Managing customers' expectations is even more challenging in the online world because of raised expectations. We need to:

1 Understand the customer's expectations for service delivery and the gap with current delivery.

2 Make clear service promises through privacy statements, promises and guarantees on security, delivery, price and customer service response times.

3 Deliver the service promise through a fast, easy-to-use site, with competitive pricing backed up by excellent customer service and perfect fulfilment.

Not rocket science – just common sense.

4.4 Fears and phobias

By the end of this section you will understand the fears and phobias that occupy some customers' minds when going online. You will also know how to address these issues.

The average consumer is not fearful of turning on the TV or radio or picking up a telephone. Perhaps the biggest difference about the Internet is the fear associated with it, and as marketers, we have to deal with this. You probably don't have these fears (since you're reading this book). But many of your potential customers do. Now we're going to ask you to do what good marketers are good at – empathize – empathize with customers – imagine how they feel when going online, particularly when going online for the first time.

WHAT ARE THE FEARS AND PHOBIAS?

Consider the fears you think your customers might suffer when they think about going online. Security risks such as stolen credit card details, hackers, hoaxes, viruses, SPAM and lack of privacy – big brother syndrome – probably top your list. Others fear having their computer taken over remotely. You may have also noted less significant anxieties such as not knowing what to do, fear of getting lost, fear of too much information or fear of inaccurate information. These fears centre on lack of control.

There are also fears about how the Internet will destroy the lives of individuals, families and so the whole of society. Safety needs such as security, protection, order and stability are of great importance in our hierarchy of needs. Finally, we have e-nasties such as cyber stalkers, hate mail, fake mail, mail bombs, cults and paedophiles lurking in children's chat-rooms. The human mind is a complex arena with its realities, its fears and its phobias. Sadly many of these fears are based on reality.

On a more positive note, excellent marketers understand their customers' fears and phobias and take actions to minimize them. The leading e-tailers not only have a great proposition, but they are perceived by the customer as low risk because they eliminate customer fears.

E-MARKETING INSIGHT

Fears diminishing but still strong

Over the past five years, the UK government has run an omnibus survey which gives great insight into customers' fears and phobias:

- The survey shows that the percentage of individuals who have accessed the Internet in the last 3 months has increased from 40% to 60%. Of course in the younger age groups the proportion is much higher (16–24 = 90%, 25–44 = 79%, 45–55 = 67%, 55–64 = 48%). This still shows many 'silver surfers' or users over 55, and indicates the potential for growth as the current population ages.

- This still leaves a substantial number who have not used the Internet who say they do not see a need for the Internet (43%), they have a lack of knowledge or confidence (37%) or costs are too high (11%).

- The main reasons for those not buying online are:

  - Have no need (26%)
  - Prefer to shop in person/see the product (35%)
  - Security concerns (19%).

- It seems as if e-retailers will need to work hard to convince non-adopters to overcome their prejudice, but the potential for success is high.

Source: ONS (2004)

Marketers alone cannot change some of the negative feelings about the Internet. The Internet makes great copy for the newspapers; it seems that the Internet is a scapegoat for many events that occur in modern society, whether this is babies being adopted over the Internet, discontented employees running amok, racism or indeed any immoral or illegal activity.

What marketers can, and must do, is to reassure customers that the problems they perceive are unlikely and act responsibly to minimize the risk of problems happening.

Follow these guidelines to achieve reassurance, gain trust and build loyalty:

1 *Provide clear and effective privacy statements.* Visit the sites of easyJet (www.easyjet.co.uk) and RS components (B2B) www.rswww.com for plain privacy statements which directly address customers' fear and phobias.

2 *Follow privacy and consumer protection guidelines in all local markets.* In 2003 the European Electronic Communications Regulations came into force to supplement existing European data protection laws. The essence of this law, implemented in the UK as the Privacy and Electronic Communications Regulations Act, is to make permission-based e-mail marketing a legal requirement. **Opt-in and opt-out are** both legal requirements for e-mail marketing to consumers (individual subscribers) in the UK. For B2B e-mail communications in the

UK this isn't currently a requirement, but it is in many European countries with fines of hundreds of thousands of Euros in some countries. It is also necessary to have clear privacy statements which inform users about **cookies** and **web analytics** tracking.

3 *Make security of customer data a priority*. This is a requirement of data protection law. For example, you should offer the strongest encryption standards possible and use firewalls and ethical hackers to maximize the safety of customer data.

4 *Present independent site certification*. Companies can use independent third-parties who set guidelines for online privacy and performance. The best known international bodies are Truste (www.truste.org) and Verisign for payment authentification (www.verisign.com). Other UK certification bodies include SafeBuy/TrustUK (www.safebuy.org.uk, www.trustuk.org.uk), Webtrader UK (www.webtraderuk.org.uk) and the IMRG Hallmark (www.imrg.org).

5 *Emphasize the excellence of service quality in all communications*. This is explained in Section 4.3 on meeting customers' expectations.

6 *Use content on the site to reassure the customer*. Explain the actions they have taken. Ask them to confirm. Allow them to revoke or cancel an action. Amazon takes customer fears about security seriously judging by the prominence and amount of content it devotes to this issue.

7 *Leading-edge design*. Marketers should challenge their site designers to make the customer experience as easy as possible by customer-centred site design. Intuitive, easy-to-use sites, where customers experience flow help to counter fears and phobias. Customers become comfortable more quickly and word-of-mouth spreads positive messages.

New approaches are needed to build trust in the networked world since conventional ways of gaining trust such as personal contact are no longer practical. Credibility and trust must be built at Internet speed. Time is of the essence. For some FMCG brands trust was built over two generations, Gap did it in ten years and Yahoo! in five years. In contrast, note that some studies show that trust is also a long-term proposition that builds slowly as people use a site, get good results, and don't feel let down or cheated.

SECTION SUMMARY 4.4

Fears and phobias

A headline in a *Harvard Business Review* recently announced: '*Price doesn't rule the web; trust does.*' The typical online customer is fearful and has many anxieties. Companies that succeed in reassuring customers by clearly communicating their security, privacy and ease-of-use backed up by real quality of service will reap the rewards through customer loyalty.

4.5 The online buying process

By the end of this section you will understand the stages buyers go through and how to ensure you address all of these stages online. You simply have to understand how customers use the new media in their purchase decision-making.

The buying process should be catered for both online and offline (**mixed-mode buying**, Chapter 2). Each stage of the purchasing process should be supported both online and offline. Let us consider a 'high-involvement' purchase such as a car or a house. Assuming this follows a simple linear buying model, what occurs at each stage?

1 *Problem recognition*. This can occur through changed circumstances such as a new job, new money or the existing car breaks down, etc. Peer pressure or clever advertising or editorial (online or offline) which highlights the problem can also help the customer to recognize it themselves. Advertising is often targeted at unconscious needs.

2 *Information search*. Having established a need, i.e. the problem is recognized, the customer gathers information. We need to understand how customers gather information – online and offline. Online the web is increasingly used for searching. Remember there is a difference between searching and surfing. Think about the timing and frequency of when online customers seek information. Get the timing and the targeting right and you create 'relevance' which allows the information through the customer's perceptual filters. Get it wrong and your information gets screened out by an uninterested audience.

3 *Evaluation*. We need to use the content on our site to communicate the features and benefits of the brand in what may be a fleeting visit to the site or an in-depth analysis. Independent reports prominently positioned on site may save the buyer from having to search elsewhere. We also need to think about how to cater for different customer buying behaviour according to Internet experience. Remember that search behaviour will differ according to familiarity with the Internet, the organization and its web site.

4 *Decision*. Some car buyers may have already physically test-driven several cars and now want to decide and buy online. Some sites help the decision by offering payment facilities that match the customer's personal financial situation. Once the decision has been made to purchase, we don't want to lose the customer at this stage, so make purchasing slick and simple. And if the customer has anxieties, give them the choice of buying through other channels by prompting with a phone number or a call-back facility.

5 *Action (sale)*. Often an appropriate incentive to 'buy now' either online or offline helps to push the buyer over the edge and into the sale. The purchase can be made online particularly if suitable reassurances are made.

6 *Post sale*. Then the real marketing begins. The sale is only the beginning of the relationship (i.e. relationship marketing and lifetime customers). Lifetime customers generate repeat sales which, in turn, generate much higher profits (some estimates suggest five times higher profits on repeat sales than new customers). Use e-mail and the web site to provide customer service and support.

Figure 4.4 summarizes how content on site can support the buying process. Produce a map for how your site supports the buying process.

Obviously the process above applies best to high-involvement purchases like a car rather than to low-involvement purchases like a can of cola. Here the model is about awareness, trial and reinforcement, followed by availability, availability availability.

B2B buying models have a specification and tender stage built in before sellers can tender or present their bids (and product information). Often, only pre-selected or preferred suppliers' information is considered. Note information search tends to be 'directed' or 'focused' rather than browsing or surfing. In fact five different types of search behaviour have been recognized and we should cater for each in site design and communications, but with the emphasis on the predominant groups.

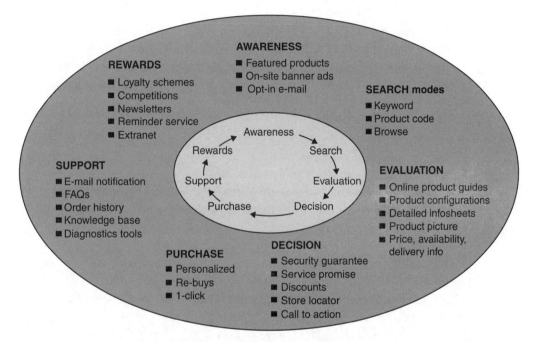

Figure 4.4   The buying process and how it can be supported by site content

i.e. the tracker is looking for specific information about a particular product. The report says: 'If they get the answers they are seeking they need little further persuasion or purchase justification before completing the purchase'. While this may not be true since they may compare on other sites, this type of shopper will be relatively easy to convert.

2 **Hunter**. Defined as follows:

> *'doesn't have a specific product in mind but knows what type of product they are looking for (e.g. digital camera, cooker) and probably has one or more product features they are looking for. The hunter uses an online shopping site to find a range of suitable products, compare them and decide which one to buy'.*

The hunter needs more help, support and guidance to reach a purchasing decision. The report says:

> *'once a potential purchase is found, they then need to justify that purchase in their own minds, and possibly to justify their purchase to others. Only then will confirmation of the purchase become a possibility'.*

3 **Explorer**. Defined as follows:

> *'doesn't even have a particular type of product in mind. They may have a well-defined shopping objective (buying a present for someone or treating themselves), a less-resolved shopping objective (buying something to 'brighten up' the lounge) or no shopping objective at all (they like the high street store and thought they would have a look at the online site)'.*

The report suggests that the explorer has a range of possible needs and many uncertainties to be resolved before committing to purchase, but the following may be helpful in persuading these shoppers to convert: 'Certain types of information, however, are particularly relevant. Suggested gift ideas, guides to product categories, lists of top selling products and information-rich promotions (What's New? What's Hot?) – these could all propel them towards a purchasing decision'.

Leading companies use web analytics data to see how activity and repeat visits vary through each day, week, month and year. A financial services provider found a traffic peak on Monday lunchtime when people looked to find out more after reviewing alternatives in the Sunday papers. A B2B company found a peak at the start of each month that corresponded with new sales promotions. A monthly competition was launched, timed to coincide with the traffic peak.

Amazingly, research by BT showed that customers seem to use the Internet and telephone more before a full moon, but how marketers can tap into this behaviour is unclear!

The online buying process

We have to support customers through each stage of the buying process: problem identification, information search, evaluation, decision, action and post sales.

We need to think about how we can combine online and offline communications to support the customer through each stage of the buying process and also support mixed-mode buying at each stage. We also need to be self-critical about how we profile customers. What are the underlying variables that might influence the customer's product purchase and usage patterns and can we track these patterns? Techniques to achieve this are described in Section 4.10 Researching the online customer. Finally, some customers want to search, compare and buy online. Others just want to browse. Does your web site accommodate all stages of the buying process?

4.6 Online information processing

By the end of this section you will understand how customers process information – what gets through and what doesn't.

The section is structured around Charles Hofacker's five stages of on-site information processing (Hofacker, 2001). The five stages are: (1) Exposure (2) Attention (3) Comprehension and perception (4) Yielding and acceptance (5) Retention. Each stage acts as a hurdle, since if the site design or content is too difficult to process, the customer cannot progress to the next stage. The e-marketer fails.

The best web site designs take into account how customers process information. Good e-marketers are aware of how the messages are processed by the customer and of the corresponding steps we can take to ensure the correct message is received.

The first stage is **exposure**. This is straightforward. If the content is not present for long enough, customers will not be able to process it. Think of splash pages, banner adverts or shockwave animations. If these change too rapidly the message will not be received.

The second stage is **attention**. The human mind has limited capacity to pick out the main messages from a screen full of single column text format without headings or graphics. Movement, text size and colour help to gain attention for key messages. Note though that studies show that the eye is immediately drawn to content, not the headings in the navigation systems. Of course, we need to be careful about using garish colours and animations as these can look amateurish and detract from the main message.

Comprehension and perception are the third of Hofacker's stages. They refer to how the customer interprets the combination of graphics, text and multimedia on a web site. The design will be most effective if it uses familiar standards or metaphors since the customer will interpret them according to previous experience and memory. Once relevant information is found, visitors sometimes want to dig deeper for more information.

Fourth, **yielding and acceptance** refers to whether the information you present is accepted by the customer. Different tactics need to be used to convince different types of people. Classically, a US audience is more convinced by features rather than benefits, while the reverse is true for a European audience. Some customers will respond to emotive appeals, perhaps reinforced by images, while others will make a more clinical evaluation based on the text. This gives us the difficult task of combining text, graphics and copy to convince each customer segment.

Finally, **retention** – how well the customer can recall their experience. A clear, distinctive site design will be retained in the customer's mind, perhaps prompting a repeat visit when the customer thinks, 'where did I see that information?' and then recalls the layout of the site. A clear site design will also be implanted in the customer's memory as a mental map which they will be able to draw on when returning to the site, increasing their flow experience.

Sites with excellent design use a range of techniques. Examine Figure 4.5 to see how the concepts in this section have been applied.

Figure 4.5 Lastminute.com attracts attention

E-MARKETING INSIGHT

Jakob Nielsen on graphics

Jakob Nielsen says:

> *'when they arrive on a page, users ignore navigation bars and other global design elements: instead they look only at the content area of the page' (www.useit.com/alertbox/20000109.html)*

Studies show that e-customers are very goal-driven and tend to ignore banner ads while focusing completely on their task. Eye-tracking studies confirm the existence of 'banner blindness' where the user's gaze never rests in the region of the screen occupied by advertising (www.useit.com/alertbox/990221.html).

Nielsen says:

> *'the most common behaviour is to hunt for information and be ruthless in ignoring details. But once the prey has been caught, users will sometimes dive in more deeply. Thus, web content needs to support both aspects of information access: foraging and consumption. Text needs to be scannable, but it also needs to provide the answers users seek' (www.useit.com/alertbox/20000514.html)*

A good compromise is to have small rectangular animated banner ads to the right of the screen which highlight the special offers. But remember about 'banner blindness'.

SECTION SUMMARY 4.6

Online information processing

Understanding how customers process information through the stages of exposure, attention, comprehension and perception, yielding and acceptance and retention can help us design sites – sites that really help us get our message across and deliver memorable messages and superior customer service.

4.7 Online relationships and loyalty

By the end of this section, you will understand the importance of lifetime customers, relationship marketing and loyalty. You will also know how to begin to explore setting up loyalty marketing schemes.

Look at the stats. Retaining existing customers is five times more profitable than acquiring new customers. US corporations lose half their customers in five years (Reicheld, 1996). All marketers know that building long-term relationships with the 'ideal customer' is essential for any sustainable business. Failure to build relationships largely caused the dotcom failures.

Recent research shows that by retaining just 5% more customers, e-companies can boost their profits by 25% to 95%. This section describes techniques to build and maintain relationships with customers using a combination of online and offline techniques.

We want to move customers up what Considine and Murray (1981) referred to as the 'ladder of loyalty'. From suspects to prospects to customers to clients to advocates who are totally loyal and are happy to spread the word about our products and services.

Remember, some customers are more likely to be loyal than others. Companies need to focus on those ideal customers that are likely to become loyal rather than the promiscuous, loss making, customers who grab incentives and run.

Many companies now only proactively market to 'ideal' customers since research suggests that 20% of existing customers are 'ideal' and generate most of your profits. Some customers break even, while other, disloyal, promiscuous, customers are loss makers. They cost you money. Low loyalty has a high cost.

Seth Godin said (exaggerating for effect) 'Focus on share of customer, not market share – fire 70% of your customers and watch your profits go up!' Some companies go further – they actually stop 'bad customers' from becoming customers (Godin, 2001). They also invest in acquiring and keeping ideal customers. For many businesses it can take at least two years before a company recoups its initial acquisition costs.

So how can we keep customers and form relationships, particularly in the cyber world?

In *Permission Marketing*, Seth Godin suggests online relationships can be likened to the relationships built through dating, with incentives important at every stage. Lindstrom and Andersen, authors of *Brand Building on the Internet*, encourage e-marketers to think of loyalty as virtual love.

Research summarized by Reicheld and Schefter (2000) showed that acquiring online customers is so expensive (20–30 per cent higher than for traditional businesses) that start-up companies may remain unprofitable for at least two to three years. The research also shows that by retaining just 5 per cent more customers, online companies can boost their profits by 25 per cent to 95 per cent. They say:

> *'but if you can keep customers loyal, their profitability accelerates much faster than in traditional businesses. It costs you less and less to service them.'*

Note that the relationship between customer loyalty and profitability has been questioned, notably by Reinartz and Kumar (2002), who discovered through analysis of four company databases that:

> *'there was little or no evidence to suggest that customers who purchase steadily from a company over time are necessarily cheaper to serve, less price sensitive, or particularly effective at bringing in new business.'*

While few would argue that the cost of acquiring customers is significantly higher than repeat ᵐmers and that some customers are unprofitable, care has to be taken with customer ion.

As in any relationship, the early stages are crucial. In relationship marketing the first ninety days are crucial. Maintaining online customer relationships is difficult. Laurie Windham says:

'That's what's so scary about customer retention in the online space. We've created this empowered, impatient customer who has a short attention span, a lot of choices, and a low barrier to switching.'

E-MARKETING INSIGHT

The *Cluetrain Manifesto* on developing relationships

The authors of the groundbreaking *Cluetrain Manifesto* (Levine *et al.*, 2000) kept for posterity as 'read only landmark' at www.cluetrain.com suggest that we should not conceive the Internet as an impassive network of hardware and software, but as a means of creating global conversations within markets – a new dynamic dialogue.

It refers to a large organization being unable to listen or respond to the 'clues' from customers demanding better service and response. Clues include high churn, rising complaints and the success of more responsive competitors.

To illustrate the danger of continuing with push marketing the authors say:

Conversations among human beings sound human. They are conducted in a human voice.

Most corporations, on the other hand, only know how to talk in the soothing, humorless monotone of the mission statement, marketing brochure, and your-call-is-important-to-us busy signal. Same old tone, same old lies. No wonder networked markets have no respect for companies unable or unwilling to speak as they do.

Corporate firewalls have kept smart employees in and smart markets out. It's going to cause real pain to tear those walls down. But the result will be a new kind of conversation. And it will be the most exciting conversation business has ever engaged in.

DEVELOPING LOYALTY

So how do you develop loyalty and strong relations with customers?

First, target and acquire the right type of customer – the ideal customer. Second, delight them. Don't just satisfy them. Ground-breaking research by Xerox some years ago revealed that between 65 and 85% of customers who defected from Xerox were actually 'satisfied customers'.

So, we need to excel beyond the five 'primary determinants of loyalty' identified by Reicheld and Schefter (2000):

1 Quality customer support.
2 On-time delivery.
3 Compelling product presentations.
4 Convenient and reasonably priced shipping and handling.
5 Clear trustworthy privacy policies.

And then delight the customer with:

1 *Extra service and added value*. There are a host of other opportunities constantly to delight and surprise the customer. Start by asking, 'What interests, passions and needs do my customers have? How can I help them?' Then see how you can add value. The difficult bit is finding the time to think about these and then time to implement them. There is no limit to relevant, timely added value ideas – many of which do not cost that much but have a high value.
2 *Personalization*. Personalization and mass customization can have a high value. They can be used to tailor information in both the web site and opt-in e-mail. Extranets can be used to provide value-added services for key accounts.
3 *Community creation*. Community creation can engage the customer and provide a hook that keeps them returning. It can be used to create a new form of added value built around the brand. Section 4.8 deals with communities.
4 *Integration*. Integration into the customer's own systems (e.g. ERP) reducing duplication of work and increasing 'lock-in' which creates a switching cost should a customer ever want to leave.
5 *Incentivization*. Traditional retention methods such as loyalty schemes and sales promotions work well. But remember – be consistent with your page layout so that your customers know where to find the special offers section. Opt-in e-mail can also alert customers to special offers and events. For both B2B and B2C organizations, think about the potential for online events. There are an infinite amount of opportunities.

There are many different approaches, but basically they embrace the same principles – focus on good customers, treat them individually and serve them excellently and outstandingly.

E-MARKETING EXCELLENCE

Dell identify loyalty drivers

Reicheld and Schefter (2000) reported that Dell Computer has created a customer experience council that has researched key loyalty drivers, identified measures to track this and put in place an action plan to improve loyalty (Table 4.1).

Table 4.1 Relationship between loyalty drivers and measures to assess their success at Dell Computer. Based on example related in Reicheld and Schefter (2000)

Loyalty drivers	Summary metric
1 Order fulfilment	Ship to target. Percentage that ship on time exactly as the customer specified.
2 Product performance	Initial field incident rate – the frequency of problems experienced by customers.
3 Post sale service and support	On-time, first-time fix – the percentage of problems fixed on the first visit by a service rep who arrives at the time promised.

SECTION SUMMARY 4.7

Online relationships and loyalty

To summarize, we need to keep 'ideal' customers for life by building strong emotional and rational bonds. Constantly find out more about their needs, serve them and then plant seeds and relevant incentives to keep them coming back again and again.

4.8 Communities

By the end of this section you will understand the benefits of building communities and be able to assess the suitability of techniques used to foster online communities and how to build active/lively online communities that improve brand equity and foster customer retention.

Man is a sociable animal. Communities or social networks are important. Whether stockbrokers or punks – they tend to group together into communities. Can your brand immerse itself within a community and thereby strengthen its relationship with customers? Communities of buyers, users, lovers, even haters can pop up all over the Internet. Better to work with communities than against them. Wouldn't it be great if you could listen to your customers and prospects talking about your brand and related issues. Imagine occasionally dropping in and asking the community a question.

Imagine them telling you their current and future needs – what they like and don't like about your company. Imagine your brand at the hub of a community? Imagine your customers using your brand as a virtual meeting place? Imagine your customers getting great value from talking to each other?

Community is a key feature of new media that distinguishes them from traditional push media. But why is community important? John Hagel (Hagel and Armstrong, 1997) has said:

> *'The rise of virtual communities in online networks has set in motion an unprecedented shift from vendors of goods and services to the customers who buy them. Vendors*

who understand this transfer of power and choose to capitalize on it by organizing virtual communities will be richly rewarded with both peerless customer loyalty and impressive economic returns.'

What is the reality behind this vision? How can we deliver the promise of community? The key to successful community is customer-centred communications. It is customer-to-customer (C2C) interaction. Customers, not suppliers, generate the content of the site, e-mail list or bulletin board.

C2C community success and essential power can be gauged by the millions of customers who used Napster and Gnutella to download MP3 music files. Using the peer-to-peer (P2P) approach, these companies created a global swap shop by acting as intermediaries enabling users to exchange files.

E-MARKETING INSIGHT

Durlacher on community

Think about these different types of community identified by Durlacher at the time of the dotcom boom but which remain valid today. What content and interaction will occur on each to support them? Which are appropriate to your marketplace?

1 *Purpose* – people who are going through the same process or trying to achieve a particular objective. Examples include those researching cars, e.g. at Autotrader (www.autotrader.co.uk) or stocks online, e.g. at the Motley Fool (www.motleyfool.co.uk).

2 *Position* – people who are in a certain circumstance such as a health disorder or in a certain stage of life such as communities set up specifically for young people and old people. Examples are teenage network Dubit (www.dubit.co.uk) which is used by FMCG brands to research youth market trends and engage opinion formers (Figure 4.6) or sites for the over 50s such as www.over50s.com and www.50connect.co.uk.

3 *Interest* – this community is for people who share an interest or passion such as sport (www.football365.com), music (www.nme.com), leisure (www.walkingworld.com). See Magicalia (www.magicalia.com) for a range of communities created in the UK.

4 *Profession* – they are important for companies promoting B2B services. For example in the dotcom boom Vertical Net (www.vertical.net) set up over 50 different communities to appeal to professionals in specific industries such as paints and coatings, the chemical industry or electronics. Some still persist, for example, E-consultancy (www.e-consultancy.com) is an online-only portal for new media specialists, but trade papers such as *Construction News* (www.cnplus.co.uk) are the dominant portals for professionals.

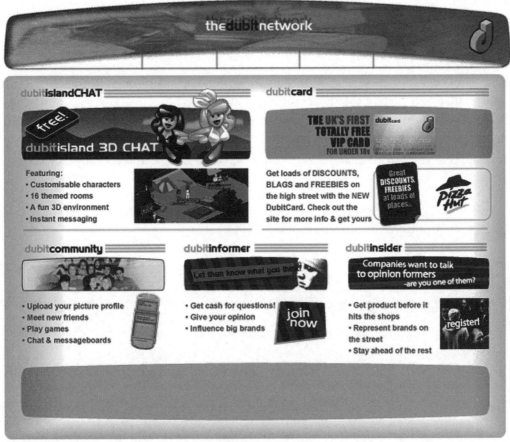

Figure 4.6 Dubit (www.dubit.co.uk)

COMMUNITY BUILDING STRATEGIES

You will notice that most of the community examples are intermediary sites that are independent of a particular manufacturer or retailer. A key question to ask before embarking on a community-building programme is: 'can customer interests be best served through a company independent community'. If the answer to this question is 'yes', then it may be best to form a community that is a brand variant, differentiated from its parent. For example, Boots the Chemist has created Handbag.com as an independent community for its female customers. Another tip, and a less costly alternative, is to promote your products through sponsorship or co-branding on an independent community site or portal. Or at a minimum get involved in the community discussions.

Roger Parker, author of *Relationship Marketing on the Web*, lists eight useful questions to ask when considering how to create a community for your customers:

1 What interests, needs or passions do many of your customers have in common?
2 What topics or concerns might your customers like to share with each other?

3 What information is likely to appeal to your customers' friends or colleagues?

4 What other types of business in your area appeal to buyers of your products and services?

5 How can you create packages or offers based on combining offers from two or more affinity partners?

6 What price, delivery, financing, or incentives can you afford to offer to friends (or colleagues) that your current customers recommend?

7 What types of incentives or rewards can you afford to provide customers who recommend friends (or colleagues) who make a purchase?

8 How can you best track purchases resulting from word-of-mouth recommendations from friends?

What about specific approaches for the B2B community? The B2B community offers great potential for high-involvement business services.

E-MARKETING EXCELLENCE

Overcoming community problems

These are examples of how companies have overcome problems with their communities.

1 *Empty communities.* A community without any people isn't a community. You need to apply your traffic building skills. What is the online value proposition of your community and how are you communicating it? Perhaps it is best if existing brands tap into a third party, independent community rather than starting your own that may not gain critical mass. For example, a baby toy manufacturer is likely to be better served by getting involved on community sites such as Babyworld (www.babyworld.com) and Babycentre (www.babycentre.co.uk) rather than starting its own community which may never gain critical mass since it is not perceived as neutral.

2 *Silent communities.* A community may have many registered members, but community is not a community if the conversation flags. This is a tricky problem. You can encourage people to join the community, but how do you get them to participate? Here are some ideas.

- Seed the community. Use a moderator to ask questions or have a weekly or monthly question written by the moderator or sourced from customers. Have a resident independent expert to answer questions. Visit the communities on Monster (www.monster.co.uk) to see these approaches in action and think about what distinguishes the quiet communities from the noisy ones.

- Make it select. Limit it to key account customers or set it up as an extranet service that is only offered to valued customers as a value-add. Members may be more likely to get involved.

- Use e-mail. With e-mail groups such as Yahoo Groups (http://uk.groups.yahoo. com) participants don't need to revisit the web site, it is always in their e-mail inbox.

3 *Critical communities.* Many communities on manufacturer or retailer sites can be critical of the brand. The Egg Free Zone for example (www.eggfreezone.com) from bank Egg had to be closed because of critical comments of its services and retailers. Think about whether this is a bad thing. It could highlight weaknesses in your service offer to customers and competitors, but enlightened companies use communities as a means to better understand their customers' needs and the failings with their services. Community is a key market research tool. Also, it may be better to control and contain these critical comments on your site rather than them being voiced elsewhere in newsgroups where you may not notice them and can less easily counter them. The computer-oriented newsgroup on Monster shows how the moderator lets criticisms go so far and then counters them or closes them off. Particular criticisms can be removed. So, a moderator is clearly needed for any company-run communities.

SECTION SUMMARY 4.8

Communities

Well-run communities strengthen relationships, trust and loyalty as well as maintaining brand awareness in the minds of the community members. Communities also allow a unique opportunity to stay close to customers, their concerns, their worries and their desires. Despite these benefits, building an active community can be time consuming, expensive and difficult. Careful moderation and seeding of topics from a subject expert may be required. An alternative approach is to hook up to an established community that has greater independence. Either way, communities are part of the dynamic dialogue and dynamic opportunities that today's marketer enjoys.

4.9 Customer profiles

We need to know who's online? What are their profiles? We need to know each customer segment and the proportion of customers who use various digital channels such as the Internet, interactive digital TV and mobile or other devices:

We need to know the proportion of customers who:

1 Have access to which channel or channels?
2 Are influenced by using which channel or channels?
3 Purchase using which channel or channels?

Let's consider each of these now.

PROFILING B2C CUSTOMERS

1 *Access to channel.* E-commerce provides a global marketplace, and this means we must review access and usage of the Internet channel at many different geographic levels: worldwide,

between continents and countries. Also we must evaluate demographic differences in access – the stereotype of the typical Internet user as male, around thirty years of age and with high disposable income no longer holds true. Many females and more senior 'silver surfers' are also active.

To understand online customer behaviour and how they are likely to respond to messages, we also need to consider the user's access location, access device and '**webographics**', all of which are constraints on site design.

Finally, we mustn't forget the non-users, who comprise more than half of the adult population in many countries.

2 *Influenced online.* Next we must look at how our audience is influenced by online media. Finding information about goods and services is a very popular online activity, but we need to capture data about online influence in the buying process for our own market.

3 *Purchased online.* Customers will only purchase products online that meet the criteria of de Kare-Silver's electronic shopping test. Research shown in Figure 4.2 suggests that an increasing proportion of people are prepared to buy online. For e-planning you need to know this data for your segment. Although we can use this information when building e-plans and when calculating the channel contribution to revenue, we still need some psychographic information to understand online customers better.

Many attempts have been made to characterize the online customers in order to tailor the online offering for them (see box 'Information sources for researching customer profiles').

PROFILING B2B CUSTOMERS

That's all very well for B2C, but what about B2B users? How should we profile online business users?

Think about the information you would want to collect when designing an online form to profile registered site B2B users. Users may be asked to enter the following organization characteristics:

- Size of company (employees or turnover)
- Industry sector and products
- Organization type (private, public, government, not for profit)
- Division
- Country and region.

What about buying cycles and budgets? You can also profile customers according to which are hot and which are cold – which are ready to buy and which are not. We also need to know the following customer variables:

- Names
- Role and responsibility from job title, function or number of staff managed

- Role in buying decision (purchasing influence)
- Department
- Product interest
- Demographics: age, sex and possibly social group.

When searching for the ideal customer, what variables, or characteristics do you use? What is your profile of your ideal customer?

We can profile business users of the Internet in a similar way to consumers:

1 *The percentage of companies with access.* In most developed countries more than three-quarters of businesses have Internet access, regardless of size, suggesting the Internet is very effective in terms of reaching companies. But does it reach the right people in the buying unit? Not necessarily, as access is not available to all employees.

2 *Influenced online.* Data indicates that the Internet is important in identifying online suppliers, with the majority identifying some suppliers online, especially in the larger companies.

3 *Purchase online.* E-mail and the web are widely used for online purchases, with extranets and EDI less important since these are the preserve of larger companies. Many of the larger blue chip companies only buy online.

E-MARKETING INSIGHT

Information sources for researching customer profiles

These are the premier sources:

1 Internet access penetration by country and continent. Visit the web site of the International Telecommunications Union (ITU) (http://www.itu.int/ti/industryoverview/index.htm). Choose Internet indicators.

2 Consumer usage behaviour (number of users, length of time and number of sites visited each month). Nielsen Netratings (www.nielsennetratings.com). UK usage only – National Statistics Omnibus Survey (www.statistics.gov.uk). Demographics and access type – e-mori (www.mori.com/emori).

3 Consumer purchase behaviour. EIAA (2004) (www.eiaa.net).

4 Business access and applications *Business In The Information Age – International Benchmarking Study 2003*. UK Department of Trade and Industry. Statistics update available online at: http://www2.bah.com/dti2003.

5 Aggregators of research about Internet usage: ClickZ Stats (www.clickz.com/stats) formerly Nua/Cyberatlas.

Customer profiles

User profiles change as Internet penetration changes. Marketers constantly need to keep a watch on who is online and who is offline – the number of connected customers, the percentage whose offline purchase is influenced online and, of course, the number who buy online. We need to research our customer geographic, demographic and psychographic segments. We also need to know why certain customer segments buy or don't buy.

4.10 Researching the online customer

In our quest to understand online customers, we need to know how to research them. Before that we need to identify what we need to know. In this section we look at the key questions and where to find the answers.

So what do you need to know about online customers? The following are key:

- Who are they – demographics and psychographics?
- What do they want – their needs – why do they buy or not buy?
- How do they buy (online or offline or mixed mode)?
- When do they buy?
- How did they find us or our competitors?

In the context of the site, we need to know, in particular, what do visitors need before, during and after they go online and when they arrive at your site? We also need to know what kind of content customers want. One way of finding out is **personas and scenario-based design**.

Modelling personas of site visitors is a powerful technique for helping increase the usability and customer centricity of a web site. Personas are essentially a 'thumbnail' description of a type of person. They have been used for a long time in research for segmentation and advertising, but since the mid-1990s have proved effective for improving web site design. Here are two simple examples for a music publisher wishing to sell music clips and sheet music to a business audience.

Persona 1 – George: George is a 45-year-old violin teacher who has used the Internet for less than a year. He accesses the Internet from home over a dial-up connection. He has never purchased online before, preferring to place orders by phone.

Persona 2 – Georgina: Georgina is a 29-year-old ad exec who has been using the Internet for five years.

You can see that these are quite different types of people who will have quite different needs.

Customer scenarios are developed for different personas. Patricia Seybold in her book *The Customer Revolution* explains them as follows:

> *'A customer scenario is a set of tasks that a particular customer wants or needs to do in order to accomplish his or her desired outcome.'*

You can see that scenarios can be developed for each persona. For an online bank, scenarios might include:

1 New customer – opening online account.
2 Existing customer – transferring an account online.
3 Existing customer – finding an additional product.

Each scenario is split up into a series of steps or tasks before the scenario is completed. These steps can be best thought of as a series of questions a visitor asks. These questions identify the different information needs of different customer types at different stages in the buying process.

The use of scenarios is a simple but very powerful web design technique that is still relatively rare in web site design. Evidence of the use of scenarios and persons in sites are when the needs of a range of audiences are accommodated with navigation, links and search to answer specific questions. Clear steps in a booking process are also an indication of the use of this approach.

The approach has the benefits of:

● Fostering customer-centricity;
● Identifying detailed information needs and steps required by customers;
● Can be used to both test existing web site designs or prototypes and to devise new designs;
● Can be used to compare and test the strength and clarity of communication of proposition on different web sites;
● Can be linked to specific marketing outcomes required by site owners.

Effective customer research also uses pre-launch research techniques such as concept testing, competitor benchmarking and usability testing (Chapter 6) as well as post-launch research such as customer profiling and tracking.

E-MARKETING INSIGHT

Using personas and scenarios to inform web site design

These are some guidelines and ideas on what can be included when developing a persona. Start or end with giving your persona a name. The detailed stages are:

1 Build personal attributes into personas:
● Demographic: age, gender, education, occupation and for B2B, company size, position in buying unit.
● Psychographic: goals, tasks, motivation.

- Webographics: web experience (months), usage location (home or work), usage platform (dial-up, broadband), usage frequency, favourite sites.

2 Remember that personas are only models of characteristics and environment:
- Design targets
- Stereotypes
- Three or four usually suffice to improve general usability, but more are needed for specific behaviours
- Choose one primary persona whom, if satisfied, means others are likely to be satisfied.

3 Different scenarios can be developed for each persona as explained further below:
Write three or four, for example:
- Information seeking scenario (leads to site registration)
- Purchase scenario – new customer (leads to sale)
- Purchase scenario – existing customer (leads to sale).

Once different personas have been developed who are representative of key site visitor types or customer types, a primary persona is sometimes identified. Wodtke (2002) says:

> *'Your primary persona needs to be a common user type who is both important to the business success of the product and needy from a design point of view – in other words, a beginner user or a technologically challenged one'.*

She also says that secondary personas can also be developed such as super-users or complete novices. Complementary personas are those that don't fit into the main categories that display unusual behaviour. Such complementary personas help 'out-of-box thinking' and offer choices or content that may appeal to all users.

An example of applying personas to explain online banking products to users is viewable at www.hsbc.co.uk.

RESEARCH TECHNIQUES

We can divide research techniques into primary data collection where we collect our own data and secondary data where we use published research. For each we need to decide the best combination of online and offline (Figure 4.7). The two main types of primary research are traditional marketing research methods and **web analytics** using server-based or browser-based techniques as shown in Table 4.2. Log files give undreamed visibility of customer behaviour, through click streams and page impressions we can find out what a customer is or is not interested in and can measure the response to our online campaigns. We can even use data mining software to profile different online behaviours.

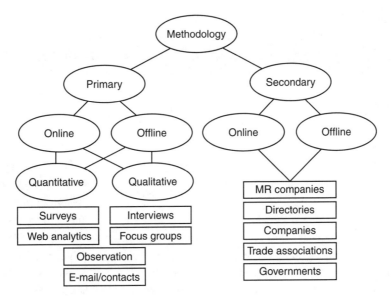

Figure 4.7 Different research techniques

Table 4.2 A comparison of different online metrics collection methods

Technique	Strengths	Weaknesses
1 Server-based logfile analysis of site activity (web analytics) Examples: www.clicktracks.com www.webtrends.com	• Directly records customer behaviour on site plus where they were referred from • Low cost	• Not based around marketing outcomes such as leads, sales. • Size, even summaries may be over 50 pages long • Doesn't directly record channel satisfaction • Undercounting and overcounting • Misleading unless interpreted carefully
2 Browser-based site activity data (web analytics) Examples: www.indextools.com www.redsheriff.com	• Greater accuracy than server-based analysis • Counts all users, unlike the panel approach	• Relatively expensive method • Similar weaknesses to server-based technique apart from accuracy • Limited demographic information
3 Panels activity and demographic data	• Provides competitor comparisons • Gives demographic profiling	• Depends on extrapolation from limited sample that may not be representative

(Continued)

Table 4.2 *(Continued)*

Technique	Strengths	Weaknesses
Examples: www.netratings.com www.comscore.com www.hitwise.co.uk	• Avoids undercounting and overcounting	
4 Outcome data, e.g. enquiries, sales, customer service e-mails	• Records marketing outcomes	• Difficulty of integrating data with other methods of data collection when collected manually or in other information systems
5 Online questionnaires. Customers are prompted randomly – every *n*th customer or after customer activity or by e-mail	• Can record customer satisfaction and profiles • Relatively cheap to create and analyse	• Difficulty of recruiting respondents who complete accurately • Sample bias – tend to be advocates or disgruntled customers who complete
6 Online focus groups; synchronous recording.	• Relatively cheap to create	• Difficult to moderate and co-ordinate • No visual cues as from offline focus groups
7 Mystery shoppers. Example customers are recruited to evaluate the site, e.g. www.emysteryshopper.com	• Structured tests give detailed feedback • Also tests integration with other channels such as e-mail and phone	• Relatively expensive • Sample must be representative

Although initially promising, we should remember the weaknesses of log file analysis indicated in Table 4.2 and consider supplementing them with browser-based analysis methods. For large B2C sites we can also use panel data to give customer numbers and profiles.

To understand the e-customer we can use online versions of traditional marketing research techniques, but more rapidly and cheaper than before. But remember there are many new issues involved with the design and execution of online questionnaires, focus groups and mystery shoppers and we need to assess the strengths and weaknesses of each technique (Table 4.2).

For all research, we must devise a methodology to minimize sample bias. We need to make sure the sample is not made solely of evangelists who love your service or critics who hate it. How do you counter this?

Remember also that the web also offers a fast, lower-cost method of researching the online customer using secondary data. Consider how well your organization uses the web to enhance its market intelligence using the sources given in the web links at the end of the chapter.

SECTION SUMMARY 4.10

Researching the online customer

Today's marketers have the most fantastic opportunity to research customers. We can track customers online, we can ask them questions online and we can have group discussions online. We can gain a closer understanding of online customers. Metrics combine new research techniques such as server log files and traditional techniques such as focus groups and questionnaires. Disciplined marketers will take the opportunity and improve their customer research by mixing online and offline research techniques.

4.11 The post-PC customer

Web access via PCs will decline as a proportion as more people use 3G phones and interactive TV to access the web. Things are changing. Here's a view of the future, its environment and what the post-PC customer might be like. By the end of this section you will have a glimpse of the future and the customers within it. Let's step into the future now.

The post-PC customer may occasionally accept payment to view some ads. The rest are screened out by both filtering software and PVRs (Section 5.9) to wall-to-wall screen TVs. Neither governments nor society permit old style intrusive advertising anymore. No more intrusive evening telephone calls from script reading intelligent agents. It is also illegal to litter anyone's doorstep or house with mail shots and inserts. Heavy fines stopped all that a long time ago. The only ads that do get inside are carried by the many millions of private media owners who rent out their cars, bikes and bodies as billboards.

The tedious task of shopping for distress purchases like petrol, electricity or memory storage is delegated completely to embedded shopping bots. Non-embedded bots spun out of control some years ago when they first appeared in three-dimensional hovering holograms – always at your side, always double checking the best price for hire cars, hotels, even drinks at the bar. Some are programmed to be polite, others aggressive or even abusive. All are programmed to be intrusive whenever anything is being bought. Delays on buses and traffic jams regularly occurred when argumentative bots engaged in lengthy negotiations. Frustration broke out. Bots attacked bots, people attacked bots and bot owners. Eventually bots were banned from buses, planes, trains and several 'peaceful supermarkets'.

Next came the great worm wars. Programming bots so they only buy your brand – for life. But, unlike humans, bots can be re-programmed by a competitor. The advertising agent worm was born. Agent eaters soon followed.

Despite being information fatigued and time compressed, the post-PC customer lives a lot longer than many bots. And certainly longer than most of the new brands that seem to come and go. The 150-year-old person has already been born.

Meanwhile, back at the ranch, microwaves insist on offering suggestions of ideal wines to go with your meal, offering instant delivery from the neighbourhood's wired-up 24-hour roving delivery van. Your fridge offers special incentives to buy Pepsi when you run out of Coke (or whichever brand owns or hires the fridge-linked database). Children happily play chess and interact with their opponents on giant vertical screens. Voice-operated computers are considered noisy and old fashioned as discrete, upmarket, thought-operated computers operate silently, but extremely effectively.

And all the time **Bluetooth** type technology facilitates ubiquitous communications which allows constant interaction between both man and machines, and machine and machine. The tectonic shift will continue.

Think of a world without TV ads, billboards and direct mail – a world where customers choose the information they want to receive. How will businesses reach their target markets in this new environment?

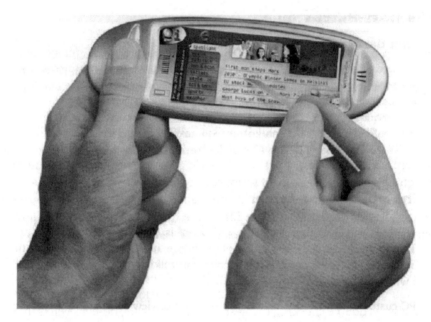

Figure 4.8   What 3G technology products could look like?

And all the time, the technology, if truly mastered, can free up time to do the important things that give the post-PC customer a genuinely higher quality of life.

SECTION SUMMARY 4.11

The post-PC customer

As Moore's Law (the observation made in 1965 by Gordon Moore, co-founder of Intel, that the number of transistors per square inch on integrated circuits had doubled every year since the integrated circuit was invented) continues to hold true, the time compressed, information fatigued and disloyal, post-PC customer seeks relationships not from brands themselves but from databases that know, understand and seemingly care about them. Witness the virtual girlfriend relationships in Japan. Relationships with shops and vending machines. Oh, and relationships with people – real, quaint, touchy feely, physical people.

CHAPTER SUMMARY

1 Consumers are motivated to venture online for a range of reasons – social, shopping, entertainment. B2B customers are driven by cost savings, speed and selling.

2 We need to understand expectations for service delivery, making promises and then deliver.

3 Online customers have many fears and phobias such as security and privacy. Companies need to reassure that with their services, the risks are minimized.

4 We have to support customers through each stage of the buying process: problem identification, information search, evaluation, decision, action and post sales. We need to account for mixed-mode buying.

5 Understanding how customers process information through the stages of exposure, attention, comprehension and perception, yielding and acceptance and retention can help us design effective sites.

6 Achieving online relationship and loyalty involves defining the ideal customers, understanding their needs and delivering them through the five 'primary determinants of loyalty' of quality customer support; on-time delivery; compelling product presentations; convenient and reasonably priced; and clear trustworthy privacy policies. We must delight the customer and add value through personalization, community, integration and incentivization.

7 Online communities can be effective in delivering **stickiness** and understanding customer motivations and fears. A key decision is whether communities are independent of or integral to the brand.

8 Profiling customers involves asking who they are (demographics and psychographics), what they need, why, how and when they buy, and identifying segments.

9 Research involves answering the profiling questions using a combination of online and offline primary and secondary techniques.

10 The post-PC customer. Companies will need to respond to new technologies to offer new forms of customer relationship that deliver customer needs.

References

Chaffey, D. (2004) Article on online value proposition published in the CIM's 'What's New in Marketing?' September 2004. Available from www.davechaffey.com/E-marketing-Insights.

Considine, R. and Murray, R. (1981) *The Great Brain Robbery*. The Great Brain Robbery, CA.

DTI (2003) *Business In The Information Age – International Benchmarking Study 2003*. UK.

de Kare-Silver, M. (2000) *eShock 2000*. Macmillan, Basingstoke.

EIAA (2004) EIAA European Media Consumption Study II. Pan-European Results October 04. Commissioned by European Interactive Advertising Association (www.eiaa.net). Completed by Millward Brown.

E-consultancy (2004) Online Retail 2004, benchmarking the user experience of UK retail sites. Available online from www.e-consultancy.com.

Godin, S. (1999) *Permission Marketing*. Simon and Schuster, New York.

Hagel, J. and Armstrong, A. (1997) *Net Gain: Expanding markets through virtual communities.* Harvard Business Press.

Hofacker, C. (2001) *Internet Marketing.* Wiley, New York, 3rd edition.

Levine, R., Locke, C., Searls, D. and Weinberger, D. (2000) *The Cluetrain Manifesto.* Perseus Books, Cambridge, MA.

Lindstrom, M. and Andersen, T. (2000) *Brand Building on the Internet.* Kogan Page, London.

ONS (2000) National Statistics Omnibus Survey – October 2000. http://www.statistics. gov.uk/press_release/Archive.asp.

ONS (2004) Office of National Statistics Internet access data from quarterly household survey. www.statistics.gov.uk.

Parker, R. (2000) *Relationship Marketing on the Web,* Adams Streetwise publication, Holbrook, MA.

Reicheld, F. (1996) *The Loyalty Effect: The Hidden Force Behind Growth, Profits, and Lasting Value.* Harvard Business School Press, Boston, MA.

Reicheld, F. and Schefter, P. (2000) E-loyalty: Your secret weapon on the Web. *Harvard Business Review,* July–August, pp. 105–113.

Reinartz, W. and Kumar, V. (2002) The Mismanagement of Customer Loyalty. *Harvard Business Review,* July, pp. 4–12.

Windham, L. (2001) *The soul of the new consumer. The Attitudes, Behaviours and Preferences of e-customers.* Allworth Press, New York.

Wodtke, C. (2002) *Information architecture: blueprints for the web.* New Riders, Indianapolis, IN.

 ## Further reading

Godin, S. (1999) *Permission Marketing.* Simon and Schuster, New York. An interesting, influential book which raises direct marketers' hackles.

Seybold, P. (1999) *Customers.com.* Century Business Books, Random House, London. Describes a customer-centric approach to business strategy with many examples drawn from the US.

Windham, L. (2001) *The soul of the new consumer. The Attitudes, Behaviours and Preferences of e-customers.* Allworth Press, New York. The title says it all! Recommended.

 ## Web links

1 *Digests of published MR data*

ClickZ Internet research	www.clickz.com/stats
Market Research.com	www.marketresearch.com
MR Web (see desk research)	www.mrweb.co.uk

2 *Directories of MR companies*

British Market Research Association	www.bmra.org.uk
Market Research Society	www.mrs.org.uk
International MR agencies	www.greenbook.org

3 *Traditional market Research Agencies*

MORI	www.mori.com/emori

| NOP | www.nopworld.com |
| Nielsen | www.nielsen.com |

4 *Government sources*

OECD	www.oecd.org
European Government	http://europa.eu.int/comm/eurostat
UK Government	www.open.gov.uk, www.ons.gov.uk
US Government	www.stat-usa.gov

5 *Online audience data*

Comscore	www.comscore.com
Hitwise	www.hitwise.com
Mori	www.mori.com/emori
Netratings	www.netratings.com
NOP World	www.nopworld.com

 **Self-test**

1 What are the main reasons why customers venture online and how should marketers use this customer knowledge?

2 How should organizations meet the expectations of online customers?

3 Given that the main fears about using the Internet are security and privacy, how should companies reassure customers?

4 Draw a diagram that summarizes the online buying process and actions that can be taken at each stage to help move the customer through the process.

5 Explain what is meant by each of these five stages of on-site information processing: (1) Exposure (2) Attention (3) Comprehension and perception (4) Yielding and acceptance (5) Retention.

6 How can customer loyalty be improved using online tools and techniques for your organization?

7 Explain how to overcome the problem of empty communities, silent communities and critical communities.

8 Identify the key variables by which you need to profile visitors to your organization's web site.

9 What are the research options for determining customers' opinions and feelings about a web presence?

10 How do you think the post-PC customer will live and what will this mean for marketers?

Chapter

5

E-tools

'E-marketing is not only about web sites. Already, in many European countries, more consumers are accessing interactive digital services through TV and mobile than via the web'.

This is where the online world begins to get really interesting. Once we move beyond the PC and into the wireless world of pervasive technology, a whole new vision appears. Always on, everywhere, easy to use, integrated marketing will exploit these new tools.

By the end of this chapter you will be able to:

- Assess the marketing opportunities arising from new digital technologies.
- Understand the advantages and disadvantages of the many different e-tools.
- Begin to integrate e-tools into different platforms and a database.

CHAPTER TOPIC	LEARNING OBJECTIVE
5.1 Introduction	To introduce the e-tools and their significance
5.2 Interactive digital TV	To understand what iDTV is and how it applies within a marketing context
5.3 Digital radio	Understand the relevance and benefits of digital radio
5.4 Mobile devices	To understand the space of mobile devices in a marketing context
5.5 Interactive kiosks	Evaluate the relevance and benefits of interactive kiosks
5.6 CD-ROMs and interactive business cards	Evaluate the relevance and benefits of CD-ROMs and interactive business cards
5.7 Miscellaneous tools	Review the significance of other e-tools
5.8 Repurposing content	Determine the complexities of marketing across integrated digital channels
5.9 Convergence	Assess the significance of the convergence phenomenon
5.10 Integrated campaigns	Define the elements of an integrated campaign

5.1 Introduction to e-tools

Through its short existence, for many, e-marketing has been synonymous with Internet marketing and web marketing. But technology is in constant flux and leading e-marketers look to new technologies to fulfil their objectives. Already interactive digital TV and mobile Internet access are used by more people than the web (Figure 5.1). Such tools are becoming increasingly important for marketing to consumers, although they are less important for marketing to businesses.

As the number of e-tools increase, so too does the number of challenges to marketers. This chapter examines the current key e-tools and considers a few more besides. We need to become familiar with all e-tools such as PCs, interactive TV, digital radio, smart phones, interactive kiosks, CD cards and a host of miscellaneous e-tools emerging in the online world. There is a section on each in this chapter. We review different e-tools and consider their advantages and disadvantages, their easy applications and natural integrations.

In some ways it's harder not to integrate the e-tools as they naturally lend themselves to integration particularly if there is a single seamless database supporting it all. A total selling proposition must somehow be maintained across all e-tools and offline communications tools also. The final section, integrated campaigns, addresses this and uses some simple but effective online integrated campaigns as an example of what we're about to see unfold as new forms of 'extended integration'.

Unfortunately content does not generally port easily across to other e-tools, e.g. from web site to TV. Or even from TV platform to TV platform. This requires repurposing, which, in turn, requires resources (skills, budgets and time). Despite the complications there is an e-tools trend towards convergence as 'all devices become equal'. A separate section addresses this. So, let's move rapidly into the changing world of e-tools.

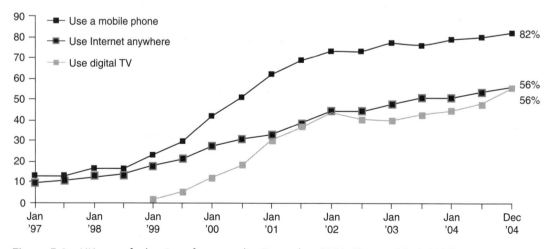

Figure 5.1   UK rate of adoption of new media, December 2004. (*Source:* Mori, 2004)

The speed of change

Figure 5.2 highlights the speed with which new technologies are adopted by consumers. The challenge for marketers is to select significant new technologies and rapidly deploy services for customers appropriate to the new medium.

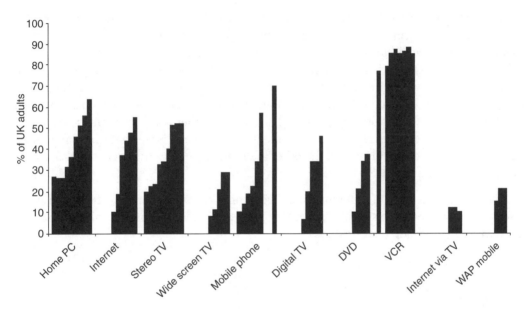

Figure 5.2 Adoption of different technologies over an 8-year period (each bar represents a single year). (*Source:* Svennivig, 2004)

SECTION SUMMARY 5.1

Introduction to e-tools

E-marketing involves not only the web access through PCs, but also other tools such as interactive digital TV, digital radio, smart phones, interactive kiosks, CD cards and a host of miscellaneous e-tools emerging in the online world. Marketers need to review the advantages and disadvantages of each and deploy them, in integration with other tools, where appropriate to achieve competitive advantage.

5.2 Interactive digital TV

TV is the most compelling content channel of all. With over a billion TVs (compared to a few hundred million PCs) you can see how **interactive digital TV** (iDTV) has huge potential.

Interactive digital TV is here and it's growing at a similar rate to Internet adoption (Figure 5.1). It's already changing the way audiences use TV with the 'red button' for user interaction now widespread both within programmes and ads. Although still embryonic and clunky, like early use of the web, it is opening up the online world in a new way. In this section, we will explore iDTV, its advantages and disadvantages and the key steps towards integrating iDTV into your e-marketing mix.

WHAT IS INTERACTIVE DIGITAL TV?

Some say interactive TV has been around for a long time – children have been using it for over ten years now through games consoles. These have made TV screens interactive and far more engaging than traditional 'linear' TV. But this is not real interactive TV that involves a new digital transmission system instead of standard signals. It converts sound and pictures into computerized digits, which are transmitted through the air by modified transmitters. The digits can be received by standard aerials, satellite dishes or by cable, but have to be decoded and turned into sound or vision (Figure 5.3). This is done either with a separate set-top box, or a decoder built-in to your television (an 'integrated' TV set). Note that only cable gives true two-way digital communications, the other alternatives require the user to dial out via a phone line to make a purchase.

Interactive digital television is different – it delivers more channels, better pictures and more interaction. For marketers this means better targeting and immediate opportunities to sell, to collect data and to develop relationships.

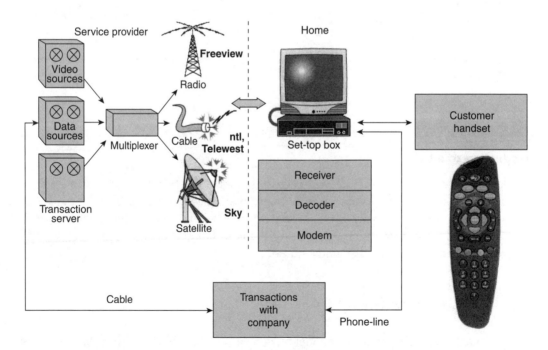

Figure 5.3   Different forms of delivery of interactive digital TV

More channels means a huge selection – more than you can ever watch in a lifetime! There is a channel for almost everyone. Many niche TV channels will emerge as markets fragment and splinter into discrete interest groups (or microsegments) such as Manchester United TV or MTV2. More interaction means more shopping, browsing, banking, gambling, games, programme participation, voting, text information services and, e-mail, of course. And it's user-friendly – you don't have to be computer literate – its simple, intuitive navigation through remote control or console should make it easy for everyone to access both programmes and the Internet. No more booting up and logging on, although it seems pedestrian to Internet broadband users. And it is perceived to be a safe, secure and private place to trade. However, it's not quite there yet and we will have to wait for higher **bandwidth** before some of these promises are delivered. But it can be used to reach adults who do not have an Internet connection.

HOW IS IDTV USED?

TV is traditionally a '**lean back**' or 'couch potato' medium where relaxation dominates. PCs and the Internet are a '**lean forward**', interactive medium. Perhaps this is why 'mad couch disease' seems to have affected some iDTV producers whose poor screen designs do nothing to nurture the coveted mouse potato! They've forgotten that iDTV is not the web. It is a different experience. A key difference is that iDTV can offer a **return path** – an interaction where the customer sends information to the provider using a phone line or cable such as voting on a TV programme or placing a brochure request after pressing the red button. However, as Curry (2001) explains, often the return path is not seamless compared to broadband or mobile phone – requiring dial-up and phone charges which restrict its adoption. Surprisingly, this is still true in this age of technological change.

Marketers have, however, a powerful new tool that connects the emotional intensity of TV with instant response and instant buying. In a world of instant gratification, interactive TV makes the perfect fit. As audiences are aroused by films they are simultaneously offered more information or special promotions via the red button. And every response captures data that in turn, builds a better profile of the household's interests. Advertisements using the red button can potentially offer full sales facilities for the immediate decision makers and store 'more info' requests for viewers who don't want the interruption now but do want the information later. And all the time they're protected by a **walled-garden** required to stop their audiences wandering off and getting lost in the online world.

E-MARKETING EXCELLENCE

Volvo integrate digital tools for their 'Mystery of Dalaro' campaign

This innovative campaign, supporting the launch of the Volvo S40, was shot in the style of a documentary purporting to be a real account of the Swedish village Dalaro where 32 people all bought a new Volvo S40 on the same day.

But Volvo has now revealed that it is Spike Jonze, the director of the films *Being John Malkovich* and *Adaptation* as well as the legendary Beastie Boys video 'Sabotage', who made the documentary. However it has said that the characters in the campaign are real residents of Dalaro and not actors.

This campaign shows how offline ad executions naturally drive visitors online. During the campaign, visits to the Volvo UK web site doubled and 435 000 digital viewers of the ad selected the red button option to view the documentary via interactive TV.

Those pressing red on iDTV saw a longer eight-minute version of the documentary, made by director Spike Jonze, featuring interviews with residents of Dalaro talking about the spooky phenomenon and had the opportunity to download brochures, thus interacting much more closely with the brand than was possible before the advent of iDTV. The documentary was also available from the web site which received 96 000 visits with 64 per cent accessing the video and several thousand requesting a brochure.

Source: Revolution (19 March 2004) (www.revolutionmagazine.com)

BENEFITS FOR THE MARKETER

Although there are many teething problems, ultimately, interactive TV offers e-marketers a new way of reaching customers. From interactive advertisements, to interactive product placement, to fully interactive programmes, to sponsored programmes, interactive TV presents a host of new opportunities. And it's not just for impulse purchases, but also more considered purchases like cars and computers. In addition to the many advantages for the viewers that include wider choice, convenient shopping, more engaging TV programmes and community participation, there are many advantages for the e-marketer:

1 Direct response mass market advertising
2 Highly targetable
3 Moves buyers through the complete buying process
4 Audience engagement through interaction
5 Brand building and positioning reinforcement
6 Brand building through community building
7 Customer-service bottleneck reduction
8 Security – less risk associated with TV than web sites
9 Controllable – highly measurable
10 Cost savings.

So iDTV has advantages and disadvantages. However, as the e-marketing insight 'The interactive viewer: myth or reality?' shows, the convenience of using a PC for digital services seems to be much higher, resulting in greater use. As a result some marketers have suspended trial iDTV services in sectors such as banking and travel, and the Sky Active service is now restricted to niche services which can pay their way such as gambling, dating, special offers and directory services. These services target an audience who have iDTV but not a PC, and this audience is large enough to warrant an investment in iDTV.

E-MARKETING INSIGHT

The interactive viewer: myth or reality?

Svennivig (2004) in his research on use of interactive media points out some of the limitations of interactive TV when he says: 'Television may not, however, be the ideal route for delivering interactive services in terms of volume of use. For a start, the medium has a central social function... This social role is not particularly compatible with the range of existing or potential services'. The research summarized by Svennivig (2004) in Figure 5.4 shows that the usage of web-based services is currently much more important than using iDTV services amongst UK audiences.

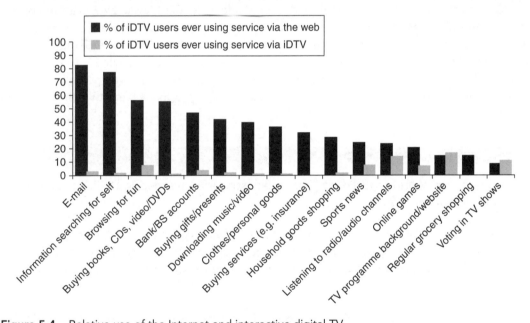

Figure 5.4   Relative use of the Internet and interactive digital TV

SECTION SUMMARY 5.2

Interactive digital TV

Interactive digital TV can be delivered to a set-top box by cable, satellite or conventional aerial. It offers a large and rapidly growing audience and interactive tools which help engagement and generate a response. Marketing approaches include new programme sponsorship, product placement; advertising opportunities abound in interactive digital TV.

5.3 Digital radio

It's now over 100 years since Marconi made the first radio broadcast. Little has changed up to now. Brace yourself for a whole new world of digital radio. This highly intrusive and highly trusted secondary activity is about to change, forever. By the end of this section, you will understand iRadio's different formats and its advantages and disadvantages as an e-tool.

WHAT IS DIGITAL RADIO?

There are two types of digital radio – digital radio and web radio – both are interactive. Digital radio is also available through iDTV, mobile and in-car.

Digital radio requires buying a new digital radio although it can be streamed just like traditional analogue web radio. Digital radio is often accompanied by a big liquid crystal display. Digital radio is now widely known as **Digital Audio Broadcasting (DAB) radio.**

Web radio or Internet radio is when existing broadcasts are streamed via the Internet and listened to using plug-ins such as Real Media or Windows Media Player. This is an important trend with radio listener auditing service Rajar reporting that in 2004 nearly 20 per cent of adults had listened to radio on the web. 'Streamies' are people who listen to web radio at home or at work. For many it means logging on to a web radio station and leaving it to play as you work. In fact, once you log on to a station it accompanies you wherever you go on the net – so you can carry on listening wherever you go online. And if you like a particular track you can order it there and then online. Sonic branding!

BENEFITS OF DIGITAL RADIO

According to the World DAB Forum, the trade association promoting DAB, the benefits of DAB for the consumer are:

> *'Aside from distortion-free reception digital sound quality, DAB offers further advantages as it has been designed for the multimedia age. DAB can carry not only audio, but also text, pictures, data and even videos – all on your radio at home and on the move!'*

For example, clips of goals or delivery of electronic programme guides are possible with DAB – an example of media converging.

For the marketer, digital radio is a proven brand builder. It is great for direct response; it increases reach of local radio to global radio; it grows the 'glocal' community; it can build communities around a brand and is a good targeting medium; and like the web it can be personalized by streaming 'radio-tailored' programmes for individual tastes.

A traditional radio campaign will drive listeners to the radio, but if they are listening online they have an instant call-to-action. In 2004, easyJet spent 60 per cent of its non-TV budget on radio and Internet advertising. *Revolution* reported Alistair Buckle, easyJet's head of marketing, explaining: 'a lot of people consume radio in different environments. Most people aren't too far away from web access to book a flight and we wanted to push that impulsive, "come-on, let's fly behaviour."'

Martin Tod, head of brand and marketing communications at Vodafone UK, says: 'We are big fans of radio and Internet advertising – there is a relationship between the two. It's easier to target radio geographically, and to use the web to reach target audiences and measure direct impact on revenue'. Revolution (2004).

Let's look at these benefits in terms of the '5 Ss of e-marketing'.

Sell

Web radio is radio with a buy button! (Cross selling opportunities are enormous.) Hear an ad for CDs, concerts or merchandise – click immediately and you have it (eventually just shout 'yes' to your voice activated radio in your car and you'll have a real dialogue)! And web radio reaches often difficult to target groups of customers such as young sophisticated international audiences.

Note that such a 'return path' is only available by web radio – with DAB, it is necessary for direct response to be achieved through other e-tools such as a web site or SMS.

Internet radio is great for integrated campaigns. Listeners may first see an ad in the newspaper or on TV, register it but not respond. When they then hear about it online, response is more seamless – they just type in the company or campaign number into their browser. Result! For example, for Christmas 2004 eBay UK ran a treasure hunt to showcase the range of products on sale through clues on the home page which prompted a search. It was advertised both in print and on web radio.

Sizzle

Radio has always been a good brand builder for the marketer. Now it is beginning to offer additional routes via new syndication and content deals which, in turn, may mean new programmes which means new sponsorship opportunities, and even new radio station opportunities. Some radio stations now offer audio ads with a banner ad or 'buy now' button when listening to web radio – you hear the ad – you click the button. Web radio also offers to do partner deals delivering niche radio to other web sites. This adds to the branding and also offers new revenue generating channels as affiliates share ad revenues and merchandise sales from the partner web radio company.

Speak

There is already a dialogue with traditional radio – people phone in, e-mail in and snail mail in. Now they can click and respond instantaneously and marketers can see what's working and what's not instantaneously. Continue the conversation later or join in a group discussion. This adds lots of 'stickiness' as people stay for many hours with a station and its site. Remember once the listener has logged on to a station, it will accompany them wherever they go on the net so they can carry on listening whatever they're doing online.

Serve

Digital radio allows you to get extra information on a track; buy the track; interact with live shows; vote. This is currently achieved through buttons but eventually will be via voice-operated systems and a good archive database. Eventually your car radio should be able to do all of this for you, add digital pictures and answer in voice.

E-MARKETING EXCELLENCE

Comet uses Virgin Radio for positioning and response

In 2004 Virgin Radio was the most popular commercial radio station in the UK. Its website receives over 1 million unique visitors per month. The Comet campaign is a typical cross-media campaign that uses on-air and web site messaging and interaction.

Campaign objectives

- Support awareness of Comet's Price Promise that they provide low prices all year round.
- Communicate that Comet has great Christmas gifts for all the family.
- Drive traffic to Comet's gift finder at comet.co.uk.
- Create competitive standout through engaging activity.

Implementation

- Listeners were invited to play 'The Price is Right' with Comet in a week-long Drivetime Show promotion.
- Each day, a prize package demonstrating Comet's wide product range was up for grabs with a higher than normal starting price.
- Two listeners then guessed ever-decreasing prices to guess the package's true low Comet price.
- The first listener to get the price right won, or the first to get the price too low lost (and the other won by default).
- On-air mentions directed listeners to Comet's gift finder which was built into a co-branded micro-site on virginradio.co.uk.
- Banner ads and a competitions area on the web site directed visitors to Gift finder.

Source: Virgin Radio (www.virginradio.co.uk)

DISADVANTAGES OF RADIO

So, radio is changing – it might not be called radio in the future. Now let's look at some of the disadvantages of digital radio:

- Bandwidth costs money and the cost of streaming increases in line with the number of listeners.
- Not as sexy as TV. TV adds credibility to a brand – 'as seen on TV'. Radio doesn't quite carry the same impact or credibility.
- Fragmenting audience as number of online stations increase. It therefore requires more work (media planning and media buying) to reach the fragmented audience.

SECTION SUMMARY 5.3

Digital radio

The future of radio is in digital radio and web radio where interaction is possible by responding to on-screen prompts such as voting or e-mail. Digital radio has many advantages including brand-building, impact, direct-response and a few disadvantages including fragmentation. It is highly portable and digital radio, in particular, presents new opportunities to many marketers.

5.4 Mobile (wireless) devices

Although many are cynical about mobiles as an Internet access device. Mobile technology is here to stay; it's popular and still evolving at a rapid pace. We are beginning to move beyond the hype, hysteria and disappointment of the early 'mobile Internet', m-commerce and the initial woeful WAP.

With penetration in many western countries already exceeding 80 per cent (see Figure 5.1, for example) and estimated mobile use worldwide exceeding 2 billion by 2007, marketers cannot ignore this potentially powerful new tool. By the end of this section you will understand these developing technologies and know how marketers can use them in different ways.

WHAT ARE MOBILE OR WIRELESS DEVICES?

First let's clarify what's what. In the beginning (1980s) there was the big bulky expensive analogue mobile – the first generation of mobile phones. Then came the second generation – smaller digital mobiles. These almost accidentally created a new phenomenon called text messaging, or SMS (short message service). Then came **WAP**, **I-mode**, **GPRS** and **EDGE** all offering greater speed and more interaction. And finally came the third generation, or **3G**, mobiles which have a single global standard wireless system called **UMTS**.

Like previous mobile technologies such as WAP, few would argue that 3G hype has exceeded the experience delivered to users. Currently 3G offers a maximum practical download speed of 384 kbps (although 2 Mbps is possible) and an upload speed of 64 kbps. So 3G is approximately six times faster than GPRS and about two-thirds of the speed of standard 512 kbps.

Some initial problems are indicated by a report by the Consumers' Association body *Which* who advised in 2004:

> *'There are teething problems with 3G phones and coverage so we recommend sticking with a 2G phone for the time being. We're not sold on 3G yet. The handsets are still fairly bulky and the network coverage is limited which means that, for some time still to come, there are likely to be problems accessing 3G services successfully and consistently'.*

These advances and their implications for the marketer are summarized in Table 5.1.

Table 5.1   Characteristics of different mobile technologies

	SMS	WAP on GSM	GPRS and 3G	I-mode
Audience size (penetration)	Large	Large	Small (<10%)	Large in Japan. Launched in Europe
Characteristics	Instnt txt msgs	A new browsing standard	Always on, also offers WAP	Similar to WAP, but introduced in Japan
Speed	9600 bps	9600 bps	GPRS: 56 kbps 3G: 384 kbps	Similar to GSM
Current audience type	Broad range of profiles	Innovators and early adopters	Innovators	Teenagers and…
Audience state of mind	No control – e-mails/text messages interrupt	Some control as there is limited browsing	Some control as there is more browsing	More control as there is lots of browsing
Cost of production (of ad/e-mail/ web site)	Low (text message and e-mail only)	Low–medium (WAP site design and traffic generation)	More costly repurposing	
Message type	Good for urgent messages (time based and location based). Limited technical detailed information	Good for urgent messages (time based and location based). Link to more technical detailed information on WAP site	Good for urgent messages (time based and location based). Link to more technical detailed information on site	Good for urgent messages (time based and location based). Link to more technical detailed information on site

Connecting laptops to the Internet can be considered as the first mobile devices and now 3G wireless services are available for remote workers. Today, smart phones are here – they carry chips that allow them to act as a mini PC as well as a phone – you probably have one. Phones now have features built in which are familiar from our PCs such as address books, diaries and have fun features such as MP3 playback and image capture. Live e-mail downloads in the Blackberry devices have taken the business world by storm. Add in **Bluetooth** technology (which allows devices to communicate without wires – as soon as they come into range) and you've got a very powerful interactive device which somehow has moved far beyond being a phone. Maybe this will herald the end of the term 'telephone' as single purpose devices will be deemed archaic. Some marketers are now considering **BlueJacking** which involves sending a message from a mobile phone (or other transmitter) to another mobile phone which is in close range via Bluetooth technology. It has potential for: (1) Viral communication; (2) Community activities (dating or gaming events); (3) Location-based services – electronic coupons as you pass a store.

Whether WAP, I-mode or other form of phone, users can now surf or browse specially built sites, extending the 5 Ss benefits derived from web sites although constrained by the smaller screen and limited graphics.

Now we're moving into location-based marketing where customers receive messages on their mobiles relevant to their geographic location (whether passing a store or arriving in an airport). Add in **voice portals** and things get even more interesting. VPs use speech recognition technology to search and find information from the web and then, the good bit – 'speak it to you' through your phone. No more dialling up, downloading and clumsy mice, all you do is dial a free number and ask the question. A related approach is **unified messaging systems** portals which act as an organizer for text, fax, e-mail and phone messaging.

SMS OR TEXT MESSAGING

Finally don't forget good old text messaging. It is huge, as the e-marketing insight 'How impt is txt msging?' shows!

For the creative marketer who respects opt-in and privacy legislation, SMS has proved a great way to get closer to customers, particularly those in the youth market who are difficult to reach with other media. These are some of the applications showcased on Text.it (www.text.it):

1 **Database building/direct response to ads/direct mail or on-pack**. This is one of the most significant applications. For example Ford engaged its audience when promoting the Ford Ka by asking consumers to text in a unique code printed on their postcard for entry into a prize draw.
2 **Location-based services**. Text for the nearest pub, club, shop or taxi. In London you can now text for the nearest available taxi!
3 **Sampling/trial**. Nestlé used an opt-in SMS database to offer samples for a new chocolate bar to consumers in its target group.

4 **Sales promotions**. Timed e-coupons can be sent out to encourage footfall in real and virtual stores. Drinks brand WKD directed its consumers to 'Peel Off and Win' on its bottles. The competition offered prizes of 3000 football club shirts, mini footballs, 10 000 referee cards, and 1 million exclusive ring tones and logos designed by WKD. Half a million people played the game, a campaign response rate of 3 per cent. A 3000 strong opt-in database of the company's 18–24-year-old customer base was created. The company plans to use this database to trial new WKD variety Silver.

5 **Rewarding with offers for brand engagement**. Valuable content on mobiles can be offered via SMS; for example, free ringtones, wallpaper, Java games or credits can be offered to consumers via text.

6 **Short codes**. These are easy-to-remember 5-digit numbers combined with text that can be used by advertisers or broadcasters for response.

7 **Offering paid-for WAP services and content**. Any service such as a ringtone delivered by WAP can be invoked from a text message. For example, Parker's Car Guides now prints ad text 'go parkers' to 89080 (a short code) for quick access to the Parker's WAP site which provides car prices on-the-go, at £1 for 10 minutes.

SMS messaging has recently been augmented by Picture Messaging or Multimedia Messaging Services (MMS). While volumes have been relatively low initially, the overlap between text messaging and e-mail marketing will decrease as there are more handsets with larger screens.

E-MARKETING INSIGHT

How impt is txt msging?

In 2004, 25 billion text messages were sent in the UK alone. The top texting days for 2002–4 show the importance of this medium for consumers:

1 26 August 2004 – 79 million text messages were sent on **the day that GCSE results were announced**.

2 New Year's Day 2004 – on **New Year's Day 2004**, the number of text messages reached 111 million, the highest recorded daily total.

3 14 February 2003 – 78 million text messages were sent by Britons on **Valentine's Day 2003**, six times more than traditional cards and a 37 per cent increase on text figures for 2002.

4 22 November 2003 – 76 million messages were sent on the day **England won the Rugby World Cup**.

5 17 March 2003 – 65.7 million messages were sent exchanging **St Patrick's Day greetings**.

6 May 2003 – 65 million text messages were sent on the last day of the **2002/3 season's Premiership**.

7 7 June 2002 – **England v. Argentina, World Cup group match**, 58 million messages sent.

WI-FI BROADENS WIRELESS INTERNET ACCESS

Wi-fi ('wireless fidelity') is the shorthand often used to describe a high-speed wireless local-area network. Wi-fi can be deployed in an office or home environment where it removes the need for cabling and adds flexibility. Wi-fi access points are now available in major airports and city cafés. We mention it for reference; it does not have additional significant direct marketing applications but we mention it since it will increase wireless access to the web. Wi-fi can be accessed from suitably equipped laptops and mobile phones.

BENEFITS OF MOBILE TECHNOLOGIES

In addition to being a new channel to market, mobiles offer marketers many other benefits. In Finland, customers buy flowers, CDs, bid in auctions, buy cola from vending machines and pay for a car wash all with their mobiles. It can be a useful customer support tool, whether reserving airline tickets, checking your bank balance or transferring money. For example, in the UK customers can see and select which airline seats they want from their mobiles.

Sales force and other employees can use their mobiles to see client history, get updates about orders and dispatch as well as feeding back research while engineers can access appointments, directions and diagnostic tools. Go Airlines use 'MADS' or text messages to drive traffic to its site. Alaska Airlines and British Airways both let passengers check in via their mobiles. There are some extremely creative approaches to mobile marketing – teaching with text messages is now available via mobile and even the National Blood Service has boosted blood donations using an integrated mobile campaign. Add in disposable mobiles and all sorts of interesting ideas occur to marketers!

You can see how mobiles can help marketers to enjoy all five of the 'S' benefits. The key question to ask is 'How can mobiles help my customers (or distributors, or suppliers, or employees)?'

E-MARKETING EXCELLENCE

I-mode creates a successful wireless proposition

I-mode is a mobile technology to watch in the future. Although I-mode is technology proprietary to NTT Docomo, it has developed a successful proposition initially with 2G and now with 3G.

In Japan, 42 million have subscribed to I-mode since its introduction in February 1999. More recently, over 3 million elsewhere have subscribed following launch in Germany, The Netherlands, France and Spain, and in 2005 adoption started in the UK. Adoption has been limited to date due to lack of handsets and competition from local mobile portals such as Vodafone Live! I-mode offers access to entertainment including paid content, games and dating, transaction services such as e-mail, Citibank accounts, Amazon.jp, databases such as travel information and information such as news CNN and local area maps.

There are 85 000 I-mode web sites: a key benefit of I-mode is that content providers create web sites for I-mode using I-HTML, a subset of HTML. This makes it relatively easy to convert any existing web site written in HTML into I-mode content. I-mode also supports Flash and Java based applications and games.

DISADVANTAGES OF MOBILE TECHNOLOGIES

There are several significant hindrances or disadvantages to bear in mind including small screens restricting content, a limited number of web sites; limited content; poorly designed sites; poor coverage causing shopping interrupts and SPAM text messages. Location-based marketing also worries some people as they feel their movements are being tracked – anyone who has seen Tom Cruise in *Minority Report* being followed around a shopping mall by personalized ads will know what we mean. There is also the cost of repurposing – traditional web sites need to be stripped down and repurposed.

SECTION SUMMARY 5.4

Mobile technologies

Smart phones and Bluetooth technology, text messaging, location-based marketing, voice portals and browser phones didn't exist a few years ago. Today they can help the market achieve all 5 Ss but with the usual caveat – don't SPAM. Phones will get faster, smaller, friendlier and eventually, become multifunctional devices integrated into most marketers' armoury and many, many customers' lives.

5.5 Interactive self-service kiosks

Interactive self-service kiosks come in all shapes and sizes. Compact and robust, they can be placed virtually anywhere that attracts passing footfall of customers. This makes them ideal not just for sales and marketing, but public information purposes and corporate communications. Although they are often known as self-service kiosks, they can also be used in-store by sales staff for demonstrations. By the end of this section you will know how kiosks can help marketers, their advantages and disadvantages.

BENEFITS OF KIOSKS

So how can marketers use interactive kiosks? Let's explore the advantages of kiosks by seeing how they help marketers to enjoy the benefits of the 5 Ss.

Sell

Kiosks (including vending machines, ATMs and other devices) can widen distribution and ultimately boost sales of both products and services. Kiosks can extend reach to passing footfall of customers. From music kiosks (that create tailored CDs) to in-store kiosks (that extend the range of stock) to bus stop mini-kiosks (that sell theatre tickets) to micro kiosks, or touch pads attached to vending machines (that create virtual outlets) the kiosk is here. And there! In fact they can be anywhere. The key is to think where to put kiosks. Where are the opportunities? Where do your target market congregate? When would they be most likely to buy? When would they like more information?

Serve

An interactive kiosk with full multimedia facilities can do everything a web site can do, better and faster as the media may be already downloaded. Kiosks can provide information, ideas and suggestions, e-mail facilities and ordering facilities. In airports they help passengers to skip check-in queues by printing boarding passes. Kiosks can be particularly valuable if used in 'downtime areas' such as waiting rooms, hospitals, motorway service stations, reception areas, airport luggage halls, even gymnasiums where kiosks can keep the mind off the pain barrier.

Speak

Kiosks can trigger a dialogue with a customer by answering FAQs, engaging interactions and collecting data from customers which, in turn, can be integrated with the Internet or your own office network. Installed in the right place kiosks can grab attention, attract interest and generate data from the ideal customer. But remember if the dialogue is going to continue the marketer must first ask for permission to do so.

Electronically enabled interaction between kiosks and consumer devices is the way of the future. In 2005, drinks brand Carling started delivering information and offers to users of Bluetooth-enabled mobiles when they access a dedicated Carling channel on a series of kiosks in the south west. Users will gain the chance to win tickets to Carling Live gigs in Bristol and London, or a pint of Carling in their local pub.

Save

Kiosks provide physical presence without the associated costs of staff and buildings. Kiosks also provide information and service 24 hours a day, 7 days a week without the enormous overtime costs of staff. Kiosks can be free-standing and unattended. In Italy, they're even used to pay local taxes. So although initially considered expensive, they can offer cost savings, particularly if they're used to their full potential.

Sizzle

And some of the potential is fulfilled when kiosks simultaneously double up as brand icons and represent the brand in some manner, shape or form. Kiosk design ranges from stunning design-led units that are almost impossible to ignore, to more practical, engineered units. Unlike the Internet, kiosks provide a controlled environment. Protected by a 'walled garden', marketers can connect customers directly to their own site and only their own site.

DISADVANTAGES OF KIOSKS

Despite the many advantages, kiosks do have their disadvantages. They can be expensive for different reasons. There is a long lead time and cost of paying specialists to design and produce them. They require installation and then there are the maintenance costs of electricity, costs of Internet connection, maintenance contracts and support. And of course, they are subject to vandalism. Finally, just as for web sites, they are moving targets requiring updates to content and new design and marketing approaches.

E-MARKETING EXCELLENCE

Vodafone rolls out kiosks worldwide

In the UK, Vodafone deployed 350 interactive kiosks at retail outlets which simulated the Vodafone Live! phone experience including games, e-mail, news and webcam pictures. When not in use, Vodafone ad campaigns can be displayed. The kiosks gave customers the opportunity to research products and allowed sales staff to demonstrate the capabilities of the service. As with web sites, kiosk interactions can be monitored to assess popular applications and products. Customer and branch manager feedback in the UK led to Vodafone rolling out the kiosks worldwide. In New Zealand, displays are state of the art with 50-inch touchscreens showing the shape of the future.

SECTION SUMMARY 5.5

Interactive self-service kiosks

In this section, we have seen how interactive kiosks can sell, serve, save, speak and sizzle. However, they do have some disadvantages such as costs, time, installation, maintenance and vandalism.

5.6 CD-ROMs, DVDs and interactive business cards

Historically, CD-ROMs were the primary channel for multimedia marketing, offering instant video, full colour photos and far greater interactive delivery of information and content. However, as the Internet grew, sales of CDs declined in favour of publishing content on the web. But there are still benefits, with firstly, CDs delivering faster full motion video and secondly, **interactive business cards**, CDs and DVDs being adopted once again to perform very specific marketing functions. By the end of this section, you will understand how CD cards can be an innovative e-tool and some of their applications and technical limitations.

BENEFITS

CDs, DVDs and cards add impact to your message, communications and distinction to your brand. They work just like regular CDs and CD-ROMs and can contain all of the same information on them, such as text, audio, images, animations, video clips, software, etc. From business-card shaped CDs to custom shaped CDs, this e-marketing tool can potentially catch and hold your customers' attention.

If you want some marketing activities which use full blown multimedia, primarily product showcases and Flash micro sites, and the web is too slow, CD technology is the way to go, offering high-density data storage with creative style that reinforces your brand.

Now consider how a CD card could deliver all 5 Ss – sell, serve, save, speak, sizzle. CD cards won't sell too many products on their own but they can support the sales team as an innovative type of sales literature or 'collateral'. They can contain product demonstrations, customer testimonies and new applications.

Cards can contain helpful information, product demonstrations, service advice, FAQs, instruction manuals, added-value products such as additional software, reports, surveys, technical tips and knowledge. CD cards combine the shape and size of a normal business card but with the added capabilities of multimedia – video, sound, graphics, animations, pictures and interaction plus links to your web site.

CD cards are not cheap. Producing a CD is a mini project and requires expertise. However, if produced in the right quantities they can be cheaper than full-colour four-page leaflets. They can carry high data content – which can replace expensive catalogues and the accompanying high cost of delivery.

In addition to bringing a new brochure to life in a new and dynamic way, CDs can come in any shape or colour – your logo, your strap line, your pack shape, or an event shape such as a football or trophy. The shape becomes part of the message, supporting long-term branding and enhancing your company's image. Different shapes and colours catch the eye and reinforce the brand if they're well produced. CDs need good underlying instructional design and professional production values can add some excitement to the brand. Not only do they look good but they can present the products in a dynamic way. They can also be used as invitations to conferences, exhibitions and special events containing maps, car park vouchers (which can be printed) and also act as bar code swipe for fast track registration and entry. And if you're in the food, cosmetics or holiday business, you can add aromas with scratch 'n' sniff CDs for the extra sizzle.

DISADVANTAGES

CD cards and DVDs are relatively unpopular compared with web media. The reasons include:

- It is relatively difficult to measure their effectiveness.
- Each project requires new multimedia skills.

- They are costly to produce in small volumes and most significantly can't be updated once created and distributed.

- They represent an additional cost on producing web site content which is always likely to be a higher priority.

- Most significantly, the usage of multimedia CDs and DVDs is less convenient than the web for customers and potential customers – they require insertion into a PC and usually some configuration and learning of the approach. Often if a customer is interested in reviewing a company's offering it is more convenient to go straight to the web site.

SECTION SUMMARY 5.6

CD-ROMs and interactive business cards

There are all types and shapes of interactive business cards, which can be used as sales force business cards, invitations to events, exhibitions and trade shows, direct mail shots and product launch press packs. CD cards can support all the 5 Ss but do require some resources for planning, designing and producing.

5.7 Miscellaneous tools

'A million businesses, a billion people and a trillion devices all interconnected…' You've heard it before? Pervasive computing combined with deep computing bringing a new interconnected world. In fact, IBM's Lou Gerstner many years ago said that he dreamed of a world made up of a trillion interconnected intelligent devices, intersecting with data-mining capability – where pervasive computing (embedded chips in doorknobs and clothes) meets deep computing (like the chess playing Deep Blue PC which calculated 200 million moves a second). By the end of this section you will start to see the interconnected future.

Do you remember in Chapter 1 we talked about the wired-up world and how everything in the household was connected to the web, from fridges and freezers to TVs and toys? Do you remember we told you that MIT's Nicholas Negroponte said that by the year 2010 there would be more wired-up Barbie dolls than wired up Americans? Teddy bears with mobile phones have since been launched. It's true. The world is becoming connected through a wide range of wireless devices. It's been happening for some time.

Computers in jackets? Phones in ties? Wearable technology has been around for some time (Figure 5.5). US Army and Military Police see wearable computers as an important part in a soldier's arsenal. But it's not just military, industry is experimenting also. Northwest Airlines, Nabisco and General Dynamics are also using wearable computers (connected to their intranets) across different business functions from customer service, distribution centres, and inspection and maintenance. And way before this, in fact in the last century, MIT staff occasionally donned 'hot badges' at parties. After keying in their personal interests, party goers wore the badges and whenever anyone with similar interests came within a few feet then both badges flashed!

Figure 5.5 Wearable PC from Xybernaut (www.xybernaut.com)

Earrings and eyeglasses embedded with instantaneous language translation, speech recognition and speech synthesis so that someone can speak to you in French and you hear it in English all help. And of course cars speak your preferred language. In fact at the end of the last century car computer power (the hidden microcomputers in cars) had more power than all the computers in the first rocket that landed on the moon. Those astronauts were true heroes.

Athletes can be heroes too. Nike have just released a running shoe with a chip in it. Why? Think for a moment why or what possible benefit it might have. The chip in the shoe allows friends or competitors to communicate and race against each other simultaneously even if they are on other sides of the world.

Then came thought-operated-computers. A glass cone (laced with neurotrophic chemicals extracted from knees to encourage nerve growth) is inserted into the brain's motor cortex. Over a period of a few months, neurones grow – and effectively, become naturally wired into the brain. This allows disabled people to control a cursor by thinking about moving parts of their body.

Add in some virtual reality and anything becomes possible. Disabled pensioners can play rugby, paraglide the world and meet new people all in a brave new world.

It has been forecast that our whole personalities will one day be downloaded into machines! We're not so sure about this but we are sure that the embedded chip will be everywhere from your washing machine to your car and everything will be connected to everything else in a seam-less wireless way. And the data pulsing through the Internet won't even be seen by humans.

The trick for marketers is first to ask how each device can help my customer, distributors, employees, etc.). Use the 5 S checklist. Also ask, what proportion of my customers want to use these devices now and in the future? Second, keep all channels integrated on a central database so that customers are reassured as the organization recognizes them regardless of which channel, whether car, TV, or running shoe. Third, stay listed with search engines, direc-tories and portals, whether voice portals or automated portals of any description. Fourth, stick close to customers. Use these new tools to listen to customer feedback. Fifth, and finally, don't let the technology blind you. Ensure common sense rules and not the technology! It can pretty much do whatever you want – if you know what you want – which is a good starting point.

SECTION SUMMARY 5.7

Miscellaneous tools

We need to be responsive to new tools that will be used by customers, distributors or employees. At the moment, some of these futuristic tools include: wearable technology, embedded chips and speech recognition and synthesis.

5.8 Repurposing content

We are witnessing the emergence of a multi-channel culture, where people access online con-tent from a range of different devices or tools. Your customers will use a range of tools for more and more 'moments of interactivity' with your brand. In an ideal world (with unlimited budgets), you would have a presence on all iDTV services, the web, WAP, I-mode, etc. Unfortunately there is no perfect content management system that seamlessly repurposes content for each tool, so for the moment, you've got to do it. Sometimes it's easier to start again and create new con-tent. In this section, you will learn about re-purposing content for different e-tools, particularly from web to WAP and web to iDTV.

What is **re-purposing**? The simplest definition of re-purposing is the adaptation of some piece of content for a new purpose to display it on a different e-tool (e.g. from web to iDTV). First, let's look at repurposing from web to WAP.

REPURPOSING FOR WAP

Part of the problem with WAP sites currently is that marketers or site designers and creators often fail to take into account the current limitations of today's mobile devices. WAP is text based. The standard code, WML (wireless mark-up language) is a simple derivative of HTML. So pictures, lavish graphics and sound get stripped out. Many WAP sites seem to be uploaded straight from web sites and therefore the text used is sometimes too long, links are broken or the information is un-navigable on a WAP browser. Today WAP designers have to design for many different mobile devices, each requiring different coding, making development more complex and expensive than simply designing for the two main web browsers and different versions.

REPURPOSING FOR INTERACTIVE TV

Interactive digital television moves TV into the online world and offers many exciting possibilities for the marketer but also many challenges to transfer content across. Internet content needs to be re-purposed for television. You can't take your web site and dump it on iDTV. It's not the web. Content must be 're-purposed', recreated or re-coded. Traditional PC-based web sites are 'lean forward' media – designed for lone viewing from 2 ft away. However software repurposing packages which automatically re-format can assist the process.

iDTV viewing is 'lean back' (relax) medium designed for group viewing from 8 ft away on a lower resolution screen. It's a different medium. Even an iDTV ad linked to a microsite needs large text and large buttons. You won't be able to read a standard web site unless you're practically on top of the set! The problem is exacerbated by different iDTV platforms, each based on different technology, making content re-purposing highly complicated. Another problem with traditional web sites – they're designed to be accessed with a point and click device, not a remote control. So no scrolling. And of course, iDTV's lower screen resolution adds to the challenge. So remember iDTV is not the web. Its design ethics, visual qualities and viewer usage are entirely different.

So how do you repurpose, say, web site content for iDTV? Same as WAP – strip out all but the text? How do you repurpose text? You don't! You start again and write a new script for voice over and moving images. Brands need to create TV experiences not heavy text and graphics. You can of course repurpose cheaply by adding a simple hyperlink button linked to an iDTV microsite.

SECTION SUMMARY 5.8

Repurposing content

Repurposing content for 'other' devices requires an awareness of the problems caused by a lack of re-purposing and an ability to think beyond the PC. Most other devices have lower screen resolutions. Many are viewed from a greater distance and have a different style of navigation to the Internet. Exploration of new technologies such as XML and Middleware is required. Think Transmedia. Create environments. Involve your audience. Test, test, test. Good luck! You'll need it!

5.9 Convergence

It's not so long ago that a phone was a phone and computer a computer. Not any more – **convergence** is here. The cumbersome days of carrying a laptop, a PDA and a phone will go. All of their functions can be carried out by a phone. By the end of this section you will know what convergence means, its fast changing nature and the key to successfully harnessing it.

Convergence means phones will be PCs and TVs, while TVs will be PCs and PCs will be TVs. Handheld devices will be both. The demand for a single device is evident from the numbers of users who already combine the use of devices. Marketers need to think about communicating with users that have multiple devices, for example making web site users aware of mobile and iDTV-based services.

Smart phones carry mini-PCs that combine telephony and computers. 3G phones can stream full motion video. You can watch your football team live on your phone, send e-mails and make some old fashioned telephone calls too. The phone is becoming more than a PC and TV combined. One of the innovators in this field is Nokia who produced the Nokia Communicator which combines a phone with PC and PDA features.

TVs go online and carry out many functions previously considered the domain of the PC. Online TVs with hard drives, memory and interactive online capacity – sounds like TV on steroids.

There's more, phones with flip-down keypads which reveal large screens. Phones with roll-up keypads. Phones with PCs. Phones with dual-mode microbrowser for WAP and HTML access and MP3.

PDAs with voice recognition. PDAs with speakers. PDAs with telephone compatibility almost brings us through the full circle…

A PDA is a phone. A phone is a PDA. A PDA is a PC. A PC is a TV. A TV is a PC is a phone.

And don't forget the humble radio – the digital radio can stream data, pictures and audio in your car or in your house. Add voice recognition and the circle seems complete with voice-operated computers, TVs, PCs, radios.

One more thing. Add some **Bluetooth** technology and the e-tools can talk to each other. Radios will not be called 'radios', nor TVs 'TVs'. These are 'old world' words will soon be left behind by the lightning quick emergence of media convergence. Moore's Law is on the rampage. What do you think the new devices will be called (we'll have to be more creative than 'personal digital assistants')?

Convergence really means convenience. If customers want to watch, roam, explore, shop, bank or communicate they can now choose whichever tool suits them. In an office it might be a PC. On a train it might be a hand-held device. At home it might be a TV or perhaps the fridge depending on which room you're in.

Key to success will be an underlying integrated database and seamless systems that recognize customers regardless of which 'converged device' they use. So everything is converging with alarming speed. Convergence means convenience. A seamless integrated database must be at the heart of whichever tool or device is used.

CONVERGENCE IN THE HOME

As well as convergence in hand-held devices we are starting to see more overlap between PC, TV, iDTV box and DVD player. Many TVs now have the iDTV box built in, perhaps a DVD recorder too. **Personal video recorders (PVRs)** or **digital video recorders (DVRs)** are consumer electronics devices that record television to a hard disk in digital format. Sky Plus and TiVo are the two best known PVR/DVR products. Many models are now also offering the facility to record onto DVDs. They enable 'time shifting' features such as pausing live TV, instant replay of interesting scenes, and skipping advertising.

At the same time we are seeing PCs that are becoming closer to TVs. Many PC manufacturers are now building PCs based on Microsoft's Media Centre edition of Windows. These contain built-in TV tuners to receive TV and wireless keyboards. They must make battles over who has the remote control seem trivial. Because PCs are generally a personal device, it is more likely that there will be several of these around the house connected by a wireless network, rather than one that everyone fights over!

E-MARKETING INSIGHT

Jeff Hawkins on convergence

Jeff Hawkins, founder of Palm and Handspring, believes total convergence is possible. He says:

> *'If you try to integrate a cellphone and a PDA and an e-mail machine and by integration one of them suffers, then people won't buy it. So the trick is, how do you do it right? But I think that's what the world wants. I think you can build a great single device'.*

(Hawkins, 2001)

As CEO of Handspring he has developed devices that incorporate conventional PDA functions such as diary and address books with other features including web access, MP3 players and even GPS navigation.

SECTION SUMMARY 5.9

Convergence

Convergence involves merging technologies into fewer devices. Functions such as speech, TV viewing, text entry, web browsing and listening to music will be available in a single, mobile device or a multi-function PC or TV.

5.10 Integrated campaigns

Marketers are beginning to integrate e-tools innovatively. We're going to show you a few examples ranging from TV shows, to cars and cola. These integrated campaigns also integrate the online tools with offline tools such as traditional TV, radio and magazine advertising, direct mail and packaging. By the end of this section you'll be able to 'think integrated' when considering e-tools.

Now consider integrated campaigns for cars. Take Audi, it has used interactive TV, WAP, web and hand-held devices. Traditionally car manufacturers use TV for brand building, awareness and re-assurance and save the detailed information for a medium you can study such as the press. iDTV can do both. WAP on the other hand can remind them or invite a call back for a test drive, while the web site can take customers through all stages of the buying model from banner ads creating awareness (and/or problem recognition) to web sites that help information search for evaluating and comparing through to booking a test drive. Again offline integration should deliver the test drive car to the door if the request comes from a prospect who fits the ideal customer profile.

E-MARKETING EXCELLENCE

MTV use integrated campaign for 'Videoclash'

Here's how MTV used C2B via an integrated campaign to help consumers become prosumers and create a video request TV show. MTV produced their first live television show to be built around SMS text messages. The programme asked viewers to become prosumers by helping MTV produce the most popular programme. Viewers were asked to vote for the video they wanted to see next from a choice of two. It's C2B – customers creating the product (well at least from a controlled menu). Customers were empowered to play director. Viewer input also became part of the programme as their comments were then run live on MTV while the winning video was played. Messages were sent in via mobile text messages or on the Internet. Using up to 50 characters of text, messages (explaining how the show worked) were sent to yourmobile.com's database and also to teen girl magazine *J17*'s database. Opinion formers were targeted through the fan sites of the artists involved in the show. The programme was explained and the fan sites relayed the information to all their fans. Of course, the artists themselves were e-mailed also. Offline ads in *J17* magazine showed a text message on a phone. Promotional postcards were also distributed in schools in the north east of England.

Finally, consider Coca-Cola's innovative Coke Auction campaign which combined sales promotions and packaging with the unique online facility of online auctions with offline radio and TV advertisements, with online e-mail viral marketing. Online auctions harness some of the Internet's unique functions. With innovation at the helm, Coca-Cola have somehow converted the normally discarded ring pulls into online currency called unsurprisingly 'Coke credits'. These credits are then used to bid for items from sports tickets to becoming stars in Coke ads (having their faces on the Coke signs) in major advertising venues.

Integrated marketing campaigns used to involve all ten offline communications tools. Today, there's more; they can be integrated with the wide variety of emerging e-tools from web to WAP to mobile to kiosks to iRadio to iDTV. Use of e-tools in campaigns makes measuring campaign effectiveness easier – we can profile who has sent e-mails or text messages. We're only seeing the start of really interesting integrated campaigns.

In the long-term, information will be 'platform neutral'. Customers will use many different e-tools. This means that marketers will send out messages using many different tools and platforms, as shown in the Tank! e-marketing insight box. Crafting messages that work across many tools is a new skill.

Integrated campaigns, in fact any customer communications, ideally need to integrate with one seamless database. Unfortunately different e-tools have different ways of delivering customer data to your database. Capturing the data in the right way is important. Customers don't care how you do it but they do expect you to remember their order, request, complaint and background details regardless of which tool they choose.

Finally, a truly integrated business brings data and systems seamlessly together, e.g. if you buy a pair of shoes from an online store you can return them to any of the store's brick and mortar locations. Total integration is required.

E-MARKETING INSIGHT

Tank! Assess the effectiveness of integrated campaign plans

The tank! multi channel testlab was a test set up to determine the best combination, frequency and timing of different media including mail, e-mail, SMS, telephone and web site. Four financial service companies were involved in the test: Abbey, Bristol & West, Tesco Personal Finance and Sainsbury's Bank.

The companies were given a choice of direct mail, SMS, e-mail, outbound telephony and a responsive web site. Their task was to sell a fictitious financial service product, using anonymously branded direct mail as the main communication. They had an opportunity to utilize up to four 'teaser' communications and four 'chaser' communications. They decided the timing and frequency of the communications in the same two-week period. Consumer panellists recruited for the test were primed to assume they were in the market for the product and to respond but only when the company did enough to convince them to act. This approach has the advantage over traditional research as panellists experienced in real life the communication schedule.

Figure 5.6 shows the winning campaign from Brand M. Points to note relative to other campaigns include:

- E-mail and SMS teaser useful in raising awareness of mail pack.
- E-mail and SMS chaser added to campaign response, creating a second campaign response.
- Initial voice chaser (pack +2 days) received highest single response of all four campaigns.
- This campaign had the highest number of touches.

Source: Tank! (www.tankgroup.com)

Brand M

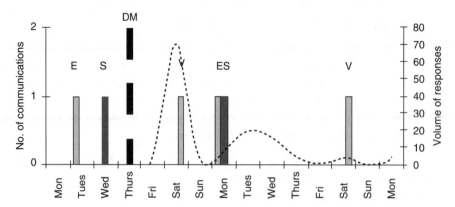

Figure 5.6   Campaign timeline for winning brand in integrated campaign contest (E, e-mail; S, SMS; V, voice; DM, direct mail pack; dashed curve = volume of responses shown on right Y axis). (*Source*: TankOnline, 2004)

SECTION SUMMARY 5.10

Integrated campaigns

From cars to cola, businesses are beginning to integrate their e-tools. Integration includes: online and offline, databases, systems and processes. Now there's a challenge!

Integrated campaigns use all ten traditional communications tools in conjunction with different forms of traditional media (TV, print, radio) and new media (iDTV, web and iRadio). Each interactive tool can be used to move the consumer through the buying process. An integrated transmedia database is required to profile the customer and provide them with customer service information about their purchase and sales history.

CHAPTER SUMMARY

1   E-marketing is not restricted to the use of the web and e-mail. It also includes interactions with customers achieved through other access devices such as interactive digital TV, digital radio, mobile phones, kiosks and CD-ROMs. The numbers of users of these services is significant.

2   Interactive digital TV has a rapidly growing audience and opportunities are available for interactive advertising, channel sponsorship or transactional e-commerce.

3   Digital radio is used in conjunction with the web for brand-building and direct response.

4   Mobile devices are widely used for messaging, which gives new opportunities for advertising and location-based services. The facility of browsing through WAP, and multimedia through 3G, will rival the web and iDTV channels.

5   Interactive kiosks can be used to reach an audience who may not access the web frequently. They are at their most powerful when used in-store to offer services tied to loyalty cards.

6 CD-ROMs and interactive business cards can be of value in generating attention about a new service where there is a high-level of access to PCs and detailed or multimedia information needs to be delivered.

7 We must track the introduction of new tools such as interactive technology, speech recognition and synthesis and deploy them where appropriate.

8 Re-purposing content for devices other than the web requires careful planning to minimize the costs of repackaging. The cost of re-purposing should be considered when deciding which technology platforms to support.

9 Convergence involves multi-functionality built into fewer devices. Functions such as speech, TV viewing, text entry, web browsing and listening to music will be available in a single, mobile device or a multi-function PC or TV.

10 Integrated campaigns involve leveraging the ten traditional communications tools across traditional and new media.

 ## References

Curry, A. (2001) What's next for interactive television. *Interactive Marketing*, Vol. 3, No. 2, October/December, pp. 128–40.

Hawkins, J. (2001) Interviews section. tnbt.com. The Next Big Thing. www.tnbt.com.

Mori (2004) MORI Technology Tracker. Available at www.mori.com/emori/tracker.shtml.

Revolution (2004) Digital finds a new ally in Radio. *Revolution*. December, 2004. www.revolutionmagazine.com.

Svennivig, M. (2004) The interactive viewer: Reality or Myth? *Interactive Marketing*. Vol. 6, No. 2, pp. 151–64.

TankOnline (2004) Personal correspondence with Tank Group (www.tankgroup.com).

 ## Further reading

BBC E-commerce (www.bbc.co.uk/e-commerce). A great summary of the latest applications of technology to boost e-commerce and digital marketing.

The New York Times Technology section (www.nytimes.com/pages/technology). People in the US look to the NYT for the latest innovations in technology and marketing.

Bookmark or subscribe to Trendspotting (www.trendspotting.com) to keep up-to-date with the latest technologies.

Wired magazine (www.wired.com) has traditionally been an earlier proponent of new technologies and how they are marketed.

 ## Web links

Clickz.com (www.clickz.com/stats). Keep up-to-date with the adoption of digital media worldwide from this searchable aggregator of analyst reports.

Digital radio in the UK, visit www.digitalradionow.com.

The World DAB Forum www.worlddab.org. Explains the marketing benefits of DAB with examples of how it is being used around the world.

Howstuffworks (www.howstuffworks.com). Good explanations with diagrams of many new technologies.

Kiosks.org (www.kiosks.org). Trade association for the mobile kiosks industry.

Text.it (www.text.it). Portal from Mobile Data Association with examples of how SMS is used in the UK for consumer and business campaigns.

Total Telecoms (www.totaltele.com). Industry news and the latest adoption levels for wireless and telecoms.

Whatis.com (www.whatis.com). Succinct explanations of terms for new technologies.

Revolution (www.revolutionmagazine.com). See 'Campaign of the month' feature for discussion of new technologies.

 ## Self-test

1 Summarize the relative importance, in terms of reach, for all the different e-tools mentioned in this chapter.

2 Describe the different marketing options of interactive digital TV available to a retailer, manufacturer and FMCG brand.

3 Distinguish between digital radio and web radio. How does web radio integrate with PC-based e-marketing?

4 Define the customer value proposition for mobile services. Explain how marketers can work with this proposition.

5 List the different marketing applications of kiosks.

6 Describe the benefits of interactive business cards and CD-ROMs. Which sectors do you think they are relevant to?

7 Summarize how some of the latest technologies, not described in Sections 1 to 6 of this chapter, may influence the future of marketing.

8 Describe approaches to content re-purposing.

9 Explain the relevance of the concept of convergence to marketers.

10 Visit the archive of a new media magazine such as *Revolution* (www.revolutionmagazine.com) and summarize the design and execution of two integrated campaigns using some of the new media described in this chapter.

Chapter **6**

Site design

'Unless a web site meets the needs of the intended users it will not meet the needs of the organization providing the web site. Web site development should be user-centred, evaluating the evolving design against user requirements'.

Bevan, 1999

OVERVIEW

This chapter will make you think about web sites a little differently. As you read through the chapter, we urge you to draw deep on your web site experiences and the key design components you observe.

OVERALL LEARNING OUTCOME

By the end of this chapter you will:

- Know what makes an excellent web site
- Be able to review the components of a site when designing an enhancement
- Understand the rules to follow and the mistakes to avoid
- Be able to converse with any web master, marketer or chief executive about improving your web site
- Be able to explore options for added value through dynamic facilities.

CHAPTER TOPIC		LEARNING OBJECTIVE
6.1	Introduction	Identify the main objectives of effective site design
6.2	Integrated design	Ensure web sites are integrated with the rest of the business
6.3	Online value proposition	Develop an online value proposition (OVP)
6.4	Customer orientation	Be able to translate customer needs into web site design
6.5	Dynamic design and personalization	Explore options for added value through dynamic facilities
6.6	Aesthetics	Identify different aspects of aesthetic design
6.7	Page design	Understand and apply best practice for page layout
6.8	Copy writing	Grasp and apply the fundamental principles of copy writing for web sites
6.9	Navigation and structure	Assess best practice for navigation and structure
6.10	Interaction	Assess best practice for interaction (including conversion rates and customer services)

6.1 Introduction to web site design

> Web site design = Function + Content + Form + Organization + Interaction

Web site design presents a challenge few have mastered. We have all used web sites that provide us with what we are looking for, and many more that don't, but what makes some sites more appealing than others? This section looks at the purpose or objectives of web sites and then the key variables required to achieve web objectives. Clarifying the key objectives and purpose of the site helps to determine the functions and content of the site. In turn content drives form and finally form drives the organization of the web site. We will also look at how interaction should be built into the site to improve the visitor experience.

So what is the purpose, or objective, of a web site? First, to help customers, or other stakeholders, ask *'How can my web site help my customers?'* For example:

- Help them buy something they need.
- Help them find information.
- Help them to save money.
- Help them to talk to the organization.
- Help them to enjoy a better web experience.

These are the 5 Ss Sell, Serve, Speak, Save and Sizzle introduced in Chapter 1 as seen from the customer perspective. Site design can help achieve the 5 Ss as follows:

- *Sell* – Growing sales can be achieved through effectively communicating our proposition and through making e-commerce facilities straightforward.
- *Serve* – We can add value through designing easy-to-use interactive services that help customers in their work and customer service enquiries.
- *Speak* – We can use the site to converse with and get closer to customers by providing tailored content and designing interactive facilities to create a dialogue, and learn about their needs.
- *Save* – Costs are saved through delivering online content and services that may have previously been achieved through print and post or face-to-face service and sales transactions.
- *Sizzle* – An excellent site design helps build the brand and reinforces the brand values through the type of content, interactivities and overall style, tone or feel.

Design priorities do vary, but many companies use the objectives of customer relationship management to serve as objectives for their site:

- *Customer acquisition* – Acquisition means winning customers – converting prospects (visitors) into customers on site.
- *Customer retention* – Retention means keeping customers – ensuring they repeat buy. Timely, personalized and relevant e-mails and offers can bring them back to you via the site.

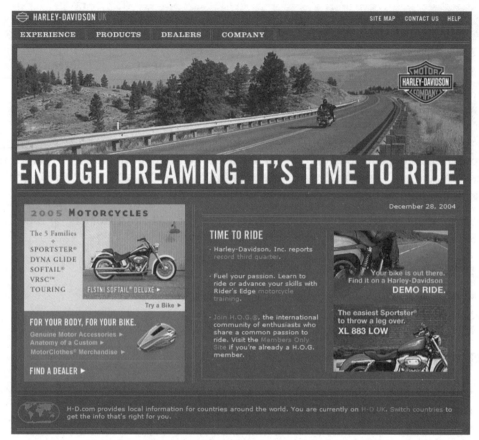

Figure 6.1 Harley-Davidson (www.harley-davidson.co.uk)

● *Customer extension* – Extension means extending the share of wallet. Selling other relevant products and services to the same customer. The database can identify customers that bought A but not B.

For each of these, design can help *convert* the visitor to the required marketing outcome. Achieving site **stickiness** increases the chance of achieving these objectives.

E-MARKETING EXCELLENCE

Harley-Davidson use the web to achieve diverse objectives

Some sites, like Harley-Davidson, are designed towards a range of objectives including acquiring new customers through detailed product information about the core product and extended product such as guarantees and rentals; developing additional revenue streams such as rentals, tours and courses and saving through making efficiency gains through helping dealers with warranty claims – thereby generating cost savings and better customer service.

KEY VARIABLES FOR WEB DESIGN OBJECTIVES

So what factors facilitate online sales and encourage visitors back again and again? What are the key variables? A Forrester survey of 8600 US consumers (www.forrester.com) showed that web users believe four main factors encouraged them to return to a site:

1 High quality content.
2 Ease of use.
3 Quick to download.
4 Updated frequently.

Other factors such as coupons and offers and leading-edge technologies were insignificant in comparison. Let's explore these four factors in more detail.

- *Content* is important. It is often said that 'content is king', but recent thinking suggests that 'context is king'. Having the right information in the right place at the right time – just when you need it – is king.
- *Ease of use* is also important: easy-to-use sites means good navigation. The form or structure of the site is neither over-complicated nor too big. You never get lost in a good site since it's always clearly signposted. Take sales – the order page should be easily found. E-commerce transactions must be easy to make and provide reassurance about security and privacy.
- *Quick to download* – Good sites also download quickly. Bad sites are cumbersome and slow. Visitors won't wait.
- *Frequently updated* – Good sites stay fresh. They put up new information which is useful, relevant and timely for their audience. This is expensive. It takes time, energy and skills to maintain a site. Does your site encourage repeat visits? Does it encourage customers to come back? Does the site offer them genuinely good reasons to return?

E-retailers also need to research what blocks purchase – what causes 'shopping cart abandonment'. Remember that for most e-tail sites, fewer than 10 per cent of new visitors make a purchase. Research presented in Figure 6.2 highlights typical problems. You can see how a

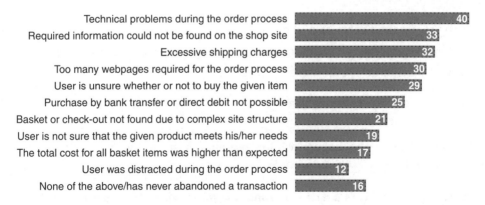

Figure 6.2   Reasons for abandoning online shopping process. (*Source:* Novomind, 2004)

combination of technical problems and poor design coupled with inadequate information can hamper the online shopper. Every site can improve its conversion rate by researching the factors that cause abandonment and improving the design to correct problems. Even Amazon still continually needs to refine its site to reduce abandonment and increase average order value.

There is more on all of these issues in the aesthetics, navigation, interaction and copywriting sections in this chapter.

KEY CONCEPTS IN WEB SITE DESIGN

Effective web site designs are today informed by two key approaches used by professional designers. These are usability and accessibility.

Usability is a concept applied to the design of a range of products which describes how easy they are to use. The British Standard/ISO Standard 'Human Centred design processes for interactive systems' defines usability as:

> *'the extent to which a product can be used by specified users to achieve specified goals with effectiveness, efficiency and satisfaction in a specified context of use'.* **(BSI, 1999).**

You can see how the concept can be readily applied to web site design – web visitors often have defined *goals* such as finding particular information or completing an action such as booking a flight or viewing an account balance.

In Jakob Nielsen's book *Designing Web Usability* (2000), he describes usability as follows.

> *'An engineering approach to website design to ensure the user interface of the site is learnable, memorable, error free, efficient and gives user satisfaction. It incorporates testing and evaluation to ensure the best use of navigation and links to access information in the shortest possible time. A companion process to information architecture'.*

In practice, usability involves two key approaches. **Expert reviews** are often performed at the beginning of a redesign project as a way of identifying problems with a previous design. **Usability testing** involves:

1 Identifying representative users of the site.

2 Asking them to perform specific tasks such as finding a product or completing an order.

3 Observing what they do and how they succeed.

The use of **personas** and **scenario-based design** which we looked at in Section 4.10 is a key approach to inform usability.

Jakob Nielsen explains the imperative for usability best in his article 'Usability 101' (www.useit.com/alertbox/20030825.html). He says:

> *'On the Web, usability is a necessary condition for survival. If a website is difficult to use, people leave. If the homepage fails to clearly state what a company offers and*

what users can do on the site, people leave. If users get lost on a website, they leave. If a website's information is hard to read or doesn't answer users' key questions, they leave. Note a pattern here?'

For these reasons, Nielsen suggests that around 10 per cent of a design project budget should be spent on usability, but often actual spend is significantly less.

For a site to be successful, the tasks or actions need to be completed:

- **Effectively** – web usability specialists measure task completion, for example, only three out of ten visitors to a web site may be able to find a telephone number of other piece of information.
- **Efficiently** – web usability specialists also measure how long it takes to complete a task on site, or the number of clicks it takes.

Web accessibility is about allowing all users of a web site interact with it regardless of disabilities they may have or the web browser or platform they are using to access the site. The visually impairment or blindness is the main audience that designing an accessible web site can help.

This quote shows the importance of the accessibility to a visually impaired user of a web site who uses a screen-reader which reads out the navigation options and content on a web site.

> *'For me being online is everything. It's my hi-fi, it's my source of income, it's my super-market, it's my telephone. It's my way in'.*

Lynn Holdsworth, screen reader user, Web Developer and Programmer. *Source:* RNIB (www.rnib.org.uk)

Remember that many countries now have specific **accessibility legislation** to which you are subject. This is often contained within disability and discrimination acts. In the UK, the relevant act is the Disability and Discrimination Act (DDA) 1995.

Recent amendments to the DDA make it unlawful to discriminate against disabled people in the way in which a company recruits and employs people; provides services; or provides education. Providing services is the part of the law that applies to web site design.

Providing accessible web sites is a requirement of Part II of the Disability and Discrimination Act published in 1999 and required by law from 2002. In the 2002 code of practice there is a legal requirement for web sites to be accessible. This is most important for sites which provide a service. The Code of Practice gives this example:

> *'An airline company provides a flight reservation and booking service to the public on its website. This is a provision of a service and is subject to the Act'.*

Links on accessibility guidelines and standards are given at the end of the chapter.

E-MARKETING INSIGHT

From AIDA to persuasion marketing

In addition to usability and accessibility, web site designers need to add persuasion into the design mix; to create a design that delivers results for the business.

ClickZ columnist Bryan Eisenberg (www.clickz.com) has been called a 'conversion guru'. He advocates persuasion marketing alongside other design principles such as usability and accessibility. He says:

> '*It's during the wireframe and storyboard phase we ask three critical questions of every page a visitor will see:*
>
> *1 What action needs to be taken?*
>
> *2 Who needs to take that action?*
>
> *3 How do we persuade that person to take the action we desire?*'

We can readily apply the AIDA model for advertising to site design to help achieve persuasion. Site designers seek to achieve Attention, then Interest, then Desire, then Action. Although the elements of this model, described by Strong (1925), are often criticized as outdated, many sites use the tried and tested AIDA model as a framework for design objectives. Here AIDA is used to generate a lead from a potential customer.

- *Attention* – The site must grab attention when the visitor first hears about it or even when the visitor actually arrives. We achieve attention through graphics, animation, interaction and easy access to relevant information.

- *Interest* – Once you have the customers' attention we have to provide more detailed information and incentives to gain interest.

- *Desire* – One approach is using the prefix 'free': free information, free screensaver, free services. Emphasizing the brand values through site design as in Figure 6.1 is another approach.

- *Action* – The call to action, e.g. to ring up, subscribe or order, should be clear and easy to use.

SECTION SUMMARY 6.1

Introduction to site design

Well designed sites have clear objectives. The 5 Ss can help you to choose objectives. Asking 'How can my web site help my customers?' also helps. But remember the highest priority marketing objectives or purpose should determine the web site design. Well designed sites have regularly updated, quality content. Both content and context are 'king'. Good sites are also designed for usability and accessibility, but remembering the principle of persuasion.

6.2 Integrated design

In this section we look at the importance of integrating the web site into all communications, customer buying modes and with the databases that help to support relationships with customers. We won't explore the ultimate integration into an e-business; this is covered in Chapter 9.

THE WEB AND INTEGRATED MARKETING COMMUNICATIONS

Although web sites do more than just communicate (remember the 5 Ss), web sites must integrate with all other communications tools, both online and offline. The web site's brand messages must be consistent with those in offline advertisements and mail-shots. Equally, new offers and major announcements such as awards won should be communicated consistently both online and offline. As the organization and the web site grows this job gets more difficult.

At a basic level of integrated communications, all offline communications should carry the web site address or **URL** and describe the **online value proposition**. Equally the web site should cater for **inbound communications** by carrying telephone, e-mail and fax number. Some sites, however don't offer e-mail facilities as they don't have the resources to answer e-mails promptly.

The integration of offline and online communications to generate traffic to the web site is described in more detail in Chapter 7 on traffic building.

It is worth remembering, however, that different customers prefer different communications tools, channels or modes, particularly when buying.

THE WEB AND BUYING MODES

The web site should integrate with different buying modes. We must take account of customers' preferences of browsing, comparing, selecting or buying products either online or offline as shown in Figure 6.3. Completing some activities of the buying process offline and some online is referred to as **mixed-mode buying**. The site design and offline marketing communications should be integrated to support mixed-mode buying.

Common buying modes include:

- *Online purchase* – Some customers want to search, compare and buy online. Does your web site accommodate all stages of the buying process? Few products can be delivered online so fulfilment is usually offline.
- *Online browse and offline purchase* – **Mixed-mode buying** is when customers like to browse, look or research, *online* and eventually purchase *offline* in a real store or in a real meeting. Some of these customers might like to browse online but purchase via fax or telephone because of security and privacy issues. Does your site have fax forms and telephone numbers for placing orders or taking further enquiries? Does your site integrate with other communications channels? Some sites also have '**call back facilities**' which allow visitors to request a telephone call from a sales staff to complete the purchase.

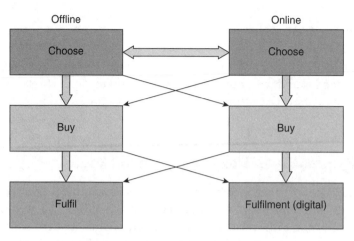

Figure 6.3 Alternative buying modes

How Dell supports mixed-mode buying

Dell supports a common buying mode of:

> *Offline choose then online choose then offline purchase*

This is done through communications tools that facilitate customer transition from offline to online and vice versa:

- *Offline choose to online choose* – If a customer reads about a particular model of a Dell computer in a magazine, it provides e-codes. These are typed in on the site's home page, so avoiding the need for the customer to navigate to the particular product page.

- *Online choose to offline purchase* – If the customer decides to proceed with the purchase, but is uncomfortable about providing their credit card details online, Dell facilitate this transition by providing a prominent telephone number on each page. This phone number is web specific, so Dell know that all inbound calls to this number are in response to web research.

HOW SHOULD THE WEB INTEGRATE WITH THE DATABASE?

Mixed-mode buying requires good systems. A web site database should, ideally, be integrated with the old, legacy, database. Enquiries coming in from offline mail-shots or online from the web site should be recorded centrally on the database and subsequently followed up carefully. An integrated database can help sales reps know which web visitors have requested a real visit or a telephone call.

Furthermore, the database and the actual design of the web site can also help to nurture marketing relationships. The database remembers customer names, preferences and behaviours. The days of being able to build an effective web site using simple HTML code are long gone. An integrated database can personalize the experience and make relevant offers that match the needs of particular customer types.

The web site needs to be integrated with databases to deliver facilities such as transactional e-commerce, personalization and customer relationship management.

The database needs to be centralized and seamless as customers access the business via PDAs, WAP watches, interactive TVs, as well as telephones and other offline routes.

The level of integration can go up and down the supply chain so that data is shared and integrated with suppliers, distributors and key customers' own IT infrastructures. Now the business is becoming an e-business (Chapter 9).

SECTION SUMMARY 6.2

Integrated design

Web activities on their own won't work. Isolated web sites are ineffectual. They need to be integrated at several different levels:

1 Communications – consistent communications whether online or offline.

2 Buying modes – marketers must facilitate customer transitions between online and offline information sources during the buying process.

3 Databases – databases must be integrated to achieve a consistent view of the customer in order to build long-term relationships.

6.3 Online value proposition

The web gives the ultimate in customer choice. There are millions of sites to choose from and thousands of new domain names are still added every day. How will you stand out?

We saw in the first section of this chapter that good sites have good content, are regularly updated, easy to use and fast to download. In addition to all of these, your site has to have a clear and strong proposition. A proposition to your visitor. A unique proposition. An **online value proposition (OVP)**.

Why should a customer visit, stay and even revisit your site? What does your site propose to visitors? Can you summarize the proposition for your site? Try to identify the proposition as you visit other web sites. Can you summarize their OVPs? Refer to Chapter 2 ReMix, since the OVP will refer to different aspects of the marketing mix. The OVP should be clearly evident to the visitor. If you don't clearly know why a customer should visit and revisit your site, how likely is it that customers will understand?

The OVP is similar to the traditional unique selling proposition used in advertising, although advertising executives can have great debates about how the cyber world is different. Ideally, we need to try to find a proposition that explains what your organization or site is offering that:

- is different from your competitors;
- is not available in the real-world;
- makes a difference to your customers' lives.

At the very least the proposition should clearly show the services you are offering and your credibility to deliver.

You then need to devise a tag line that accompanies your brand identity and URL to drive home your web proposition in all communications, both web-based and real world. The proposition can also be detailed as a series of key messages (Figure 6.4).

Figure 6.4   Firebox (www.firebox.com) exhibits a clear, detailed online value proposition

So, we have our proposition. What next?

1 First we need to leverage the proposition in traffic building. The proposition can be combined with the **URL** or web address and be in all advertising, as an e-mail signature and included in all marketing collateral.

2 We need to state clearly the proposition on-site. Many sites are designed so that their proposition is prominent on the home page and may be referred to on every page at the top or top left as part of the organization's identity. Others make the visitor work too hard to understand the proposition.

3 We need to deliver on the proposition through all interactions a customer has including online and offline fulfilment and service.

The following section on customer orientation examines what customers want, what's important and what's affordable.

E-MARKETING INSIGHT

Different views on the value proposition

These comments epitomize traditional meanings of the 'value prop' which can all be translated into an online environment.

A conventional view of the value proposition is provided by Knox *et al.* (2003) in their review of approaches to customer relationship management. They say a value proposition is:

> *'an offer defined in terms of the target customers, the benefits offered to these customers, and the price charged relative to the competition'.*

Similarly, Rayport and Jaworski (2004) suggest that construction of a value proposition requires consideration of (1) Target segments, (2) Focal customer benefits, (3) Resources to deliver the benefits package in a superior manner to competitors. However, branding advocates believe that the value proposition is more than the sum of product features, prices and benefits. They argue that it also encompasses the totality of the experience that the customer has when selecting, purchasing and using the product. We will see that these customer experiences and also service quality are very important online. For example, Molineux (2002) states that:

> *'the value proposition describes the total customer experience with the firm and in its alliance partners over time, rather than [being limited to] that communicated at the point of sale'.*

To summarize, we can say that:

1 The offer forming the OVP should be developed specifically for specific target customer segments (see the Firebox example in Figure 6.4).

2 The OVP is not limited to the customer experience on-site but involves how it links to other channels as part of a multi-channel buying process.

3 The product or service offer and experience that form the OVP must be based on in-depth research of which factors govern purchase and loyalty behaviour and refined according to actual experience of the OVP by customers.

What should be specific elements of an OVP? Remember from Chapter 4 the 6 Cs that e-customers demand: Content, Customization, Community, Convenience, Choice and Cost reduction. These can all be built into the OVP.

SECTION SUMMARY 6.3

Value proposition

In addition to good content, regular updates, ease-of-use and downloads, good sites to have clear and strong online value propositions. OVPs require a lot of thought and refining. The hard work is rewarded as a good OVP distinguishes your site and also, simultaneously, helps to focus the marketing effort and the customer's mind.

6.4 Customer orientation

Defining, first, the purpose of your web site and second, your audience, are fundamental stages of web site development. The answers drive the kind of content required; content drives the form required and form drives the structure of the site. Usability and accessibility as defined at the start of this chapter are also a key element of customer orientation.

There are many different types of audiences including your competitors, shareholders, employees, the press and customers to name a few (Table 6.1). **Customer orientation** is about trying to achieve the impossible – trying to provide content to appeal to a wide range of audiences. It's also about prioritizing your content for your key audiences and their key needs. Look at www.cisco.com, www.ibm.com and www.ni.com as examples of B2B sites that

Table 6.1 Different types of web site audience

Customers vary by	Staff	Third parties
New or existing prospects	New or existing	New or existing
Size of prospect companies (e.g. small, medium or large)	Different departments	Suppliers
Market type, e.g. different vertical markets	Sales staff for different markets	Distributors
Location (by country)	Location (by country)	Investors
Members of buying process (decision makers, influencers, buyers)		Media students

efficiently connect their audience with the information they need. In this section we focus on the core audience – different types of customer.

As far as customers are concerned, you must remember that your web site exists for one reason and one reason only – to help customers. The big question is 'how can my web site help my customers?'

A customer-orientated web site starts with customers and their needs. The site will not only fulfil basic customer needs, it may even delight customers by fully understanding and satisfying the different needs which different customers have. So ask customers! Try thinking about the types of services you can offer customers. Identify their key tasks and goals and make these options prominent. These may be services you offer already such as giving the status of an order, new added value services that don't cost much, or there may be new services that customers can operate themselves. Also ask customers what they think of your existing site. Ask them how you can improve your web site – what would they like to see there?

Rosenfeld and Morville (2002) suggest four stages of research that help achieve customer orientation:

1 Identify different audiences.

2 Rank importance of each to business.

3 List the three most important information needs of audience.

4 Ask representatives of each audience type to develop their own wish lists.

Customer orientation can create competitive advantage. Customer-orientated web sites are relatively rare compared to product-orientated web sites. Product-orientated web sites tend to show lots of products (or services) and their features. Benefits are buried as are any attempts to identify customer needs. Product benefits are never matched to specific customer needs. These sites never ask 'How can I help my customer?'

Although we have said we want to provide content to appeal to a wide range of audiences, providing detailed content to all audiences may well be undesirable (since our messages to priority target segments may be diluted) or impractical (resources are limited). So we need to

E-MARKETING INSIGHT

Defining contexts of use

Nigel Bevan of usability specialists Serco refers to customer orientation in terms of contexts of use. He suggests designers should ask:

- Who are the important users?
- What is their purpose for accessing the site?
- How frequently will they visit the site?

- What experience and expertise do they have?
- What nationality are they? Can they read English?
- What type of information are they looking for?
- How will they want to use the information: read it on the screen, print it or download it?
- What type of browsers will they use? How fast will their communication links be?
- How large a screen/window will they use, with how many colours?

(*Source:* Bevan, 1999)

E-MARKETING EXCELLENCE

Customer orientation in practice

Figure 6.5 is an example of the principle of customer orientation in action. In the first edition of *eMarketing eXcellence*, we noted that retail site DIY.com is targeted at a range of users of DIY products, so it was designed around three zones: products, advice and inspiration. Experts who know what they want go straight to the product section and buy what they need. Less experienced users with queries on what to purchase can gain advice from an expert just as they would in store and novices may visit the inspiration zone which includes room mock-ups with lists of the products needed to create a particular look. Note that now, through usability testing and assessing web analytics, most customers simply need to be connected with a product as quickly as possible. There is a prominent search box at the centre of the screen with a detailed list of product departments forming the main navigation on the left. Key user tasks are in the buttons at the top of the screen and Advice and Services have been limited to this area which will result in fewer visitors knowing about value-added services and advice.

An alternative approach is used by Guinness (www.guinness.com) who at the time of the first edition had three site zones '*like it, live it, love it*'. This has now transformed to: 'Knowing (education for students), Seeing (ads) and Doing (web store and downloads).

ask which key audiences should we concentrate resources on? A good starting point is to ask the question, 'Who is my ideal customer?'

IDEAL CUSTOMERS

If you don't know your ideal customers, then you probably don't know your worst customers. If you can't define these you cannot target them. If you don't know who they are, it's unlikely that you'll find them.

You will probably find that there are several types (or segments) in which your ideal customers exist. For which different types of customer do we need to offer what kind of content? Customer-orientated web site professionals constantly ask these questions. They spend time defining their target customers and then finding ways to satisfy them.

Figure 6.5 B&Q web site DIY.com illustrates customer orientation (www.diy.com)

Of course global markets complicate matters. And after all aren't we all in global markets, particularly since web sites propel us into the global arena. For example, Asian customers might expect to see lots of red and gold in a financial site. Westerners might see red as trouble, warning or debt ('in the red').

Let's keep it simple. Consider your own local customers. Who are they? What is their profile? Why do they buy? Many businesses do not know who their customers are. They have got names and addresses but they haven't got profiles or clusters that describe their characteristics.

As well as customer segments, we also need to think about how the backgrounds of visitors to our site will vary. Visitors have different levels of familiarity with the Internet, your organization, your products and your site. Customer-orientated web sites are built to accommodate all of these different levels of **familiarity**.

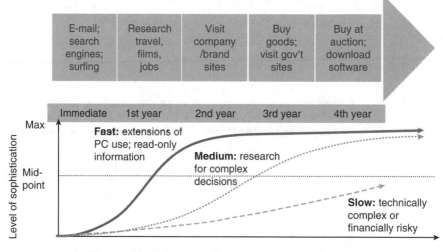

Figure 6.6 Stages of familiarity with the Internet. (*Source:* Forrester Technographics (www.forrester.com))

Customer orientation focuses the web site design around customers, particularly ideal customers. The ultimate customer orientation has to be personalization combined with a dynamic dialogue relevant to customers' needs and wants and not a dialogue focused on products or services.

E-MARKETING INSIGHT

The Four Familiarities

Research by Forrester suggests that users pass through different stages of familiarity and confidence as they use different Internet facilities. Site design should try to accommodate this by allowing for users with different levels of experience. Remember that thousands of people use the Internet for the first time every day – they could be on your site.

We can identify other forms of familiarity that good sites take account of. Our 'four familiarities' are:

1 *Familiarity with the net.* See above.

2 *Familiarity with your organization.* For those who don't know, you need content to explain who you are, your OVP and a statement of credibility through 'About us' options and customer testimonials.

3 *Familiarity with your products.* Even existing customers may not know the full range of your product offering. Many companies have parts of pages, or post-transaction pages to educate customers about the range of products.

4 *Familiarity with your site.* Site maps, Search and Help options are 'must have', not 'nice to have' options for a web site since you may lose potential customers if you cannot help them when they are astray.

Customer orientation

A customer-oriented site provides easy access to content and services tailored for a range of audiences. But resources for content development should be targeted at ideal customers.

Site design should allow for different levels of experience or familiarity amongst its audience including familiarity with the net, the organization, its products and its web site.

6.5 Dynamic design and personalization

The most important sound in the world is your own name. Remembering customer names and their needs is a personal thing. Web sites can get personal. Internet-based personalization delivers customized content and services for the individual either through web pages, e-mail or push-technology. In this section we are going to look at what **personalization** is and what its components are. This topic is also reviewed from a different perspective in Section 8.6 where the concepts of **customization**, **mass customization** and **individualization** are explained.

Today's marketers have a dream opportunity – to personalize their services, and web sites in particular. Web technology, combined with database technology, increase the marketer's memory so that any number of customers can be recognized, preferences remembered and served immediately.

A typical personalization service is that provided by the portals such as Yahoo! and Excite that enables users to personalize the web site by configuring their home page so that it delivers the information they are most interested in – whether weather, football scores or share prices. Some sites even create personalized products.

Personalization also helps to Sell, Serve, Speak and Sizzle:

- *Sell* – personalization can make it easier for customers to select their products. A customer of an online supermarket does not want to select a new shopping basket of goods each time they shop. Example: Tesco (www.tesco.com).

- *Serve* – a customer who uses an online travel booking service does not want to have to key in the same journey details if it is a common itinerary. Instead personalization enables them to save their itinerary. Example: Expedia (www.expedia.com).

- *Speak* – through personalization a customer can select the type of communications they want to receive from a company as part of permission marketing. For example, a customer may just want to hear about major product launches via e-mail, but not receive a weekly e-mail. Example: Siebel (www.siebel.com).

- *Sizzle* – all of the above can help add value, strengthen the brand and develop the relationship.

Note though, that we missed out Save, since web-based personalization tends to be expensive to create and maintain. A less-costly, e-mail-based approach may be best for many companies. Personalized e-mails can be pushed out to customers reminding them and helping them in many different ways.

Remember also that personalization can create barriers since passwords and log-ins are required and easily forgotten. This is where **cookies** work well, but remember the legal requirements for using cookies. Cookies identify customers and provide a link to stored data about their preferences without the need for passwords.

Even if the customer can remember the password they often forget to remember to return to a particular web site to view personalized web page content. They may be too busy. E-mail can remind them or even make it easier by presenting the information or offer directly. Personalized opt-in e-mail offers an alternative route to keeping the dialogue alive.

OPTIONS FOR PERSONALIZATION

Personalization can occur through displaying different information depending on customer specific or dynamic environment variables. Examples, many of which are illustrated by Figure 6.7, include:

- *Customer or company name*. A site can be personal on a simple level by referring to returning customers by name.
- *Date or time*. Updating the date or time on site using **JavaScript** can be used to highlight a dynamic, up-to-date online presence that is worth returning to.
- *Country*. Sites can identify the origin of a visitor based on their **IP address** and deliver content accordingly. IBM.com automatically **redirects** customers to their own country site.
- *Customer preferences*. Personalization of content on a web site can be set up by a customer clicking or selecting different types of content. This can be used to build data collected via registration forms, questionnaires, cookies and of course purchases. However, the most effective personalization is arguably unobtrusive; Amazon gives recommendations of books based on past purchases without requiring the user to register their preferences.
- *News and events*. Results, surveys or press releases can be automatically posted to the site.
- *Referrer string*. Content can potentially be personalized according to which site the visitor previously visited and in particular the keyphrase typed into a search engine, e.g. an insurer has used the type of insurance searched for to tailor messages for new visitors.
- *Location*. Internet phones enabled with WAP make it is possible to send promotions to a customer as they pass a shop. Whether this is desirable is another matter!

Note however that personalization can be expensive to implement. It requires complex software and up-to-date databases. As such it is most commonly used by retailers and major portals who hope to have frequent interactions with customers.

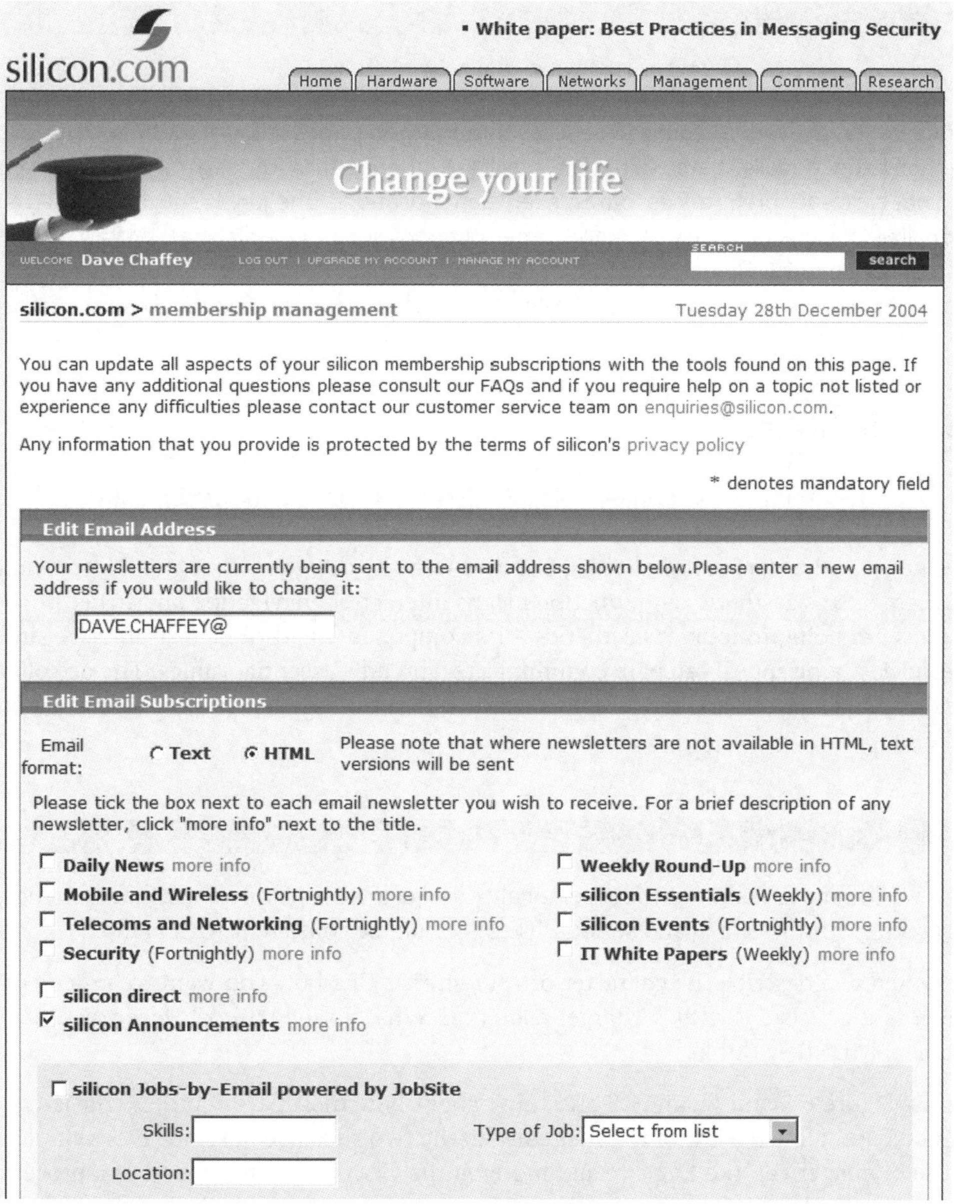

Figure 6.7 Personalization for IS professionals at Silicon.com (www.silicon.com)

E-MARKETING EXCELLENCE

Ordnance Survey personalize maps

Map maker Ordnance Survey offers the OS Select service (www.osselect.co.uk) which enables customers to centre their map on their home or favourite destinations to offer a personalized map complete with their own cover title and photo.

SECTION SUMMARY 6.5

Dynamic design and personalization

Personalization delivers customized services through web pages and e-mail and rich media, e.g. voice activated e-mails. Personalization can be triggered through several dynamic variables including: customer preferences, dates, events and locations. The jury is still out on the value of personalized web sites. It may work for some situations such as media sites, portals or complex e-tail catalogue sites. Remembering names shows respect. Recognizing customers and their preferences sows seeds of good relationships and better business. The database is vital to this.

6.6 Aesthetics

Aesthetics = Graphics + Colour + Style + Layout and Typography

As we noted at the start of this chapter, effective web site design includes both form and function. Form means aesthetics and function means interaction, navigation and structure. In this section we're going to look at aesthetics – its components and the constraints. A site with powerful aesthetic appeal can help communicate a brand's essential values. The use of graphics, colour, style, layout and typography create aesthetics. Together these create a personality for the site.

SITE PERSONALITY

Words we could use to describe site personality are just as for people: formal, fun or engaging, entertaining or professional and serious. These should be consistent with brand.

How would you describe the character of your site? Is this how you want to be seen or positioned? Is it consistent with the target audience? What do they think? Have you asked your customers what they think?

Contrast Figure 6.8 and Figure 6.9 and think about how their personality is consistent with their audience. Note that since the first edition, the two sites have become more similar with less use of imagery on the Egg site and more on the Cisco site. This is part of a process that has been referred to as 'web site undesign'. Increased use of text at the expense of graphics has been driven by a wish to improve usability, accessibility and search engine optimization.

SITE STYLE

Some sites are information intensive and other sites are graphics intensive. **Information-intensive sites** may appear cluttered because of the amount of text blocks, but the intention is to make best use of screen real estate and project an image of information depth and value to the visitor. Retail sites often fall into this category. With **graphics-intensive sites** there is relatively little text; graphics and animations are used to create an impression. FMCG brand sites often use this approach with an introductory graphical screen or splash screen. Again

Figure 6.8 Cisco B2B site – networking products (www.cisco.com)

Figure 6.9 Egg B2C site – financial products (www.egg.com)

contrast Figure 6.8 and Figure 6.9 and think about the extent to which they are information or graphics intensive.

WHAT ARE THE DESIGN CONSTRAINTS?

There are many design constraints or challenges under which web designers operate. Unfortunately the list of constraints is long and sometimes neglected, to disastrous effect:

1 *Modems and download time*. Slow modems take longer to download graphics – if the visitor waits! Although broadband access is growing rapidly, at the time of writing over half of home users still had a dial-up connection. Good designers optimize graphics for fast downloading and then test using a slow modem across phone lines. Remember the top sites download in less than a second. Also remember the eight second rule of thumb that shows the majority of initial visitors to a site will not hang around to wait for it to download if it takes longer than this.

2 *Screen resolution*. Today a relatively small proportion of users have lower screen resolutions of 640×480 or 1024×768 pixels; the majority have 1024×768 pixels or greater. But if designers use resolutions much greater than the average user, the screens may be difficult to read for the majority. Fluid designs are best for many sites where the content maximizes the space on the screen. So, we recommend designing for the majority as long as you are compliant with accessibility law.

3 *Number of colours*. Some users have monitors capable of displaying 16 million colours giving photo-realism while others may only have the PC to set up to display 256 colours.

4 *Browsers*. Different types of **web browsers** such as Microsoft Internet Explorer, Mozilla Firefox and Opera and different versions of browsers such as version 6.0 or 7.0 may display graphics or text slightly differently. An e-commerce site tested under one browser may fail completely under another.

5 *Plug-ins and download time*. If the site requires **plug-ins** that the user doesn't have you will be cutting down the size of your audience by the number of people who are unable or unprepared to download these plug-ins.

6 *Font sizes*. The facility for the user to change font size – choosing large fonts on some sites causes unsightly overlap between the different design elements, but this capability is required for accessibility.

As a result of these constraints, design of web sites is a constant compromise between what looks visually appealing and modern and what works for the older browsers, with slower modems the *lowest common denominator*.

What are the implications of all these constraints? First, if you use experienced web designers you will not have time to worry about these issues. Second, many designers cater for the lowest common denominator so that no one is excluded. Third, offer choice – offer the user choice between 'high-tech' or 'low tech'. For example ask the visitor if they want sound effects, video clips, etc. Some will, some won't, some can't (perhaps because of office constraints or company firewalls). But at least you are meeting their needs.

Finally, when discussing site design with suppliers you may hear them refer to GIF and JPEG files. These are graphics standards. GIFs are typically used for banner adverts, icons and text in graphical menus. JPEGs are typically used for photographic images such as photos of products or people. To use these graphics effectively, designers need to use special graphical techniques such as **browser-safe palettes**, **anti-aliasing** and **dithering** here, but evidence of shoddy sites, some from well-known brands, shows that not all designers have these skills.

TYPOGRAPHY

The web gives enormous scope for users to vary font size and type through their web browsers, but many users do not use this facility. Given this, site designers should specify font characteristics through the <FONT> HTML command. There are some general traps to avoid when using fonts.

> *The XYZ Company offer you the opportunity to take part in our online competition* *exclusively for customers who have made several purchases over the last year.*

1 Never use underline in body text as a reader will think it's a hyperlink.

2 Avoid using italics as it is difficult to read on screen.

3 San-serif font styles such as Arial or Verdana work best on the web, as they look sharper on the screen and are therefore easier to read.

SECTION SUMMARY 6.6

Aesthetics

Aesthetics comprises graphics, colour, style and personality. Many web sites indulge in over-elaborate graphics and ignore their audiences' capability, and patience, to view them. Web designers must consider the constraints of variable modems, screen resolutions, colour displays, browsers and of course audiences. Many designers don't like designing for the lowest common denominator but it does give you the widest audience.

6.7 Page design

In this section we will explore the components of good page layout and the difference between frames and tables. The main layout elements of a web page we want to include throughout a website for consistency are usually:

- Company name and logo for identity.
- Menu (and submenus) for navigation.
- Footer for reference to copyright and privacy information (usually in small text).
- Page title for content, e.g. product information.

From a usability standpoint, for most applications it is important that the main elements of each page, in particular headers, footers and navigation systems such as left, top or right navigation are consistent on each page. Designers use a **page template** to create this consistency. Most **content management systems (CMS)** are based on a defined page template for the whole site, or parts of the site. Using a capable CMS is essential to the consistency and management of any large site since it will enable **content owners** in different parts of the organization to update the content they are responsible for. Some good open source CMSs are now available such as Plone (www.plone.org) which is used for the page templates for Dave Chaffey's E-marketing portal (www.davechaffey.com) making it easy to add new articles and news items.

When creating the design, **wireframes** are used by web designers to indicate the eventual layout for web page templates by showing where navigation elements and different types of content will appear on the page. Figure 6.10 shows that the wireframe is so called because it just consists of an outline of the page with the 'wires' of content separating different areas of content or navigation shown by white space. A wireframe can be created for all types of similar page groups, identified at the blueprint (site map) stage of creating the information architecture. Wireframes are useful for agencies and clients to discuss the way a web site will be laid out without getting distracted by colour, style or messaging issues which should be covered separately as a creative planning activity.

Wodtke (2002) describes a wireframe (sometimes known as a schematic) as:

> *'a basic outline of an individual page, drawn to indicate the elements of a page, their relationships, and their relative importance'.*

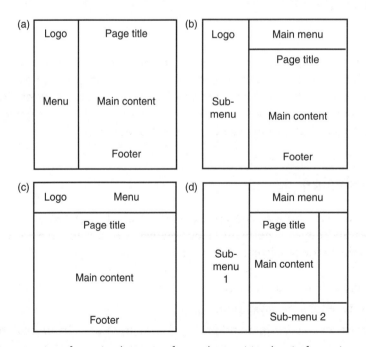

Figure 6.10   Some options for main elements of page layout (simple wireframes)

There are many different options for layout of this information shown on the page (Figure 6.10). In addition there may be announcements or special offers, which can be more effective if they occupy a consistent position on screen. Examples include: links to product and service information; special offers or promotions; incentives to register; contact phone numbers; company news and PR.

The limited space on a page requires: concise writing (more so than brochures); chunking or breaking text into units of 5–6 lines at most; use of lists with headline text in larger font; generally never including too much on a single page. The art of writing succinctly for the web is addressed in Section 6.8 on copy writing.

Remember, too that using hyperlinks can help achieve flow within copy, either by linking to sections further down a page or linking to another page.

E-MARKETING INSIGHT

Users spend most of their time on other sites

Jakob Nielsen says:

> *'Users spend most of their time on other sites. This means that users prefer your site to work the same way as all the other sites they already know... Think Yahoo and Amazon. Think "shopping cart" and the silly little icon. Think blue text links'. (Nielsen, 2000b)*

Web site designers face a difficult challenge in that they want their site to be memorable and differentiated from competitors. On the other hand, for ease of use, standardization of web features that users are familiar with is desirable. Think about the merit of these features of standardization:

- Widely used standards for labels such as Home, Main page, Search, Find, Browse, FAQ, Help, About us and Contact us.
- Logo top left, hyperlink to home pages.
- Main menu left margin or at top.
- Signposts of content at top or top left of page.
- Don't use non-standard text hyperlinks e.g. non-underlined links.

FRAMES AND TABLES – TO FRAME OR NOT TO FRAME?

In the early days of the web there used to be discussions about whether to use **frames** instead of **tables** for layout. Today, the battle is won and frames are no longer widely used (except for specialist applications such as library catalogues or the shopping basket system on www.tesco.com) since there are difficulties with printing, bookmarking and when visitors arrive via a search engine.

E-MARKETING INSIGHT

Jakob Nielsen's ten good deeds in web site design

As you scan this list from Jakob Nielsen's usability site UseIt (www.useit.com) think about whether your site has these characteristics, which you consider most important and where they fit with Sections 5, 6, and 7 of this chapter.

1 Place your name and logo on every page and make the logo a link to the home page (except on the home page itself, where the logo should not be a link: never have a link that points right back to the current page).

2 Provide search if the site has more than 100 pages.

3 Write straightforward and simple headlines and page titles that clearly explain what the page is about and that will make sense when read out-of-context in a search engine results listing.

4 Structure the page to facilitate scanning and help users ignore large chunks of the page in a single glance: for example, use grouping and subheadings to break a long list into several smaller units.

5 Instead of cramming everything about a product or topic into a single, infinite page, use hypertext to structure the content space into a starting page that provides an overview and several secondary pages that each focus on a specific topic. The goal is to allow users to avoid wasting time on those subtopics that don't concern them.

6 Use product photos, but avoid cluttered and bloated product family pages with lots of photos. Instead have a small photo on each of the individual product pages and link the photo to one or more bigger ones that show as much detail as users need. This varies depending on type of product. Some products may even need zoomable or rotatable photos, but reserve all such advanced features for the secondary pages. The primary product page must be fast and should be limited to a thumbnail shot.

7 Use relevance-enhanced image reduction when preparing small photos and images: instead of simply resizing the original image to a tiny and unreadable thumbnail, zoom in on the most relevant detail and use a combination of cropping and resizing.

8 Use link titles to provide users with a preview of where each link will take them, before they have clicked on it.

9 Ensure that all important pages are accessible for users with disabilities, especially visually impaired users.

10 Do the same as everybody else: if most big websites do something in a certain way, then follow along since users will expect things to work the same on your site. Remember Jakob's Law of the Web User Experience: users spend most of their time on other sites, so that's where they form their expectations of how the web works.

Finally, always test your design with real users as a reality check. People do things in odd and unexpected ways, so even the most carefully planned project will learn from usability testing.

Source: Nielsen (1999b)

SECTION SUMMARY 6.7

Page design

Consistent layout is important. Key messages, menus, links, page size and frames versus tables all need to be considered carefully for effective web use.

6.8 Copywriting

Copywriting for the web is an evolving art form, but many of the rules for good copywriting are as for any media. This section explores the basic rules.

Possibly the most important rule is don't assume your visitors have full knowledge of your company, its products and services. Remember the four familiarities described in Section 6.4. So, don't use internal jargon about products, services or departments and avoid indecipherable acronyms!

So what should you do? How should you write copy for your web site? A simple mnemonic for web copywriting is CRABS; aim for Chunking, Relevance, Accuracy, Brevity and Scannability.

Chunking, Brevity and Scannability go together. Many visitors briefly scan pages looking for headlines, followed by short, brief, digestible chunky paragraphs of 5 or 6 lines maximum which can be hyperlinked to further detail for those that want to 'drill down' for more information. Other visitors scan, move on and quickly find what they need elsewhere on the site. Section 6.9 on structure and navigation explores this in more detail.

In addition to chunky, brief and scannable, the copy must be relevant and useful to the target audience. This is where 'content is king' becomes 'context is king' – relevant information available at the right time in the right place. The copy must satisfy their needs and not yours, i.e. start with benefits instead of features (Figure 6.11). You can create benefits out of features by adding the three magic words: 'which means that…' after a feature.

Remember that you are copywriting not only for your human audience, but also the search engine spiders or robots which read (index) the words you use in your copy. So words used

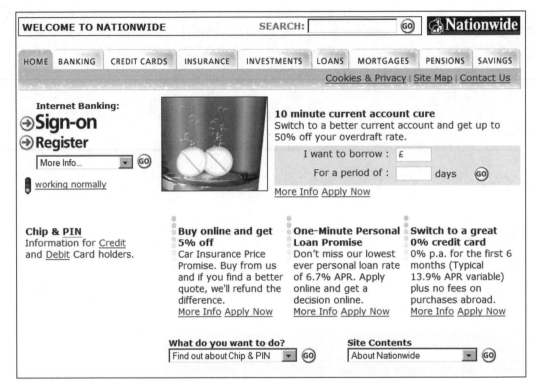

Figure 6.11 Nationwide insurance exhibits clear features and benefits (www.nationwide.co.uk)

should include keyphrases that users are likely to search on within search engines (see Chapter 7 on search engine optimization).

And as with any genuinely good writing, it must be accurate to win credibility and loyalty in the long term. Don't promise what you cannot deliver. Do not cheat customers. It kills repeat business as well as new, referred business.

So, use CRABS (chunky, relevant, accurate, brief and scannable) to write good web copy. And remember, don't leave the best until last because, first, readers who scan will miss it, and, second, some readers won't scroll.

And last but not least – don't forget nomenclature, or names, used for headings and sign-posting. Different nametags and signposts can give a very different feeling. Eyetracking research (www.poynter.org) suggests that on the web, customers' eyes are drawn first to the headings rather than the graphics. Test different headings to see which give the best **clickthrough**.

E-MARKETING INSIGHT

Gerry McGovern's top ten rules of copywriting

These are ten copywriting rules from Gerry McGovern (www.gerrymcgovern.com). As you read through these, think about whether these rules apply for other media and also whether your organization achieves them on your web site.

1 *Be honest*. Paper never refused ink. Websites never refused hype. If you can't deliver within twenty-four hours, then don't promise to.

2 *Be simple, clear and precise*. Time is the scarcest resource, so never use five sentences when one will do. Avoid jargon. People are confused enough today.

3 *State your offer clearly*. What exactly is it that you sell?

4 *Tell them about your products' limitations*.

5 *Have a clear call to action*. If they like what you have to offer how do they go about buying it?

6 *Tell them quickly if they're not a customer you can supply*. There's nothing I find more frustrating than finding out at the last moment that they can't deliver.

7 *Edit! Edit! Edit!* There has never been an article that cannot be made shorter.

8 *Give them detail*. If they feel like finding out more about a particular product feature, then give them that opportunity. (That's what hypertext is for!)

9 *Write for the web*. Avoid the customer having to download Word documents, Powerpoints or PDF unless offered as an alternative for convenience. (Note that Google and other search engines do now index these documents.)

10 *Leave it at 9!* If you want to create a '10 Rules' but can only find 9, leave it at 9.

SECTION SUMMARY 6.8

Copywriting

Copywriting for web sites is different to brochures and mail shots – think CRABS – chunky, relevant, accurate and brief. Write for scannability and watch the detail – even words used in signposts create a different feel or personality to the site.

6.9 Navigation and structure

Ease of use = Structure + Navigation + Page layout + Interaction

Ease of use is number two of the key factors that make customers return to web sites. To achieve ease of use we need to structure our site so that users can easily navigate. **Navigation** describes how users move from one page to the next using navigational tools such as menus and hyperlinks. We also need a suitable page layout that makes it easy for visitors to find information on the page and the right types and amounts of interactivity as described in separate sections.

This section examines structure and navigation to ensure that first, all sections of your web site are easily accessible, and second, visitors enjoy the satisfying experience of finding what they want.

SITE STRUCTURE

Web site **structure** is the big picture of how content is grouped and how different pages relate to others. Without a planned structure, a site can soon end up as a 'spaghetti site'. This may leave visitors dazed, disorientated, confused and frustrated. If they cannot achieve **flow control**, they may not return.

A planned site structure with clear hierarchies will allow the user to build up a 'mental map' of the site. As we will see later, this can be reinforced by clear sign-posting and labelling.

There is a formal process that professional site designers use to create an effective structure known as an **information architecture**. Rosenfeld and Morville (2002) point out the importance of designing an information architecture when they say:

> '*It is important to recognize that every information system, be it a book or an intranet, has an information architecture. "Well developed" is the key here, as most sites don't have a planned information architecture at all. They are analogous to buildings that weren't architected in advance*'.

They describe an information architecture as:

1 '*The combination of organization, labelling, and navigation schemes within an information system.*
2 *The structural design of an information space to facilitate task completion and intuitive access to content.*
3 *The art and science of structuring and classifying web sites and intranets to help people find and manage information.*
4 *An emerging discipline and community of practice focused on bring principles of design and architecture to the digital landscape*'.

Rosenfeld and Morville (2002)

Creating an information architecture requires specialist techniques. For example **card sorting or web classification** categorize web objects (i.e. documents and applications) in order to facilitate user task completion or information goals. **Blueprints** are then produced which show the relationships between pages and other content components, and can be used to portray organization, navigation and labelling systems. They are often thought of, and referred to, as site maps or site structure diagrams and have much in common with these, except that they are used as a design device clearly showing grouping of information and linkages between pages, rather than a page on the web site used to assist navigation.

The depth of the site is one aspect of creating an information architecture. This is important since it will determine the number of clicks a user has to make to find the information they need. The balance is between shallow and deep.

Which of Figure 6.12 (a) or (b) would you say is best? Most would agree that a shallow site structure is best since it takes fewer clicks for the customer to find the information they need. A good rule of thumb is that, even for a large site, **three clicks** should be sufficient to enable the user to find their area of interest. Placing an order should never be more than three clicks away. How deep is your site?

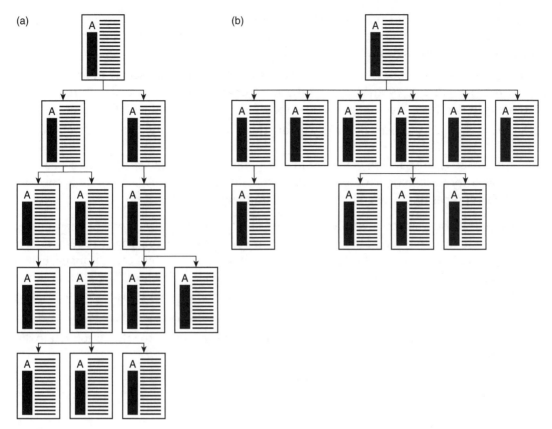

Figure 6.12 Alternative site structures: (a) deep, (b) shallow

However, site design is an art, not a science. If you selected the deep structure you will have had your reasons – the user has more simple choices at each stage in comparison with the shallow structure. In fact, the correct answer is probably a compromise between the two!

ACHIEVING FLOW

Good web designers try to enable '**flow**'. Flow is a concept that describes the degree of control or power a consumer has over the site. If customers can easily find the information they want through clicking on menu options and graphics they will feel in control and this will be an enjoyable experience. We can use buttons and hyperlinks within copy to help achieve flow, but this is often neglected.

NAVIGATION RULES

Here are three navigation rules for a navigational template that is used throughout the site:

1 *Keep it simple*. Not too many buttons. Psychologists who have analysed the behaviour of computer users in labs say the magic number is seven (or fewer). Any more than seven and the

user will find it difficult to choose. Seven or less keeps it simple. You can use nesting or pop-up menus to avoid the need for too many menus or too many menu items. Simplicity is necessary to avoid confusing the user.

2 *Be consistent*. Consistency is helpful since we want to avoid a user seeing different menus and page layouts as they move around the site. For example, the menu structures for customer support should be similar to those for when browsing product information.

3 *Signposts*. Signposts to help visitors by telling them where they are within the web site.

We also need to clearly label the different folders or directories on the site so they act as a reference point for describing particular types of content on the site. A URL strategy specifies how different types of content will be placed in different folders.

For example, if you visit the buy-to-let property web site That's Property (www.thatsproperty.co.uk), look at how the web address details vary as you move from one page to another. Here each page is defined in a different folder. This is a common approach of content management systems. Each folder effectively has a single file in it named index.htm. The URL becomes more meaningful and memorable rather than gobbledygook which is not well indexed by search engines.

A further example is where site owners have to make a decision how to refer to content in different countries – either in the form:

http://<country-name>.<company-name>.com

or the more common

http://www.<companyname.com>.com/<country-name>

E-MARKETING INSIGHT

Jakob Nielsen on navigation

Nielsen (2000c) suggests that the designer of navigation systems should consider the following information that a site user wants to know:

- *Where am I?* The user needs to know where they are on the site and this can be indicated by highlighting the current location and clear titling of pages. This as *context*. *Consistency* of menu locations on different pages is also required to aid cognition. Users also need to know where they are on the web. This can be indicated by a logo, which by convention is at the top or top left of a site.

- *Where have I been*? This is difficult to indicate on a site, but for task-oriented activities such as purchasing a product can show the user that they are at the *n*th stage of an operation such as making a purchase.

- *Where do I want to go?* This is the main navigation system which gives options for future functions.

NAVIGATION TYPES

Most web sites have several types of navigation. These include:

- *Global navigation* – These are site-wide navigation schemes. Examples for a B2B site are: Products, Solutions, Clients, Support. They often occur at the top or bottom of a site, but may occur down the side.
- *Local navigation* – More detailed navigation to find elements in an immediate area – for example, Products may be broken down further.
- *Contextual navigation* – Navigation specific to a page or group of pages which may be in the body copy or in slots such as Related products.
- *Breadcrumbs* – Used to indicate where the visitor is on the site. For an example see: www.davechaffey.com/E-marketing. As you navigate around this site you will see, just below the top menu, a list of pages showing where you are and allowing you easily to visit a higher point in the structure. These are so named from the trail of breadcrumbs Hansel and Gretel left in the forest to go back to their house.

On a customer-facing web site, there are a number of alternative approaches to navigation. The most important are:

- Product-based
- Organization-structure based
- Visit-based: first time/repeat visitor
- Task-based or need related
- Relationship-based: customer/non-customer
- Customer type based
- Company need
  - Calls-to-action
  - Campaign related
  - Branding.

How many of these are appropriate to your web site? How many are you missing? Note that many companies only adopt some of these, with the product-centric or organization structure common. Often key navigation approaches may be missed such as task, relationship or customer type-based. It is always a balance between accommodating a range of audience needs and avoiding confusing visitors through too many navigation options.

E-MARKETING EXCELLENCE

Navigation at the BBC

The BBC site (www.bbc.co.uk) is a great example of a site that achieves consistency, simplicity and context and has a clear URL strategy. Visit the site and navigate around different areas such as News (www.bbc.co.uk/news), Sport (www.bbc.co.uk/sport), Football (www.bbc.co.uk/sport/football) and Radio 1 (www.bbc.co.uk/radio1). You will see that there is clear signposting at the top of each page, which part of the site you are on and there are changes in colour and style associated with each part of the site. You will also notice that the site has a well thought through information architecture with each section having a clear URL.

SECTION SUMMARY 6.9

Navigation and structure

So navigation and structure can in themselves satisfy or dissatisfy customers. You need a strong information architecture. Well thought through navigation options are needed to promote flow experiences. Keep the page layout simple, consistent and clearly signposted, and you're on your way to success.

6.10 Interaction

Interaction helps to engage web site visitors by giving them some two-way communications plus greater involvement and control over their web experience. This section explores the types and benefits of interactions.

DIFFERENT TYPES OF INTERACTIVITY

We can identify several basic interactive mechanisms:

- A simple mouse click on an image or an arrow to find more information or to look at the next item in a sequence (mouse event).
- Placing the mouse over a text menu option may give feedback by changing the colour of the text (mouse rollover).
- Selection from drop-down boxes.
- Drag and drop.
- Typing requirements into a box and then searching through a catalogue.
- Slider, same choice: small, medium or large.

Remember also that there are many other types of interactions that add value to the user experience such as simulations, calculators, crosswords, quizzes, helpful information and turbine optimizers (Chapter 1).

Good interactions reinforce brand values – like Fedex's delivery update service. In addition to all of these automated interactions, web sites can also have real staff interaction, e.g. where

callback technology invites a customer to request phone contact, **live chat sessions** or **co-browsing** involving a real-time web dialogue.

USING INTERACTIVITY TO MOVE CUSTOMERS THROUGH THE BUYING PROCESS

Now consider how interactions and two-way communications can help move a customer through several stages of the buying process, which was introduced in Chapter 4.

1 *Learning*. Help customers learn about you – your company, your products, features and their benefits. Interaction helps a customer to learn because involvement deepens the learning process. Interactive techniques include:

- Simulations or interactive demonstrations of products, e.g. the National Instruments Product advisor (www.ni.com/advisor).
- Animations that explain different features or benefits of a product (e.g. www.nike.com).
- Tailoring – by product category or segment, e.g. Dell asks users to state whether they are a small, medium or large company. The site tailors itself accordingly (www.dell.com).
- Selection choice – online toy e-tailers allow section by age of child, by type of toy and by brand (for example, www.fisherprice.com).
- Downloads of detailed technical sheets often presented as **PDF** files, e.g. Siebel (www.siebel.com/resource-library) has hundreds of documents needed to support different people involved in the buying decision for a complex product.
- Testimonials or case studies, e.g. www.accenture.com has client successes for each of its offerings.
- 'E-mail a friend' facility. This can be used to alert a colleague or make them aware of a product or service.

2 *Deciding*. There are many kinds of interactions that can help customers to choose your product. Here's a small selection:

- An **interactive product selector** (Figure 2.3). This will help customers choose between different options if it is well-designed.
- **Callback facility**. Human advice may be helpful in guiding the user through selection. To achieve this, some sites include callback facilities where a customer types in their name and phone number and specifies a time when the company should ring back.
- **Chat facility**. Some companies also include chat facilities where a human customer service representative types an immediate response to the customers' queries. This approach is more efficient than bouncing e-mails between suppliers and customers over a long period. LivePerson (www.liveperson.com) illustrates this type of interaction. Co-browsing or screen-sharing can also help.
- **On-site search engines**. These help customers find what they're looking for quickly. They are popular features and some companies have improved conversion to sale greatly by improving the clarity of the results they return. Site maps are a related feature.
- **'E-mail a friend' facility**. This can be used to alert a colleague or friend or to help accelerate a shared decision on a purchase within an organization.

Some e-tailers such as Lands' End (www.landsend.com) use a range of communications techniques to interact with the customer, including e-mail, call-back and chat (Lands' End live) – all helping the customer to decide.

3 *Buying*. Leading the customer through the purchase can help break down reluctance to buy online or **shopping cart abandonment** as shown by Figure 6.2. Established e-tailers use techniques such as:

- Leading the customer through the purchase in clearly numbered stages.
- Minimizing the number of stages.
- Offering an incentive to 'buy now'.
- Understanding purchasing objections and information needs at each stage of the checkout process and providing appropriate information within the checkout area.

Figure 6.13 Sky – clearly indicate stage in purchasing process (www.sky.com)

- Location selection tool – find your nearest dealer by typing in a postal or ZIP code.

- Voucher systems that are printed out on a customer's printer, then redeemed in store.

- Including a phone number on site to encourage purchase by phone where the customer prefers this.

- Detailed content to reassure about security and privacy.

This remains an important, but hugely challenging area despite the use of techniques such as usability analysis and web analytics.

4 *After-sales support.* After-sales support techniques for interactive support include:

- Searchable FAQs – Easyjet (www.easyjet.com) have worked at improving their FAQs by analysing online and offline customer service queries and then presenting FAQs when the customer selects the 'Contact us' option.

- Interactive support tools – Epson allow customers to diagnose their problems with printers by prompting them to select their problem from pre-configured choices and then suggesting solutions (www.epson.co.uk/support).

- Customer feedback – After customers have used the interactive support tool they have the option of interacting via a questionnaire on how useful the support was.

- The methods used for product selection, namely call-back, chat or community discussion forums, can also be used. Some companies such as Cisco have found that customers can help solve other customers' problems.

Finally, all the interaction techniques we have reviewed in this section can also be viewed as a means of collecting marketing research. Web stats or web logs from your site reveal customer preferences, responses and problems.

E-MARKETING EXCELLENCE

Using interactions for research

Consider these examples of how interactive can be used to gather customer intelligence:

- *Customer preferences* – For example, Dell can see the proportion of users clicking on 'small, medium and large' customers' to gain an appreciation of the role of the Internet in reaching these segments.

- *Responses to promotions* – When the Carphone Warehouse analyses response to online vouchers they can analyse regional differences in use of the Internet and response to promotion.

- *Customer problems* – Epson can use information from its interactive support tool to find out the type of problems customers experience with products and feed this information through into both customer service and new product development.

SECTION SUMMARY 6.10

Interactions

Appropriate interactions add satisfaction, value and flow to the web site. They help customers to learn about features and benefits, choose products and enjoy better after-sales service. It's worth considering!

CHAPTER SUMMARY

1 Site design should be determined by clear marketing objectives. Key concepts for an effective design are usability, accessibility and persuasion.

2 Web site design needs to be integrated with other marketing activities, in particular outbound and inbound communications, buying modes and databases.

3 Each site should have a clear online value proposition (OVP) that differentiates the site from competitors, and defines services not available in the real world which positively impacts the customer's lives. The OVP should be communicated offline, online and on the site itself and should be delivered.

4 Customer orientation involves grouping access to content and services that meet the needs of an audience made up of different stakeholders and customer segments with different familiarity with the net, the organization, its services and its site.

5 Customized services can be delivered through personalization of web pages and e-mail. These help build relationships as data can be gathered about customers' needs and services provided that match these needs more closely.

6 Site aesthetics are an important consideration in design since the combination of graphics, colour, style, layout and typography define a site's personality and style, which are important in branding. Designers have to work under the constraints of and test for many technology variations including download speed, screen resolution, browsers and plug-ins.

7 Page layout is important to providing a clear consistent message throughout the site. This is achieved through standard locations for menus, logos, names, signposts and content.

8 Copywriting for the web shares much in common with other media. 'CRABS' highlights the importance of Chunking, Relevance, Accuracy, Brevity and Scannability.

9 Ease of use is achieved by creating a sound information architecture and then designing navigation tools and structures that enable a smooth flow for site visitors. Minimizing clicks to find content, simplicity, consistency and signposts can all help achieve this.

10 Providing interactive content in addition to static content can help support the customer throughout the buying process through product selection tools, callback facilities and direct or indirect customer service tools.

References

Bevan, N. (1999) Usability issues in web site design. *Proceedings of the 6th Interactive Publishing Conference, November 1999*. Available online at www.usability.serco.com.

British Standards Institute (1999) BS 13407 Human Centred design processes for interactive systems. British Standards Institute.

Knox, S., Maklan, S., Payne, A., Peppard, J. and Ryals, L. (2003) *Customer Relationship Management: Perspectives from the Marketplace*. Butterworth-Heinemann, Oxford.

Lynch, P. and Horton, S. (2002) *Web style guide. Basic design principles for creating web sites*. Yale University Press, 2nd edition.

Molineux, P. (2002) *Exploiting CRM. Connecting with customers*. Hodder & Stoughton, London.

Nielsen, J. (1999a) Web Research: Believe the Data. *Jakob Nielsen's Alertbox*, 11 July. www.useit.com/alertbox/990611.html.

Nielsen, J. (1999b) Ten Good Deeds in Web Design. *Jakob Nielsen's Alertbox*, 3 October. www.useit.com/alertbox/991003.html.

Nielsen, J. (2000a) *Designing Web Usability*. New Riders Publishing, USA.

Nielsen, J. (2000b) End of Web Design. *Jakob Nielsen's Alertbox*, 23 July. www.useit.com/alertbox/000623.html.

Nielsen, J. (2000c) *Details in Study Methodology Can Give Misleading Results*. Jakob Nielsen's Alertbox, 21 February. www.useit.com/alertbox/990221.html.

Novomind (2004) E-commerce research by Novomind/Faz Institute. Hamburg, Germany, 27 October. www.novomind.com.

Rayport, J. and Jaworski, B. (2004) *Introduction to E-commerce*. McGraw-Hill, New York, 2nd edition.

Rosenfeld, L. and Morville, P. (2002) *Information Architecture for the World Wide Web*. O'Reilly, Sebastopol, CA, 2nd edition.

Strong, E.K. (1925) *The Psychology of Selling and Advertising*. McGraw-Hill Book Co., New York.

Wodtke, C. (2002) *Information architecture: blueprints for the web*. New Riders, Indianapolis, IN.

Further reading

Van Duyne, D., Landay, J. and Hong, J. (2001). *The Design of Sites. Patterns, Principles, and Processes for Crafting a Customer-Centered Web Experience*. Addison-Wesley, Reading, MA. An in-depth analysis of web site design with many examples. All web site designers will learn some new tips from this book.

Krug, S. (2000) *Don't Make Me Think*. New Riders. A commonsense introduction to this topic.

Nielsen, J. (2000) *Designing Web Usability*. New Riders Publishing, USA. The original classic book on web site design. Now superseded by others in this list.

Rosenfeld, L. and Morville, P. (2002) *Information Architecture for the World Wide Web*. O'Reilly, Sebastopol, CA, 2nd edition. A structured, fairly academic description of how to approach information architecture.

Lynch, P. and Horton, S. (2002) *Web style guide. Basic design principles for creating web sites*. Yale University Press, 2nd edition. A great online resource available at: www.webstyleguide.com.

 Web links

Disability and Discrimination Act. Code of practice including reference to web sites available from www.disability.gov.uk/dda.

Jakob Nielsen's UseIt (www.useit.com). Detailed guidelines (alertboxes) and summaries of research into usability of web media.

User Interface Engineering. Articles on usability that often provide a counterpoint to those of Nielsen. (www.uie.com).

Royal National Institute for the Blind web accessibility guidelines (www.rnib.org.uk/accessibility).

Usability News (www.usabilitynews.com).

Usability resources (www.usabilityfirst.com).

Worldwide Web consortium web accessibility guidelines (www.w3.org/WAI).

 **Self-test**

1 Explain the linkage between site design and marketing objectives.

2 Describe a scenario where on-site and offline marketing communications can be integrated to support mixed-mode buying.

3 Explain how OVP differs from USP and define the OVP for your organization.

4 How would you assess whether a web site had good customer orientation?

5 Describe the benefits of different types of personalization.

6 What are the constraints on using graphical elements to produce a site with strong visual appeal?

7 Draw a diagram summarizing the main page elements of your organization's web site.

8 Write down six rules for effective web copywriting.

9 Explain the concept of flow.

10 Describe the link between web site design and supporting customers through stages of the buying process.

Chapter 7

Traffic building

'*If you build it, they will come*'. This famous line proved true in the 1989 film *Field of Dreams*, but unfortunately, it doesn't apply to web sites. If you want to maximize visitors to your site and to acquire new customers online you have to work hard to master the full range of online and offline marketing tools.

Having a great web site is absolutely no use if no one uses it. It's a bit like having a 'better mousetrap'. You know the story 'show me a better mousetrap and the world will beat a path to my door'. Sadly it's not always the best products that succeed but rather reasonably good ones that (a) everyone knows about and (b) everyone can easily find when they need them. The same is true of web sites. This chapter shows you how to build traffic – how to acquire the right visitors to your site in order to achieve the right marketing outcomes for you.

OVERALL LEARNING OUTCOME

By the end of this chapter you will be able to:

- Evaluate the range of options for traffic building
- Develop a plan to balance the options for traffic building
- Identify success factors for different online communications tools.

CHAPTER TOPIC	LEARNING OBJECTIVE
7.1 Introduction	Assess different options for traffic building
7.2 Search engine marketing	Use different approaches to improve a site's listing in search engines including search engine optimization (SEO) and pay per click (PPC)
7.3 Online PR	Manage your reputation online through supporting journalists and maximizing your representation on portals
7.4 Online partnerships	Use links building, affiliate marketing and online sponsorships to exploit the network effect of the Internet
7.5 Interactive advertising	Identify the elements of a successful online ad campaign
7.6 Opt-in e-mail	Build traffic and relationships through opt-in e-mail
7.7 Viral marketing	Assess the relevance of viral marketing
7.8 Offline traffic building	Create a balance between offline and online promotion techniques
7.9 Control	Monitor the effectiveness of traffic building
7.10 Resourcing	Construct a traffic building plan

7.1 Introduction to traffic building

Generating traffic is vital to achieving e-marketing objectives, no matter whether the aim is sell, speak, serve, save or sizzle (see Chapter 1). What are the key characteristics of effective traffic building? In this section we will introduce three key aspects of traffic building:

1 *Targets* – specific objectives for traffic building need to be developed before embarking on a traffic building campaign. Traffic building objectives are essentially tactics to achieve wider e-marketing objectives.

2 *Techniques* – traffic building involves combining new online and traditional offline communication techniques to promote the web site proposition and so encourage visits. Achieving the correct mix of traffic-building techniques is vital, but difficult.

3 *Timing* – when should traffic building occur? Some e-marketers may consider traffic building to be a continuous process, but others may view it as a specific campaign, perhaps to launch a site, new product or promotion.

TARGETS

Typical traffic targets include the quantity, quality and cost of traffic. Although a successful site is often referred to in terms of quantity, such as the number of visitors, it is the traffic quality that really indicates the success of a traffic building campaign. Remember that generating traffic is not limited to driving visitors to your own web site. Traffic-building can also be effective on the third-party sites that your audience use. For example, a manufacturer of nappies may decide to create or sponsor a microsite on a third-party site such as www.babyworld.com or www.babycentre.co.uk. See the box 'Lexus achieve opt-ins through *Guardian* microsite' as an example of this type of microsite campaign. This case also shows the marketer can track online campaigns to assess their return on investment.

Traffic quality can be assessed by asking two questions about site visitors. First, are they within the target audience for the web site? Second, do they respond in line with the communications objectives, i.e. do they convert to the site outcomes you require?

Cost can be considered in terms of the cost of getting the visitor to the site, and the cost of achieving the outcomes during their visit. Experienced online marketers control their traffic building through managing the cost per acquisition (CPA) (sometimes cost per action). Depending on context and market, CPA may refer to different outcomes. Typical cost targets include:

- cost per acquisition – of a visitor (**cost per click, CPC**)
- cost per acquisition – of a lead
- cost per acquisition – of a sale (**allowable customer acquisition cost**).

CPA is typically equivalent to cost per sale (CPS) but may also apply to cost per visitor, lead or enquiry or other type of outcome since direct product sales are not practical or appropriate for all web sites. For a car manufacturer, for example, CPA might refer to the cost of generating a brochure or test drive request.

The value of sales should also be considered. Online retailers calculate sales value in terms of the value from the first sale (**average order value, AOV**) and campaign **return on investment (ROI)**. Companies should also model **customer lifetime value (LTV)**. Leading e-marketers select online referrers (i.e. choice of portal) not only by minimizing CPA, but also through maximizing new visitors with the highest potential LTV.

Costs and value should be compared for different sources of traffic such as **referrals** of visitors from **online adverts** on different sites or different search key phrases. To be able to measure cost per action effectively, we need to be able track a visitor from different referrer sources from when they first arrive on the web site through to when the action (sale or enquiry) is taken. This is sometimes referred to as 'tagging visitors'. Costs are considered further in Section 7.10 on resourcing.

E-MARKETING EXCELLENCE

Lexus achieve opt-ins through *Guardian* microsite

In 2004, Toyota invested £200 000 in a sponsored microsite campaign to support the launch of the Lexus RX300 SUV. The site, themed around how we use our time, was connected with the Proms and other summer events. The site achieved 90 000 page impressions and also registered more than 5500 competition entries with a 48 per cent opt-in to future communications from Lexus – so database building through direct response was one of the results, and this is not usually achieved through offline sponsorship. A prominent brochure request panel was also used, but this proved less successful achieving only 73 requests. Likewise a PDA initiative only gathered 30 e-mail addresses. The effectiveness of the sponsorship was increased by a range of ads targeting relevant content on the *Guardian* site and through e-mail ads of which 700 000 impressions were served. Another success factor of the microsite was its topical focus on our lack of time today, with editorial titled 'Too tired for sex' driving interest from elsewhere in the site and other media.

This case shows the importance of monitoring cost per acquisition of a lead, so that e-marketers can refine future work.

Source: Interactive Advertising Bureau UK (www.iabuk.net)

TECHNIQUES

The traffic building techniques we will cover are summarized in Figure 7.1. You may have heard of many of the online techniques that use the network effect of the Internet to drive traffic to a site, such as viral marketing, affiliates and search engine optimization. The promotional mix for traffic building typically includes a range of online and offline techniques, each with their own strengths and weaknesses, which will be explored in later sections of this chapter. Van Doren *et al.* (2000) provide an overview of the range of techniques.

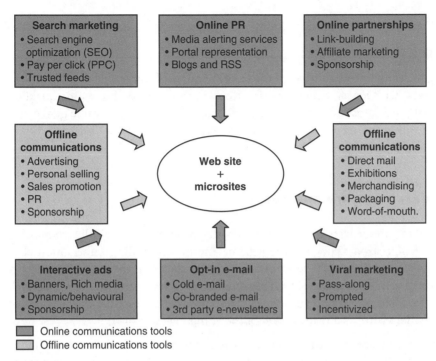

Figure 7.1 Options available in the communications mix for traffic building

Traditional advertising is based around campaigns that run for a fixed duration. Specific campaigns are also used for traffic building. These are often tied into a particular event such as the launch or re-launch of a web site. For example a banner advert campaign may last for a period of two months following a re-launch. In addition to campaigns there are also **continuous traffic building activities**. Companies should ensure that there is sufficient investment in continuous online marketing activities shown in Figure 7.1 including search marketing, affiliate marketing and sponsorship.

E-MARKETING INSIGHT

Gordon Pincott of Millward Brown on site promotion

Pincott (2000) suggests there are two key issues in site promotion. First there should be a media strategy which will mainly be determined by how to reach the target audience. This will define the online promotion techniques described in this chapter and where to advertise online. Second there is the creative strategy. Brown says that 'the dominant online marketing paradigm is one of direct response'. However, he goes on to suggest that all site promotion will 'influence perceptions of the brand'.

Introduction to traffic building

Targeting, techniques and timing are three key aspects of traffic building and their relevance should be assessed for all techniques described in this chapter. It is traffic quality, not quantity, that really indicates the success of a traffic building campaign. Traffic quality is high if site visitors are within the target audience for the web site and if they respond in line with the communications objectives.

7.2 Search engine marketing

How important are **search engines** for web site promotion? Typically, the answer is 'very important'. The reason? They are the primary method of finding information about a company and its products. Over 90 per cent of web users state that they use search engines to find information. If your organization is not registered with a search engine, you make it difficult for a prospect or customer to find you unless they know or successfully guess your web address (if the potential visitor is already aware of the company or brand).

The importance of effective search marketing is suggested by Figure 7.2 which shows that the higher the rank of your company and products in the **search engine results pages (SERPS)** the more visitors you will receive. It is widely thought that it is essential to be in the top three sites listed in the results from a search, but Figure 7.2 and the box 'Understanding consumer search engine behaviour' shows some visitors can still be delivered from lower rankings.

You need to avoid being in the Internet black hole shown in Figure 7.3. Of the billions of web pages that have been created, many are not listed at all on search engines because companies are not registered with the search engine for indexing or the site content is inaccessible. Alternatively, pages may be indexed, but no effort has been taken to improve the company's ranking. Make sure this doesn't apply to your site. Ensure that you are visible in at least the top ten search engines and that dynamic information held in databases is visible through techniques such as **URL rewriting**.

Remember though, that search engine marketing is only one online digital communications tool. For established brands, we commonly see from web analytics that more than half of site visitors arrive at a site, not through search engines, but direct through typing in the web address or following a bookmark (web analytics tools label these as 'no referrer'). The volume of direct visitors shows the power of branding, PR and offline communications in driving visitor traffic. In 2003, Statmarket (www.statmarket.com) reported that direct navigation accounted for 65% of site visits worldwide, with 21% following links and just 14% arriving by search engines. For first-time visits, however, search marketing is generally found to be over 20%.

We will now review the three main search engine marketing techniques for making a company and its products visible through search engines:

1 Search engine optimization (SEO)
2 Pay per click (PPC)
3 Trusted feed including paid-for-inclusion.

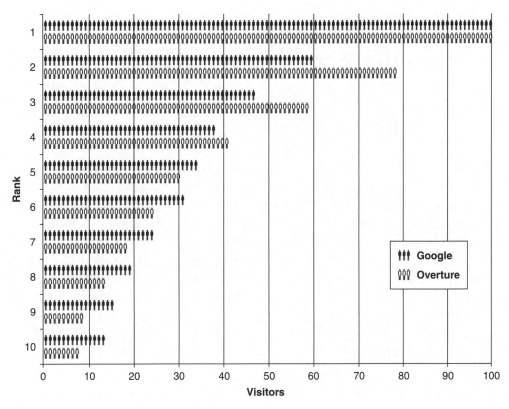

Figure 7.2 Relative traffic projections based on the ranking on search engine results pages. Visitor numbers are shown relative to 100 for position 1. (*Source:* Atlas DMT, 2004)

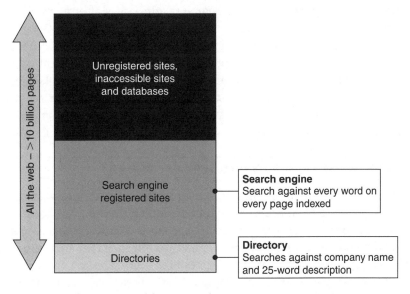

Figure 7.3 Proportion of sites accessible via search engines

Understanding consumer search engine behaviour

Search marketing firm iProspect conducted research on how we search; the results are instructive:

- Over half of Internet users search at least once a day.

- 81.7% will start a new search if they can't find it in the first three pages (typically 30 results). So, to some extent, it is a myth that if you are not in the top ten you will receive no visitors – it depends on the quality and relevance of the listing also. The detailed figures were: 22.6% try another search after first few results; a further 18.6% after reviewing the first page (41.2% cumulative); 25% after checking the first two pages (67% cumulative) and 14.6% the first three pages (81.7% cumulative)

- Users tend to choose the natural search results in preference to the paid search listings, according to a sample. Figures for selection of natural search were 60.8% for Yahoo! and 72.3% for Google. This figure increases for experienced users. This suggests that companies who concentrate on paid listings only are limiting their visibility.

- Around half use search toolbars from one of the providers such as Google, Yahoo! or MSN (these are plug-ins for searching which are added to the browser).

Source: iProspect research, Spring 2004 (www.iprospect.com)

SEARCH ENGINE OPTIMIZATION (SEO)

Search engine optimization involves achieving the highest position or ranking practical in the **natural or organic listings** on the search engine results pages after a specific combination of keywords (or keyphrase) has been typed in. In search engines such as Google, Yahoo! and MSN Search, the natural listings are on the left as shown in Figure 7.4(a), although there may also be sponsored links above these. The position or ranking is dependent on an algorithm used by each search engine to match relevant site page content with the keyphrase entered. There is no charge for these listings to be displayed or when a link relevant to your site is clicked upon. However, you may need to pay a search engine optimization firm to advise or undertake optimization work to make your web pages appear higher in the rankings.

How are the search engine results pages produced?

To optimize your position in different search engines, it helps to understand the basis on which SERPS are generated and ordered. By understanding this you can boost your position higher than your competitors and so achieve higher levels of traffic. Search engines compile an index by sending out **spiders** or **robots** to crawl around sites that are registered with that search engine. The spider compiles an index containing every word on every page against the page address. It weights the index according to different parameters using an algorithm specific for each search engine and then stores the index as part of a database on a web server.

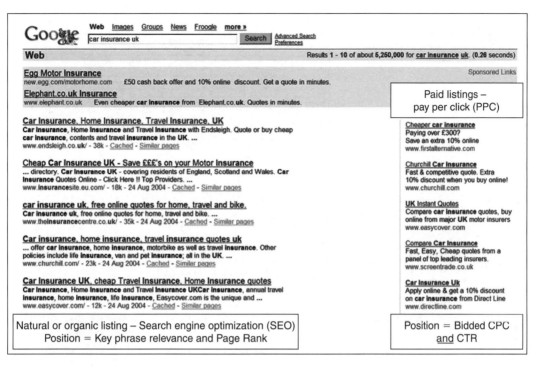

Figure 7.4 (a) Google search engine results page for keyphrase 'car insurance uk'

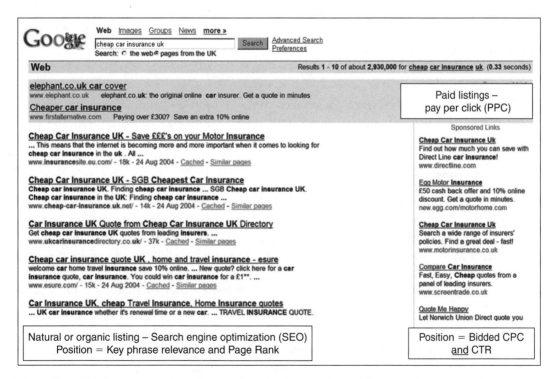

Figure 7.4 (b) Google search engine results page for keyphrase 'cheap car insurance uk'

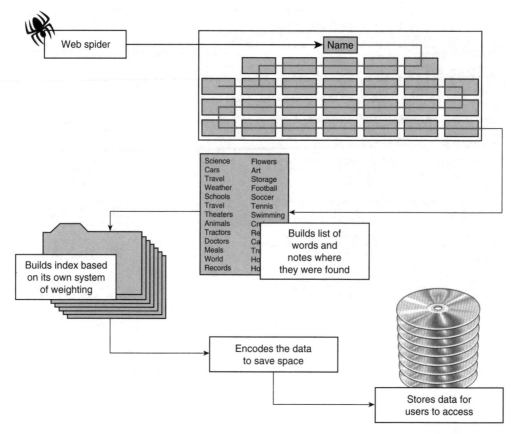

Figure 7.5 Stages involved in search engine indexing

This index is what is searched when potential customers type in key words. Google is rumoured to use at least 100 factors within its search ranking algorithm and we will explore the most important ones of these in a moment.

Search engine registration

For success in SEO, the first thing you need to check is that you are registered with all the main search engines. While some unscrupulous search marketing companies offer to register you on the 'top 1000 search engines', in reality, registering on the top 10 to 20 search engines in the countries you operate will probably account for more than 95 per cent of the potential visitors. To find out the most popular search engines in different countries, use online panel data from www.netratings.com, ISP analysis from Hitwise (www.hitwise.com) or compilations at SearchEngineWatch (www.searchenginewatch.com/reports).

How do you achieve registration? The good news is that registration with many search engines is free if you find the 'Add a URL' page (e.g. www.google.com/addurl.html) where you supply your home page URL and Google will then automatically index all the linked pages. It is recommended that automated submission tools are not used since these can be considered a **search engine spamming** technique. In fact, if you have links from other companies that are registered with a search engine, many search engines will automatically index your site without the need to submit a URL. You can check that you are registered with search engines by:

1 Reviewing **web analytics** data which will show the frequency with which the main search robots crawl your site.
2 Using web analytics referrer information to find out which search engines your site visitors originate from, and the pages they use.
3 Checking the number of pages that have been successfully indexed on your site. For example, in Google the search 'inurl:www.davechaffey.com' lists all the pages of Dave's site indexed by Google and gives the total number in the top right of the SERPS.

Keyphrase analysis

The key to successful search engine optimization and pay per click is achieving **keyphrase** relevance since this is what the search engines strive for – to match the combination of keywords typed into the search box to the most relevant destination content page. Notice that we say 'keyphrase' (short for keyword phrase), rather than 'key word' since search engines such as Google attribute more relevance when there is a phrase match on a page. Despite this, many search companies and commentators talk about optimizing your 'keywords' and in our opinion pay insufficient attention to **keyphrase analysis**.

You can see from comparing Figure 7.4(a) with Figure 7.4(b) that some well-known companies are visible for one search phrase, but not the other. Other companies who have done the appropriate analysis are visible for both.

Key sources for identifying the keyphrases your customers are likely to type when searching for your products include your market knowledge, competitors' sites, key phrases from visitors who arrive at your site (from web analytics), the internal site search tool and the keyphrase analysis tools from vendors such as Overture (www.overture.com) listed at the end of the chapter. When completing keyphrase analysis we need to understand different qualifiers that users type in. For example, this list of seven different types of keyphrases is taken from an Overture representative talking at Search Engine Strategies in 2004. We have added examples for 'car insurance':

1 Comparison/quality – compare car insurance
2 Adjective (price/product qualifiers) – cheap car insurance, woman car insurance
3 Intended use – high mileage car insurance
4 Product type – holiday car insurance
5 Vendor – Churchill car insurance
6 Location – car insurance UK
7 Action request – buy car insurance.

You can see some of these types of keyphrases by using the Overture keyterm suggestion tool. For example for a single month in the UK, the most popular phrases related to car insurance were:

1 Car insurance, 1 423 350

2 Cheap car insurance, 71 979

3 Car insurance quote, 32 857

4 Woman car insurance, 21 087

5 Young driver car insurance, 17 175

6 Performance car insurance, 12 379

7 Car insurance uk, 11 719

8 AA car insurance, 7956

9 Online car insurance quote, 7423

10 Car insurance company, 7186.

This data suggests the importance of ranking well for high-volume keyphrases such as 'cheap car insurance' and 'car insurance uk'.

Improving search engine ranking through SEO

Although each search engine has its own algorithm with many weighting factors that change through time, fortunately there are common factors that influence search engine rankings. These are, in approximate order of importance:

1 *Frequency of occurrence in body copy*. The number of times the keyphrase is repeated in the text of the web page is a key factor in determining the SERPS position for a keyphrase. Copy can be written to increase the number of times a word or phrase is used (technically, its **keyphrase density**) and ultimately boost position in the search engine. Note though that search engines make checks that a phrase is not repeated too many times such as 'cheap flights … cheap flights … cheap flights … cheap flights … cheap flights … cheap flights … cheap flights … cheap flights …' and will not list the page if this key phrase density is too high or it believes '**search engine spamming**' has occurred. Relevance is also increased by a gamut of legitimate 'tricks' such as including the keyphrase in headings (<H1>, <H2>), **link anchor text** in links and using a higher density towards the start of the document.

2 *Number of inbound links (page rank)*. The more links you have from good quality sites, the better your ranking will be. Evaluation of inbound links or backlinks to determine ranking is one of the key reasons Google became popular. **Page rank** helps Google deliver relevant results since it counts each link from another site as a vote. However, not all votes are equal – Google gives greater weight to links from pages which themselves have high page rank and where the link anchor text or adjacent text contains text relevant to the keyphrase. For keyphrases where there is a lot of competition such as 'car insurance', the quantity and quality of inbound links may even be more important than keyphrase density in determining your ranking.

3 *Inclusion in directories*. This is important since it can assist in boosting page rank. **Web direc-tories or catalogues** are often included on the same site as a search engine, but are constructed and presented differently to search engines. Directories are not constructed automatically by robots and spiders, but are generated manually. A real person will place each reference to a site in a category. After you submit your URL to a site such as Yahoo! or Business.com (for which a fee is payable) or the Open Directory (www.dmoz.org, which is currently free) it will be reviewed by a human and then included if it is thought to be of a suitable standard. Another difference is that directories do not give comprehensive access to all web pages. When you search a directory, you are not searching the entire web, but the list of company names, categories and for Yahoo!, the 25 word description of the site.

4 *Title HTML tag*. The keywords in the title tag of a web page that appears at the top of a browser window are indicated in the HTML code by the <TITLE> keyword. This is significant in search engine listings since if a keyphrase appears in a title it is more likely to be listed highly than if it is only in the body text of a page. It follows that each page on a site should have a specific title giving the name of a company and the product, service or offer featured on a page. Greater weighting is given to keyphrases at the left of the title tag and those with a higher **keyphrase density**. The title HTML tag is also vital in search marketing since this is typically the text underlined within the SERPS which forms a hyperlink through to your web site. If the title tag appearing on the search results page is a relevant call-to-action that demonstrates relevance you will receive more clicks which equals more visits (incidentally Google will monitor clickthroughs to your site and will determine that your content is relevant too and boost position accordingly).

5 *Meta-tags*. **Meta-tags** are part of the HTML file, typed in by web page creators, which is read by the search engine spider or robot. They are effectively hidden from users, but are used by some search engines when robots or spiders compile their index. In the past, search engines assigned more relevance to a site containing keyphrases in its meta-tags than one that didn't. **Search engine spamming** of meta-tags resulted in this being an inaccurate method of assessing relevance and Google has reported that it assigns no relevance to meta-tags. However, other search engines such as 'Yahoo! Search' do assign some relevance to meta-tags, so it is best practice to incorporate these and to change them for each page with distinct content. There are two important meta-tags which are specified at the top of an HTML page using the <meta name=""> HTML keyword:

1 The '**keywords**' meta-tag highlights the key topics covered on a web page.
2 Example: <meta name="keywords" content="book, books, shop, store, book shop, bookstore, publisher, bookshop, general, interest, departments,">
3 The '**description**' meta-tag denotes the information that will be displayed in the listing of web sites in the web browser when a web page is found.
4 Example: <meta name="description" content="The largest online book store in the world.">
5 Other meta-tags are used to give other information such as the type of tool used to create the web page. Remember that incorporating the names of competitors is now not only underhand, but case law in the UK has demonstrated it is illegal.

6 *Hidden graphic text*. A site that uses a lot of graphical material and/or plug-ins, is less likely to be listed highly. The only text on which the page will be indexed will be

the <TITLE> keyword. To improve on this, graphical images can have hidden text associated with them that is not seen by the user (unless graphical images are turned off), but will be seen and indexed by the search engine. For example text about a company name and products can be assigned to a company logo using the 'ALT' tag as follows:

<IMG NAME='Logo' SRC='logo.gif' ALT="Eastern Engineering – lathes and milling machines">

Again due to **search engine spamming** this factor is assigned lesser relevance than previously, but it is best practice to use this since it is also required by accessibility law (screen-readers used by the blind and visually impaired read-out the ALT tags).

E-MARKETING EXCELLENCE

Danny Sullivan on search engine optimization

A shock for graphic designers, Danny Sullivan, editor of respected Search Engine Watch (www.searchenginewatch.com) says:

'Search engines prefer big, dumb and ugly pages'.

He also emphasizes the importance of the title tag; he says:

'After the page content itself, the title tag is the most important. Keep the title short, attractive, and enticing, and it will work well both for search engines and people reading a description of your page'.

PAY PER CLICK (PPC) SEARCH MARKETING

Pay per click (PPC) search marketing or paid listings is similar to conventional advertising; here a relevant text ad with a link to a company page is displayed when the user of a search engine types in a specific phrase. A series of text ads usually labelled as 'sponsored links' are displayed as is shown on right of Figure 7.4. Unlike conventional advertising, the advertiser doesn't pay when the ad is displayed, but only when the ad is clicked on which then leads to a visit to the advertiser's web site – hence pay per click! Most clicks result in a visit to the site, although there may be a small (usually less than 5–10 per cent) attrition that cannot be controlled, but you should be aware of. The relative ranking of these 'paid performance placements' is typically based on the highest bidded **cost per click** (CPC) value for each key word phrase. The company that is prepared to pay the most per click gets top spot. Google also takes the relative clickthrough rates of the ads into account when ranking the sponsored links, so ads that do not appear relevant, because fewer people are clicking on them, will drop down or may even disappear off the listing.

Paid search listings, or sponsored links, are very important to achieve visibility in all search engines when an organization is in a competitive market. If, for example, a company is promoting online insurance, gambling or retail products, there will be many companies competing using the search engine optimization techniques described in the previous section. Often, the companies that are appearing at the top of the listing will be small companies or affiliates. Such companies are less constrained by branding guidelines and may be able to use less ethical search engine marketing techniques that are close to search engine spamming. If you look at sites near the top of the listings for any of the keyphrases above, you will find that they are often ugly pages that look bad, but search engines like. Furthermore, smaller organizations can be more nimble, they can respond faster to changes in search engine ranking algorithms, sometimes referred to as the **Google Dance,** by changing the look and feel or structure of their site. A small company can make changes in hours or days: for a large organization it may take weeks, months and in some cases, years.

Managing pay per click

To participate in PPC, clients or their agencies commonly use PPC ad networks or brokers to place and report on pay per click ads on different search engines. Two of the most important PPC ad networks are Overture (www.overture.com) which is owned by Yahoo! and Espotting (www.espotting.com). For example, in Europe, in 2004, placing an ad on Overture would enable advertisers to display the ad on Yahoo!, MSN and ISP Wanadoo. It is necessary to deal direct with Google, who have their own PPC ad programme known as Google adwords (http://adwords.google.com).

Different advertisers bid on particular key words through a web-based PPC management interface provided by the network to achieve the listing that they want. Typical aims are to be top, or to be in the top three or five sponsored ad links. Espotting estimates that 97 per cent of its traffic to its advertisers' destination sites is from the top five positions.

Advertisers decide on the maximum cost per click (CPC) they are prepared to pay. If this is more than the current top position, the cost per click will be reduced so that it is just sufficient for you to be top. If your bid is less than the current cost per click of the top position, you will be placed according to the relative ranking of your bid.

A minimum bid of 10p is typical, with a maximum capping on bids and amounts spent per month possible. If this sounds cheap, remember that some marketers spend millions annually on search marketing for a wide range of keyphrases. For products with a high potential value to the company such as life insurance, the cost per click can, amazingly, exceed £10.

With PPC as for any other media, media buyers carefully evaluate the advertising costs in relation to the initial purchase value or lifetime value they feel they will achieve from the average customer. As well as considering the cost per click (CPC), you need to think about the conversion rate when the visitor arrives at your site. Clearly, an ad could be effective in generating clickthroughs or traffic, but not achieve the outcome required on the web site such as generating a lead or online sale. This could be because there is a poor incentive, call-to-action or the profile of the visitors is simply wrong. One implication of this is it will often be more cost-effective if targeted microsites or landing pages are created specifically for certain keyphrases to convert users to making an enquiry or sale. These can be part of the site structure, so clicking on a 'car insurance' ad will take the visitor through to the car insurance page on a site rather than a home page. This is not a form of advertising to use unless the effectiveness of the web site in converting visitors to buyers is known.

Table 7.1 shows how cost per click differs between different keywords from generic to specific. It also shows the impact of different conversion rates on the overall CPA. It can be seen that niche terms that better indicate interest in a specific product such as 'women's car insurance' demand a higher fee (this may not be true for less competitive categories where niche terms can be cheaper). The table also shows the cost of PPC search in competitive categories. Advertising just on these four keywords to achieve a high ranking would cost €33 000 in a single day!

The cost per acquisition (CPA) can be calculated as follows:

$$\text{Cost per acquisition} = (100/\text{Conversion rate \%}) \times \text{Cost per click}$$

Table 7.1 Variation in cost per click for different key phrases in Google UK, 2004

Keywords	Clicks/Day	Average CPC	Cost/Day	Average position	CPA @ 25% conversion	CPA @ 10% conversion
Overall	5,714	€5.9	€33,317	1.3	€23.4	€58.4
'insurance'	3,800	€5.4	€20,396	1.3	€21.5	€53.7
'car insurance'	1,700	€6.6	€11,119	1.2	€26.2	€65.5
'cheap car insurance'	210	€8.4	€1,757	1.1	€33.5	€83.7
'women's car insurance'	4.1	€10.5	€43	1.0	€42.2	€105.4

Given the range in costs, two types of strategy can be pursued in PPC search engine advertising. If budget permits, a premium strategy can be followed to compete with the major competitors who are bidding the highest amounts on popular keywords. Such a strategy is based on being able to achieve an acceptable conversion rate once the customers are driven through to the web site. A lower-cost strategy involves bidding on lower cost, less popular phrases. These will generate less traffic, so it will be necessary to devise a lot of these phrases to match the traffic from premium keywords.

Optimizing pay per click

Each PPC keyphrase ideally needs to be managed individually in order to make sure that the bid (amount per click) remains competitive in order to show up in the top of the results. Experienced PPC marketers broaden the range of keyphrases to include lower volume phrases. Since each advertiser will typically manage thousands of keywords to generate clickthroughs, manual bidding soon becomes impractical. An example of the scale of a campaign on the Espotting network in 2003 is given below.

Some search engines include their own bid management tools, but if you or your agency is using different pay per click services such as Overture, Espotting and Google, it makes sense to use a single tool to manage them all. It also makes comparison of performance easier too. **Bid management software** such as Atlas One Point (www.atlasonepoint.com) and BidBuddy (www.bidbuddy.co.uk) can be used across a range of PPC services to manage keyphrases across multiple PPC ad networks and optimize the costs of search engine advertising.

The current CPC is regularly reviewed and your bid is reduced or increased to maintain the position you want according to different strategies and ROI limits with amounts capped such that advertisers do not pay more than the maximum they have deposited.

As more marketers have become aware of the benefits of PPC, competition has increased and this has driven up the cost per click (CPC) and so reduced its profitability. When writing the second edition, the average increase in CPC in the US was 25 per cent in a single quarter alone. We will soon reach the point where those bidding top will be the companies with the most efficient web sites for conversion to outcome and the highest potential lifetime value for cross-selling.

Beware of the fake clicks

Whenever the principle of PPC marketing is described to marketers, very soon a light bulb comes on and they ask, 'so we can click on competitors and bankrupt them'. Well actually no. The PPC ad networks detect multiple clicks from the same computer (IP address) and say they filter them out. However, there are techniques to mimic multiple clicks from different locations such as software tools to fake clicks and even services where you can pay a team of people across the world to click on these links. It is estimated that in competitive markets one in five of the clicks may be fake. While this can be factored into the conversion rates you will achieve, ultimately this could destroy PPC advertising. We believe, that in the longer term, PPC will move to something similar to an affiliate model when marketers only pay when a sale or some other outcome on a site occurs.

E-MARKETING EXCELLENCE

PriceRunner boost sales through the Espotting network

The campaign:

- PriceRunner purchased 15 000 + keyphrases
- These included variants on the generic term: 'cars' and also highly targeted keyphrases such as: '4x4', 'buying a saloon', 'BMW Z3'.
- The URL link for all keywords took consumers straight to the relevant pages.

The result:

- 25 000 click-throughs
- 26% went on to a retailer from PriceRunner and 18% conducted a sale
- Cost £3000 = Sales £1.2 million.

PriceRunner MD Jamal Hirani said simply 'Pay per click is the best form of advertising we have found'.

Source: Espotting (www.espotting.com)

This form of search advertising is less widely used, so we will only cover it briefly. In trusted feed, the ad or search listings content is automatically uploaded to a search engine from a catalogue or document database in a fixed format which often uses the XML data exchange standard (see http://www.w3.org/XML). This technique is mainly used by retailers who have large product catalogues for which prices and product descriptions may vary and so potentially become out-of-date in the SERPs. A related technique is **paid for inclusion (PFI)**. Here, PPC ads are placed within the search listings of some search engines interspersed with the organic results. In paid inclusion, the advertiser specifies pages with specific URLs for incorporation into the search engine organic listings. There is typically a fixed set-up fee and then also a PPC arrangement when the ad is clicked on. A crucial difference with other PPC types is that the position of the result in the search engine listings is not paid according to price bid, but the normal algorithm rules of that search engine to produce the organic listings. The service most commonly used for PFI is Overture Sitematch (www.overture.com) which supplies search engines such as Yahoo! and MSN. Note that Google does not offer trusted feed in its main search results at the time of writing (but it does offer a free XML feed to its main Froogle shopping catalogue).

SECTION SUMMARY 7.2

Search engines

Ensure you employ someone who is knowledgeable to optimize your position with search engines. Remember, the main techniques are:

1 Ensure you are represented on the main search engines.
2 Complete keyphrase analysis to identify phrases relevant to your market.
3 Start a search engine optimization initiative. This may involve restructuring your site to make it more accessible to search engines and including relevant keyphrases in the body copy, title tag and other page elements.
4 Maximize links from and to different sites – run a link-building campaign.
5 Review the relevance of pay per click advertising and trusted feeds and be sure to devote sufficient resources to deliver ROI from these.

7.3 Online PR

Online PR or e-PR leverages the network effect of the Internet. Remember the term 'Internet' is a contraction of 'interconnected networks'! Mentions of your brand or site on other sites are powerful in shaping opinions and driving visitors to your site. Furthermore, as we saw in the section on search engine optimization, the more quality backlinks there are from other sites to your site, the higher your site will be ranked in the natural or organic listings of the search engines.

Ranchhod *et al.* (2002) identify four key differences between online PR and traditional PR:

1 *The audience is connected to organizations.* Previously, there was detachment – PR people issued press releases which were distributed over the newswires, picked up by the media and then published in their outlets. These authors say:

> *'the communication channel was uni-directional. The institutions communicated and the audiences consumed the information. Even when the communication was considered a two-way process, the institutions had the resources to send information to audiences through a very wide pipeline, while the audiences had only a minuscule pipeline for communicating back to the institutions'.*

2 *The members of the audience are connected to each other.* Through publishing their own web sites or though e-mail, information can be rapidly distributed from person to person and group to group. The authors say:

> *'Today, a company's activity can be discussed and debated over the Internet, with or without the knowledge of that organization. In the new environment everybody is a communicator, and the institution is just part of the network'.*

3 *The audience has access to other information.* Often in the past, the communicator was able to make a statement where it would be difficult for the average audience member to challenge – the Internet facilitates rapid comparison of statements. The authors say:

> *'It takes a matter of minutes to access multiple sources of information over the Internet. Any statement made can be dissected, analysed, discussed and challenged within hours by interested individuals. In the connected world, information does not exist in a vacuum'.*

4 *Audiences pull information.* This point is similar to the last one. Previously there were limited channels in terms of television and press. Today there are many sources and channels of information – this makes it more difficult for the message to be seen. The authors say:

> *'Until recently, television offered only a few channels. People communicated with one another by post and by phone. In this conditions, it was easy for a public relations practitioner to make a message stand out'.*

Activities that are part of online PR include:

1 *Communicating with media (journalists) online.* Communicating with media (journalists) online uses the Internet as a new conduit to disseminate press releases through e-mail and on site. Options include setting up a press-release area on the web site; creating e-mail alerts about news, which journalists and other third parties can sign up to; and submitting your news stories or releases to online news feeds. Examples include: PR

Newswire: (www.prnewswire.com), Internetwire (www.internetwire.com/iwire/home), PressBox (www.pressbox.co.uk); PRWeb: (www.prweb.com) and Business Wire (www.businesswire.com).

2 *Link-building*. Link building is a key activity for search engine optimization. However, agencies involved with managing online PR need to understand the principles in order to support SEO. We consider this in more detail in Section 7.4 on partnerships.

3 *Blogs and RSS*. Web logs or **'blogs'** give an easy method of publishing web pages which are best described as online journals, diaries or news or events listings. Business blogs are created by people within an organization. They can be useful in showing the expertise of those within an organization, but need to be carefully controlled to avoid releasing damaging information. An example of a business blog used to showcase the expertise of its analysts is the Jupiter Research Analyst Weblogs (http://weblogs.jupiterresearch.com). **Really Simple Syndication (RSS)** is an extension of blogging where a blog, news or any type of content is received by specialist reader software such as RSS reader (www.rssreader.com). It offers a method of receiving news that uses a different broadcast method to e-mail, so is not subject to the same conflicts with SPAM or SPAM filters.

4 *Managing how your brand is presented on third-party sites*. 'Maximizing favourable mentions' implies minimizing unfavourable mentions of your company, brands, products or web sites on other third-party web sites. So online reputation management is an important part of online PR also. Googlealert (www.googlealert.com) and Google Alerts (www.google.com/alerts) will alert you when any new pages appear that contain a search phrase such as your company or brand names.

5 *Creating a buzz – viral marketing*. Viral marketing is discussed in Section 7.7.

Naturally, web addresses should also be quoted for all offline PR activity to complete the campaign's objective in driving traffic to the site.

E-MARKETING INSIGHT

Use PR to increase PR

Mike Grehan, a UK search engine marketing specialist, stresses the importance of the web to PR. He puts it this way (Grehan, 2004):

'Both online and off, the process is much the same when using PR to increase awareness, differentiate yourself from the crowd and improve perception.

Many offline PR companies now employ staff with specialist online skills. The web itself offers a plethora of news sites and services. And, of course, there are thousands and thousands of newsletters and zines covering just about every topic under the sun.

Never before has there been a better opportunity to get your message to the broadest geographic and multi-demographic audience. But you need to understand the pitfalls on both sides'.

In the article he also emphasizes the importance of link-building activities to build Page Rank – the 'PR' referred to in the title.

PORTALS

Understanding **portals** is a key to successful online PR and link-building. Portals are web sites that act as a gateway to the information on the Internet by providing search engines, directories and other services such as communities, personalized news or free e-mail. They are some of the best-known brands on the Internet such as Google, Yahoo!, MSN, Wanadoo, The BBC and more specialist portals. A good understanding of the types of portals available is important to maximizing traffic on a site. **Representation** is the watchword. Your organization, its products and services need to be represented on as wide a range of sites as possible.

There are three main types of portal to consider. **Horizontal portals** are the well-known portals mentioned above that offer a range of content and services to a broad audience. **Vertical portals** are specialist portals with a more targeted audience in comparison with a horizontal portal. B2B vertical portals which are online extensions of trade papers are important for companies promoting B2B services. One example is Construction News (www.cnplus.co.uk). **Geographical portals** are those centred on a particular locality which may include versions of horizontal and vertical portals. This may be a town, city, country or continent. Many horizontal and vertical portals will have geographic variants. In the United States Yahoo! has specific content for different metropolitan areas. Elsewhere country-specific versions such as www.yahoo.co.fr, www.yahoo.au, www.yahoo.de and www.yahoo.co.uk have been launched.

SECTION SUMMARY 7.3

Online PR

1 Online PR is maximizing favourable mentions of your company, brands, products or web sites on third-party web sites that are likely to be visited by your target audience.

2 An important part of this is online reputation management, which is controlling the reputation of an organization through monitoring and controlling messages placed about that organization.

3 There are four main differences between online PR and traditional PR: the audience is connected to the organizations; the members of the audience are connected to each other; the audience has access to other information; audiences pull information.

4 Activities that can be considered as online PR include: communicating with media (journalists) online; link-building; blogs and RSS; managing how your brand is presented on third-party sites; creating a buzz – viral marketing.

7.4 Online partnerships

We showed in Chapter 2 that partnerships are an important part of today's marketing mix. The same is true online. Resources must be devoted to managing your online partners. Many large organizations have specific staff to manage these relationships. In smaller organizations it is often neglected – a big missed opportunity. There are three key types of online partnerships that need to be managed: link-building, affiliate marketing and online sponsorship. All should involve a structured approach to managing links through to your site.

LINK-BUILDING

Link-building is a key activity for search engine optimization. It's simple logic! More quality links from relevant sites mean more quality visitors and more marketing outcomes. **Reciprocal links** are agreed between yourself and another organization. You should pro-actively seek out, using existing contacts and search engines, sites with a similar audience to yours. If a site looks suitable, the owner should be contacted with the offer of a reciprocal link. You should develop mini banner ads and standard link text summarizing your **Online value proposition** that you use for exchange. Remember that search engines ranking is dependent on the number of links into their site, so this is a further reason for this. From an SEO perspective inbound links without a corresponding outbound link are superior, but it is still worthwhile exchanging links with relevant partner sites.

E-MARKETING INSIGHT

Ken McGaffin on why linking matters

McGaffin (2004) provides a great introduction to link-building. The main principle of link-building is as he says:

> *'Create great content, link to great content and great content will link to you'.*

However, a structured link building campaign is also needed to maximize the number of quality inbound or backlinks which are from sites that have a high page rank and from pages with the right content and anchor text. Ken McGaffin recommends these stages in his report at www.linkingmatters.com:

1 Who links to you now?

2 Who links to your competitors?

3 Which sites could link to you?

4 Understand why external sites would link to you.

5 Set objectives.

6 Make sure your site is link friendly.

7 Which links are on your site?

8 Ask for inbound links.

9 Track and improve.

Tip: Use 'link:site' in Google to see the number of quality links into a page on your site as judged by Google with a high pagecount, e.g. www.google.com/search?q=link% 3Awww.linkingmatters.com.

AFFILIATE MARKETING

Affiliate marketing has become very popular with e-retailers since many achieve over 20 per cent of their online sales through affiliates. The great thing about affiliate marketing for the e-retailer is that the advertiser does not pay until the product has been purchased or a lead generated. It is sometimes referred to as 'zero risk advertising'. Contrast this with nearly all forms of offline promotion where there is not a direct link between the cost of promotion and the revenue gained. Affiliate marketing also contrasts with pay per click search engine marketing, where the retailer has to pay for the visitor irrespective of whether they purchase anything. As a result it is relatively easy to control affiliate expenditure and a company can readily ensure that spend is below the allowable cost of customer acquisition. However, affiliate marketing still has challenges in that affiliates can be potential competitors in search optimization and pay per click (driving up bid prices) and they may harm your brand by association if they refer to pornography or gambling on their site, for instance. Time needs to be allocated to manage these relationships. Affiliates can be rewarded for their loyalty to encourage more referrals by tiered programmes such as that run by Amazon.

Amazon was one of the earliest adopters of **affiliate marketing** and it now has hundreds of thousands of affiliates who drive visitors to Amazon through links in return for commission on products sold. Internet legend records that Jeff Bezos, the creator of Amazon, was chatting to someone at a cocktail party who wanted to sell books about divorce via her web site. Subsequently, Amazon.com launched its Associates Program in July 1996 and it is still going strong. Figure 7.6 summarizes the affiliate marketing process. To manage the process of finding affiliates, updating product information, tracking clicks and making payments, many companies use an **affiliate network** or **affiliate manager** such as Commission Junction (www.cj.com) or Trade Doubler (www.tradedoubler.com). Since the affiliate network takes a cut on each

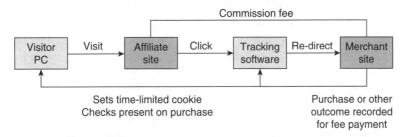

Figure 7.6 The affiliate marketing model (note that the tracking software and fee payment may be managed through an independent affiliate network manager)

sale, many merchants also try to set-up separate relationships with preferred affiliates often known as 'super affiliates'. Affiliate marketing is often thought to apply solely to e-retailers where the affiliate is paid if there is a purchase on the merchant site. In fact, payment can occur for any action which is recorded on the destination site, for example, through a 'thank you' post-transaction page after filling a form. This could be a quote for insurance, trial of a piece of software or registration for download of a paper.

E-MARKETING EXCELLENCE

ASOS.com (As Seen On Screen) builds more traffic with affiliates

ASOS.com is a fashion Internet store specializing in designer brands worn by celebrities (think, the Beckhams). In 2004, they were number two on hitwise.com above Top Shop, Figleaves.com, La Redoute, Marks & Spencer and Laura Ashley.

The ASOS affiliate programme drives between 25 and 30 per cent of ASOS online sales. Affiliates are offered between 7 and 10 per cent commission and there are also many hybrid deals in place. ASOS say that their affiliate programme is popular with affiliates since conversion rates are good and they offer affiliate incentives.

Source: E-consultancy Buyers Guide on Affiliates (www.e-consultancy.com)

ONLINE SPONSORSHIP

Online sponsorship is not straightforward. It's not just a case of mirroring existing 'real world' sponsorship arrangements in the 'virtual world'. There are many additional opportunities for sponsorship online which can be sought out, even if you don't have a big budget at your disposal.

Ryan and Whiteman (2000) define online sponsorship as:

> *'the linking of a brand with related content or context for the purpose of creating brand awareness and strengthening brand appeal in a form that is clearly distinguishable from a banner, button, or other standardized ad unit'.*

For the advertiser, online sponsorship has the benefit that their name is associated with an online brand that the site visitor is already familiar with. So, for users of the ISP Wanadoo, with whom they are familiar, sponsorship builds on this existing relationship and trust. Closely related is online 'co-branding' where there is an association between two brands.

Paid-for sponsorship of another site, or part of it, especially a portal for an extended period, is another way to develop permanent links. Co-branding is a lower-cost method of sponsorship and can exploit synergies between different companies. The e-marketing excellence box featured in Section 7.1 'Lexus achieve opt-ins through *Guardian* microsite' shows that sponsorship does not have to directly drive visitors to a brand site – it may be more effective if interaction occurs on the media owner's microsite.

A great business-to-business example of online sponsorship is offered by WebTrends who sponsor the customer information channel on ClickZ.com (www.clickz.com/experts). They combine this sponsorship with different ads each month offering e-marketers information about different topics such as search marketing, retention and conversion marketing through detailed whitepapers and 'Take 10' online video presentation by industry experts which could be downloaded by registered users. The objective of these ads was to encourage prospects to subscribe to the WebTrends WebResults e-newsletter and to assess purchase intent at signup enabling follow-up telemarketing by regional distributors. WebTrends reported the following results over a single year of sponsorship:

- List built to 100 000 WebResults total subscribers.
- 18 000 'Take 10' presentations.
- 13 500 seminar attendees.

E-MARKETING INSIGHT

How effective are online sponsorships?

A study by Performance Research (2001) compared differences in the perception of the online audience to banner ads and sponsorships. Respondents were shown a series of web page screens; for each, half of the respondents were shown a similar version with a banner advertisement, and the remaining half were shown a nearly identical image with web sponsorship identifications (such as 'Sponsored by', 'Powered by' and 'in association with').

The results were illuminating. Of the 500 respondents, ratings for different aspects of perception were:

- Trustworthy (28% for sponsorships to 15% for ads)
- Credible (28 to 16%)
- In tune with their interests (32 to 17%)
- Likely to enhance site experience (33% to 17%)
- More likely to consider purchasing a sponsor's product or service (41% to 23%)
- Less obtrusive (66% to 34%).

SECTION SUMMARY 7.4

Online partnerships

We reviewed three key types of online partnerships:

1 Link-building; obtaining links from third-party sites to a company site. This should be performed in a structured manner to maximize visitors from third-party sites and to help increase page rank within Google.

2 Affiliate marketing; a commission-based arrangement where referring sites are paid a fee for sales, leads or visitors. It is potentially a large source of quality traffic for e-retailers.

3 Online sponsorship; a long-term arrangement to associate a brand with a site, or part of a site.

7.5 Interactive advertising

A visitor who clicks on an **interactive (banner) ad** at an ad site is then **referred** through to the site of the company who paid for the banner ad which links through to a **destination site** as indicated by Figure 7.7. Many organizations link interactive ads to a specific campaign **microsite**. This provides content tailored to the campaign that appears immediately on click-through without the distractions of a link to the standard site. It can be independent of the media owner site, or it can be part of it, which can potentially improve response.

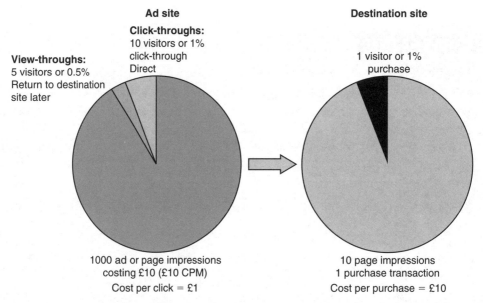

Figure 7.7   Measurement of interactive ads

Although banner advertising is often thought of simply as a traffic building technique, there are several alternative objectives which were first summarized by Cartellerieri *et al.* (1997):

- *Deliver content.* Information on-site to help communicate a company's offering.

- *Enable transaction.* An e-tailer intending to use banner ads to increase sales.

- *Shape attitudes.* An advert that is consistent with a company brand can help build brand awareness. Research services such as Dynamic Logic (www.dynamiclogic.com) are used by savvy online advertisers to assess the effectiveness of creative in terms of traditional branding metrics such as message association, brand awareness and purchase intent.

- *Solicit response.* An advert may be intended to identify new leads or as a start for two-way communication.

- *Encourage retention.* The advert may be placed to remind about the company and its service.

Online ads are one of the main revenue models for online media owners so there is a lot of research into how to make them effective. Here we will summarize the issues involved in interactive advertising by setting out five questions to ask when working with agencies when first exploring interactive advertising.

Q1. Mix of offline and online media (are we spending enough?)

The first question to ask is how much are you spending on online elements of campaigns, or, put another way – what is your optimal media mix to increase awareness and purchase intent within your target markets?

For any given campaign, media selection and the proportion of spend on online media will often be left to the media planner. But, depending on the agency used, they may play it safe by putting the ad spend into what they are familiar with and what may be most rewarding – offline media. Many **cross-media optimization studies (XMOS)** have shown that the optimal mix for low-involvement products is surprisingly high, with online advertising at 10–15 per cent of total spend.

E-MARKETING INSIGHT

XMOS studies show importance of online spend

XMOS research is designed to help marketers and their agencies answer the question 'What is the optimal mix of advertising vehicles across different media, in terms of frequency, reach and budget allocation, for a given campaign to achieve its marketing goals?' The mix between online and offline spend is varied to maximize campaign metrics such as reach, brand awareness and purchase intent. Table 7.2 summarizes the optimal mix identified for four famous brands. For example, Dove found that increasing the level of interactive advertising to 15% would have resulted in an increase in overall brand awareness of 8%. The proportion of online is small, but remember that many companies are spending less than 1% of their ad budgets online meaning that offline frequency is too high and they may not be reaching many consumers.

Table 7.2   Optimum media mix suggested by XMOS studies

Brand	TV	Magazine	Online
Colgate	75%	14%	11%
Kleenex	70%	20%	10%
Dove	72%	13%	15%
McDonald's	71%	16% (radio)	13%

Source: IAB (2004)

Q2. Are we exploiting the full range of ad formats?

The classic 468 × 60 rotating GIF banner ad is virtually dead – many online veterans suffer from 'banner blindness' – we simply filter out this content. Media owners now provide a choice of larger, richer formats which web users are more likely to notice. Research has shown that message association and awareness building is much higher for Flash-based ads, **rich media** ads and larger format rectangles and skyscrapers. Visit the rich media ads at www.eyeblaster.com or www.tangozebra.com and you will agree that they definitely can't be ignored.

Other online ad terms you will hear include '**interstitial**' (intermediate adverts before another page appears); and **superstitials** (pop-up adverts which require interaction by the user to close them down). Online advertisers face a constant battle with users who deploy pop-up blockers, or, less commonly, ad-blocking software. This is one reason why, in the UK in 2004, 40 per cent of online ad-spend is in PPC – it is more visible – can't be blocked (yet). Some media sites such as *The Guardian* now charge a premium for those users who don't want to see ads.

Q3. Are your ad buys smart?

Banner advertising is purchased for a specific period. It may be purchased for the ad to be shown or served on:

- The run-of-site (the entire site) and roadblocks
- A relevant section of site
- According to keywords entered on a search engine (the PPC model described earlier in the chapter).

Payment is typically according to the number of customers who view the page as a cost per thousand (CPM or CPT) ad or page impressions. Typical CPM is in the range of £10–£50. Other options that benefit the advertiser if they can be agreed are: per clickthrough, e.g. Valueclick (www.valueclick.co.uk) or per action such as a purchase on the destination site.

Q4. Are you using all the targeting options?

Online ads can be targeted through:

1 Purchasing on a site (or part of site) with a particular visitor profile
2 Purchasing at a particular time of day or week
3 Online behaviour – the ultimate in **dynamic ad targeting** according to types of content used. For example FT.com using software from Revenue Science can identify users in eight segments: business education, institutional investor, IT, luxury and consumer, management, personal finance, travel and private equity.

Banner ad networks provide the facility to advertise on a range of properties and target in a range of ways, as shown in the e-marketing excellence box.

Effective online advertisers build in flexibility to change targeting through time. Best practice is to start wide and then narrow focus – allow 20 per cent budget for high performing ad placements (high CTR and conversion).

E-MARKETING EXCELLENCE

Options for targeting advertising

Leading online media owners such as MSN (www.msn.com) and FT (www.ft.com) offer a range options for targeting:

1 Content targeting. Placement of advertising message on a particular interest site or within an entire interest category such as: automotive, business and finance or health.

2 Behavioural targeting. An audience can be targeted according to how they use the web or an individual site. For example, advertisers can select business users by delivering advertisements on Monday to Friday between 9 and 5, or leisure users by targeting messages in the evening hours. Ads can be targeted according to the types of content viewed, even when in a different part of the site.

3 User targeting. This enables advertisements to be placed according to specific traits of the audience including their geographic location (based on country or post code), domain type (e.g. educational users with addresses ending in .edu or .ac.uk can be targeted), business size or type according to SIC code or even by the company they work for based on the company domain name. This is possible where users create a profile on a site such as Yahoo! (www.yahoo.com) or FT (www.ft.com) or through automated analysis of the type of content they consume.

4 Tech targeting. This is based on user hardware, software and Internet access provider.

Q5. Are you using creative effectively?

Avantmarketer (www.avantmarketer.com) summarizes these tips for effective online creative:

- Brand the first frame with a brand identity (or the top of skyscrapers).
- Tell a story, but each frame should stand alone.
- Ditch 'Click here!', instead use an action verb such as 'Sign-up now' or 'Download our whitepaper' (many would advise using 'Click here' for some ad types).
- Use high contrast.
- Keep it simple – only use a few elements in ad creative.
- Include a human face where possible.
- Flash makes producing higher impact ads more practical.

Choosing creative for different ad placements is difficult to predict and requires hard work. In an iMediaConnection interview, ING Direct VP of Marketing, Jurie Pieterse highlighted:

> *'Another lesson we learned is the importance of creative. It's critical to invest in developing various creative executions to test them for best performance and constantly*

introduce new challengers to the top performers. We've also learned there's no single top creative unit – different creative executions and sizes perform differently from publisher to publisher'.

iMediaConnection (2003)

Finally, consider your options for online sponsorship which is closely related to interactive advertising (online sponsorship is covered in Section 7.4 Online partnerships).

SECTION SUMMARY 7.5

Interactive ads

Interactive advertisements can help build site traffic, but also have a role in building brand recognition. Rich media and large format ads are effective in targeting visitors through placements on specialized portals and dynamic or behavioural ad targeting. Acquiring customers by banners paid for by CPM is relatively expensive and alternative forms of promotion or payment according to results is preferable.

7.6 Opt-in e-mail

Savvy e-marketers understand that **opt-in e-mail** is a powerful online communications tool. As with direct mail it is most widely used for direct response, but e-newsletters in particular can also achieve branding objectives. It enables a targeted message to be pushed out to a customer to inform and remind and they are certain to view at least the subject line within their e-mail inbox, even if is only to delete it. Contrast this with the web – a pull medium where customers will only visit your site if there is a reason or a prompt to do this. But there is a problem; in the minds of many Internet users, e-mail is evil. It is **SPAM**, unsolicited e-mail sent by unscrupulous traders. Some say SPAM stands for 'Sending Persistent Annoying E-mail', but it actually originates from the Monty Python sketch. Remember that SPAM is now outlawed in many countries.

To achieve the potential benefits of opt-in e-mail, marketers should take careful measures to avoid SPAM. This section explains how to achieve this.

Opt-in is the key to successful e-mail marketing. Customer choice is the watchword. Before starting an e-mail dialogue with customers, companies must ask them to provide their e-mail address and then give them the option of 'opting into' further communications and selecting their communications preferences, for example the frequency of e-mail and type of content. Privacy law in many countries requires that they should proactively opt-in to by checking a box (showing consent in some way). E-mail lists can also be rented where customers have opted in to receive e-mail.

Opt-in e-mail options for customer acquisition

For acquiring new visitors and customers to a site, there are three main options for e-mail marketing. From the point of view of the recipient, these are:

1 *Cold e-mail campaign.* In this case, the recipient receives an opt-in e-mail from an organization who has rented an e-mail list from a consumer e-mail list provider such as Experian

(www.experian.com), Claritas (www.claritas.com) or IPT Limited (www.myoffers.co.uk) or a business e-mail list provider such as Mardev (www.mardev.com), Corpdata (www.corpdata.com) or trade publishers/event providers such as VNU. Although they have agreed to receive offers by e-mail, the e-mail is effectively cold. For example, a credit card provider could send a cold e-mail to a list member who is not currently their member. It is important to use some form of '**statement of origination**' otherwise the message may be considered SPAM. Cold e-mails tend to have higher CPAs than other forms of online marketing, but different lists should still be evaluated.

2 *Co-branded e-mail*. Here, the recipient receives an e-mail with an offer from a company they have a reasonably strong affinity with. For example, the same credit card company could partner with a mobile service provider such as Vodafone and send out the offer to their customer (who has opted-in to receive e-mails from third parties). Although this can be considered a form of cold e-mail, it is warmer since there is a stronger relationship with one of the brands and the subject line and creative will refer to both brands. Co-branded e-mails tend to be more responsive than cold e-mails to rented lists since the relationship exists and fewer offers tend to be given.

3 *Third-party e-newsletter*. In this visitor acquisition option, a company publicizes itself in a third-party e-newsletter. This could be in the form of an ad, sponsorship or PR (editorial) which links through to a destination site. These placements may be set-up as part of an interactive advertising ad buy since many e-newsletters also have permanent versions on the web site. Since e-newsletter recipients tend to engage with them by scanning the headlines or reading them if they have time, e-newsletter placements can be relatively cost effective.

Opt-in e-mail options for prospect conversion and customer retention (house-list)

E-mail is most widely used as a prospect conversion and customer retention tool using an opt-in house-list of prospects and customers who have given permission to a company to contact them. For example, Lastminute.com has built a house list of over 10 million prospects and customers across Europe. Successful e-mail marketers adopt a strategic approach to e-mail and develop a contact or **touch strategy** that plans the frequency and content of e-mail communications. Some options include:

- *Conversion e-mail* – someone visits a web site and expresses interest in a product or service by registering and providing their e-mail address although they do not buy. Automated follow-up e-mails can be sent out to persuade the recipient to trial the service. For example, betting company William Hill found that automated follow-up e-mails converted twice as many registrants to place their first bet compared to registrants who did not receive an e-mail.

- *Regular e-newsletter type* – consider options of different frequency such as weekly, monthly or quarterly with different content for different audiences and segments.

- *House-list campaign* – these are periodic e-mails to support different objectives such as encouraging trial of a service or newly launched product, repeat purchases or reactivation of customers who no longer use a service.

- *Event-triggered* – these tend to be less regular and are sent out perhaps every 3 or 6 months when there is news of a new product launch or an exceptional offer.

● *E-mail sequence* – software can send out a series of e-mails with the interval between e-mails determined by the marketer.

Think about which approaches you use now and which others may you consider. You can read more about how e-mail is used strategically as part of Customer Relationship Management in *Total E-mail Marketing* (Chaffey, 2003) another book in this series, and also in Section 8.2 on **permission marketing**.

E-MARKETING EXCELLENCE

MAD use sequential e-mail to assist conversion

MAD (www.mad.co.uk) is a marketing-specific portal accessed through online subscriptions. It offers a trial one-month subscription to its service. During this period, a series of e-mails is used to help convert the prospect to a full subscription. E-mails are sent out at approximately 3, 10, 25 and 28 days to encourage a subscription before the trial lapses.

E-MAIL MARKETING SUCCESS FACTORS

Effective e-mail marketing shares much in common with effective direct e-mail copy. We suggest you use the mnemonic 'CRITICAL' as a checklist for e-mail marketing success factors. CRITICAL is a checklist of questions to ask about your e-mail campaigns (Chaffey, 2003). It stands for:

● *Creative* – This assesses the design of the e-mail including its layout, use of colour and image and the copy (see below).
● *Relevance* – Does the offer and creative of the e-mail meet the needs of the recipients?
● *Incentive* (or offer) – The WIFM factor or 'What's in it for me' for the recipient. What benefit does the recipient gain from clicking on the hyperlink(s) in the e-mail? For example, a prize draw is a common offer for B2C brands.
● *Targeting and timing* – Targeting is related to the relevance. Is a single message sent to all prospects or customers on the list or are e-mails with tailored creative, incentive and copy sent to the different segments on the list? Timing refers to when the e-mail is received; the time of day, day of the week, point in the month and even the year; does it relate to any particular events. There is also the relative timing – when is it received compared to other marketing communications – this depends on the integration.
● *Integration* – Are the e-mail campaigns part of your integrated marketing communications? Questions to ask include: are the creative and copy consistent with my brand? Does the message reinforce other communications? Does the timing of the e-mail campaign fit with offline communications?
● *Copy* – This is part of the creative and refers to the structure, style and explanation of the offer together with the location of hyperlinks in the e-mail.

- *Attributes* (of the e-mail) – Assess the message characteristics such as the subject line, from address, to address, date/time of receipt and format (HTML or text). Send out Multipart/ MIME messages which can display HTML or text according to the capability of the e-mail reader. Offer choice of HTML or text to match users' preferences.

- *Landing page* (or microsite) – These are terms given for the page(s) reached after the recipient clicks on a link in the e-mail. Typically, on clickthrough, the recipient will be presented with an online form to profile or learn more about them. Designing the page so the form is easy to complete can affect the overall success of the campaign.

Designing direct e-mail copy is as involved as designing direct mail and many similar principles apply. Effective e-mail should:

- Grab attention in subject line and body.
- Be brief and be relevant to target.
- Be personalized – Not Dear Valued Customer, but Dear Ms Smith.
- Provide opt-out or unsubscribe option by law.
- Hyperlink to web site for more detailed content.
- Have clear call-to-action at the start and end of the message.
- Be tested for effectiveness.
- Operate within legal and ethical constraints for a country.

SECTION SUMMARY 7.6

Opt-in e-mail

E-mail is an effective push online communications method. It is essential that e-mail is opt-in, otherwise it is illegal SPAM. Consider options for customer acquisition including cold e-mail, co-branded e-mails and placements in third-party e-mails. For house list e-mails, experiment with achieving the correct frequency, or give customers the choice. Consider automated event triggered e-mails. Work hard on e-mail design and maintaining up-to-date lists. Stay within the law.

7.7 Viral marketing

Ideally, viral marketing is a clever idea, a shocking idea, or a highly informative idea which makes compulsive viewing. It can be a video clip, TV ad, a cartoon, a funny picture, a poem, song, political message, or a news item. It's so amazing that it makes people want to pass it on.

Viral marketing harnesses the network effect of the Internet and can be effective in reaching a large number of people rapidly in the same way as a computer virus can affect many machines around the world.

Like most buzz words 'viral marketing' means different things to different people. A viral marketing execution certainly needs to create a buzz to be successful. The two main forms of viral marketing are best known as 'word-of-mouth' and 'word-of-mouse'. Both rely on networks of people to spread the word.

To make a viral campaign happen, Justin Kirby of viral marketing specialists DMC (www.dmc.co.uk) suggests there are three things that are needed (Kirby, 2003):

1 Creative material – the 'viral agent'. This includes the creative message or offer and how it is spread (text, image, video).
2 Seeding. Identifying web sites, blogs or people to send e-mail to start the virus spreading.
3 Tracking. To monitor the effect and to assess the return from the cost of developing the viral agent and seeding.

We distinguish between these types of viral e-mail mechanisms.

1 *Pass along e-mail viral*. This is where e-mail alone is used to spread the message. It is an e-mail with a link to a site such as a video or an attachment. Towards the end of a commercial e-mail it does no harm to prompt the first recipient to forward the e-mail along to interested friends or colleagues. Even if only one in 100 responds to this prompt, it is still worth it. The dramatic growth of Hotmail, reaching 10 million subscribers in just over a year, was effectively down to pass-along as people received e-mails with a signature promoting the service. Word-of-mouth helped too.
Pass-along or forwarding has worked well for video clips, either where they are attached to the e-mail or the e-mail contains a link to download the clip. If the e-mail has the 'WOW!' factor, of which more later, a lot more than one in 100 will forward the e-mail. This mechanism is what most people consider to be viral, but there are the other mechanisms that follow too.
2 *Web facilitated viral (e-mail prompt)*. Here, the e-mail contains a link/graphic to a web page with 'e-mail a friend' or 'e-mail a colleague'. A web form is used to collect data of the e-mail address to which the e-mail should be forwarded, sometimes with an optional message. The company then sends a separate message to the friend or colleague.
3 *Web facilitated viral (web prompt)*. Here it is the web page such as a product catalogue or white paper which contains a link/graphic to 'e-mail a friend' or colleague. A web form is again used to collect data and an e-mail is subsequently sent.
4 *Incentivized viral*. This is distinct from the types above since the e-mail address is not freely given. This is what we need to make viral really take-off. By offering some reward for providing someone else's address we can dramatically increase referrals. A common offer is to gain an additional entry for entry into a prize draw. Referring more friends gains more entries to the prize draw. With the right offer, this can more than double response. The incentive is offered either by e-mail (option 2 above) or on a web page (option 3). In this case, there is a risk of breaking privacy laws since the consent of the e-mail recipient may not be freely given. Usually only a single follow-up e-mail by the brand is permitted. So you should check with the lawyers if considering this.

5 *Web-link viral*. But online viral isn't just limited to e-mail. If you click on any of the links in this article – that can also be considered to be online viral marketing or you could call it online PR. Links in discussion group postings or **blogs** that are from an individual are also in this category. Either way, it's important when seeding the campaign to try to get as many targeted online and offline mentions of the viral agent as you can.

E-MARKETING INSIGHT

Seth Godin and the ideavirus

Godin (2001) writes about the importance of the ideavirus as a marketing tool. He describes it as 'digitally augmented word-of-mouth' and viral marketing is seen as one form of the ideavirus. What differences does the ideavirus have from word-of-mouth? First, transmission is more rapid, second, transmission tends to reach a larger audience and third, it can be persistent – reference to a negative comment about a product or a service on a site such as Epinions (www.epinions.com) remains online to be read at a later time. Godin emphasizes the importance of starting small with a niche audience he describes as a 'hive' and then using advocates in spreading the virus – he refers to them as 'sneezers'.

SECTION SUMMARY 7.7

Viral marketing

With viral techniques, traffic is built either through using e-mail (virtual word-of-mouth) or real-world word-of-mouth to spread the message from one person to the next.

7.8 Offline traffic building

In this section we will see that offline communications is a key component of the e-communications mix. Companies need to decide on whether advertising is *incidental* or *specific*; whether specialist messages need to be communicated and the mix of techniques used. All ten offline communications tools from Smith and Taylor (2004) can and should be used to build online traffic. These ten tools are referred to in Table 2.1. They are: advertising, selling, sales promotion, PR, sponsorship, direct mail, exhibitions, merchandising, packaging, and word-of-mouth – can be used to communicate or promote in the online or offline world.

How significant is offline promotion? After evaluating the range of online promotion techniques available, you may be asking yourself, 'if all these online techniques are effective, why do companies spend so much on offline advertising?' In fact, the spend on online advertising is dwarfed by spend on advertising in traditional media such as print, TV and radio. At the start of the new millennium global online advertising spend was around 1 per cent of total advertising. On average, it has still not reached double figures, but some leading adopters are now spending more than 10 per cent of their budget online.

To summarize, a key decision for e-marketers is deciding on balance of spend between online and offline promotion as we will see in Section 7.10 on resourcing.

WHAT ARE WE COMMUNICATING OFFLINE?

Important aspects of the online brand to communicate are:

- The URL (of course)
- Online value proposition (see Section 6.3)
- Traditional brand values
- Sales promotions and offers.

Let us now briefly consider four of the main tools, advertising, word-of-mouth, PR and direct mail.

Advertising

Early attempts by many traditional clicks and mortar companies to advertise their online offering were limited to **incidental advertising** where the company's web site address was added as a footnote to the advert with no attempt to explain the online proposition or drive a web response. For dotcoms, it is vital to use offline advertising to communicate their **online value proposition** in specific adverts and traditional companies are increasingly using this approach as more sales are achieved online. Online recruitment agency Monster.com saw its traffic quadruple in the 24 hours following adverts in the prime US superbowl spot. Many organizations now run **web response ad campaigns** where one of the main objectives is to achieve web site visits. The web may be used to request a sample, enter a competition, find further information or if appropriate, buy online. Enlightened FMCG brands are now using offline advertising in conjunction with the web to get customers to interact with their brand, profile them and add value.

Word-of-mouth

Word of mouth is a powerful technique of offline promotion. An urban myth is that if someone successfully buys a book online they will tell 10 other people, but if fulfilment is poor, they will tell 20 people! Offline communications techniques such as PR and advertising should be aimed at stimulating word-of-mouth and online viral techniques can also promote this.

PR

PR is a powerful and relatively low-cost form of offline communications. There is good demand amongst the general and specialist media for stories about e-everything. PR can leverage events such as site launches and re-launches with new services, particularly when they are first in a sector. Press releases can be issued through normal channels, but using e-mail linked to the full story on the web site to get information to the journalists faster. Options for getting mentions on the new online-only news sources should be explored. Some defensive, reactive PR may be necessary by scanning press releases on other company sites. The scope for PR stunts related to web sites is limitless. In the US a town, Half.com, has been renamed to be the first dotcom town.

Direct mail and physical reminders

Physical reminders about web site offers are important since most of our customers will spend more time in the real-world than the virtual world. What is in our customers' hands and on their desk top will act as a prompt to visit your site and overcome the weakness of the web as a pull medium. Examples include brochures, catalogues, business cards, point of sale material, trade shows, direct mail sales promotions, postcards (in magazines), inserts (in magazines), password reminders (for extranets).

E-MARKETING INSIGHT

Jay Walker of Priceline on offline promotion

Jay Walker, co-founder of Priceline.com, a cybermediary for consumer products, has said: 'Priceline.com has been about building a brand as opposed to building traffic. In advertising, you're building a larger context around who you are as a company. To do that, online advertising just doesn't cut it'. In its first 12 months, Priceline.com spent $40 million to $50 million on old-media advertising.

SECTION SUMMARY 7.8

Offline promotion

Specific offline communications are vital to traffic building for both dotcoms and clicks and mortar companies. Traditional advertising, PR and direct mail are all essential to communicate the URL and IVP. Remember that although we have reviewed online and offline traffic building techniques separately, they need to be part of integrated e-marketing communications.

7.9 Control

This section summarizes how the offline techniques described in other sections of this chapter can be harnessed together and their effectiveness can be assessed. We explore: measuring traffic origin, content and quality. It is closely linked to Section 7.10 on resourcing which explains how the different techniques should be balanced. Key control questions that managers need to answer are:

1 *How is budget allocated?* This is covered in more detail in the resourcing section where it will be seen that often the typical amount spent on online and offline promotion is similar.

2 *How is the contribution of different promotional tools calculated?* The contribution can only be calculated if the right control processes are in place. Using data from server log files the following referrals can be measured directly: affiliate sites, banner ads, partners and links. Market research can be used to estimate customer acquisition from other sources such as: traditional advertising, word of mouth and PR.

3 *What is the cost of acquisition?* The cost of customer acquisition is important when assessing each promotion technique. As mentioned above, cost of acquisition can be measured as the cost of acquiring a visitor to site, the cost of acquiring a lead or a customer who makes a purchase. The suitability of each measure will depend on the type of site, but for media sites selling advertising space, cost of visitor acquisition would be most relevant and for e-tailers, cost of customer acquisition will be relevant.

4 *What is traffic quality?* Traffic quality is dependent on whether visitors are within the target group of customers and their propensity to buy. A key measure for traffic quality is **conversion rate** which is calculated by dividing the number of new customers by new visitors. **Repeat visits** are also important to traffic quality. To see whether these objectives are being achieved, customers need to be **tagged** through time, but remember the privacy law implications. **Web analytics** are one method of achieving this.

E-MARKETING INSIGHT

Identifying the contribution from different referrers

With a little forethought, it is possible to collect good information about the contribution of traffic from different referrers. Here are some suggestions:

- Don't link through to the home page, but use a microsite specific to each campaign or referrer (sometimes called a CURL, or campaign specific URL).
- Use a different web page or directory for different advertisers, e.g. www.name.com/promotion_name, if necessary a number of pages can be used for different referrers, which then **redirect** through to a common page.
- Enable the referrers option in the server log file (see below) to collect information about the relative importance of different referrers.
- Ask the customer how they were referred through conventional or online questionnaires.

WEB ANALYTICS

Valuable information on the effectiveness of promotion is available from **web analytics tools**. These software tools record 'site statistics' such as the volume of traffic, its source (referring sites) and which content is popular on site including **clickstreams** of each visit. Two alternative technical approaches are commonly used to capture this information. Traditionally, server-based tools such as WebTrends or Urchin have been popular. These work by summarizing across different time periods, all the events recorded in a transaction log file every time a web page or graphic is downloaded for viewing by a site visitor. More recently, browser-based measurement tools such as HitBox, Indextools, WebTrends and Red Sheriff have become more popular since these are more accurate. Browser-based tools work by including a small piece of Javascript in each page which records the page view on a separate (remote) server. Browser based tools such as that shown in Figure 7.8 have the advantage that information can be accessed in real time and visits to pages are recorded each time a page

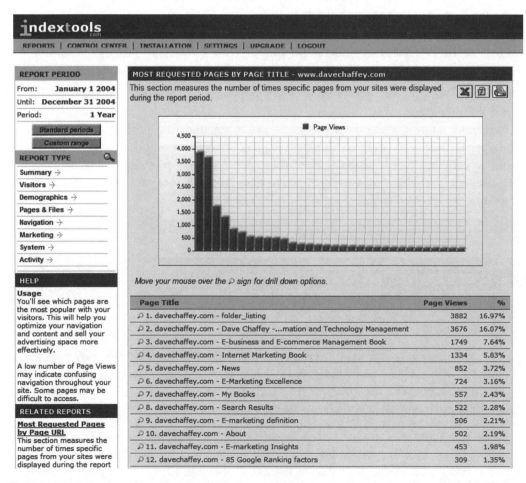

Figure 7.8 Example web analytics tool used to record the most popular pages on DaveChaffey.com (www. davechaffey.com)

is viewed. This contrasts with the server-based approach where repeat visits may not be identified if the pages have already been loaded and are cached by the browser or a server. A combination of tools is often used since server-based tools are best for managing server load, page errors and identifying crawling by search robots. Often the hosting company will provide basic visitor statistics, however the full insight possible from a tool such as Clicktracks (www.clicktracks.com) or the tools mentioned above is needed to really drive your results from digital marketing.

The type of information available from web analytics software includes:

1 *Referring sites*. The proportion of visitors from different sites indicates the relative importance of referrers.

2 *Referral time*. The time of arrival of visitors can be used to plan the timing of future campaigns.

3 *Search engine keywords*. Search engine keyphrases indicate the behaviour of customers trying to find your site. Using the important keywords in web site copy in PPC search can help your position in search engine listings.

4 *Conversion rates*. Conversion to key outcome pages such as registration pages or purchase pages can be calculated to understand the effectiveness of site design, messaging and incentives.

5 *Stickiness*. The duration of visitors on site can be used to assess whether visitors are finding what they require.

6 *Repeat visits*. During a campaign we need to see whether the proportion of visitors on the site are new or existing customers. Cookies or registration on a web site need to be used to estimate repeat visitors. Here there are relatively few new users, so a banner campaign is probably not currently active and most visitors are looking for technical support.

E-MARKETING INSIGHT

Eric Peterson demystifies web analytics

Eric, an analyst specializing in web analytics, defines it as:

> *'Web analytics is the assessment of a variety of data, including web traffic, web-based transactions, web server performance, usability studies, user submitted information (i.e. surveys), and related sources to help create a generalized understanding of the visitor experience online'.*

Note that in addition to what are commonly referred to as 'site statistics', sales transactions, usability and researching customers' views through surveys are also included. The definition could also refer to comparison of site visitor volumes and demographics relative to competitors using panels and ISP collected data.

We believe, though, that the definition can be improved further – it suggests analysis for the sake of it – whereas the purpose of analytics should be emphasized. Our definition is:

'Web analytics is the customer-centred evaluation of the effectiveness of Internet-based marketing in order to improve the business contribution of online channels to an organization'.

Sources: Peterson (2004), www.davechaffey.com

PANEL DATA AND AUDITING

In addition to measuring traffic directly from a site, it is also possible to use **panel data** to estimate your traffic, break it down by socio-demographic characteristics and compare it to competitors. A panel member is profiled in terms of socio-demographics and software is installed on their PC to monitor the sites they visit. Examples of online panel data providers are Nielsen Netratings (www.netratings.com) and Comscore (www.comscore.com). Similar data is available from Hitwise (www.hitwise.com) which aggregates data from ISPs it has signed agreements with to show the relative popularity of sites (online audience share) within a sector. Other competitor data such as sites popular with your visitors before and after they visit your site and keyphrases used to reach competitor sites are used.

SECTION SUMMARY 7.9

Control

Control activities should target assessing the effectiveness of promotion campaigns against objectives of: traffic volume; traffic quality (marketing outcomes); cost of visitor and customer acquisition for different promotional techniques. Log file analysers and panel data are important in making this evaluation.

7.10 Resourcing

Resourcing is about achieving the correct balance of investment between traffic building and other e-marketing activities. Other aspects of resourcing that must be balanced are between online and offline promotion and between campaign and continuous traffic building activities.

Table 7.3 provides an example of the promotional mix for a fictitious company. There are a range of promotional techniques comprising the total budget. Which would you say are most cost effective in terms of their contribution to revenue? It is apparent that the lower-cost methods shown at the bottom of the table including affiliates, word-of-mouth, PR and link building are all effective.

Table 7.3 Relative effectiveness of different forms of marketing communications

Media	Budget (%)	Contribution (%)	Effectiveness
Print (off)	20	10	0.5
TV (off)	25	10	0.25
Radio (off)	10	5	0.5
PR (off)	5	15	3
WoM (off)	0	25	Infinite
Banners (on)	20	20	1
Affiliate (on)	20	10	0.5
Links (on)	0	3	Infinite
Search engine registration (on)	0	2	Infinite

Watson *et al.* (2000), although dated, does suggest the different levels of effectiveness of media for digital marketing. Therefore, constant monitoring of integration is crucial.

BALANCE BETWEEN TRAFFIC BUILDING AND OTHER E-MARKETING COSTS

You also need to be clear about what is the right balance between expenditure on:

1 Web-design or creation

2 Service or maintenance

3 Traffic building (promotion).

It has been suggested that many European sites have allocated resources between design, service and traffic in the ratio 5 to 2 to 1. However, for many US sites, these were in the order 1 to 2 to 5, i.e. with the emphasis firmly on traffic. You need to review carefully what is right for your business.

Figure 7.9 shows two alternatives for balancing these three variables. Figure 7.9 (a) is a model where traffic building expenditure exceeds service and design. This is more typical for a dot-company that needs to promote its brand. Figure 7.9 (b) is a model where traffic building expenditure is less than service and design. This is more typical for a traditional bricks and mortar company that already has a brand recognition and an established customer base. What is the balance of your investment to date? In retrospect has it been right?

BALANCE BETWEEN ONLINE AND OFFLINE PROMOTION

Defining the correct balance between online and offline promotion is another key aspect of resourcing. Which of the options in Figure 7.10 would you say is the best balance for your organization? Surveys indicate that for many companies, situation (b) is most common. However there is a general trend to higher spend on online promotion, possibly because of better targeting and a direct response between advertising and site visits.

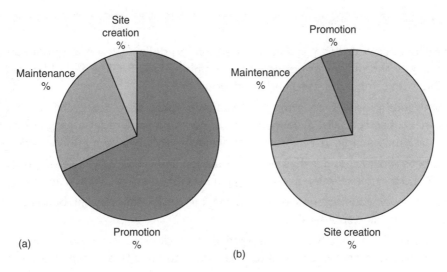

Figure 7.9 Alternatives for balance between expenditure on e-marketing

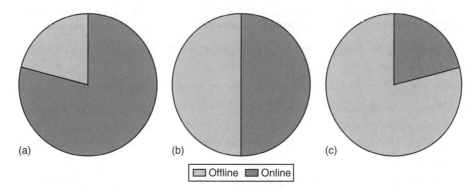

Figure 7.10 Alternative options for investment in online and offline traffic building

---

BALANCE OF CAMPAIGN AND CONTINUOUS TRAFFIC BUILDING

It would be a mistake to spend an entire promotion budget on campaigns. A proportion should be left for expenditure required every month of the year for search engine re-registration and updating; updating copy to improve search engine positions; link building; managing long-term sponsorship arrangements and direct opt-in e-mail.

SECTION SUMMARY 7.10

Resourcing

Resourcing is about achieving the right balance of: promotion, service and design; online and offline promotion and campaign activities and continuous traffic building. For campaigns, resourcing decisions include: banner run length, ad-weighting, targeting and campaign size.

CHAPTER SUMMARY

1 Traffic building or visitor acquisition is dependent on defining the appropriate *targets* of traffic quantity and quality, using the correct combination of online and offline *techniques* and using both campaign-based and continuous *timing*.

2 An organization presence on a range of search engines should be achieved and then optimized by using specialist techniques such as rewriting copy, redesign and link-building. Pay per click marketing can be essential to achieve visibility in competitive markets.

3 Organizations should consider their online reputation and visibility by reviewing options for online PR and their representation on a range of portals: horizontal, vertical and geographic.

4 You should review your potential online partners to drive visitors by link-building, affiliate marketing and online sponsorship.

5 A wide range of different types of interactive ads including skyscraper, large rectangle and rich-media formats can be used to refer traffic to the site and can also be used for brand building.

6 Opt-in e-mail is an effective method of communications since it is a push method delivering information to the mail inbox of the audience. E-mail options include newsletters, promotional campaigns and as a conversion tool.

7 Viral e-marketing techniques involve transmitting a marketing message using the word-of-mouth or online word-of-mouth (e-mail and chat).

8 Offline communications are essential to achieve reach amongst an audience to increase awareness and explain the Internet value proposition.

9 Control supported by web analytics software should be in place to assess the effectiveness of promotional campaigns against objectives of traffic volume, traffic quality and cost of acquisition.

10 Resourcing issues involve budgeting a suitable expenditure on site creation, maintenance and advertising; getting the right balance between the mix of online and offline promotional techniques and campaign-based and continuous traffic building.

 ## References

Atlas DMT (2004) The Atlas Rank Report: How Search Engine Rank Impacts Traffic. Available from Research Insights, http://www.atlasdmt.com/insights.

Cartellerieri, C., Parsons, A., Rao, V. and Zeisser, M. (1997) The real impact of Internet advertising. *The Mckinsey Quarterly*, Vol. 3, pp. 44–63.

Chaffey, D. (2003) *Total E-mail Marketing*. Butterworth-Heinemann, Elsevier, Oxford.

Van Doren, D., Fechner, D. and Green-Adelsberger, K. (2000) Promotional strategies on the World Wide Web. *Journal of Marketing Communications*, Vol. 6, pp. 21–35.

Farris, J. and Langendorf, L. (2001) Engaging customers in e-business, How to build sales, relationships and results with e-mail. White paper available online at www.e2software.com.

Grehan, M. (2004) Increase your PR by increasing your PR. *E-marketing News*, November. http://www.e-marketing-news.co.uk/november.html#pr.

Godin, S. (2001) *Unleashing the ideavirus*. Available online at: www.ideavirus.com.

Hoffman, D.L. and Novak, T.P. (2000) How to acquire customers on the web. *Harvard Business Review*, May–June, pp. 179–88. Available online at: http://ecommerce.vanderbilt.edu/papers.html.

IAB (2004) XMOS research centre. Interactive Advertising Bureau (www.iab.net/xmos).

iMediaConnection (2003) Interview with ING Direct VP of Marketing, Jurie Pieterse http://www.imediaconnection.com/content/1333.asp.

Kirby, J. (2003) Online viral marketing: next big thing or yesterday's fling? New Media Knowledge, March. http://www.nmk.co.uk/knowledge_network/kn_item.cfm?ItemID=4884&ThreadID=46.

Performance Research (2001) Performance Research Study 'Mastering Sponsorship On-Line'. http://www.performanceresearch.com/web-based-sponsorships.htm.

Peterson, E.T. (2004) *Web Analytics Demystified: A Marketer's Guide to Understanding How Your Web Site Affects Your Business*. Available from www.webanalyticsdemystified.com.

McGaffin, K. (2004) *Linking Matters. How To Create An Effective Linking Strategy To Promote Your Web Site*. Published at www.linkingmatters.com.

Pincott, G. (2000) Web site promotion strategy. White paper from Millward Brown Intelliquest. Available online at www.intelliquest.com.

Ranchhod, A., Gurau, C. and Lace, J. (2002) On-line messages: developing an integrated communications model for biotechnology companies. *Qualitative Market Research: An International Journal*, 5(1), 6–18.

Ryan, J. and Whiteman, N. (2000) Online Advertising Glossary: Sponsorships. ClickZ Media Selling channel, 15 May.

Smith, P.R. and Taylor, J. (2004) *Marketing Communications – An integrated approach*. Kogan Page, London, 4th edition.

Watson, R., Zinkhan, G. and Pitt, L. (2000) Integrated Internet Marketing. *Communications of the ACM*, June, Vol. 43, No, 6, pp. 97–102.

Williamson, D. (2001) Lastminute.com sets off Easter campaign. *Revolution*, 4 April.

 ## Further reading

Hoffman, D.L. and Novak, T.P. (2000) How to acquire customers on the web. *Harvard Business Review*, May–June, pp. 179–88. Available online at: http://ecommerce.vanderbilt.edu/papers.html.

 ## Web links

Atlas DMT Research Insights, (www.atlasdmt.com/insights). Detailed research on effectiveness of search marketing and advertising such as impact of frequency and reach on ad effectiveness.

ClickZ (www.clickz.com). An excellent portal for the online marketer to learn more, with channels for different e-tools such as e-mail marketing, search and ad buying.

Doubleclick Knowledge Central (www.doubleclick.com/knowledge_central). US, European and Asian trends on responsiveness to e-mail and advertising campaigns.

E-consultancy (www.e-consultancy.com). One of the best sources for details about traffic building tools such as search and affiliates. Includes specific channels on each with buyers' guides and best practice guides.

E-metrics (www.emetrics.org). Articles and insights about web analytics collated by Jim Sterne of Target Marketing.

Email Reaction (www.emailreaction.com). Knowledge section contains detailed articles by Dave Chaffey on success factors for e-mail marketing.

iMediaConnection (www.imediaconnection.com). 'State of the art' articles and guidance on interactive advertising techniques.

Searchenginewatch (www.searchenginewatch.com). This is the premier source for keeping up-to-date on the significance of different search engines and the techniques they use.

Search Engine Marketing Professional Association (www.sempo.org). SEMPO is a 'non-profit professional association working to increase awareness and promote the value of Search Engine Marketing worldwide'. Good introduction to search marketing, articles, case studies and a glossary.

Keyword suggestion tools

The latest version of these tools is available at:

http://www.davechaffey.com/E-marketing/C7-Traffic-Building/Keyword-research-tools

Netratings (www.netratings.com). Panel data summarizing the popularity of the main portals and the total number of active Internet users in many countries.

Pay Per Click Analyst (www.ppcanalyst.com). An update-source on latest developments in paid listings by industry experts.

 **Self-test**

1 Define appropriate measures for traffic building quantity and quality for a campaign for your organization's site.

2 Distinguish between the operation of a search engine and a directory. What are the implications for promotion of a company?

3 List the relevant portals your company *should be* and *is* represented on. Include horizontal portals, vertical portals and geographical portals.

4 What approaches should be used in a link building campaign?

5 Assess the relevance of banner advertising to your organization through reviewing their advantages and disadvantages.

6 Summarize the elements of effective opt-in e-mail.

7 List the different types of viral marketing campaigns for which you have been a recipient. Which could be effective for your own organization?

8 Explain why offline communications are significant. What should be their aims?

9 Review the suitability of different forms of measuring the effectiveness of a web campaign including server log file analysis, traditional market research and audience panels.

10 Audit the current balance of online and offline traffic building techniques used in your organization, producing a summary as for Table 7.1.

Chapter 8

E-CRM

'... Database marketing only works if the customer benefits from it
... building a relationship with the customer to improve loyalty and repeat
sales. CRM advocates often (wrongly) see CRM as advantageous mainly to
the company trying to manipulate the customers'.

McKim and Hughes, 2001

OVERVIEW

Online customer relationship management is packed with fundamental commonsense principles. Surprisingly many companies do not adhere to them. Serving and nurturing customers into lifetime customers makes sense as existing customers are, on average, five times more profitable. At the heart of this is a good database – the marketer's memory bank, which if used correctly, creates arguably the most valuable asset in any company.

OVERALL LEARNING OUTCOME

By the end of this chapter you will be able to:

- Apply basic customer relationship management principles in the online world
- Appreciate the careful planning required to create the perfect database
- Begin to develop and nurture a properly integrated, multi-channel database.

CHAPTER TOPIC	LEARNING OBJECTIVE
8.1 Introduction	Understand the significance of e-CRM
8.2 Relationship marketing	Explain the basic principles of relationship marketing
8.3 Database marketing	Grasp the basic principles of database marketing
8.4 E-CRM	Specify what new media add to CRM
8.5 Profiling	Know how to approach profiling
8.6 Personalization	Know the options for personalizing web sites, opt-in e-mails, prices and promotions
8.7 Incoming e-mails	Develop a strategy for managing inbound e-mail
8.8 Control issues	Develop a control strategy
8.9 Cleaning the database	Assess approaches to database cleaning
8.10 Making it happen	Outline a plan to achieve e-CRM

8.1 Introduction to CRM

This section introduces **e-CRM**, explains what it is, how it is inextricably linked with database marketing, why e-CRM is so important and how the other sections in this chapter fit together.

So first, what is e-CRM? Customer relations management with an 'e'. Ultimately, e-CRM cannot be separated from CRM, it needs to be integrated and seamless. However, some organizations do have specific e-CRM initiatives or staff responsible for e-CRM. Both CRM and e-CRM are not just about technology and databases, it's not just a process or a way of doing things, it requires, in fact, a complete customer culture.

In many ways there's nothing new here since good marketers have been taking care of their customers for many decades now. What is new is the lack of CRM in the fast moving online world:

- A world where customer expectations are often higher than those of the offline world.
- A world where customers' raised expectations are regularly crushed by successful offline companies.
- A world where customer e-mails are left unanswered for days.
- A world where immediate responses are expected but more often than not, are not delivered.
- A world where satisfying customers is simply not enough to keep them.
- A world of consolidating relationships ... where surfers visit fewer sites but spend longer with them.

So nothing is really new other than higher expectations, fickle customers, patterns of consolidation and some new technology!

SOME E-CRM BENEFITS AND CHALLENGES

There is e-CRM software which enhances our ability to understand customers and enquirers, their needs, names, interests and a lot more. We can get closer to them. Speak with them. One of the 5 Ss – the five fundamental benefits of e-marketing discussed in Chapter 1.

A dynamic dialogue that is instantaneous, relevant, value adding and information gleaning:

- recognizes and remembers each customer by name and need
- answers questions often automatically ... and ideally, personally
- asks questions, collects information and builds a better profile, particularly of those ideal, lifetime customers.

The real power of online marketing lies in its potential to build relationships and create long-term value. Companies who have risen to the challenge of e-CRM have a '360-degree view of their customers'. This in turn generates real loyalty from lifetime customers who readily share valuable data with you.

Have you got the software to exploit the valuable data you can collect from customers? Most don't. Have you got the processes in place to ensure excellent service – that keeps customers coming back for more? Have you got staff trained to use the software?

Keeping existing customers coming back for more is more profitable than acquiring new customers. It therefore makes a lot of sense to nurture the captured customers into lifetime friends. CRM and e-CRM helps to keep ideal customers. Customer retention can be improved by improving CRM. The returns on this investment are large.

The online world presents new challenges when nurturing customer relationships. This e-CRM chapter has sections on the key elements including two introductory-level sections on CRM itself and relationship marketing, database marketing as well as personalization, profiling, managing incoming e-mails and implementing e-CRM.

Remember CRM or, e-CRM, in particular, is not about technology, it's not just a process or way of doing things, it requires, in fact, a complete customer culture. The challenge is yours.

Given these benefits of e-CRM, many companies have attempted to implement CRM technologies to help give a 'single view of the customer'. But beware, the failure rate of CRM projects is even higher than other types of IT project. Gartner reported that 50 per cent of CRM projects completely failed to live up to expectations and a further 20 per cent substantially failed to live up to their expectations (Mazur, 2004). The challenge of CRM is that it is not just an immense technological challenge, but about also a challenge because of the change management needed for changes in process and role of staff.

SECTION SUMMARY 8.1

Introduction to e-CRM

Customer relationship management is well established as an approach to acquiring customers and then retaining them to develop a higher life-time value for each customer. Managing CRM online and integrating it with offline CRM activities introduces new challenges. We need to think about how we can use online tools to have a more dynamic dialogue with the customer, answering their questions, understanding their needs, profiling them and then delivering appropriate services and communications.

8.2 Introduction to relationship marketing

By the end of this section you should be able to see how relationship marketing and permission-based marketing are essential to CRM and e-CRM.

What is **relationship marketing**? Marketing is all about relationships. Relationships with customers, lapsed customers and potential customers. There are also relationships with suppliers, partners and even internal audiences (staff). So although relationship marketing involves more than just customers, we're focusing on customers, hence CRM – customer relationship management. True CRM involves treating each customer differently according to their characteristics as described in the e-marketing Insight box below.

Relationship marketing shifts marketing away from short-term **transactional marketing** (with its one-off sales) towards developing longer lasting relationships which, ideally, develop into lifetime customers. This obviously generates more profitable repeat business as well as increased share of wallet or customer share.

E-MARKETING INSIGHT

Peppers and Rogers on building one-to-one relationships

Peppers and Rogers (1999) have applied their work on building one-to-one relationships with the customer to the web. They suggest the IDIC approach as a framework for using the web effectively to form and build relationships. IDIC stands for:

1 *Customer identification.* This stresses the need to identify each customer on their first web site visit and subsequent visits. Common methods for identification are use of cookies or asking a customer to log on to a site.

2 *Customer differentiation.* This refers to building a profile to help segment customers into groups which share characteristics and can be evaluated according to company value. Peppers and Rogers suggest Most Valuable Customers, Most Growable Customers and Below Zero Customers.

3 *Customer interaction.* These are interactions provided on site such as customer service questions or creating a tailored product.

4 *Customized communications.* This refers to personalization or mass-customization of content or e-mails according to the segmentation achieved at the acquisition stage.

PERMISSION MARKETING

Building relationships is a delicate affair. Marketers have to gain permission first, then trust and ultimately, loyalty. It's all commonsense stuff. Sticking to basic marketing tenets of identifying, anticipating and satisfying customer needs relentlessly helps to build relationships. But how do you do this? First, adopt a 'permission based marketing', approach as developed by the now classic *Permission Marketing* by Seth Godin (Godin, 1999). There are several steps towards permission marketing:

1 *Gaining permission.* The first step is to get customer's permission to give them information. Winning this permission, in the customer's time compressed world, is a valuable asset.

2 *Collaboration.* Marketing is a collaborative activity – where marketers help customers to buy and customers help marketers to sell.

3 *Dialogue.* A dialogue emerges whether via web site e-mails, discussion rooms or real conversations in focus groups or even real meetings between customers and sales reps.

Permission marketers develop the relationship and win further permission to talk on a regular basis. Some excellent permission-based marketers actually get permission to place orders

Figure 8.1 The design of the That's Property buy-to-let portal emphasizes gaining permission (www.thatsproperty.co.uk)

on the customer's behalf. Other permission-based marketers even deliver right into the customer's buildings without the customer opening the door! They become part of the customer's systems.

In developing the relationship there are a series of stages through which the customer moves. There are several approaches, one of which is the ladder of loyalty (Considine and Murray, 1981) from Suspects to Prospects to Customers to Clients to Advocates.

When a customer '**opts-in**' for further e-mail, they give permission to be e-mailed. This is a first step in using their permission to develop the relationship. Do not abuse this permission. Make sure you don't pass their details on to other marketers. Ensure your future contact with the customer always adds value.

Remember you have to respect this relationship – this special permission you have. Be brave enough to offer the customer the option to '**opt-out**'. The number of existing customers that opt out from further contact is known as the '**churn rate**'. Obviously good marketers watch the churn rate closely, and try to understand how it varies.

E-MARKETING INSIGHT

Seth Godin on permission marketing

The concept of permission marketing is best summarized by three magic words. Seth Godin said:

'Permission marketing is ... anticipated, relevant and personal'

He goes on to describe the essential concepts of permission marketing as 'dating the customer':

1 Offer the prospect an incentive to volunteer (achieve opt-in)
2 Use the attention offered by the prospect, offer a curriculum over time, teach the consumer about your product or service (enable the customer to learn more)
3 Reinforce the incentive to guarantee that the prospect maintains the permission (offer opt-out, but minimize the likelihood for this)
4 Offer additional incentives to get even more permission from the consumer (learn more about the customer through time)
5 Over time, leverage the permission to change consumer behaviour towards profits (deepen the relation through converting from prospect to customer and triallist to loyalist).

E-MARKETING INSIGHT

Victor Ross on permission marketing

Not everyone sees permission marketing as a marketing panacea – interruption marketing is still required to start the dialogue. Victor Ross, a fellow of the Institute of Direct Marketing, says in reviewing Seth Godin's *Permission Marketing* (Ross, 2001): 'This book and the concept behind it need to be debunked before they gain cult status'. He suggests that much of the approach is not new:

'the large number of direct marketers who start the selling process with an ad offering information, and take it from there with a graduated programme of data collection and follow-ups will wonder how it is they have been practising permission marketing for all this time without knowing'.

Authors note: Despite this, we believe that Seth Godin's permission marketing is a significant contribution since it highlights the importance of a key principle of digital marketing in a clear and colourful way.

MANAGING THE DIALOGUE

Too much contact can wear out the relationship. The key to building the best relationship is to have the right number of contacts of the right type at the right time for specific customers. Markets are always changing, so your communications needs to be flexible and capable of individualized, personalized, responses. See the discussion on **contact strategy** in Section 2.8.

Don't forget that relationships are two-way conversations. It involves as much listening as talking, e-mailing, mobile messaging, telesales, advertising, etc. Watch clickthroughs on different e-newsletter topics, news pages, special offers and forums as well the incoming flow of communications. Give the customer a chance to talk to you, taking the time to listen and tell the other party how what they have told you has been acted upon, or at least heard!

Tell customers what they have told you, maybe in the form of order acknowledgement or consolidated feedback from surveys, etc. Showing them how this has changed what you do/how you do it is an important part of building a relationship. All part of the ongoing dialogue. Remember 'Markets are conversations!' Database-driven marketing allows the dialogue to become a dynamic dialogue – responsive, relevant and fast moving.

E-MARKETING INSIGHT

E-permission marketing principles

It is now over five years since Seth Godin launched his permission marketing mantra. So, we need to ask, 'how can the original principles of permission marketing be applied by today's online marketer?' We would emphasize these key developments of permission marketing principles, what we call 'e-permission marketing principles'.

1 *Offer selective opt-in to communications.* Offer choice in communications preferences to the customer to ensure more relevant communications. Some customers may not want a weekly e-newsletter, rather they may only want to hear about new product releases. Remember opt-in is a legal requirement in many countries. Four key opt-in options, selected by tick-box, are:

- *Content* – news, products, offers, events
- *Frequency* – weekly, monthly, quarterly, or alerts
- *Channel* – e-mail, direct mail, phone or SMS
- *Format* – text versus HTML.

2 *Create a common customer profile.* A structured approach to customer data capture is needed otherwise some data will be missed, as is the case with the utility company that collected 80 000 e-mail addresses, but forgot to ask for the postcode for geo-targeting! This can be achieved through a common customer profile – a definition of all the database fields that are relevant to the marketer in order to understand and target the customer with a relevant offering. It sounds obvious, but …

3 *Offer a range of opt-in incentives.* Many web sites now have 'free-win-save' incentives to encourage opt-in, but often it is one incentive fits all visitors. Different incentives for different audiences will generate a higher volume of permission, particularly for business-to-business web sites. We can also gauge the characteristics of the respondent by the type of incentives or communications they have requested, without the need to ask them.

4 *Don't make opt-out too easy.* Our view is that we often make it too easy to unsubscribe. Although offering some form of opt-out is now a legal requirement in many countries due to privacy laws, a single click to unsubscribe is making it too easy. Instead, wise e-permission marketers use the concept of 'My Profile'. Instead of unsubscribe, they offer a link to a web form to update a profile, which includes the option to unsubscribe. The use of 'My Profile' can be tied to the principle of 'selective opt-in' – you could call it selective opt-out.

5 *Watch don't ask.* The need to ask interruptive questions can be reduced through the use of monitoring of clicks to better understand customer needs and to trigger follow-up communications. Some examples:

- Monitoring click-through to different types of content or offer
- Monitoring the engagement of individual customers with e-mail communications
- Follow-up reminder to those who don't open the e-mail first time.

6 *Create an outbound contact strategy.* Online permission marketers need a plan for the number, frequency and type of online and offline communications and offers. This is a contact or touch strategy. The contact strategy should indicate: (1) Frequency (e.g. minimum once per quarter and maximum once per month); (2) Interval (e.g. there must be a gap of at least one week or one month between communications); (3) Content and offers (we may want to limit or achieve a certain number of prize draws or information-led offers); (4) Links between online communications and offline communications; (5) A control strategy (a mechanism to make sure these guidelines are adhered to – for example using a single 'focal point' for checking all communications before creation dispatch).

Source: This is a summary of an article by Dave Chaffey for *What's New in Marketing* (www.davechaffey.com/E-marketing-Insights)

SECTION SUMMARY 8.2

Relationship marketing

Relationship marketing is at the heart of e-CRM. It requires a longer-term perspective, a lifetime value perspective built on permission, trust and listening and responding to customers to build longer, lasting success.

8.3 Database marketing

The database and **database marketing** is at the heart of e-CRM. By the end of this section you will understand what a database is, the complications that can arise, the types of data fields and the importance of linking it all to a clear marketing programme.

It has been said that 'The driving force underlying modern CRM systems is the customer database'. The repository of information on customers and prospects from all sources and channels – whether web sites, interactive TV, sales reps or customer service staff.

The database and profiling software is a vital part of e-CRM since it enhances our ability to understand customers and enquirers, their needs, names, interests and a lot more. We can get closer to them. It helps achieve the dynamic dialogue of permission marketing which:

- recognizes and remembers each customer by name and need
- answers questions often automatically and, ideally, personally
- asks questions, collects information and builds a better profile, particularly of those ideal lifetime customers
- delivers communications that are instantaneous, relevant and value adding.

WHAT IS STORED IN THE DATABASE?

A database is more than a list of names. A database is distinguished by the amount and quality of relevant marketing data held on each customer or prospect. It should identify best ('ideal') customers and worst customers. The worst customers have 'negative value'; these are customers who claim early on insurance, are bad debtors, or are intensive users of free services. There are two types of information kept on a database that a simple mailing list does not provide: historical data and predictive data. Smith and Taylor (2004) describe **historical data** as 'transactional' or 'back' data which includes names addresses, recency and frequency of purchases, responses to offers and value of purchases. They say **predictive data** identifies which groups or subgroups are more likely to respond to a specific offer. This is done through statistical scoring: customer attributes (e.g. house type, business type, past behaviour, etc.) are given scores that help to indicate their future behaviour.

This begs the question – what kind of data, or 'fields' should be captured? In addition to capturing a customer's name and address, there are obviously other kinds, or 'fields', of data worth capturing both for B2C and B2B businesses. **FRAC** is a useful mnemonic. It stands for: Frequency, Recency, Amount and Category of purchase. This is a basic statement relating to four categories of the type of information gathered when carrying out relationship marketing, and in no way addresses what the real issues behind RM are. There is a lot of other useful data worth collecting also such as promotions history or responses to specific promotions, share of wallet or customer share (potential spend), timing of spend and more. In B2B, we are interested in business type (SIC codes), size of business, holding companies and subsidiaries, competitive products bought, etc.

WHICH SOFTWARE TOOLS ARE REQUIRED?

Every organization has lots of useful data on its customers. This can be very simple and well organized, or incredibly complex. Unfortunately many organizations have several databases, each set up at different times with no ability to cross-reference the data within them. Typically, there is the old 'legacy' database for traditional direct mail and a completely separate web-based database built specifically for web site visitors. Fortunately there is **middleware** software that allows these disparate databases to talk to each other. There are also standard off-the-shelf software packages that allow basic cross-referencing of different data-fields as well as mail-merge facilities for 'snail' mail and e-mail.

Then comes the really interesting software – **data mining** software that drills down into the data warehouses to find correlations and profiles buried deep with the layers of data. Data mining can reveal surprising correlations some of which help to profile an organization's own customers and then look for similar types elsewhere.

There is an increasing growth in complex database generation because of the obvious links between data capture and web marketing – when you have a visitor to your web site you have a great opportunity to capture data about that visitor, especially if you use **cookie** technology. But remember data captured for data's sake does not make a good database. What will you do with the data? If, for example, key predictive data identifies a customer who is likely to defect – what is the strategy? How will you separate offers between ideal and negative value customers? It is important to be clear about why you are creating a database in the first place. If there are no clear objectives then the database is an expensive, unused toy.

Rohner (2001) says 'Without a corresponding marketing programme, database marketing should not be introduced'. You must be clear what you want to do with the database. What kind of **contact strategy** will you have? A sequence of **opt-in** e-mails, snail mails, telephone calls, personal visits or what? What kind of responses and offers will be date triggered (e.g. three months after purchase), event triggered (e.g. Christmas time), purchase triggered (bought Item A but not Item B)? What is the sequence of contacts for each of these? Be clear about what you want to achieve with your e-CRM system.

Active database marketers know that databases deteriorate over time: people die, change job, move house. So the database asset has to be maintained, cleaned or updated. The cleaning process costs resources, but is crucial if the database is going to be used to its optimum. See Section 8.9 Cleaning the database.

Finally, it is essential to have a seamless, integrated database that works across all different platforms. So a customer is recognized and remembered and serviced in a personalized way whether they access the company by telephone, web site, interactive TV, or mobile phone. Integrating the databases presents a big challenge.

E-MARKETING EXCELLENCE

Abbey cares about data and cuts costs and gets closer to customer

Abbey Bank treats data as a critical corporate asset and has a board-level agreed strategy and method for managing it. The bank has created a 'data superstore' (data warehouse) that can be accessed by any authorized user or application within the bank.

By using Avellino Discovery, in the first two years Abbey:

- Achieved more efficient integration of Abbey Bank data into the central data architecture, delivering £1 million (US$1.5m) net present value (NPV).
- Migrated data into the central data architecture faster and with more accuracy. The total benefit is estimated at £2.5 million ($4m) NPV.
- Completed data-cleansing activities achieving £1.7 million ($2.7m) in savings.
- Achieved more accurate bad debt provisioning and credit scoring, leading to well over £10 million ($16m) in NPV benefits.

'We estimate that Avellino Discovery has delivered benefits to the bank worth some £15.2m,' said Christine Craven, Head of Retail Information at Abbey. 'Without Discovery, we estimate that it would take around five man-years to manually check the 29 million records that need migrating from the data warehouse into a new customer database. With Discovery automating much of the process, we estimate this activity will instead take around three man-months'.

Jean Knight, head of information quality at Abbey, says the old system took 40 hours to analyse one field in five million records. The bank is introducing new software that takes just three hours to complete the same task.

Source: Based on Avellino case studies (www.avellino.com)

SECTION SUMMARY 8.3

Database marketing

Although the database and database marketing is at the heart of e-CRM it goes way beyond simply collecting data. You now know the importance of linking the database to a clear marketing programme; the types of data fields – the complications that can arise; how mining can help to profile different types of customers (including best and worst) and the importance of maintaining and cleaning the database. A carefully planned, integrated and managed database can reap huge rewards.

8.4　E-CRM

This section shows how e-CRM draws on the basic principles of CRM, relationship marketing and database marketing. By the end of it you will also know how to (a) list the CRM stages and (b) keep the relationship alive.

WHAT DOES THAT 'E' ADD TO CRM?

Relationship marketing is all about building relationships with all external parties involved in marketing. CRM focuses specifically on the relationship with customers and e-CRM focuses even further on the electronic relationship with customers.

CRM software is used to manage these electronic relationships. Ebner *et al.* (2002) define this software as 'the systems that allow companies to plan and analyse marketing campaigns, to identify sales leads, and to manage their customer contacts and call centres'.

This means that marketers can deliver cheaper, faster and more flexible CRM. *Cheaper* since although software can be expensive initially, if it is carefully chosen and utilized fully, it can deliver significant savings particularly when much of the dialogue is both personalized and automated. *Faster* since much e-CRM is automated and so responses are almost instantaneous, e.g. when visitors register on a web site acknowledgement is now almost instantaneous. Similarly when placing orders via web sites most sites now automatically respond by acknowledging the order immediately. Many e-customers expect this now. *More flexible* CRM since systems should be readily updated to accommodate new products and new promotion techniques for new media.

The CRM software also enables permission marketing to be achieved – from the customer's point of view it means that the relationship, and communications in particular, are *more relevant, more tailored* and often *more interactive*.

With its customer orientation CRM helps marketers by growing longer lasting customer relationships. So both lifetime value and customer share grow. The best relationships are those where both partners feel they are equal and can build respect for each other through mutual understanding. From the customer's point of view it means that the relationship, and communications in particular, are more relevant, tailored and often interactive. Speedy responses and considered responses are always appreciated by customers. In fact complaining customers can become friends for life if their problems are dealt with swiftly and professionally. So it follows that resources have to be allocated towards monitoring customer feedback and dealing with the specific non-standard problems on a one-to-one basis. For example, many companies have found online chat (Live Person) and telephone call-back systems activated when customers fill in an online form are effective for moving customers from a virtual world relationship to a more involving real-world relationship with contact centre staff. However, such systems are resource incentive and customer expectations must be met so that they don't have to wait for that chat session or phone call.

E-CRM software is also important to *automate* the way the dialogue with the customer is initiated and then the relationship built through a series of targeted, tailored, timed e-mail and direct mail communications. The box 'Tesco.com automates relationship building' shows how this is achieved.

E-MARKETING EXCELLENCE

Tesco.com automates relationship building through web, e-mail and direct mail

Tesco.com uses software to monitor events that occur in the customer lifecycle. The examples below show that a sequence of follow-up communications are triggered after an event. Communications after event 1 are intended to achieve the objective of converting a web site visitor to action; communications after event 2 are intended to move the customer from a first-time purchaser to a regular purchaser and for event 3 to reactivate lapsed purchasers.

Trigger event 1: Customer first registers on site (but does not buy)

- Auto-response (AR) 1: 2 days after registration e-mail sent offering phone assistance and £5 discount off first purchase to encourage trial.

Trigger event 2: Customer first purchases online

- AR1: Immediate order confirmation.
- AR2: Five days after purchase, e-mail sent with link to online customer satisfaction survey asking about quality of service from driver and picker (e.g. item quality and substitutions).
- AR3: Two weeks after first purchase, direct mail offering tips on how to use service and £5 discount on next purchases intended to encourage re-use of online services.
- AR4: Generic monthly e-newsletter with online exclusive offers.
- AR5: Bi-weekly alert with personalized offers for customer.
- AR6: After three months, £5 discount for next shop.
- AR7: Quarterly mailing of coupons.

Trigger event 3: Customer does not purchase for an extended period

- AR1: Dormancy detected. Reactivation e-mail with survey of how the customer is finding the service (to identify and problems) and a £5 incentive.
- AR2: A further discount incentive is used in order to encourage continued usage the after first shop after a break.

KEEPING THE RELATIONSHIP ALIVE

All relationships can get stale unless you work hard at it. This means your web site needs to be updated and kept fresh and tailored – your offerings need to be more attractive than those of the competition. How can you keep the relationship alive – without changing so much that you are no longer the organization they wanted to have a relationship with in the first place? DRAMA – that's how!

- *Dialogue.* An organization should offer customers ways to talk to them – every message sent should allow for a response. Every unsolicited communication from them should receive a swift and relevant response. The organization *must* show that it listens and can talk and tell too!
- *Relevancy.* The beauty of e-CRM is that mass communication can be personal and made relevant to the recipient, indeed the customer's expectation of relevance will be so high that it is dangerous to send bulk messages that are not tailored to that one person's/company's needs.

- *Accuracy*. e-CRM opens the door for poor information management as does any other form of direct communication – but this time the problem might well have originated with the customer themselves, e.g. they mis-spell a name, enter digits incorrectly, etc. when data is captured. Data must be checked, must be updated and must be kept 'clean'. Equally, any information you give to customers must be double checked (as in all good communication) to ensure total accuracy.

- *Magic*. This is what makes the difference! The extra dimension that makes people want to be your customer. There is much talk of customer delight – go one better and aim for customer amazement! The Internet allows for special effects, deliveries of technically advanced packages of information presented in very appealing ways – animation, sound, interaction, prizes, incentives, collection schemes – these are all pretty much expected by customers nowadays, so what will you do that is different? Will it be your creative execution? The links with famous personalities whom you sponsor or hire? The very personal touch of a one-to-one advisor whether delivered by a virtual **avatar** adviser (Figure 8.2) or a human online chat, the best free software downloads available? *Magic* is what should be the goal – and never guess what it might be, carry out research to find out what your customers want it to be…

- *Access*. 'I feel like we're drifting apart!' Don't let your relationship wither due to lack of contact, but also be sure you are not smothering the relationship with over attentiveness! If you have a scheme to get your customers to visit you regularly (let's say they have to visit you every week

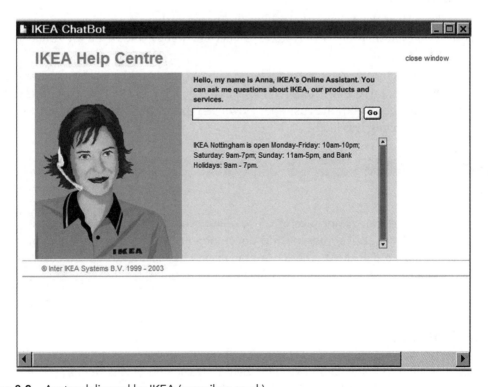

Figure 8.2   Avatar delivered by IKEA (www.ikea.co.uk)

for a year to collect all the cards in a deck of cards to be able to get an opportunity to have a free trip to Las Vegas, you must keep them going with spot prizes, because a year is a very long time to wait!) then be sure there is something worth seeing when they do visit! Getting someone to access your site is one thing – entertaining them, informing them, having what they want when they get there is something else – and cannot be ignored.

So now let us get down to the nitty-gritty of e-CRM – what are the specific stages? There are many different approaches to the CRM or e-CRM stages or cycle such as the ladder of loyalty or the customer development cycle of selection, acquisition, retention and extension. Here is another approach to the CRM cycle.

1 *Attract!* Obviously this is where traditional off-line communication as well as on-line communication about your offering is being designed to bring customers to your site. From TV advertising to banner ads and hot-spots, getting them to your site will only be possible if (a) they know what you are offering and are interested, and (b) they know where you are and how to get to you.

2 *Capture data.* The Internet is a splendid mechanism for capturing data – the prospect has the keyboard and screen in front of them and you can incentivize the giving of data.

3 *Get closer.* Get to know them better. It is not surprising that there is reluctance on the part of many individuals to give personal data away to an Internet screen. So, it is often better to gather more information about a person slowly and over time, as the trust builds between you and them.

4 *Embrace them.* Make your customer feel loved! Approach them with offers, prizes, rewards, incentives and information as well as experiences that show them you are thinking about *them*.

5 *Golden handcuffs.* Once you get them to show some loyalty, build a system whereby things are too good for them to leave! Tailored information or services to suit them specifically. Or services that integrate with the customer's own systems or lifestyle. These switching costs which making leaving less likely.

SECTION SUMMARY 8.4

E-CRM

E-CRM draws on the basic principles of CRM, relationship marketing and database marketing. There are a clear set of stages in CRM development. You have to work hard at keeping the relationship alive (DRAMA). There are many benefits including lifetime customers and increased share of wallet which help to grow your business.

8.5 Profiling

Profiling helps you to know your customers better. By the end of this section you will know what profiling is, how it works and how it can help marketers.

WHICH INFORMATION IS NEEDED FOR PROFILING?

Who is your customer? This is a classic marketing question. Do you really know who they are? What are your customers' key characteristics? What characteristics separate your **ideal customers** from your average customers? What is the profile of your ideal customer? Is it different from your worst, **negative value customers**? Surprisingly, many companies cannot answer these questions. If you don't know your customer profiles, how can you (a) satisfy them better, and (b) find other customers like them?

A **customer profile** can take everything you know about the customer and everything you know about people who are like that customer. It can then be layered with all the psychological and sociological theory that suggests how that person will react to a specific offer or promotion. This helps you to tailor offers that work better for both your customers and your business.

APPROACHES TO PROFILING

Profiling is a continuous activity. Continually collecting customer information, mining it and using it to profile and target more successfully. It is crucial to know what fields or data should be collected.

A simple example of this is the classic, timeless, grandfather clock story. A marketer with a huge database decided to market a limited edition upmarket grandfather clock. After some consideration they targeted 45–65-year-olds, upper income living in large detached houses. They ran a test mailing which generated 60 orders. They then used the 60 responses to build a better profile of the actual customer. Using a more accurate customer profile, they then targeted a different segment of their database and sold every single clock!

Profile data can be gathered from several sources: internally from the customer's own input on a web form, tracking mechanisms and questionnaires, or externally from research companies and data bureaux. Data can be complex and of massive volume – it might be that you have to hire a computer bureau to crunch the data to turn it into useful information. An example of building a profile through an online conversation with customers is given in the box 'Tektronix build customer intimacy with virtual conversations with their customers'.

One of the toughest jobs is to know which data matters most – especially where there is conflicting data. Some customers will give you incorrect information – consciously or unconsciously. You have to come up with ways to acquire the information in the first place, and then make it useful to your organization – validation.

The issue of the invasion of privacy is a difficult one. Laws, ethics and codes of practice come into play. Ethics have a role, but, the main arbiters of 'how much contact is too much contact?' are the customers themselves. They will show you how ready they are to be communicated with by their response. You have to gain their permission.

Asking for information is a delicate affair. You cannot be too greedy. Beyond the basic information, you may need to offer incentives for more information or simply wait for the relationship to develop and permission to ask for more. But remember customers value their privacy. Let your customers see your privacy policy posted clearly on your web site and any other access point customers may have with you.

Of course, it is one thing to collect profile information, it is quite another to use it and derive value from it. *Marketing Business* (Mazur, 2004) noted that it is increasingly acknowledged by organizations of all sizes, shapes and sectors that their most valuable asset is their customer information. Ironically, it also seems to be one of the least understood and most poorly managed areas. It was reported that 50 per cent of FTSE 1000 companies still do not have a robust and single view of their customers. Often, no one is in overall charge of the data and there is a failure to invest in developing processes and systems to help staff contribute to data collection, quality and usage. Far too often the same message and creative is sent to everyone on a list.

E-MARKETING EXCELLENCE

Tektronix build customer intimacy with virtual conversations with their customers

B2B test and measurement company Tektronix (www.tektronix.com) uses e-mail as a strategic communications tool to build relationships with its customers. Tektronix uses regular e-newsletters and periodic personalized e-mail 'e-blasts' about product launches and promotions based on a detailed personal 'myTek' profile. Tektronix also uses a novel form of e-mail marketing to create greater intimacy with its customers. This uses technology that generates a dialogue with the e-mail recipient rather than completion of a simple online form.

The goal in using e-mail in this way is to:

- Increase registration form completion rates to get more leads.
- Pre-qualify leads so the sales team don't waste their efforts.
- Build intimacy by educating leads with useful materials on products that are right for them.

When the customer receives an e-mail it links to a form titled 'A virtual conversation with Tektronix' (Figure 8.3). They are then led through a series of questions on different forms to help better understand their characteristics and needs and offering relevant white-papers in return. The questions are carefully tuned so that different customers see different questions and are offered different whitepapers according to their interests. With these 'skip patterns' the average respondent sees around 8 questions although there may be 20 or so in total.

SECTION SUMMARY 8.5

Profiling

Profiling helps you to:

- see your customers more clearly
- identify similar ones outside your organization
- separate your best from worst customers

- make more tailored tempting offerings relevant to specific customer profiles
- build lifetime relationships
- enjoy lifetime value from them.

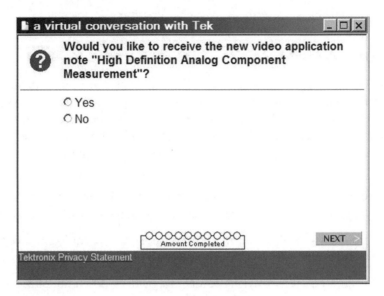

Figure 8.3   E-mail dialogue for Tektronix (www.tektronix.com)

8.6 Personalization

Specialized software combined with an up-to-date and well-cleaned database allows marketers to personalize communications such as e-mails, voice mails (voice activated e-mails), snail mails (traditional direct mail), SMS text messages (for mobiles) and most interestingly, web sites – personalized web sites. Chapter 6 on site design includes a section dedicated to personalized web sites.

WHY PERSONALIZATION?

The most important sound in the world is …. your own name! We all appreciate it when people remember our names. It's personal. It's a compliment – an expression of respect. By the end of this section you'll know how personalization helps to build relationships and the issues that arise. Some call it affectionately, 'the personal touch', when a restaurant remembers your favourite wine or preferred table .The database enhances the marketer's memory of customer names, needs, interests and preferences.

Personalization enhances the relationship. Personalized web pages help to create a sense of ownership. Not of the customer by the marketer, but of the site by the customer!

When you make a customer feel that their home page is truly theirs, that the offers you make available to them are theirs, that the information they access is put together just for them, then you allow the customer to own you.

This enhanced service helps to sell while also providing the platform for ongoing dialogue ('Speak') and enhancing the brand personality. So personalization delivers four of the 5 Ss benefits of e-marketing. Which 'S' is missing? Save – personalization software does cost money. And the larger the customer base gets the more complex the personalization becomes. For this reason many organizations stick with a less sophisticated mass web site.

APPROACHES TO PERSONALIZATION

There are three distinct approaches to personalization: customization, individualization and group-characterization. **Customization** is the easiest to see in action: it allows the visitor to the website to select and set up their specific preferences. **Individualization** goes beyond this fixed setting and uses patterns of your own behavior (and not any other user's – they know it's you because of your login and password choices) to deliver specific content to you that follows your patterns of contact.

In **group-characterization** you receive a recommendation based the preferences of people 'like' you, using approaches based on collaborative filtering and case-based reasoning.

Mass customization is where different products, services or content is produced for different segments – sometimes hundreds of different segments.

Personalization is different. It is truly one-to-one. Particularly when not only the web site and communications are personalized but the product is personalized.

The concept appears powerful, but as with everything there are always exceptions where things go wrong – Murphy's Law – what can wrong will go wrong! Here are two examples where personalization goes wrong – passwords and personalized products.

Take personalized sites – many of them require users to log in with a password which they inevitably lose. So the personalization is lost in frustration of having to remember, find or recreate a password. Many visitors give up and leave the site. The use of cookies here can avoid the need for passwords and log-ins. Note new privacy laws require e-marketers to explain the use of cookies within the privacy policy and seek permission before placing a cookie on the end-user's PC.

Now consider personalized products and possible problems … consider Nike's web site which invited customers to personalize or make their own shoes by stitching on their own personal logo. One customer filled out the online form, sent the $50 and chose 'sweatshop' as a personal logo. Nike refused. The publicity soared.

E-MARKETING EXCELLENCE

Gartner on personalization

There are many options for online personalization – these are some, from simple to complex recommended by Gartner (www.gartner.com). How many of these do you use?

Addressing customers personally

- Address customers/prospects by name in print communication.
- Address customers/prospects by name in electronic communication.

Real-time personalization

- Keyword query to change content.
- Clickstream data to dynamically change web site content.
- Collaborative filtering to classify visitors and serve content.

Customer-profile personalization

- Geographic personalization to tailor messages in traditional media.
- Demographic personalization to tailor messages in traditional media.
- Give web site visitors control over content from set preferences.
- Demographic personalization to tailor online messages.
- Geographic personalization to tailor online messages.
- Registration data to change web site content.

E-MARKETING INSIGHT

Overpersonalization leads to over familiarity

Although personalization is important, it is possible to overpersonalize. UK Online For Business reported that American Express call centres discovered that customers resented being greeted in person until they had said who they were; the practice was swiftly discontinued.

Likewise, e-CRM systems make it possible to identify an individual responding to an e-mail and downloading product information or a price list on a web site. While a follow-up phone call is obviously well timed, the call needs to be scripted carefully. It sounds like Big Brother if you say 'we see you downloaded a pricelist this morning'. It is much better to talk more generally about checking to see whether the customer needs any assistance in selecting a product.

SECTION SUMMARY 8.6

Personalization

There are pros and cons for the different levels of personalization. To summarize: It requires resources. It requires a well-kept database. It does create a feeling of ownership. It does have some specific challenges (Murphy's Law), but can, if well executed, enhance customer relationships.

8.7 Incoming e-mails

Surprisingly, many major blue chip companies insult their customers by ignoring or misman-aging their incoming e-mails – lose sales, raise anger and damage the brands which they have spent fortunes building. By the end of this section you will know how to reduce the incoming quantity, reduce the workload of outgoing responses while growing strong customer relations.

Incoming e-mails can be sales enquiries, complaints, after-sales service requests and much more. They provide a direct conduit to the marketplace. Having made the effort to create a dialogue you need to have the systems, procedures and resources in place to manage this new communications channel. You must have systems in place that:

1 Receive, sort and route the incoming e-mails.
2 Generate an automatic 'message received' response or not, depending on what you have decided is best for your customers.
3 Provide a suitable response regardless of the quantity received.

This all sounds very simple, but it demands good planning and foresight. The quantity of incoming e-mails can be reduced, without jeopardizing the relationship, by:

1 FAQs allow for many issues to be dealt with without the customer contacting you directly.
2 Search facilities allow for customers to find out more about a topic without having to contact you directly.
3 Linked websites and other locations can allow customers to research a topic across the web without having to contact you directly. It is worth looking at other web sites and their FAQs.

Even once you have removed many of the most repetitive reasons for e-mail, there will still be some incoming communication that can be dealt with through fairly standard answers. This is where pre-prepared standard template responses come in!

And template responses can be used without human input thanks to intelligent software that matches words in incoming e-mail to potential responses. So, for example, when the right count of critical word matches a certain topic, a specific relevant standard template response is sent. It can even be personalized. There are arguments for and against this type of response. It would be nice to think that nothing could match the way in which a human responds to another human, but this is not always the case.

When using real customer service or e-CRM staff, you need well trained, knowledgeable staff who, if they don't know the answer to a question at least know where to look to find it. There are always some e-mails that require a human response – so don't ignore human training as well as system design! And if your site has real-time text messaging facilities which give live e-mail answers or call back facilities where you request a telephone call, remember these require different skills – e-mail skills and telephone skills are different.

Staff need to be managed. They need to be set goals for response, set performance standards, trained, motivated and monitored. Ignore people management at your peril.

SECTION SUMMARY 8.7

Incoming e-mails

Systems help to categorize incoming e-mails. FAQs reduce the workload. Standard templates reduce workloads. Intelligent systems also use standard templates. Real staff also answer e-mails. They need to be trained and managed … if incoming e-mails are going to help customer relations to blossom.

8.8 Control issues

In this section we examine six typical e-CRM control issues that confront marketers regularly: inexperience, un-integrated systems, information overload, high churn rate, spiralling cleaning costs and changing regulations. By the end of this section you will know how to begin to deal with them.

1 *Inexperience*. You have to start good management from within, but there is no reason why you can't try to learn some lessons from outside too! Some of these forms of advice come free, others have a fee attached. The best way to learn about the sort of information that is available for those setting up and managing database and e-CRM systems is to visit some of the organizations who offer such services.

2 *Un-integrated systems*. Having systems and sub-systems that don't talk to each other – either online or offline – is one of the most common challenges, and one that has to be overcome without all the data, on all the systems, having to be re-created! The expensive way to tackle this is to get in new hardware and software and 're-capture' all the data. A better way is to work with a company that has the skills, scope and track record to do the job. There are many companies who offer to integrate your systems.

3 *Information overload*. Information overload means too much data. Even when your databases are integrated the amount of data can grow too large to manage properly. Again, by using systems that have been designed to solve this very issue you can break down seemingly huge tasks into a series of smaller, more manageable tasks. This eases workflow and aids planning.

4 *High churn rate*. Imagine this. Everything it seems is working well, but the 'churn rate', or customer defection rate, is high. The result of high churn rate is high recruitment costs and high data capture costs, as well as increasing the required rate of cleaning. One solution is to investigate the reasons for the high churn rate, e.g. are your introductory offers too good to miss, but your subsequent offerings not meeting customer expectations?

5 *Spiralling cleaning costs*. Cleaning costs can escalate. Remember that a dirty database is a bad database. It is essential to maintain the integrity of the database. However, there can be pressure to reduce cleaning costs by either de-duplicating less often, or less thoroughly. Whilst the relentless search for cost savings is constant, cutting costs here could well be your most expensive false economy.

6 *Changing regulations.* Industry rules and regulations keep changing or evolving (e.g. privacy laws) and therefore stop you being as creative as you would like. CRM and especially the e-CRM industry can only survive and thrive if it has the confidence of the customers. Every practitioner should strive to protect and enhance that trust in all their dealings. Don't forget to read up on the changing laws and regulations particularly if you attract international customers.

E-MARKETING EXCELLENCE

Richard Beal of Direct Line on a single data view

According to *The Financial Times* (Dempsey, 2000), Richard Beal believes that the key to effective control of CRM lies not in trying to enforce one single view of the customer (although Direct Line does have a large database of customer information). He uses a Japanese *kaizen* or continuous improvement approach. This does not involve a huge team of call centre agents employing a single approach to callers, but small groups of staff trying out different ways of handling calls.

For Richard Beal the strategic goal of this CRM project is cross-selling. Direct Line has expanded into home insurance and now offers loans via the Internet. This approach gives it the ability to identify a loan application that comes from a customer who might also benefit from one of its credit card schemes. The Chordiant software it uses allows a customer to bounce between web contact and a telephone conversation. Direct Line believes this flexibility is the key to converting queries into sales.

Richard Beal says 'We have found that people want a hybrid, they will commence an inquiry over the Internet but do not feel comfortable carrying out the whole transaction online'.

SECTION SUMMARY 8.8

Control issues

Be aware of some of the e-CRM issues that lie ahead of you including inexperience, unintegrated systems, information overload, high churn rate, spiralling cleaning costs and changing regulations. Now is the time to learn more about dealing with them if you are to enjoy excellent customer relations.

8.9 Cleaning the database

The database is arguably a company's greatest asset yet it can turn into a liability if not managed carefully. By the end of this section you'll know why and how it can be done.

Your database is an asset. You must maintain its integrity. Like all assets it needs to be maintained otherwise it becomes a liability – harassing uninterested people, duplicating e-mails and snail mails, calling people the wrong name – in a word making a nuisance of yourself and damaging your brand not to mention wasting time and money. Horror stories abound.

The excuse that you have an old system or worse, several old systems, which present too big a task is a weak excuse. Some organizations manage to put off setting up effective cleaning systems for years by having some sort of committee or group looking into a new super-system, costing the project and then realizing that technological developments have moved ahead.

And all the time, the working group has been costing huge sums of money to operate and very little, if anything, has been invested in keeping the databases in question clean and up to date. This is a very poor, but frequently observed, business practice. You must try to keep cleaning, even whilst discussions about changes and upgrades continue.

In addition to old systems, databases can be dirty or incorrect for several reasons:

- Information has been captured incorrectly.
- Information about the person has changed.
- Specific requests have emerged.
- Duplicate files occur.

APPROACHES TO CLEANING DATABASES

There are many methods of keeping databases clean, some are proactive and some are responsive.

Let's start with the minimum requirement – responsiveness. Respond to changes in data. It needs to be updated continually. And remember, as with any communication, online or offline, the recipient should be given the chance to inform you, either (a) how their information should be corrected, or (b) if they want to be taken off your database. The web place is an obvious place to achieve this, but this facility is only usually offered by e-tailers.

Maybe the members of your database want to tell you that they didn't like a specific mail shot, that they continue to receive three copies of something from you, that they do not wish to receive e-mails about pet insurance but they do about car insurance, or even more unusual items that you cannot imagine. To maintain a good relationship, you must be flexible and allow for a wide-ranging dialogue. This requires good systems and procedures as well as trained customer-service staff.

A free-flowing and flexible dialogue can be encouraged by: freephone numbers, a dedicated web page and a dedicated e-mail address, and mailback/faxback special request sheets. The aim is to get any unusual request into the system quickly and accurately, allow someone to have responsibility for checking that it is routed to the right place/person within the organization, and to be able to follow-up should the database member request it.

Sometimes it's not enough to listen – you have to go out and ask. Being pro-active means you have much better databases because you take responsibility for your data being correct. So:

- Regularly contact (by mail or e-mail) inactive database members.
- Regularly scan your records for possible duplication.
- Regularly cross-reference your new records against your old.

As with all business processes, you can do the cleaning yourself in-house, or subcontract, or outsource, the service – i.e. you can buy in the planning and design and then run it yourself, etc. There are many companies that specialize in software that manages customer relationships via mail, e-mail, telephone and sales force. It is worth having a look at some of them.

SECTION SUMMARY 8.9

Cleaning the database

The database is an asset. It needs to be maintained and cleaned. You can do it yourself in-house or subcontract outside. You can be responsive through customers helping to clean the database and you can be pro-active by actively cleaning yourself. Either way, cleaning is essential if your database is to remain an extremely valuable asset.

8.10 Making it happen

So how do you make it happen – how do you establish excellent e-CRM? Many organizations have to start from scratch. By the end of this section you'll know what's involved when setting up an e-CRM system.

It is quite common for a team to be developed to create a database marketing and e-CRM system. They will have to develop project teams made up of the users of the system, analysts to understand their requirements, technical staff to create the system and a project manager with sufficient time to devote to the job.

Systems development should follow a structured approach, going through several stages as shown in Figure 8.4. Note though that, just as for web site development, prototyping is the most effective approach since it enables the system to be tailored through users' experience of early versions of the system.

MANAGING THE DATABASE

The database is the core of the CRM system. The database administrator/manager (DBA) has many responsibilities here:

1 *Database design.* Ensuring the design is effective in allowing customer data to be accessed rapidly and queries performed.
2 *Data quality.* Ensuring data is accurate, relevant and timely.
3 *Data security.* Ensuring data cannot be compromised by attacks from inside or outside the organization.
4 *Data backup and recovery.* Ensuring that data can be restored if there are system failures or attacks.

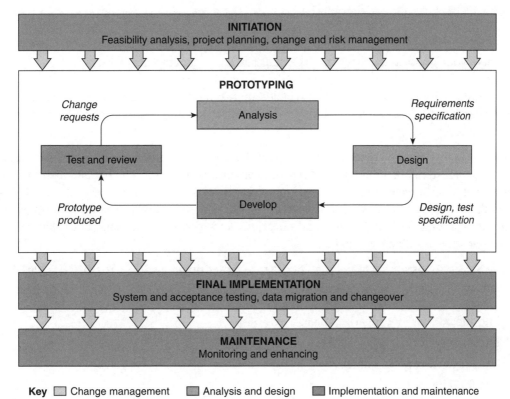

Figure 8.4   Systems development lifecycle including prototyping

5 *User co-ordination.* This involves specifying who has access to the information retrieval and who has access to information input. Too many uncontrolled inputs mean files get changed and deleted by too many different people. The database spins out of control.

6 *Performance monitoring.* Checking the system is coping with the demand placed on it by users.

There's one more part of the DBA's job – to communicate with clarity to the whole of the rest of the organization the advantages of database marketing.

COSTS AND TIMESCALES

When it comes to the crunch question of 'how much does it all cost?', there are many variables to consider:

1 The set-up costs of the system.
2 The type of system.
3 The scope of the system.
4 The size of the system.
5 The choice made about the DBMS.

6 The maintenance programme.

7 The use you make of it!

8 Where your physical database management system is geographically located.

It is a complex job, but once all these variables are taken into consideration, a task breakdown can be performed and analysis, design, set-up, maintenance and running schedule of costs can be calculated.

What's missing? Staff – customer service staff. They are a key component, particularly when handling wide-ranging, non-standard requests or complaints. Here's a crucial question. How many customer service staff should you employ? How many customer service staff do you think AOL employs? Well AOL has created a customer service army of 6000 employees and contract workers who handle technical questions and inquiries (Newell, 2000). How many customer service staff do you need?

The other key question is 'how long does it take to set up an e-CRM system?' The variables are similar to cost:

1 Time allowed for investigative stage.

2 Time allowed for design.

3 Time for writing programmes.

4 Time for data capture/reassessment/input.

5 Time for trials, piloting, testing and de-bugging.

SECTION SUMMARY 8.10

Making it happen

An effective CRM programme needs a strong project manager who can unite the business and technical team members. A defined database administrator is also required who will champion the system and own it to ensure appropriate data quality, security and performance. Planning using the systems development lifecycle provides a framework for costing, scheduling and monitoring the project. Remember also that CRM programmes should never end; they evolve.

CHAPTER SUMMARY

1 **e-CRM** operates in an environment where customers demand quality services from organizations. Since it is technology based it can be used to increase the speed, frequency and relevance of interactions, while remembering that human contact is the best for some situations.

2 **Relationship marketing** involves a long-term rather than transactional approach to customers. It is built on building up permission, trust, listening and then responding to customers.

3 **Database marketing** is key to e-CRM since the database can be used to understand customer needs through profiling and data mining, segment customers and manage integrated marketing direct marketing campaigns.

4 **e-CRM** provides DRAMA (dialogue, relevancy, accuracy, magic and access) to marketing communications. A good approach to the CRM cycle is attract, capture data, get closer, embrace and golden handcuffs.

5 **Profiling** helps to identify groups of customers and rank them according to their importance to the company. Appropriate communications and offers can then be developed for these groups with the aim of building long-term relationships with them.

6 **Personalization** refers to tailoring of a range of communications from e-mails to web sites. These can be individual (one-to-one) or to segments (mass customization). Personalization can occur due to user selection (customization), marketing rules (individualization) and group characterization such as collaborative filtering.

7 **If incoming e-mails** are mismanaged, this can destroy customer relationships. Procedure must be put in place to sort and route the incoming e-mails, notify receipt and provide a suitable response. Contact strategies such as FAQ and using the phone where appropriate can minimize the volume of e-mails and maximize the clear-up rate.

8 Control must occur to achieve avoid e-CRM problems such as inexperience, un-integrated systems, information overload, high churn rate, spiralling cleaning costs and changing regulations.

9 Cleaning the database is important to minimize marketing costs and improve relationships. Approaches are responsive where customer requests are implemented rapidly and proactive where regular planned cleaning occurs.

10 An effective CRM programme needs a strong project manager to achieve staff involvement across the business and ensure the implementation is well planned, so delivering on time. A good quality database administrator is important to champion the system and to deliver data quality, security and performance.

References

Broadvision (2001) Case study of Aviall (www.broadvision.com).

Considine, R. and Murray, R. (1981) *The Great Brain Robbery*. The Great Brain Robbery, CA.

Information Week (2001) Scaling Up: Prudential's Very Large Database Pays Off. *Information Week*. 15 January. http://www.informationweek.com/820/database.htm.

Dempsey, M. (2000) Direct Line: Strategic goal of this CRM project is cross-selling. Financial services case study, *Financial Times*, 7 June.

Ebner, M., Hu, A., Levitt, D. and McCrory, J. (2002) How to rescue CRM. *The McKinsey Quarterly*, No. 4.

Godin, S. (1999) *Permission Marketing*. Simon and Schuster, New York.

Mazur, L. (2004) Detica IT Survey Nov 2003. *Marketing Business*, Feb 2004.

McKim, B. and Hughes, A. (2001) How to measure CRM success. Database Marketing Institute, 9 March, www.dbmarketing/articles/Art198.htm.

Newell, F. (2000) *Loyalty.com*. McGraw-Hill.

O'Neill (2001) Seeking definition. *The next big thing*. www.tnbt.com. 7 March.

Peppers, D. and Rogers, M. (1999) *The One to One Fieldbook*. Currency/Doubleday, NY.

Rohner, K. (2001) *Marketing in the cyber age – the why, the what and the how*. Wiley, New York, NY.

Ross, V. (2001) Review of Permission Marketing by Godin (1999). *Interactive Marketing*, Vol. 2, No. 3, Jan–March.

Siebel (2001) BMC Software case study from Siebel web site: http://www.siebel.com/ case_studies/HighTech/BMC.pdf.

Smith, P. and Taylor, J. (2004) *Marketing Communications – an integrated approach*. Kogan Page, London, 4th edition.

 ## Further reading

Ebner, M., Hu, A., Levitt, D. and McCrory, J. (2002) How to rescue CRM. *The McKinsey Quarterly*, No. 4.

Godin, S. (1999) *Permission Marketing*. Simon and Schuster, New York. An interesting and influential book.

Newell, F. (2000) *Loyalty.com*. McGraw-Hill. An accessible book, with US examples of the principle of loyalty.

Reicheld, F. and Schefter, P. (2000) E-loyalty: Your secret weapon on the Web. *Harvard Business Review*, July–August, pp. 105–13. An essential, short summary of achieving customer loyalty using online techniques.

Seybold, P. (1999) *Customers.com*. Century Business Books, Random House, London. Describes a customer centric approach to business strategy with many examples drawn from the US.

 ## Web links

CRMGuru (www.crmguru.com). Forum, plus some white papers.

Database Marketing Institute (www.dbmarketing.com). Great practical guidelines and presentations on traditional database marketing and online marketing.

ECCS (www.eccs.uk.com). European Centre for Customer Strategies – good best practice articles, but many dated.

E-Loyalty (www.e-loyalty.com). An introduction to achieving online loyalty by Ellen Reid-Smith.

InsightExec (www.insightexec.com). Portal focusing on traditional and online CRM.

JimNovo.com (www.jimnovo.com). A specialist on online CRM, Jim's site has many practical insights about analysing and following up according to online purchase behaviour including the excellent 'Drilling Down' guide.

Peppers and Rogers (*The One to One Fieldbook*) (www.1to1.com). Contains interesting articles, case studies and supplier guides.

Self-test

1 How do database marketing, relationship building, direct marketing and CRM relate to each other?

2 Describe different staged approaches to relationship building.

3 Explain the concept of data mining.

4 How do we use DRAMA to keep customer relationships alive?

5 How, when and why should profiling occur for an organization you are familiar with.

6 Summarize the benefits and disadvantages of personalization.

7 Describe the management issues of incoming e-mails.

8 Explain these six issues of e-CRM control: inexperience, un-integrated systems, information overload, high churn rate, spiralling cleaning costs and changing regulations.

9 Describe approaches to database cleaning.

10 Produce an outline list of the main activities that need to occur for e-CRM implementation and maintenance.

Chapter **9**

E-business

'Businesses have invested heavily in ICT of all sorts over the last three years, and in many cases found themselves with an expensive depreciating asset, and less than hoped for benefits. Businesses are now seeking to use ICTs more shrewdly to unlock business value'.

DTI, 2003

OVERVIEW

The dotcom shake-out has left more professional players in the marketplace. Clicks and mortar companies generally outperform pure-play Internet companies. Why didn't these new e-businesses survive? Where did they go wrong? The answer is that they weren't e-businesses. They weren't even businesses since many were ignorant of business essentials such as the need to integrate front-office systems with back-office systems, keeping close to customers, delivering real added value, having clear propositions, carefully targeted at the right customers, etc. This chapter clarifies what is meant by e-business, a much abused concept.

OVERALL LEARNING OUTCOME

By the end of this chapter you will:

- Know what an e-business really is – what its components are.
- Understand the risks, resources and rewards associated with running an e-business.
- Be able to outline approaches to e-business.

CHAPTER TOPIC		LEARNING OBJECTIVE
9.1	Introduction	Understand the context of e-business
9.2	E-business architecture	Identify the components of an e-business architecture
9.3	An e-business value framework	Distinguish between and understand links between buy-side, sell-side and in-side e-business
9.4	Buy-side applications	Define the opportunities and marketing relevance of buy-side applications
9.5	In-side applications	Define the opportunities and marketing relevance of in-side applications
9.6	Sell-side applications	Define the opportunities and marketing relevance of sell-side applications
9.7	Creating the e-business	Identify the main elements of moving to e-business
9.8	E-business security	Outline the main risks and solutions to e-business security
9.9	E-business success criteria	Specify criteria for e-business success
9.10	Why did the dotcoms become dot-bombs?	Specify criteria for e-business failure

9.1 Introduction to e-business

E-business impacts absolutely everything about a business! It is far bigger than **e-marketing**. But what exactly is it? What does e-business entail? What are the components, the issues and the obstacles facing e-business? This chapter addresses all these questions and more. By the end of this first section you will know exactly what it is and will be able to discuss it comfortably with colleagues.

So what exactly is e-business? There are several definitions. Deloitte & Touche Consulting Group use this definition:

> *'The use of electronic networks for business (usually with web technology)'.*

Here's IBM's definition:

> *e-business (e' biz' nis) 'The transformation of key business processes through the use of Internet technologies'.*

Technology can transform key business processes out of the old **value chain** and into new, dynamic, **value networks** through the integration, automation and extension of processes both inside and outside a company. This usually means letting go – handing over information and empowerment to employees, strategic partners, customers, distributors and other stakeholders.

The old value chain started with the purchasing of raw materials to the production of goods and services to their distribution, marketing, sales and after sales service. The new **value networks** reshuffle the sequence so that customers, distributors and partners are involved more as the business integrates into a flexible, faster moving, customer driven extended network of online partners. We will explore this initially using the business value framework.

Creating an e-business offers a golden opportunity to analyse and improve your whole business – its operations, processes and procedures as well as strategic partners – a fresh opportunity to re-engineer a company.

Perhaps one of the greatest impacts of the Internet is that it has forced many business to rethink all of their 'cherished perceptions and ideas'. Building an e-business help managers to adopt what the Zen Buddhists call 'the beginner's mind'.

Having said that, the term 'e-business' probably won't exist in a few years as most businesses will be using 'e-business' as part of their normal procedures. But reviewing business processes and re-engineering of companies will continue long after e-business has integrated itself into the business architecture. But what's normal tomorrow is not necessarily normal today. E-business can create new business models that take little notice of convention.

In this chapter we will show you how value networks have replaced the old value chain model. We will break it down into a simple business value framework that will help you to build an e-business architecture. We will take this further and help you to make this happen, i.e. how to create an e-business. We will also help you assess whether your e-business idea will make a profit. We will show you why many e-businesses fail and how to avoid failure with the help of a handy checklist.

Beyond the risk assessment of a new e-business, there are other risks in the online world. Could your board of directors be taken to court on the grounds of negligence if proper security measures and/or proper back-up systems are not in place? We will address these other issues in subsequent sections.

Finally, please note that e-business should never be seen as an end itself. Like a web site (which is a small part of e-business), it is a journey not a destination. You create your e-business with the hope that it will help customers, followed by suppliers, partners, distributors. Combine this with a drive for continual improvement and you can see why it's an ongoing journey.

This chapter explores the challenges and changes involved in creating an e-business. For many, these are uncharted waters.

Remember even e-business can learn from history – sixteenth century Florentine philosopher, Niccolo Machiavelli, once said: 'There is nothing more difficult to take in hand, more perilous to conduct, or more uncertain in its success, than to take the lead in the introduction of a new order of things'.

Fortunately, you don't have to take the lead as others are already there. You can learn from their mistakes and adopt best practice demonstrated in this book. You must, however, be prepared to change your ways of doing business. More recently, American business guru Peter Drucker said: 'A time of turbulence is a dangerous time, but its greatest danger is the temptation to deny reality'. So let's get on with it and explore e-business.

E-MARKETING EXCELLENCE

Yorkshire Water revises business processes

As part of the move to e-business, Yorkshire Water implemented SAP R/3 and SAP business-to-business procurement with the aim of increasing the efficiency of business processes, e-procurement, and improved supplier management. Systems development manager Dave Murphy explains how change was achieved:

'We ran a whole series of different computer systems which had been written by our own staff in the late eighties. They were heavily tailored to Yorkshire Water's needs and they were held together by bits of string and sticky tape'.

SAP was chosen as the result of a selection procedure since around 87% of business requirements were fulfilled by the software. Murphy says:

'To bridge the gap between 87% and 100%, Yorkshire Water preferred to adapt its business processes rather than the software. We didn't customize the software package because we realized that these business changes were a good thing'.

To give an indication of the areas of the business affected by the change, the following modules were implemented in a ten-month period:

- Sales and distribution (SD)
- Financials (FI)
- Controlling (CO)
- Materials management (MM)
- Project systems (PS)
- Time sheet (CATS)
- Payroll
- Human resources (HR)
- Asset accounting (AA).

Source: SAP web site (www.sap.com/uk)

SECTION SUMMARY 9.1

Introduction to e-business

E-business is bigger than e-marketing. It involves using technology to facilitate improvements to business processes and increase the efficiency of internal and external information flows with customers, suppliers and distributors. Rigid value chains are changed to flexible, responsive value networks.

9.2 E-business architecture

The e-business architecture brings together the systems, processes and applications used by all parts of the business. The e-business architecture connects these different processes, or applications, across both internal departments and external partners. 'Applications are like building blocks – they have to be put together carefully and systematically' to create a solid e-business architecture, state Kalakota and Robinson (2000). They say that good e-business design integrates applications so they 'work together like a well oiled machine to manage, organize, route and run a business'.

This e-business architecture transforms data into useful information available to the right person at the right time in the right place – which these days means anyplace, anywhere in the world. For example, using workflow technology can achieve 'intelligent routing' of an important e-mail query from a key account customer to someone who can act on it swiftly. It's easy to see how excellent information creates competitive advantage.

WHICH BUSINESS ARE YOU IN?

E-business is more than just transplanting existing business practices and processes into online applications. It is disruptive. The Internet and e-business certainly has the capacity to disrupt the old ways of doing business. E-business provides a golden opportunity to rethink the whole business – how it operates, who does what, where and when. E-business affects every aspect of a business.

Take the value chain – it's no longer valid. Even newer, customer focused, non-linear businesses are realizing that only parts of a company create real value and generate profit, while other parts don't. In other words some bits are profitable and other bits lose money.

So many businesses find other companies that can do those bits or certain processes better and outsource, or subcontract, seamlessly with a new strategic partner.

This drives a big question. What are the core competencies? They are those core skills that your business is better at than any one else. E-business may involve some businesses becoming modular, or molecular – shrinking back to their core competencies while outsourcing everything else. For example, about 70 per cent of Cisco's hardware goes directly from connected partner producers to customers without Cisco ever seeing it. E-businesses consists of 'business webs' or '**value networks**' – connected boxes of contracts. These value networks of production, distribution and service partners are glued together by the Internet. The Internet has revolutionized the global supply chain and inventory management for many companies.

Here is a shocking statement from John Hagel at the World Economic Forum (Kirkpatrick, 2001):

> *'Companies that design and brand their own products, build and package them, and deliver them to their customers will soon no longer exist'.*

This then begs the question 'What business am I in?' Established companies are not even sure what their core competencies are. Worse still, they no longer know who, where or what competition is. 'Who is my competitor?' is a difficult question, even if you do know what business you are in you may not know who's competing against you as today's competition is boundary-less, category-less and now sometimes just a minute part of the value network (or the old value chain). For example, different collaborators may form a consortium to bid for an engineering contract which will be difficult to counter by their competitors since they have limited knowledge about this new organization.

The weak links in the old value chain are now being picked off by new 'plug and play' companies (who are better at a particular process or that part of the chain) and who offer themselves as partners in an extended network – the value network – a kind of loose confederation. It can cause major shocks to established businesses. Plug and play companies can almost pop up overnight and slice your market up, and by time you've woken a chunk of the market is gone.

Responding to e-business is complex, but one way of simplifying it is to consider a basic framework which simplifies and clusters many of these applications together. The next section explores this in more detail.

Meanwhile just remember the e-business architecture must deliver a fast, error free, integrated service that is secure, robust, reliable and scalable. Not much to ask!

E-MARKETING INSIGHT

The Internet's chameleon qualities

Francis (2000) says: 'The Internet is not simply a new distribution channel, or a new way to communicate. It is many other things: a marketplace, an information system, a tool for manufacturing goods and services. It makes a difference to a whole range of things that managers do every day, from locating a new supplier to co-ordinating a project to collecting and managing customer data. Each of these, in turn, affects corporate life in many different ways. The changes that the Internet brings are simply more pervasive and varied than anything that has gone before. Even electricity did not promise so many new ways of doing things'.

E-MARKETING INSIGHT

Beyond the value chain concept

Chaffey (2004) suggests that although the value chain concept still helps to start the thought process about increasing business efficiency and customer value, it has inherent weaknesses:

1 More applicable to manufacturing rather than services.
2 A one-way chain involving push, ignores need to highlight customers' needs (through market research) and responsiveness through innovation and new product development, e.g. Cisco have feedback forms and forums on their site that enable them to collect information from customers and channel partners that can feed through to new product development.
3 Tends to ignore the idea of value networks.

SECTION SUMMARY 9.2

E-business architecture

Constructing the e-business architecture means somehow bringing together the systems, processes and applications from all parts of the business, both inside and outside. Not much to ask!

9.3 An e-business value framework

We're going to use a basic e-business framework as an overview of some of the components and key processes that are required to run a business.

Let us keep it simple. Let us ignore legal departments, accounting, HR and IT departments and assume that they have to be integrated into any business systems. So, let's just break up the business into those aspects that perform buy-side, in-side and sell-side processes (Figure 9.1). This identifies three key areas in which to achieve e-business performance. There are other approaches to this. But for now, let's just stick with this simple model.

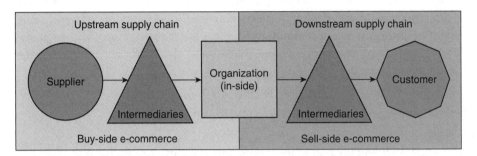

Figure 9.1 A simple e-business value framework

BUY-SIDE E-BUSINESS

The buy-side is B2B – buying raw materials and or services. It can include procurement, inbound logistics, and warehousing. Here, the business's **extranet** is used to open up certain aspects of the business (applications and data) to an exclusive audience of carefully selected suppliers to allow: faster and easier trade with suppliers, manufacturers and/or distributors; collaboration with suppliers, manufacturers and/or distributors so that they move from 'independence to interdependence' sharing data to improve operational efficiency and ultimately customer satisfaction.

Reduced working capital is achieved as efficient systems allow 'just-in-time' deliveries thereby removing vast quantities of cash tied up in stock (working capital) as shown by the e-marketing excellence box on Shell Chemical in Section 3.4. This is an 'extended enterprise' where partner suppliers and distributors work much more closely together. Supply chain management applications are commonly used.

IN-SIDE E-BUSINESS

The in-side is sometimes known as B2E – business to employee – involving internal processes and communications. This could be manufacturing, management or operations. Here the **intranet** empowers employees by opening up access to key information and applications. Any of these internal processes can be outsourced. Excellent B2E systems are vital if a small core internal team is going to run a tight ship.

Now the intranet can be used to:

- Improve communications between business and employee as employees can find information more easily and communicate with each other via discussion groups.
- Evolve from competency to 'responsive knowledge workers'.
- Use collaboration and knowledge management tools.

Typical applications used here are business analytics or intelligence, knowledge management and decision support tools and or **enterprise resource planning** (ERP) applications. Many of these are extended into partners, i.e. extended ERP – Dell and Ford.

SELL-SIDE E-BUSINESS

The sell side involves processes and applications that help sell to and service customers, whether directly or indirectly through intermediaries. E-CRM applications and selling chain management applications are commonly used. Here the **extranet** provides exclusive use to strategic intermediary partners such as distributors and also to key account or registered customers. Extranets can be used to:

- Sell to customers directly and indirectly through intermediaries.
- Move from online occasional sales to lifetime loyalty relationships.
- Serve them better and manage customer relations.
- Speak to them individually and tailor one-to-one offerings drawn from the database.

There are also many applications:

- CRM
- ERP
- Supply chain management
- Selling chain management
- Operating resource management
- Enterprise application integration (EAI)
- Business analytics
- Knowledge management
- Decision support apps.

Remember that isolated, stand alone applications will soon be history. For new e-businesses, options for **business models** and **revenue models** will also have to be reviewed. Some of the options for business models are shown in the box 'Paul Timmers on business models' and for revenue models in the box 'Yahoo! Business and revenue models'. **Revenue models** specifically describe different techniques for generation of income. For existing companies, the standard revenue model is the income from sales of products or services. This may be either for selling direct from the manufacturer or supplier of the service, or through an intermediary who will take a cut of the selling price. Other options for generating revenue include selling advertising space or **affiliate** revenues.

E-MARKETING INSIGHT

Paul Timmers on business models

Timmers (1999) identifies no less than eleven different types of business model that can be facilitated by the web as follows:

1 *E-shop* – Marketing of a company or shop via web.

2 *E-procurement* – Electronic tendering and procurement of goods and services.

3 *E-malls* – A collection of e-shops such as the now defunct BarclaySquare. (This model didn't prove sustainable. The nearest equivalent is price comparison sites such as Pricerunner (www.pricerunner.com) which link through to different e-shops.)

4 *E-auctions* – These can be for B2C, e.g. eBay (www.ebay.com) or B2C, e.g. QXL (www.qxl.com).

5 *Virtual communities* – These can be B2C communities such as Xoom (www.xoom.com) or B2B communities such as Vertical Net (www.vertical.net). These are important for their potential in e-marketing and are described in the Focus on Virtual Communities section in Chapter 6 of Timmers' book.

6 *Collaboration platforms* – These enable collaboration between businesses or individuals, e.g. Yahoo Groups! (www.yahoo.com) services.

7 *Third-party marketplaces* – Marketplaces such as EC21 (www.ec21.com).

8 *Value-chain integrators* – Offer a range of services across the value-chain.

9 *Value-chain service providers* – Specialize in providing functions for a specific part of the value-chain such as the logistics company UPS (www.ups.com).

10 *Information brokerage* – Providing information for consumers and businesses, often to assist in making the buying decision or for business operations or leisure.

11 *Trust and other services* – An example is Truste (www.truste.org), who authenticate the quality of service provided by companies trading on the web.

E-MARKETING EXCELLENCE

Yahoo! Business and revenue models

Chaffey (2004) describes three different perspectives for considering business and revenue models shown in Figure 9.2. It can be seen that Yahoo! has been one of the more successful Internet pureplays since it has developed a range of revenue sources through growth and acquisition.

1 *Marketplace position perspective.* Here Yahoo! is both a retailer and a marketplace intermediary.

2 *Revenue model perspective.* Yahoo! has commission-based sales through Yahoo! shopping and also has advertising as a revenue model.

3 *Commercial arrangement perspective.* Yahoo! is involved in all three types of commercial arrangement shown.

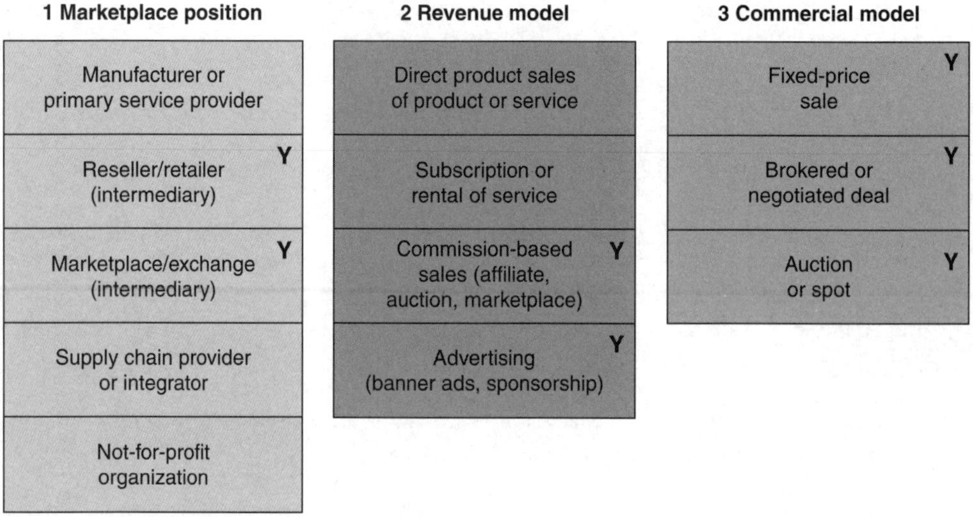

1 Marketplace position	2 Revenue model	3 Commercial model
Manufacturer or primary service provider	Direct product sales of product or service	Fixed-price sale Y
Reseller/retailer (intermediary) Y	Subscription or rental of service	Brokered or negotiated deal Y
Marketplace/exchange (intermediary) Y	Commission-based sales (affiliate, auction, marketplace) Y	Auction or spot Y
Supply chain provider or integrator	Advertising (banner ads, sponsorship) Y	
Not-for-profit organization		

Figure 9.2 Alternative perspectives on business and revenue models

---

SECTION SUMMARY 9.3

An e-business value framework

A simple business framework for assessing e-business change is:

- Buy-side e-business – extranets used for buying raw materials and or services. It can include procurement, inbound logistics, and warehousing.

- In-side e-business – intranets used for optimizing internal processes and communications. This could be manufacturing, management or operations.

- Sell-side e-business – extranets for exclusive use by strategic intermediary partners such as distributors and key account or registered customers.

Together these elements of the framework help to optimize supply chain management.

9.4 Buy-side applications

Internet technology can be used to open up the purchasing, in bound logistics, stock management and re-ordering system to an exclusive audience of carefully selected suppliers who gain direct access to the company's back office systems via the exclusive external Internet, the company's extranet. This way, the organization gets to trade with suppliers, manufacturers and/or distributors more accurately, more swiftly and more easily as cumbersome paperwork processes are abandoned and faster, easier, smarter systems are opened up to supply partners. Advanced supply chain integration becomes easier with e-business technology. This, in turn, strengthens the partnership relationship.

Chaffey (2004) suggests that the stage models can be developed for the buy-side in the same way as for the sell-side (Section 1.12). The following levels of sophistication in *product sourcing applications* can be identified:

- *Level I*. No use of the web for product sourcing and no electronic integration with suppliers.
- *Level II*. Review and selection from competing suppliers using intermediary web sites, B2B exchanges and supplier web sites. Orders placed by conventional means.
- *Level III*. Orders placed electronically through EDI, via intermediary sites, exchanges or supplier sites. No integration between organization's systems and supplier's systems. Rekeying of orders necessary into procurement or accounting systems.
- *Level IV*. Orders placed electronically with integration with company's procurement systems.
- *Level V*. Orders placed electronically with full integration of company's procurement, manufacturing requirements planning and stock control systems.

As part of strategy development, the current level can be identified and then target levels set for the future.

PARTNER RELATIONSHIP MANAGEMENT (PRM)

Rather than the 'them and us' of buyers versus suppliers, the 'partners' develop common goals and common measures to monitor their joint performance. This creates an atmosphere of collaboration and co-operation where opportunities and problems are identified and solved together.

Both the supplier and buyer move from 'independence to interdependence' sharing data to improve operational efficiency and ultimately, customer satisfaction. The original organization now builds a network of trusted partners, a network, or an **'extended enterprise'**, where partner suppliers and distributors work much more closely together courtesy of web technology.

DRIVING FORCES FOR PRM

Forming such buy-side links can be proactive. Some companies, like GEC, will not trade with suppliers if they cannot both integrate and trade online. In return, the buyers can easily relay current sales and stock levels in real time to suppliers. For example, a supermarket (buyer) can collect, analyse and disseminate sales and other data via the Internet to its suppliers. Within seconds, information on actual sales, store inventory and shelf space is available to suppliers (via a standard browser). It can be downloaded right into the supplier's own ERP (enterprise resource planning) spreadsheet and other systems.

This data can also be used in sophisticated forecasting systems which combine historical trends with current sales demand to predict how much will be bought. This in turn helps both the suppliers and the retail stores to improve promotional planning as they can monitor early responses to, say, advertising campaigns more quickly. This in turn, facilitates further collaboration particularly if joint promotions or exclusive promotions are created. The partnership grows stronger. They can even have newsflashes about specific product sales.

All very exciting stuff, but you can probably guess what can be a major barrier to all of this culture – organizations not used to sharing data and accessing each other's ERPs. The security risks and fears associated may require a gigantic cultural leap. We look at this in more detail in Section 9.7 Creating an e-business.

There is one other interesting point, in fact a new phenomenon created by tight online supply chain management, and that is **negative working capital**. Working capital refers to money tied up in stocks and debtors, money that is required to run a business. It is possible for a company to reduce stock by having suppliers deliver as and when orders come in. This **'just-in-time'** delivery obviously reduces stock and the cash it ties up. In addition cash is boosted if customer payments are taken (when the order is placed) before paying suppliers. This creates negative working capital.

E-MARKETING EXCELLENCE

Virgin Atlantic Airlines select Tranmit Sprinter

Nick Wildgoose, Head of Purchasing, says:

'In evaluating IT systems, we have several criteria in mind including ease of use, which is vital to user acceptance, and ease of integration, which is key to minimizing disruption and costs. Tranmit's product satisfied these criteria but also allowed us to implement a solution that reflected the reality of the marketplace. Whether our suppliers generate invoices on paper or electronically we need to be able to push ahead in line with our commitment to innovation and service. This software allows us to do that without leaving our business partners behind'.

Figure 9.3 shows how the solution chosen supports management of paper invoices, an intermediate step before all invoices are electronic.

E-MARKETING INSIGHT

Dell and Ford and the Extended Enterprise

When Dell receive an order from Ford Motor via the PremierPages extranet, Dell knows immediately what type of worker is ordering and what kind of PC is required. Dell assembles the hardware and installs the software including Ford-specific configuration code that's stored at Dell. That's an integrated supply chain as part of the Ford or Dell Extended Enterprise.

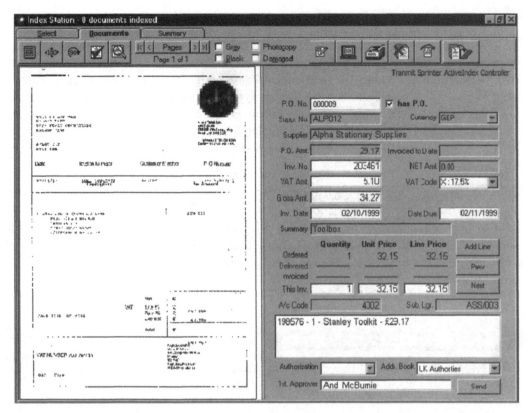

Figure 9.3 Document management and workflow component of Tranmit (with permission of Tranmit). (*Source:* Tranmit (www.tranmit.co.uk))

SECTION SUMMARY 9.4

Buy-side applications

Perfect information about customers, distribution partners and supplier partners can tighten the supply chain and create competitive advantage.

9.5 In-side applications

This section explores how web technology can help the besieged employee to do a better job. How the business can communicate more easily with employees and how employees can communicate with the organization and work with each other more easily.

This is crucial as grand strategies don't work if they are poorly executed. Some estimates suggest that *up to 40 per cent potential return on marketing spend is lost by employees*. In some cases these staff are the brand builders engaged in hundreds of millions of 'brand moments'. Staff communications become even more important here.

The internal Internet, the **intranet**, can change the way people work together. Replace cumbersome paper-based systems. Reduce information overload. Create 'responsive knowledge workers'. Use collaboration and knowledge management tools to make better decisions. On top of this an e-HR department can create virtual classrooms to support 'just-in-time learning' and longer, more structured learning involving both individuals and collaborative team efforts. But careful consideration needs to be given to avoid drowning in a sea of e-mails that clog systems and people. Knowledge management, properly implemented, is key to success.

With over 1000 new books published every day, hundreds of thousands of new web pages every day and a growing number of e-mails, it's not surprising that many managers feel overwhelmed by information. In the US it's a medical condition known as 'information fatigue syndrome'. The Novartis box describes an actual case where managers had too much information and a paper-based system that didn't work. They sought an intranet solution.

E-MARKETING EXCELLENCE

Novartis select Autonomy for knowledge management

John McCulloch, Manager, Executive Information Systems says:

'Novartis is a world leader in pharmaceuticals, healthcare, agribusiness and nutrition. That means we handle a vast amount of complex information daily, both from internal and external sources. Until now, that has cost us a great deal of time and money in manual processes, but Autonomy's technology can automate the whole process from start to finish. We are delighted to be bringing the technology on board'.

Novartis implemented Autonomy Portal-in-a-Box™ to provide an automated infrastructure for the handling and personalization of the complex information generated internally as well as research papers, market intelligence and breaking news from outside. The system not only aggregates and personalizes an enormous amount of content without incurring large labour costs in the form of staff to read, manually tag and hyperlink each piece of information, but also dynamically and continuously understands individual needs and preferences in order to deliver compelling and timely content.

Personalization occurs by automatic profiling of employees by analysing the ideas in the text they read and write in company documents, e-mail and web sites visited. Important information is automatically delivered to top managers by alert flashing icons, based on their interests and professional expertise, as soon as it is available, without the user having to waste valuable time actively searching for it.

Source: Autonomy web site (www.autonomy.com)

E-MARKETING EXCELLENCE

ASDA's intranet

Supermarket ASDA had the information management problems of unreliable distribution of documents to 230 stores; too much information with managers complaining of being 'inundated' with communication while frustrated by loss and late arrival of certain documents. Managers wanted information in a format that can be searched and the facility to share their ideas with their colleagues without simply increasing the volume of e-mail.

An intranet was created that was intended to add value to communications from a user's point of view by identifying and prioritizing applications with most business benefit. It also optimized the cost and time taken for authors to create information – real emphasis was placed on sustainability of applications. A further aim was to encourage a broad church of ASDA House departments to become involved in the development programme – to build internal awareness. The intranet gave staff access to:

- Merchandise briefs
- Daily weather forecasts
- Press releases and internal announcements
- HR policies
- Customer service information
- Checkout queue length reports
- Store performance self-assessment system
- Peer-based discussion groups.

Staff are also encouraged to add to and amend the information – authors of textual information are assisted by background routines that automatically validate the completion of fields, create hypertext links, index documents for the search facility and delete obsolete documents. Workflow processes facilitate quality control and approval of material prior to publication.

SECTION SUMMARY 9.5

In-side applications

In-side applications use intranets to share knowledge amongst employees while avoiding problems of information overload.

9.6 Sell-side applications

The sell-side involves processes and applications that help to both sell and service customers whether directly or indirectly.

Sell side applications include transactional e-commerce sites, e-commerce selling chain management applications and **e-CRM** apps. CRM is also considered in Sections 3.10, 4.7 and 8.4.

Relationship marketing helps nurture lifetime customers whose repeat sales generate much higher profits than new customers. Managing the customer relationship makes cross selling and upselling helpful rather than intrusive.

In many ways CRM is not anything new since good marketers have always taken care of their customers. What is new is the lack of CRM in the fast moving online world. A world where the higher expectations of online customer are regularly crushed by sloppy e-marketing. Surprisingly, excellence in the offline world is often forgotten in the online world even by major players: e-mails are left unanswered for days.

So major efforts are required to keep online customers loyal. Have you got the processes in place to ensure excellent service? Do you remember customers, their names, needs, past preferences when they contact you? Is there a seamless system that recognizes customers, whether they access you through iDTV, i-kiosks, web radio, mobile phones or good old traditional PC-accessed Internet web sites? Does your system help you to paint a total picture of each online customer?

Have you got the software to exploit the valuable data you can collect from customers? Most organizations don't. The reality is that many companies have a diverse range of incompatible applications combined with dirty data (unclean data).

It therefore makes a lot of sense to nurture the captured customers into lifetime friends, particularly if they're ideal customers. The returns on this investment are large.

The online world presents new challenges when nurturing customer relationships. One particular challenge is the tension between security and customer convenience – the hassle of hard to remember passwords versus easy access.

SECTION SUMMARY 9.6

Sell-side applications

E-CRM is all about common sense yet so many major companies abandon common sense and treat customers dismally. The database is an asset that must be maintained and used to enhance relationships.

9.7 Creating the e-business

So how do you create an e-business? How do you go about it? Here are seven steps to e-business.

1. ESTABLISH THE VISION

Creating an e-business requires a clear vision of where you want to be. How you want your business to grow, expand, extend and operate in a new collaborative environment. One thing that must be absolutely clear is the vision – what you want the e-business to do and what benefits it will bring.

After that you find the technology and team to do this. Not the other way around. Technology should not drive the vision – customer needs and partner collaboration requirements should drive the vision. Technology will do whatever it is asked. Do not let technology control the vision. You control the technology. You control the vision.

2. GET SENIOR MANAGEMENT SUPPORT (AND RESOURCES)

Creating an e-business whether a brand new, pure play dotcom, or a mixed-mode clicks and mortar (online and offline) business requires careful consideration, research, planning, testing and implementation – a lot of energy and effort. It requires a team of dedicated staff, fully supported by top management.

One measure of this is whether there is budget available for the resources required even just to research it – as this requires time, people and money. Top management support is a must otherwise emotions, tensions and energy are unnecessarily aroused, exhausted and frustrated. Another senior management challenge is to create a culture that welcomes change rather than resists it. A culture of shared responsibility where empowered employees own their own employability.

3. SELECT A PROJECT TEAM AND ANALYSE REQUIREMENTS

You need a strong project leader and a cross-functional team from inside and outside the organization. Task the group with identifying what the requirements of the e-business might be – what processes need to link together – who needs to link with whom … what information they need and when. Run 'discovery workshops'. Allow partners access to internal systems in real time. Project management skills are essential.

4. REVISIT THE VALUE NETWORK (AND CORE COMPETENCIES – WHAT BUSINESS ARE WE IN?)

This is the big one. Businesses are breaking up their old value chains and reconstructing themselves around their core competencies – their 'global core'. The other parts of the old chain (whether logistics, procurement, HR or even marketing) are fulfilled by a web of strategic partnerships. There appears to be a not so subtle shift from the delivery of work to the co-ordination of work. Focusing on core competencies forces managers to ask a fundamental question – what business are we in? Remember the 'outsource fiends'? There are many issues arising around 'down sizing' and outsourcing including dying concepts such as staff loyalty and staff morale.

5. DESIGN AN E-BUSINESS ARCHITECTURE

Having decided what business you're in and what are your core competencies, the next question is 'What are the processes involved in running the business?' What needs to be linked to what? The value network reaches beyond the enterprise and into the extended enterprise's network of collaborative partners – suppliers, distributors, producers and others. Whether extended to outside strategic partners or kept within the e-business architecture, it has to create a seamless flow of information between different functions and departments. Both inside and outside the company itself. Does the front end integrate with the back end? Can it be built stage-by-stage? Is it scalable? Is it robust and secure? What is the risk assessment?

6. DEVELOP, PILOT, TRAIN AND ROLL-OUT

The integrated applications obviously have to be developed – although many of them are off the shelf. The danger of tailor-made or proprietary apps is that they can take so long to develop that they emerge as 'still born' solutions – out of date before released. The systems are tested rigorously, bugs extracted, staff are trained and eventually the e-business is ready to roll out. One of the delicate roll-out issues that has to be addressed earlier is whether to integrate the e-business with the main business, separate it but keep it in the same premises or spin it off as a separate and reintegrate it later. Staff buy-in is essential. Time, money and effort has to be spent bringing them on board otherwise they resist and resent the new e-business systems.

7. BENCHMARK, MEASURE AND MONITOR

As mentioned earlier, e-business, like a web site, is not a destination but, rather, a journey. A journey towards continual improvement. So the whole operation is regularly reviewed, benchmarked and reported for improvements. New technology will continue to roll out – better, faster, easier, seamless and sensible. Remember Moore's Law. The key is not to constantly update bits and pieces as it can be disruptive to have the processes changing all the time without the staff buying into the idea. So good management skills are required to harness the technology and the delicate continual drive towards constant improvement ... to constantly delight customers and partners.

How long do you think a major e-business project might take to go through all these stages? Answer: 24–56 weeks for a large company, 10–16 weeks for a small company.

SECTION SUMMARY 9.7

Becoming an e-business

The seven steps to becoming an e-business are:

1 Establish the vision.
2 Get senior management support (and resources).
3 Select a project team and analyse requirements.
4 Revisit the value network (and core competencies).

5 Design an e-business architecture.

6 Develop, pilot, train and roll-out.

7 Benchmark, measure and monitor.

9.8 E-business security

There are thousands of hackers, vandals and viruses, at large at any given time. It's disturbing, whether you are concerned about the privacy of your personal data, or the potential risk to your organization. Businesses and customers get damaged. Kids, conmen, criminals and competitors, not to mention pressure groups, political groups, government intelligence agencies and many more want to break through security systems.

In the corporate world, popular targets for activists include: large corporations, news outlets, banking/finance, hate groups, political sites, e-commerce, personal/credit card data and computer security sites. What's left?

The excitement of building a new dynamic e-business combined with the race to market exposes many companies to significant new risks. This is the case as the extended enterprise opens up systems and data to external parties. Poorly designed systems thrown together by technical whizz-kids often ignore the wide variety of risks lurking out there.

E-BUSINESS SECURITY THREATS

Check the list of different types of security breaches. You will know of some of these risks, but who is responsible for managing the threats to your organization and are they covering all the bases? These are some of the threats:

- *Credit card fraud.* Imagine having your card details sucked into cyberspace and used by someone else? Or imagine customers denying receipt of goods delivered? Almost half of Visa's card disputes are Internet-related. Elsewhere it's higher. For the e-tailer the percentage of fraudulent purchases on sites can run to double figures. On top of this returns can be high.

- *Distributed denial of service (DDOS).* This effectively denies access to your site when hackers flood network routers from lots of different sites with an overwhelming amount of traffic to targeted web sites. They effectively shut down the sites.

- *Cyber graffiti.* Hackers can alter your web site, insert nasty images, false information, false testimonials and even direct customers to another site. Non-hackers can put up rogue sites sounding very similar to your own and attracting lots of your customers. Spot the difference between: Investsmartindia.com and Investmartindia.com.

- *Alien computer control.* If you have a permanent (broadband) Internet connection (cable or ADSL), you're constantly open and vulnerable to the outside world. Any hacker can easily gain access to your computer by using network scanning tools which track poorly protected systems. Then an alien or remote third party controls your PC. Such hijacking is technically known as a 'Trojan horse' after the classical assault on Troy. See Figure 9.4 for an example of a SPAM hoax about such an attack.

---

eMarketing Fright:
From: ealym@x.com
To: paul@y.com
Subject: A Trojan Horse is on your PC

Hi, I am from Belgium and you'll not believe me, but a Trojan Horse is on your PC. I've scanned
the network ports on the Internet. (I know, that's illegal) And I have found your pc. Your pc is open
on the Internet for everybody! Because the services.exe Trojan is running on your system. Check
this, open the task manager and try to stop that! You'll see, you can't stop this Trojan. When you
use win98/me you can't see the Trojan.
On my system was this Trojan too!
And I've found a tool to kill that bad thing.
I hope that I've helped you too!
Sorry for my bad English!
greets.

Figure 9.4 Example hoax e-mail received by P.R. Smith – threats, hoaxes and real problems
are everywhere

- *Chat room undesirables.* Even without permanent connections, your chat rooms can be invaded by uninvited and unwanted third parties such as racists. They post obscene messages or more subtle racist arguments to often vulnerable audiences. In 2001 Telextext had to close its SMS-based chat service because of racist taunting by rival football fans.

- *Intellectual property theft.* On top of this, theft of intellectual property happens all the time – software, music, information downloaded, copied and passed on. Sometimes it's duplicated and sold commercially by unauthorized pirates. Worse still, pirating is effectively legal in some countries where there is no IPR law.

- *Competitive information.* Another type of intellectual property also gets stolen – sensitive company information, particularly competitive information and databases of customers.

- *Anything that damages your data.* Viruses, for instance, can have huge legal implications since without properly used back-up systems directors can be liable for any damage to their own business.

Apart from damage done to the business, security violations can also end in downstream negligence litigation.

E-BUSINESS SECURITY SOLUTIONS

Good security starts with a security policy. Do you have one? System security is part of a wider security policy that should include physical (lost laptop, stolen PC) and procedural security (to avoid disaffected employees deliberately formatting a disk or sending information out).

It's good to build security in early to the design of an e-business as it's hard to retrofit security to an operational system under attack: 'Design security in rather than inspect security breaches out'.

Tough decisions are required, e.g. convenience and security don't always work together. For instance, passwords are a nuisance but do offer at least a minimal level of security. Equally, risk can be reduced by asking customers to pre-register before purchasing anything or clearing payment before goods are despatched.

There are many other technological, physical and procedural controls required:

- *Contracts*. Clauses that define the security processes to be used may have to be incorporated into contracts with companies you do business with online.
- *Trend and exception monitoring*. Visa contact cardholders if any 'out of character' purchases are made and AmEx offer temporary numbers that are valid for a predetermined (1–2 hours) shopping period and amount.
- *Public key technology and cryptography*. Web servers and browsers can be setup easily to encrypt or seal all communications. Public key encryption basically confirms the identity of an individual or company as established by an intermediary trusted by your company; proves a transaction originated with that individual or company, so it cannot subsequently be denied (often called non-repudiation); and seals data, such as transactions, or e-mails to prevent the contents being altered.
- *Intrusion detection routines*. These scan for attacks such as denial of service or access to a site via a competitor. They are often part of a **firewall** solution which is a specialized server at the gateway to a company that is used to keep out unwanted intruders.
- *Virus scanners*. These should be set-up to monitor continuously and kept updated to the latest version.
- *Audit trails*. You need to record good audit trails of key events, particularly security related events and transaction records. Do you audit the information that should be retained to help resolution of disputed electronic transactions?
- *Back-up*. Back-up is crucial if your business depends on being online. Do you have good back-up and recovery procedures? Is your web site content stored separately?

The best systems in the world aren't going to help if people don't use them properly. A security solution is only as strong as its weakest link and lapses such as assigning 'no brainer' passwords like 'password' or the day of the week create gaping holes for even the most novice hacker.

E-MARKETING INSIGHT

Some commonsense security guidelines

Here's some simple commonsense advice from the Institute of Public Relations:

1 Turn on antivirus software (and update it).
2 Know the original creator of e-mails with attachments.
3 Know the purpose of the attachment before opening it.
4 Don't be fooled by e-mail virus hoaxes.
5 Update IRC Internet Chat Software products.

6 Be wary of newsgroups and mail lists.

7 Keep informed.

8 Be paranoid.

9 Write-protect floppies before inserting into other user's computers.

10 Back-up, back-up, back-up!

SECTION SUMMARY 9.8

E-business security

There are many security challenges out there including:

- Credit card fraud
- Distributed denial of service
- Web site defacing
- Controlling your computer undesirables
- Populating your chat rooms
- Intellectual property theft
- Sensitive data theft.

Fortunately there are many solutions, from firewalls to filters and encryption. But remember constant vigilance is required in this fast changing online world.

9.9 E-business success criteria

By the end of this section you will understand the key characteristics of successful e-businesses. In this section we review nine criteria. The more of these criteria you can score in the better: creating an e-business is like a decathlon!

Starting an e-business or repurposing an existing one is not like starting an ordinary business; but many of the criteria for success are the same for non-e-businesses … good business principles and practice are applicable anywhere …

THE NINE SUCCESS CRITERIA

1 *A clicks and mortar parent provides cash flow and resources.* Despite popular opinion, many dot-coms are now profitable or at least forecasting profitability! Most of them however are not stand-alone e-businesses, but clicks and mortar businesses. This is no surprise: it merely shows that 'mothering' works: the e-business is brought into this world and nurtured by a caring parent which allows it to develop its individuality before eventually it becomes self-supporting and leaves home.

That parent could be an existing model business: big retailer develops online sales; big service co-develops online customer relationship management system ... or the parent is an investor group providing financial succour and ideally some business acumen and skills too.

Besides the e-businesses in profit already (capable of leaving home ...), many more are approaching profitability. So what makes the successful ones work?

2 *An existing brand provides brand awareness and a customer base.* Building on existing brands: most companies now realize their brand equity is transferable to e-business. In fact, customers are so wary of the plethora of unheard-of online suppliers – it is reassuring for them to find a traditional brand.

3 *Existing management team and structure.* Existing management and organizational structures can help if it means your e-business doesn't have to resource, from day one, all the functions needed to run a business but which don't directly lead to the creation of value: personnel, finance, property, perhaps IT even. Even so, you need a management that is quick-witted and flexible and capable of allowing the e-business venture to grow somewhat off the cuff: rigid adherence to plan can cause it to fail.

4 *Value network already in place.* The value network must be in place from supply-side to customer service, fulfilment and despatch. Or if it isn't, focus on putting it in place; or maybe a bit of both: Tesco's online shopping relies in part on the existing supply chain (buying goods, distributing them to supermarkets) and in part on a new added element (staff to pick orders from shelves, vans to provide delivery service).

5 *If not, ability to find suppliers and partners to create the value network for fulfilment.* Creating the value network is a tricky call for traditional retailers who are geared up to hand you a bag of goods at a till, but have no infrastructure to handle orders, pick stock from shelves, pack and despatch and then handle your phone enquiry three days later. The successful e-business gets this right: where the e-business value network is different from the one in the mother business, they create the network ... Get fulfilment wrong and you can damage the reputation of the mother business too.

6 *E-business enables re-engineering of existing business.* Business process re-engineering (BPR) might be a partial by-product of building an e-business. Or, it could be a business opportunity in itself: e-business enables the traditional firm to re-engineer itself and achieve new scale – for example Vacuum-Cleaners Direct which grew from £170 000 sales to over £1 m. So, get it right and you can transform a small business into, well, at least a not so small business. And all because there is now a better product/service for the customer. Whether you have expanded the market or simply shifted market share in your direction ... do you care?

7 *Realistic pace of development.* Develop at a realistic pace and do not try to grow too fast too soon – Tesco deliberately ran the service from certain flagship stores only until they had got all parts of the value network running smoothly.

8 *E-business operates in a marketable niche.* Considering operating in an existing or new niche – as value networks get more complex and as e-businesses find there are missing components, there are opportunities to be the provider of these. You can create an e-business which has its own virtues as a niche activity. Particularly if the e-business enables you

resolve problems of marketing and distribution because it is the best way to target your customers.

9 *Additional benefits of bricks and mortar.* What else can a bricks and mortar mother-business bring to the e-business?

- Confidence for investors: they can smell and taste a real business and recognize the brand; as pure-play dotcoms started to fail, investors got over the greedy rush and worried about the potential failure of non-recognized brands.
- More than likely, a firm cash flow to give the e-business working capital.
- More than likely, purchasing power through scale and therefore lower costs than new-start rivals.

Finally, like any business venture, you need to get the three Ts right … timing, timing and timing.

E-MARKETING INSIGHT

IBM's seven primary components of e-business management

IBM (2001) suggest these are the main components required for e-business management:

1 Mission – purpose and approach to managing e-business.
2 Organization – structure and reporting relationships and connections between e-business resources and their counterparts in other areas of the enterprise.
3 Roles and responsibilities to define work activities of groups and individuals.
4 Processes that define the sequence of activities and outcomes.
5 Measures to ensure accountability and improvement.
6 Policies for achieving standards.
7 Content model to provide consistency and quality of content.

E-MARKETING INSIGHT

Morgan Stanley Dean Witter also provides a check-list of success criteria for subscribers to its Internet Market Study Service.

- Sustainable market position with first-mover advantage.
- Clear broad distribution plans; reach and market share.
- Customer focus.
- Stickiness and customer loyalty.

- Rapidly growing customer base.
- Opportunity to increase customer 'touch' points.
- Extensible product lines.
- Annuity-like business with sustainable operating leverage assisted by barriers to entry.
- Low-cost infrastructure and development.
- Strong business momentum.

SECTION SUMMARY 9.9

E-business success criteria

From this section you now know some of the factors which markedly improve the chances of success. First of these is having a clicks-and-mortar parent to provide succour, resources, economies of scale, investor confidence; you should be able to make a virtue of existing management structures and expertise … but it is not vital provided you establish the value network you need and create a niche in which to operate and offer a significant value/service proposition to your customers.

9.10 Why did the dotcoms become dot-bombs?

Some dotcoms are now profitable. That means most are not, and that excludes the already failed ones! There are lots of casualties out there. You won't have got this far without having read of the many spectacular failures: Boo.com, Clickmango, eToys. There is even an influential web-site that tracks failing e-businesses and marks their downfall (www.fuckedcompany.com). What's gone wrong? By the end of this section you'll know why they failed and how failure could have been avoided. The reasons given are also typical in e-business failure – you will be able to apply these tests to your own or another company's plans and assess the risk factors and then be able to revise the plan to increase the chances of success.

We will show you why they failed and how failure could have been avoided. But long before anyone thought of e-business, it was an accepted truth that most new businesses fail. So before you consider the e-biz aspects of your e-business, ensure that the non-e-specific aspects are all working and on-track.

THE NINE FAILURE CRITERIA

1 *Bad idea in the first place; there is no market*. Much of the talk of the new economy is about new **business models** and **revenue models** (see Section 9.3). Clearly, if these fail, the business will fail. The important patterns in failure all have to do with time: you run out of cash, the

environment changes, investor appetite changes, markets change, morale changes. But that doesn't mean you can't control these to a great extent. Many dotcoms did not have crystal clear propositions that actually satisfied real needs. A clever bit of web technology is not a proposition, a solution nor even a product.

2 *Bad production or delivery*. Above all though, is failure down to the product or service itself? Was it just a bad idea in the first place; sometimes there is a gap in the market because there really is no market (the proverbial 'coals to Newcastle')! However the ideas may have been good but wrecked by bad production or delivery.

3 *Management inexperience or inflexibility*. If management is a key to success it can also be a key to failure: e-business bosses are typically younger than leaders of traditional companies. They may lack business experience in key areas and failure results. Equally, traditional managers often can't cope with fledgling enterprises: they lack the flexibility, creativity and sheer nerve to do anything other than stick to Plan A. The e-business has to be able to respond to trend changes and rapidly alter plans. Sometimes investors are their own worst enemies – lack of financial control at boo.com – whose fault was that?

4 *Failure to create a niche*. Failure to create a niche and stick to it until it works: to move from profit-seeking to profit making, you need to sell more not spend more: yet too many e-businesses do the latter: opening European offices, further developing the technology without addressing the reasons why they are not making profits. Going for the niche is all very well, but customers are pragmatists and expect to see a whole product: they won't buy your brilliant idea if you can't manufacture it, sell it, deliver it and service it. Hence the failure so far of schemes to reward Internet usage.

5 *Trying to create the e-business in isolation from the whole of the value network*. One solution is to address the value network problem: should the new e-business try and create the entire network or reel in partners and associates with specialisms in each segment? Maybe even embrace suppliers as partners?

6 *Company focused on the product or service and not on the customer's needs*. If the e-business failed to focus on customer need business failure is guaranteed. It is too easy in the flush of enthusiasm for a new idea to forget to ask: does anyone want to buy this?

7 *Product/service badly marketed*. Underestimate the marketing and you'll fail: this is the myth of 100 million users. Without a mother business to fall back on, there is a lot of marketing to do. Thus you now find a www address on almost every product label and every newspaper and outdoor advert. Remembering marketing's four Ps – product, price, placement and promotion. Market leaders are not always the best of breed of a product, but are nearly always the best marketed.

8 *Investor panic*. Numerous examples show that investor enthusiasm can rapidly evaporate if results are not delivered.

9 *Technology not ready or not delivering*. Technology solutions take time to develop and redefine if not delivering, in the meantime the brand and revenue stream will be damaged.

E-MARKETING INSIGHT

Michael Porter on strategy and the Internet

Michael Porter attacks those who have suggested that the Internet invalidates his well known strategy models. He says:

> *'Many have assumed that the Internet changes everything, rendering all the old rules about companies and competition obsolete. That may be a natural reaction, but it is a dangerous one … decisions that have eroded the attractiveness of their industries and undermined their own competitive advantages'.*

He gives the example of some industries using the Internet to change the basis of competition away from quality, features and service and towards price, making it harder for anyone in their industries to turn a profit.

In reviewing industry structure, he reinterprets the well-known five forces model concluding that many of the effects of the Internet, such as commoditization, are damaging to industry. He re-iterates the importance of six fundamental principles of strategic positioning:

1 The right goal: superior long-term return on investment.

2 A value proposition distinct from those of the competition.

3 A distinctive value chain to achieve competitive advantage.

4 Trade-offs in products or services may be required to achieve distinction.

5 Strategy defines how all elements of what a company does fit together.

6 Strategy involves continuity of direction.

Source: Porter (2001).

E-MARKETING INSIGHT

Seth Neiman on failures caused by running out of time

Seth Neiman of Cross-Venture Partners in a letter to Red Herring:

> *'There are some very important patterns in failure, and they all have to do with time. Failure in a start-up happens when you run out of cash and depends on whether or not you can get more. In addition, the environment can change, investor appetite can change, markets can change, and morale can change. So the patterns are embedded in the way a company spends its time – and, of course, its cash. The easiest way to waste time is to constantly change strategy and the execution plan driving it. Start-ups have*

to be incredibly agile in their reactions, but the senior team must separate momentary tactical shifts from real strategic change. If they don't, they will draw a zigzag line to their goal and waste time and money along the way'.

SECTION SUMMARY 9.10

Why did the dotcoms become dot-bombs?

In this section we have examined some of the reasons why dotcoms fail. Fom bad basic ideas, no market, no value network, no managerial experience, no marketing – it would almost be a joke if people's jobs, lives and careers were not at stake!

CHAPTER SUMMARY

1 E-business is larger than e-marketing. It involves using technology to facilitate improvements to business processes and increase the efficiency of internal and external information flows with customers, suppliers and distributors.

2 An e-business architecture needs to be defined that brings together systems, processes and applications from across the business.

3 The development of an e-business framework should consider buy-side, sell-side and in-side applications.

4 Buy-side applications involve setting up extranet links for e-procurement and supply chain management to reduce costs and optimize delivery of a service of a product. New purchasing approaches such as auctions may be used.

5 In-side applications involve creating intranets to improve knowledge management and assist in decision making to improve business performance.

6 Sell-side applications involve creating extranets to manage distributor channels (partner relationship management) or directly manage the relationship with the customer (customer relationship management).

7 Steps in creating the e-business are defined: (1) Establish the vision; (2) Get senior management support; (3) Identify requirements; (4) Revisit the value network (and core competencies); (5) Design an e-business architecture; (6) Develop, pilot, train and roll-out; (7) Benchmark, measure and monitor.

8 There are many security threats to the e-business such as fraud, theft and accidents. Security solutions such as firewalls, encryption and back-up should be put in place to counter these.

9 Nine e-business success criteria are defined. They are: the presence of a clicks-and-mortar parent providing cash flow and resources; an existing brand to provide brand awareness and a customer base; an existing management team and structure; value network

already in place; ability to find suppliers and partners to create the value network for fulfilment; e-business enables re-engineering of existing business; realistic pace of development; e-business operates in a marketable niche and additional benefits of bricks and mortar.

10 Nine e-business failure criteria are defined, many which have resulted in the death of dotcoms. They are: bad idea in the first place – there is no market; management inexperience or inflexibility; failure to create a niche; trying to create the e-business in isolation from the whole of the value network; company focused on the product or service and not on the customer's needs; product/service badly marketed; investor panic and technology not ready or not delivering.

 ## References

Cairncross, F. (2000) eManagement – Inside the machine, *The Economist*, 18 November.

Chaffey, D. (2004) *E-business and e-commerce management: Strategy, implementation and applications*. Pearson Education, Harlow, 2nd edition.

Deise, M., Nowikow, C., King, P. and Wright, A. (2000) *Executive's guide to e-business. From tactics to strategy*. John Wiley and Sons, New York.

DTI (2003) Business In The Information Age – International Benchmarking Study. Available from http://www2.bah.com/dti2003.

Francis, P.H. (2000) *Production Creation: The Heart of the Enterprise from Engineering to e-Commerce*. Free Press, New York.

Kirkpatrick, D. (2001) Great Leap Forward: From Davos, Talk of Death. *Fortune*, March 5.

IBM (2001) Managing e-business: The Top Ten Myths. White paper at www.ibm.com/services/whitepapers.

Kalakota, R. and Robinson, M. (2000) *e-business. Roadmap for Success*. Addison Wesley, Reading. MA.

Lister, J. (1999) *Pointing employees in the same direction, Building a successful eBusiness*, CBI/Caspian.

Porter, M. (2001) Strategy and the Internet. *Harvard Business Review*, March, pp. 63–78.

Timmers, P. (1999) *Electronic commerce strategies and models for business-to-business trading*. John Wiley series in information systems, Chichester.

 ## Further reading

Chaffey, D. (2004) *E-business and e-commerce management: Strategy, implementation and applications*. Pearson Education, Harlow, 2nd edition. Free updates at www.davechaffey.com/E-business. Part 1 describes e-business concepts, Part 2 describes approaches to e-business strategy for buy-side, sell-side and in-side e-commerce, and Part 3 describes practical issues of implementation such as change management and user-centred design.

Deise, M., Nowikow, C., King, P. and Wright, A. (2000) *Executive's guide to e-business. From tactics to strategy*. John Wiley and Sons, New York. Suggests approaches to e-business according to four snapshots and their impact on organizations, people, processes and technology. The snapshots are: channel enhancement, value chain integration, industry transformation and convergence.

Kalakota, R. and Robinson, M. (2000) *e-business. Roadmap for Success*. Addison Wesley, Reading. MA. Good introductory book on approaches to e-business divided into buy-side and sell-side.

 ## Web links

E-consultancy.com (www.e-consultancy.com). A digest of white papers and articles about managing e-business and e-commerce.

IBM (www.ibm.com/services/whitepapers/). A digest of white papers including Managing E-business: Top ten myths. What's your best e-business model?

IT Toolbox (www.ebusiness.ittoolbox.com). Resources including white papers and supplier information.

BRINT (A business researcher's interests) Ebiz (www.brint.com/ebiz/). Well established management portal providing articles, news and discussion groups.

 ## Self-test

1 Devise an explanation of e-business for a colleague in the context of your organization.

2 What are the key elements of an e-business architecture?

3 Explain buy-side, in-side and sell-side components of the e-business framework.

4 Describe how buy-side enhancements could improve your organizational performance.

5 Describe how in-side enhancements could improve your organizational performance.

6 Describe how sell-side enhancements could improve your organizational performance.

7 What are the important e-elements of an e-business strategy?

8 Summarize the main security threats to your business and describe solutions to each threat.

9 Make notes on the nine e-business criteria for success, explaining which are missing or not relevant to your business.

10 Outline the factors that may contribute to e-business failure.

10

E-planning

'There's no point rowing harder if you're rowing in the wrong direction'.

Ohmae, 1999

E-marketing is fundamentally the discipline of marketing set in the context of the e-business e-environment. So not surprisingly, the successful e-marketing plan is based on traditional marketing disciplines and planning techniques, adapted for the new media environment and then mixed with new media techniques. This chapter shows you how to do this, based on the well-established principles of the SOSTAC® Planning System.

By the end of this chapter you will be able to:

- Draw up an outline e-marketing plan
- Analyse the situation
- Draw up realistic objectives
- Begin to develop sensible strategies
- Develop appropriate tactics
- Execute the tactics with detailed action plans
- Control, monitor, measure, report and adjust.

CHAPTER TOPIC	LEARNING OBJECTIVE
10.1 Introduction	Describe the context and main components of an e-plan
10.2 Situation analysis	Assess the main aspects of situation analysis
10.3 Objectives	Define the key objectives of an e-plan
10.4 Strategies	Explain the difference between strategy, objectives and tactics and devise e-strategies
10.5 Tactics	Outline the different e-tools that can be deployed as part of tactics
10.6 Actions	Create an outline implementation plan
10.7 Control	Build in a review process into your plans
10.8 Resources	Identify the key resources required and allocate these to achieve your e-marketing objectives

10.1 Introduction to e-marketing planning

By the end of this chapter you will know what an e-marketing plan is, its key components and how they fit together. Without a plan, an organization drifts unknowingly and can end up anywhere – usually sinking, without cash and without direction – just like so many of the dot-bombs.

Planning is essential. It helps you to stop constant fire-fighting, desperately searching for funds, panicking and paying higher prices (like rush rates). Planning puts you in control and reduces stress. It also gives direction to the team so they can work in harmony.

There are many types of plans. Corporate plans and business plans incorporate the long-term corporate strategy which includes diversification and acquisition strategies, systems and funding. Then there are marketing plans that must help to fulfil the overall corporate objectives. Then there are e-marketing plans that have to integrate with the offline, traditional marketing plan in many ways.

E-marketing plans do not occur in isolation, but are most effective when integrated with offline marketing communications channels such as phone, direct-mail or face-to-face selling. Online channels should also be used to support the whole buying process from pre-sale to sale to post-sale and the continuing development of customer relationships.

Although the e-marketing plan can span right across an organization's functions (e.g. customer feedback, customer service, product enhancement, sales, finance/payment, delivery, administration and marketing), e-marketing plans tend to be linked strongly to marketing communications plans. The reality is that any e-marketing plan needs to be a part of a marketing communications plan and it also should be part of a broader marketing plan. Needless to say the e-plan should also fit in with the overall business plan. For those organizations that want a separate e-marketing plan (or a separate section for e-marketing), this chapter will help you.

For a traditional business, an overall corporate or business plan covers systems, procedures, resources and structure, while a marketing plan covers the sales, distribution, communications and delivery of the product or service.

An e-business plan addresses all the processes and systems required to run a business including the 'buy-side' processes, the 'in-side' processes and the 'sell-side' processes discussed in Chapter 9. We are going to look specifically at an e-marketing plan. Although it has to integrate with all the marketing activities both online and offline, managers with specific responsibilities for e-marketing activities are asked for e-plans or e-marketing plans.

Figure 10.1 shows the typical relationship between different plans. The corporate plan guides the marketing and e-business plan, both of which, in turn, guide the e-marketing plan. The plans are integrated so that developing the e-marketing plan may give insights that help to update other plans. Different organizations have different plans of different scope and timeframes, but what is important is to agree the plans used, their timeframes and how they integrate with each other.

Long- versus short-term plans

We can distinguish between short term (1 year) plans, medium term (2–3 year) plans and longer term (3–5 year) plans. All these plans can use SOSTAC®. For example all these plans include

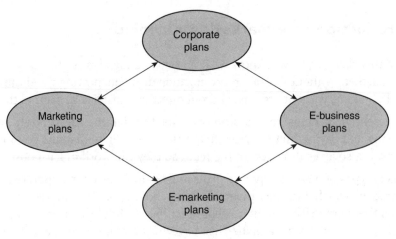

Figure 10.1 The relationship between different types of plans

strategy and tactics sections. Strategy gives clear guidance and direction for all subsequent tactical details. Strategy for a short-term plan summarizes how the one-year objectives will be achieved while strategy for a long-term plan summarizes how the long-term objective will be achieved.

Some feel that strategy is by definition deemed to have a longer term and more enduring perspective while tactics are shorter term and more flexible.

Longer-term e-marketing plans should place emphasis on three key areas. First, early identification of significant changes in the macro-environment and changes to competitive forces in the micro-environment. Second, developing value propositions for customers using online services as part of their buying process. Third, definition of the technology infrastructure and information architecture to deliver these value propositions.

New technologies and new information architectures such as a customer relationship management systems and integrated databases can take several years to specify, select and implement. Database, CRM, integration of e-business architecture and business processes are all long term when making plans and major decisions.

The shorter term operational e-marketing plan can then address the mix of communications techniques such as search marketing and online advertising (Chapter 7), used to acquire new customers and the tools used to engage and retain customers online such as incentive programmes and opt-in e-mail marketing.

SOSTAC® PLANNING

To help you, we'll structure this chapter by using a simple aide mémoire, called SOSTAC. **SOSTAC**® is used by thousands of professionals to produce all kinds of plans – corporate plan, marketing plan, e-marketing plan, advertising plans.

SOSTAC stands for: Situation, Objectives and Strategy, Tactics, Action and Control (Figure 1.1):

- *Situation analysis* means 'where are we now?' How many of your customers are online? How many are buying or influenced online? What is the growth forecast? What are your competitors doing? What is the impact of the new intermediaries? What's working for them? What seems to work online and offline and what seems not to? How have you performed online? What's changing in the online world?

- *Objectives* means 'where are we going, or where do we want to be?' Why go on-line? What are the benefits, what is the purpose of going to all of this effort? Remember the 5 Ss? Good objectives are quantified and also contain strict timescales.

- *Strategy* means 'how do we get there?' Strategy summarizes how to fulfil the objectives. Which segments? What propositions? What level of integration between tools, database and e-CRM? Which evolutionary web site stages? What sequence of e-tools, e.g. web first, then WAP then interactive TV?

- *Tactics* are the details of strategy. Breaking the tactical e-tools and techniques into more detail. Highlighting, on say, a Gantt chart, exactly which tactics occur when, e.g. a series of banner ads or a series of opt-in e-mails, or a roll-out of kiosks, or perhaps a series of iDTV ads. Tactics explain how to implement the strategy.

- *Action* is the details of tactics. What actions have to be taken to create a banner ad, a kiosk, an interactive TV ad, an opt-in e-mail campaign? Each is a mini project. Everything degenerates into work! Arguably, this is the weakest part of the planning process for most companies.

- *Control* questions whether you know if you are succeeding or failing – before it is too late. This is why control systems measure and monitor regularly the key online measurables – visitors, durations, enquiries, subscriptions, sales, conversion rates, churn rates, loyalty levels and more.

Your e-marketing plan should also be reviewed and revised frequently. Quick reactions are required. If something isn't working – find out why and change it. Constantly improve. In addition to regular detailed measurements, review your overall plan once a quarter and be prepared to revise and re-present it to senior management every six months.

Don't forget, a plan without resources will fail. So you need to budget for the 3Ms, the three key resources. These are:

- Men (and women) – human resources
- Money – budgets
- Minutes – time scales and time horizons for production, delivery, service, etc.

All aspects of SOSTAC® must be thought through. The next sections will take you through each of the SOSTAC and 3M concepts. At the end, you will be able to plan your e-marketing with confidence.

SECTION SUMMARY 10.1

Introduction to e-marketing planning

E-marketing plans must support, and be integrated with, corporate/business plans and marketing plans. SOSTAC stands for: Situation, Objectives and Strategy, Tactics, Action and Control.

10.2 Situation analysis

Situation analysis is the first part of the e-marketing plan. It explains 'where are we now?' After this you can define where you want to go (see Objectives in Section 10.3). We need to analyse both internally and externally – internally within the organization, and externally, the business environment affecting our online business situation.

The traditional tried and tested analytical areas are:

- *KPIs* – key performance indicators which identify the business's success criteria, results, data and measurements against benchmarks
- *SWOT analysis* – identifying internal strengths, and weaknesses, as well as external opportunities and threats.
- *PEST* – political, economic, social and technological variables that shape your marketplace.
- *Customers* – how many are online, how many prefer iDTV – are there new channel segments emerging?
- *Competitors* – who are they? New online adversaries or the same old competitors as always?
- *Distributors* – are new, online, intermediaries emerging while old offline distributors are being wiped out (disintermediation)?

INTERNAL ANALYSIS

The internal analysis looks at key performance indicators (KPIs). Common KPIs used to assess online activities include:

- Enquiries
- Sales
- Market share
- ROI (Return on Investment)
- **Online revenue contribution** (see Section 10.3).

Other KPIs include:

- **Unique visitors** – the number of separate, individual visitors who visit the site (typically over a month).
- Total numbers of **sessions** or **visits** to a web site (forget '**hits**' – these are a spurious measure, since when a web page is downloaded to the PC, a number of separate data transfers or hits takes place, usually one for each HTML and graphics file. Techies need to measure hits because this helps them plan the resources needed to run the sites efficiently; you as an e-marketer should measure **page impressions** because that's the real measure of customer traffic to your site and for an advertiser equates with other familiar measures such as 'opportunities to view').
- **Repeat visits**. Average number of visits per individual. Total number of sessions divided by the number of unique visitors. Update your site more often and people come back more

often. **Cookies** can help track repeat visits. Remember to get permission before placing any cookies on someone else's PC.

- **Duration** – average length of time visitors spend on your site (but remember that for some areas of the site such as online sales or customer service you may want to minimize duration). A similar measure is number of pages viewed per visitor. Also see the box on the much abused term '**stickiness**'.
- **Subscription rates** – numbers of visitors subscribing for services such as an opt-in e-mail and newsletters
- **Conversion rates** – the percentage of visitors converting to subscribers (or becoming customers). This is critical to e-marketing. Let's take an example. Say 2% of 5000 visitors to a site in a month convert to 100 customers who place an order. £10 000 cost divided by 100 conversions = £100 cost per order. Now imagine you can double your conversion rate, or better still quadruple it to 8%, you then get £25 cost per order. The leverage impact caused by improved conversion rates is huge – revenues go up and % marketing costs go down. Certainly worth keeping an eye on.
- **Churn rates** – percentage of subscribers withdrawing or unsubscribing.
- **Click through rates (CTR)** – from a banner ad or web link on another site to your own.
- Other – there are many others, e.g. some consider winning awards to be a high-profile KPI.

All of the preceding KPIs can be quantified and used as objectives, which can be constantly measured. The control section explains how frequently each KPI is measured and by whom.

Costs also need to be analysed. These metrics are also considered as part of control (Section 10.7). Internal analysis will also review the success of an organization's resources, processes and structure in delivering customer value, satisfaction and loyalty. Market research of customers and partners will be needed to determine their opinions.

Remember that numbers out of context are meaningless. Sales of £1m – is this good news or bad news? If last year's sales were £500K then this is good news but if they were £2m then this is bad news. Imagine the previous year's sales were £500K, this year's sales are £1m and the market had quadrupled in size? Although your sales have doubled your market share has halved! This is bad news in the long run. So remember all indicators are relative – leading, backwards and across. Leading to show what future results will be, backwards over time – to see the trend and across your industry – to see how competitive you are.

E-MARKETING EXCELLENCE

Use of independent auditing by Handbag.com for KPIs

Handbag.com use the ABC Electronic auditing service (www.abce.org.uk). This is used to prove the reach and engagement of audience with the site for potential advertisers. The basic figures for total qualifying traffic for the period 1–30 November 2000 were:

Page impressions:	2 874 798
Visits:	733 218
Users:	367 071

By January 2004, the corresponding figures for a single month were:

Page impressions:	24 291 888
Visits:	1 633 173
Users:	876 031

Additional KPI ratios can then be calculated from this data, for example:

Average page views per visit = 2 874 798/733 218 = 3.9 in 2000, increasing to 14.9 in 2004 showing that the 'stickiness' of the site has increased.

Average visits per user = 733 218/367 071 = 1.9 in 2000, decreasing to 1.86 in 2004 showing that the number of repeat visits in a set period has not increased in line with increased site stickiness.

E-MARKETING INSIGHT

Cutler and Sterne on stickiness

Cutler and Sterne (2001) say 'Little consensus has emerged as to how to calculate stickiness, and many stickiness formulas are potentially valid, actionable and consistent'. Some other commentators use stickiness to refer to how long visitors stay on a site according to the number of different pages of content they view (page impressions divided by visits), while others use it to refer to repeat visits (total visits divided by number of unique visitors). Cutler and Sterne (2001) present a stickiness formula they believe is 'particularly succinct':

$$Stickiness = Frequency \times Duration \times Total\ site\ reach$$

Where

$$Frequency = Number\ of\ visits/Number\ of\ unique\ users\ (in\ time\ period\ T)$$

And

$$Duration = Total\ amount\ of\ time\ spent\ viewing\ pages/$$
$$Number\ of\ visits\ in\ time\ period\ T.$$

STRENGTHS AND WEAKNESSES

A situation analysis usually includes an analysis of strengths and weaknesses. What do you think might be your online strengths and weaknesses? Which tactical tools are you particularly good at? You may review the following:

- Customer database – is it large, live, clean and integrated? Can you deliver personalized communications (1-2-1) through every communications tool both online and offline?

- Online customer care – is it sloppy or outstanding? Has your speed of response or speed of resolution increased or decreased? Do you measure it?
- Web site – is it a user-centred design that is effective in converting visitors to outcomes? Do you use customer scenarios and usability testing?
- Integrated database – does it link all online and offline tools together?
- Opt-in e-mail campaigns – are these generating results?
- Web links – are **referrals** being generated from a range of sources?
- Banner ads or sponsorship – are click-through rates and customer acquisition costs favourable?
- Mobile marketing – what are your experiences (if relevant) with mobile phone campaigns?
- Interactive TV – if it's relevant to your marketplace, have you any experience with it?

EXTERNAL ANALYSIS

The external analysis includes customers, competitors and the uncontrollable opportunities and threats. E-marketing is overflowing with new opportunities and threats thrown up by the constant waves of change.

Consider customers, how are they changing? How many are on line? Do you have a similar proportion of your customers buying online? If not, why not? Figure 10.2 shows the picture you need to build up of customer activity showing demand for your online services. This compares the role of online channels such as the web site as a means of reaching, influencing and directly delivering sales. We need to ask – How many buy exclusively online? How many browse online and shop offline? How many use price comparison sites? How many are happy

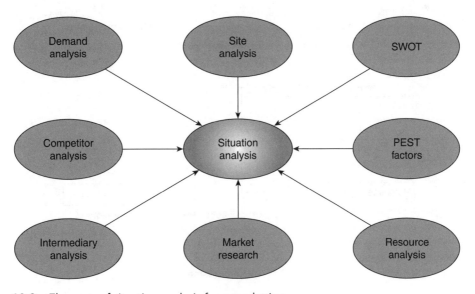

Figure 10.2 Elements of situation analysis for e-marketing

to give you permission to e-mail them, text message them or even snail mail them? Are the numbers changing?

Are your competitors online? What do they offer on their web sites that you don't? Who are they? Are there new online players entering your market? If not why not? Are they pure dot-coms or are they clicks and mortar? Are they stable?

A further issue is distributors such as online intermediaries. Are there new intermediaries you could partner with, are your competitors already working with them?

So, effectively, the analysis is not a one-off annual analysis. It's an ongoing observation of your marketplace known as **environmental scanning** which includes regularly checking stats, web sites, customer surveys and reading reports.

OPPORTUNITIES AND THREATS

The OT in SWOT, the 'opportunities and threats', are churned up by the relentless tide of change. They can be from the PEST factors:

- Political laws or regulations that affect your online marketing (such as the UK PECR – Privacy and Electronic Communications Regulations).
- Economic – variables impact all markets.
- Social – the trends that shape future online behaviour.
- Technology – are you abreast with developments – have you got an overview of the emerging technology?

To summarize this section, refer to all the options for analysis we have reviewed in Figure 10.3.

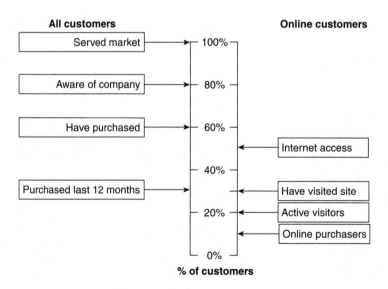

Figure 10.3 Assessing customer adoption of online services

Situation analysis

Your situation analysis should include KPI; customers; competitors and intermediaries as well as the uncontrollable PEST factors. Now you know where you are, the next section will help you to determine your online destiny – where you want to go (your objectives).

10.3 Objectives

While the situation analysis explains 'where you are now', objectives clarify where you are going – where you want to be. By the end of this section you'll know what are the realistic objectives of an e-marketing plan, and what benefits each of these objectives can yield for your business.

There are five broad benefits, reasons or objectives of e-marketing. These can be summarized as the 5 Ss (see Chapter 1). You must decide whether all or only some are going to drive your e-marketing plan.

- *Sell* – Grow sales (through wider distribution to customers you can't service offline or perhaps a wider product range than in local store, or better prices).
- *Serve* – Add value (give customers extra benefits online: or product development in response to online dialogue).
- *Speak* – Get closer to customers by tracking them, asking them questions, conducting online interviews, creating a dialogue, monitoring chat rooms, learning about them.
- *Save* – Save costs: of service, sales transactions and administration, print and post. Can you reduce transaction costs and therefore either make online sales more profitable? Or use cost-savings to enable you to cut prices, which in turn could enable you to generate greater market share?
- *Sizzle* – Extend the brand online. Reinforce brand values in a totally new medium. The web scores very highly as a medium for creating brand awareness and recognition.

Specific objectives are created for each. Consider sales – a typical objective might be:

> *'To grow the business with online sales, e.g. to generate at least 30% of sales online. Within 6 months'.*

Or

> *'To generate an extra £100 000 worth of sales online by December'.*

These objectives can be further broken down, e.g. to achieve £100 000 of online sales means you have to generate 1000 online customers spending on average £100. If, say, your conversion rate of visitors to customers was a high 10 per cent then this means you have to generate 10 000 visitors to your site. You can use the KPIs (key performance indicators) mentioned in Section 10.2 to help you quantify the main objectives and the subsequent detailed objectives.

Specific targets for the **online revenue contribution** for different e-channels should be set for the future as shown in Figure 10.4 and illustrated in the box on Sandvik Steel. Objectives should be set for the percentage of customers who are reached or influenced by each channel (or brand awareness in the target market) and the percentage of sales to be achieved through the channel. The online revenue contribution should also consider **cannibalization** – are online sales achieved at the expense of traditional offline channels?

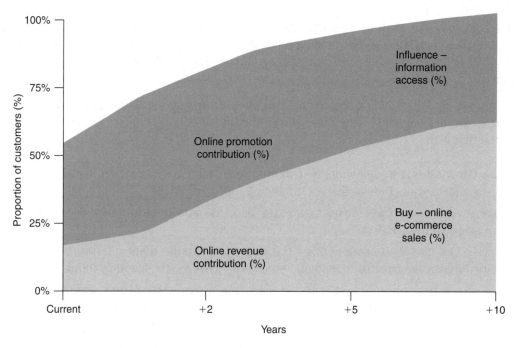

Figure 10.4   An example of objective targets for revenue contribution

Another major objective might be to build brand awareness, e.g. to create brand awareness among 50 per cent of our target market through online activities. Equally it might be to use the online opportunity to create some excitement around the brand ('sizzle'). Interactive TV and text messaging come to mind as do reactive viral marketing techniques.

Another major online objective might be to consolidate relationships and increase loyalty from 50 to 75 per cent among a high-spending customer segment during the year.

And so on.

There are many types of objectives. They will, of course, be under-pinned by either financial objectives (sales, profit margin, cash flow), or communication objectives (positioning, branding, awareness, e-CRM …).

Whatever the objective, it ultimately has to be measurable. Therefore your objectives need to be quantifiable and to have a deadline.

Finally be realistic about what is achievable – interactive technology means e-marketing offers enormous potential for data gathering and analysis, but many advertisers and marketers expect just too much!

So ask, are your objectives well-defined and properly thought through? Are they SMART? Specific, Measurable, Achievable, Realistic and Time-related.

E-MARKETING EXCELLENCE

Sandvik Steel's sets detailed objectives by markets and segments

The Financial Times (Fisher, 2001) reported a range of variation in **online revenue contribution**. At the time of the article, only a small part of all orders were transacted over the web. Nordic countries are leading the way. Around 20% of all orders from Denmark are online, as are 31% of those from Sweden. The proportion in the US, however, is only 3%, since most business goes through distributors and is conducted by EDI (electronic data interchange). Over the next six months, the company hopes to raise the US figure to 40% and in two years, between 40 and 50% of total orders are planned to come via the web.

Annika Roos, marketing manager at Sandvik Steel, was reported as saying: 'by the end of December, 2001, we want a confirmation from at least 80% of key customers that they consider the extranet to be a major reason to deal with Sandvik. Our aim is to have 200 key customers using the extranet at the end of June 2001'.

SECTION SUMMARY 10.3

Objectives

The 5 Ss (Sell, Serve, Speak, Save and Sizzle) are a useful starting point for objectives. Ultimately objectives have to be SMART. Finally objectives help you to focus on where you want to get to. Now you're ready to move on to how to get there, the next section shows you just how to do this – Strategy.

10.4 Strategy

There is much confusion about the difference between strategy and tactics. Strategy summarizes 'how do we get there?' Objectives list 'where we want to go'. Strategy summarizes how to achieve the objectives and guides all the subsequent detailed tactical decisions. Strategy is influenced by both the prioritization of objectives (sell, serve, speak, save and sizzle) and of course, the amount of resources available (see Section 10.8). Strategy should also exploit distinctive competitive advantage. Play to your strengths (assuming the market/ customers want your strengths).

Strategy is crucial. Get it wrong and all your hard work is wasted. As Kenichi Ohmae (1999) said 'There's no point rowing harder if you're rowing in the wrong direction'. Hard work is wasted if the strategy is wrong. Take some examples of absurd strategies. Imagine building an amazing WAP site, but none of your customers use WAP phones. Or imagine building a transactional web site to take orders yet the majority of your market only browses online and always shops offline. Or missing the early adopters in your target market by avoiding inter-active TV advertising. Or worse, still, reaching them through interactive TV but not having the back office systems and fulfilment services required to, say, deliver pizzas within 30 min-utes, or offer a test-drive the next day. Integrating procedures and redesigning business processes is strategic and tends to be longer term.

Strategy summarizes how the objectives will be achieved. So let us say the overall marketing objective is to achieve a 50 per cent increase in sales. The strategy that rolls out could be based on expanding the marketplace and securing new customers, attacking a particular competitor's customers or simply to reduce churn (lost customers) and get more of your existing customers to re-order. Three different strategies: one for market expansion, one for competitor attack and one for customer retention. There are many other approaches to e-marketing strategy.

So what goes into an e-marketing strategy – whatever it takes to achieve your objectives. The e-marketing strategy focuses on what you're going to do in the 'e' world. It can include prop-ositions (which summarize the online mix). Will your online proposition be different to your offline proposition? Or integrated? Can you succinctly tell your boss what your strategy is? If you were managing someone else who was hatching an e-marketing strategy, you would want to know the big picture, e.g. are we going into interactive TV linked to an automated response service and fulfilment house or linked to a tele-sales team or integrated into high street kiosks or B2B exhibition kiosks. Strategy helps it all to fit together and avoids ad hoc tactical patchworks which usually, in the end, cause more complications. For some strategists, strat-egy is all about establishing an integrated database between your web site and all other com-munications points. For others it is developing the web site from 1-stage to 2-stage to 3-stage e-marketing (e.g. fully integrated automated database driven linking opt-in e-mail and snail mails). Others develop an Internet strategy, an intranet strategy and an extranet strategy. These are longer-term strategic perspectives. For a few, e-marketing strategies are just about traffic building – a shorter-term strategic perspective.

Ideally an experienced strategist would create strategy by thinking purely about how to achieve the objectives with the resources available. Having generated several strategic options, the best strategy is carefully chosen and this then eventually cascades down into the tactical details. However, in reality, because there is little good solid experience of making strategies, many practitioners tend to move to what they're good at – tactics, e.g. banner ads, virals and opt-in e-mails. Having developed a range of exciting tactics, they then sit back and try to make sense of it all or try to tie it all together, summarize it and then call it a traffic strategy (retrospective strategy making)! This can work if (a) it all integrates sensibly (b) you can test it against at least another two strategic alternatives.

Other strategists draw from marketing warfare, e.g. full frontal attack (comparative marketing on web sites); flanking attack using the web site to highlight areas of weakness among competitors (surround bigger players by creating an array of micro sites and web rings around an area so that smaller players cannot complete). See the e-marketing insight box 'Timothy Cummings on competitive strategies' for more.

STRATEGIC QUESTIONS

Some of the questions that an e-marketing strategy can answer are:

- What segments are being targeted online? Who is the target market?
- Should new or existing products be sold into all existing segments and markets, or can specific or new segments and markets be targeted? Different options are often reviewed using the Ansoff matrix shown in Figure 10.5.

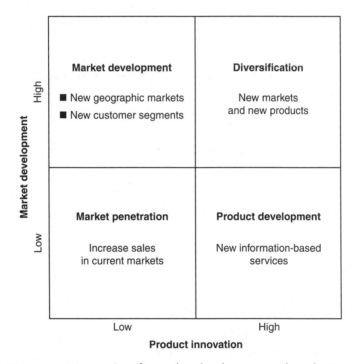

Figure 10.5   Matrix summarizing options for market development and product innovation

- Source of differentiation – what is the **online value proposition**? Can new digital products or services be developed?
- How do we deal with competition? See the box 'Timothy Cummings on competitive strategies'.
- What level of interaction on site – brochure, two-way interactive sales support, online sales or full CRM. What stage of 'e'volution is required? Will the other stages follow in subsequent years?

- What level of database integration is required? Can the customer be dealt with as a recognizable individual with unique preferences regardless of how the customer comes into contact, e.g. web, WAP, iDTV, telephone call centre, etc.?
- Will the online channels complement the company's offline channels or will it replace them? See 'Compliment or replace?' below.
- Web sites or WAP sites or both? How important are these compared to other channels to market?
- How relevant are interactive TV, kiosks or mobile marketing?

COMPLEMENT OR REPLACE?

An e-marketing strategy should define the level of resources directed at different channels. Essentially, the question is will the online channels complement the company's other channels or will it replace other channels? Gulati and Garino (2000) describe it as 'Getting the right mix of bricks and clicks'. If it is believed that sales through digital channels will primarily replace other channels, then it is important to invest in the technical, human and organizational resources to achieve this. A replace strategy was chosen by airlines such as easyJet and Ryanair who now sell over 90 per cent of their tickets online. To assess the replace versus complement strategy alternatives, Kumar (1999) provides a framework. He suggests that replacement is most likely to happen when:

1 Customer access to the Internet is high.
2 The Internet can offer a better value proposition than other media (i.e. propensity to purchase online is high).
3 The product can be delivered over the Internet (it can be argued that this is not essential).
4 The product can be standardized (the user does not usually need to view to purchase).

If at least two of Kumar's conditions are met there may be a replacement effect. For example, purchase of travel services or insurance online fulfils criteria 1, 2 and 4.

STRATEGIC COMPONENTS – STOP AND SIT

One way to remember some of the key components of marketing strategy is the acronym STOP and SIT. First of all, strategy must be focused on crystal clear *Segments (S)*, and the selected *Target Markets (T)*. *Positioning (P)* is a fundamental part of the overall customer proposition or offering, e.g. what exactly is the product, its price and perceived value in the marketplace? Can this be summarized into a strong proposition? STP is a fundamental part of any marketing strategy. Assuming it helps to fulfil the *overall objectives (O)*, then the remaining components are *Sequence or Stages (S)*, *Integration (I)* and *Tools (T)*.

Sequence and stages embrace a couple of strategic e-issues. Sequence means should there be a sequence of tools, e.g. which comes first, a web site before interactive TV before mobile? More importantly, should the business have a series of online stages of web evolution (see the evolutionary stages of Quelch and Klein (1996) in Section 1.12.). Are the web site processes and databases integrated and accessible for other transactions, whether WAP, web kiosks, iDTV or telephone? Can the online activities be integrated with the offline processes and databases? Or should it have a web site at all – for FMCG goods, perhaps just microsites attached to other portals are most appropriate. These are strategic questions for the online marketer.

E-marketing strategy guides the choice of target markets, positioning and propositions which in turn guide combination of the optimum mix, sequence of e-tools (such as web sites, opt-in e-mail, e-sponsorship, viral marketing), service level and evolutionary stage (from brochure-ware sites to two-way interactive sites to fully integrated e-business systems). One ultimate (medium to long term) part of e-marketing strategy is the development of the dynamic dialogue and the eventual full use of the integrated database potential. Regardless of how the customer comes into contact, he or she must be dealt with as a recognizable individual with unique preferences.

The overall balance of the marketing mix is strategic and the details of the mix are tactical. For example deciding whether to heavily discount prices and raising a high profile in a broad array of down-market online web sites and communities is strategic. The tactical details would list the sites and communities and relevant prices in detail.

So the components of e-marketing strategy can include:

- Target markets, positioning and propositions
- Positioning and ultimately, online value propositions
- Crystal clear objectives (does the strategy fulfil what you want to achieve online?)
- Evolutionary stage (what stage you want to be at)
- Online marketing mix (particularly service levels)
- Optimum mix of tactical e-tools (web site, banner ads, etc.)
- Dynamic dialogue (ongoing with the customer)
- Integrated database (recognize and remember each customer whether via web or telephone).

Remember STOP and SIT, the components that any marketing strategy should include. Segmentation, Targeting and Positioning – fundamental to any strategy – state very clearly who you're after and how you'll be positioned (this can include varying propositions for different target markets, or can you state the OVP?). 'O' for objective – don't forget objective – the strategy shouldn't simply restate the objective but should fulfil the objective. 'S' for Sequence of activities, how everything integrates and time scales (are there a series of stages or key dates?). Now can you summarize all that into a few strategic options? A good e-marketing strategy is more than just communications, it integrates into the guts of a business (value propositions and modus operandi/processes). Ultimately it should outline clearly (and succinctly) how the objectives will be achieved.

RANDOM STRATEGY

E-marketing strategy is lacking in many businesses. This contributes to ad hoc tactical approaches that are short term and often unfocused. Here's a selection of examples of some elements of e-marketing strategies that do not constitute a full strategy. You will see vastly different approaches to this crucial aspect of planning:

'by creating a seamless interface between online and offline, integrated by the underlying database ...'

'by moving through the three evolutionary stages over an 18-month period means the race is on to get our e-strategy on track ...'

'integrate website, database and CRM to efficiently automate a two-way dialogue between customers and our business. ...'

'by establishing a presence on several different portals ...'

'to own a particular content sector online rather than try to sell a specific product'.

Lever took a major strategic shift to change Persil from a product-centric portal (product information) to a customer-centric portal (two main sections: Time In and Time Out – lifestyle and time for yourself – relaxation, minding your skin, diet and kids, time with kids ... tips for a happy family ... get creative with kids section ...). This is an online brand experience integrated into TV, press and Internet campaigns.

You can see how each of these statements fits particular components from STOP and SIT.

Implicit in all strategic choices is resource. The strategy will in the end be constrained by the resource available and its allocation (see Section 10.8). For example, when trying to allocate resources between web site design, web site service and web site traffic generation, whichever strategy you choose, try to generate a few strategic alternatives before deciding the final e-marketing strategy. Remember the first strategy that comes to mind is not necessarily the best one.

Finally, you may generate different propositions (with different mixes) for different markets. This is perfectly acceptable. But ensure each strategy includes the key components (STOP and SIT) and works within the limited resources available (3Ms).

E-MARKETING EXCELLENCE

Hamleys selects a niche strategy

Financial Times (2000) describes how Hamleys (www.hamleys.com) has used the web to acquire new customers from overseas markets – the majority of its sales are in the USA, despite its London base. Instead of simply increasing sales to existing customers, the site has given Hamleys the opportunity to attract new customers who, according to the article, spend more on an average visit to the site than visitors to the London shop. The strategy used was to target customers looking for specialist collectibles that were difficult to obtain elsewhere such as Steiff bears and die-cast figures. While its London store stocks around 40 000 toys, the site offers only a small fraction of that number. There are already numerous toyshops online offering cheap, plentiful toys aimed at the mass market. A visit to the current site suggests that the strategy has been revised since the article was written.

E-MARKETING INSIGHT

Timothy Cummings on competitive strategies

Cummings (2001) applies well-known military strategies to e-marketing. The strategies are not exclusive. They are:

1 *Full-frontal attack*, e.g. use of comparative marketing on web sites.

2 *Flanking attack*, e.g. use the web site to strike at areas in which competitors are weak such as price or service.

3 *Surround and cut-off*, e.g. larger companies use their resources to provide web site communications that are targeted at micromarkets. Smaller companies cannot compete with the resources needed.

4 *Blocking attack*, e.g. closing out competitors by offering additional services to customers.

5 *Guerrilla attack, e.g.* direct attack of competitors using guerrilla tactics such as online PR. The easyJet online competition to guess the losses of rival airline Go is an example of these tactics.

6 *Niche defence*, e.g. specializing through providing superior content or services to competitors.

7 *Territorial defence*, e.g. developing leading communities for particular segments or countries in advance of a competitor.

8 *Mobile defence*, e.g. developing new online functionality that is one step ahead of the competitors.

9 *Stealth defence*, e.g. minimizing web content about a new service, so existing players find it difficult to find out about the new service. The service is promoted through direct sales, networking and word-of-mouth.

10 *Diplomatic nous*, e.g. Partnering with content providers to increase the value of your site compared to competitors.

One of the best books on e-marketing strategy was written over two thousand years ago by Tsun Tzu, a Chinese military genius who was conscious of the environment and understood the importance of alliances and market intelligence (translated by Wing, 1989).

SECTION SUMMARY 10.4

Strategy

Strategy is the big picture. It summarizes how you're going to get there. STOP and SIT combined with resource allocation (constraints) present at least some of the components required as part of an e-strategy.

Now you're ready to move on to the details of strategy – tactics. The next section explores them in more detail.

10.5 Tactics

Tactics are the details of strategy. You need to list all the e-tools you plan to use, in the sequence or stages set out in the strategy.

THE DIFFERENCE BETWEEN STRATEGY AND TACTICS

Tactics tend to be short term and flexible, whereas strategy is longer term and more enduring. But tactics must also be developed only after the strategy is agreed and set. It is tempting to do the reverse: have a bright idea for a new marketing initiative or a new service offering and rush it into play without a strategic context. Tactics don't drive strategy. You don't plan the journey until you have decided where you want to go.

It is easy to muddle strategy and tactics. Here's an easy example: let's say your strategy is to create an effective eCRM programme (because one of your objectives is to increase repeat sales and reduce customer churn). To deliver this strategy, you decide to have four tactics – four moments of contact with each customer over the next six months: these will be an e-mail acknowledging the order, a follow-up e-mail to check delivery was OK, a real Christmas card, and a personalized e-mail and newsletter. These are the detailed tactics that support the strategy.

Your plans will need to be set down clearly. The best tool for this is a Gantt chart that lists all the tactical activities across all the e-tools throughout the weeks and months of the planning period. So you can see what's happening when.

Also your strategy will have gone through approval and budget processes and will be set for a defined period. Whereas your ability to make swift and effective tactical responses to the changing environment will be a key factor in determining your success. Especially in e-business and e-marketing, where change happens so quickly. For example you may know at the start how you plan to implement the strategy; but what if a competitor steals a march, or an e-tool you were planning to use fails? You must think on your feet, be first to react.

E-MARKETING TACTICS

E-marketing tactics focuses on deciding the optimum marketing mix. This was described in detail in Chapter 2 ReMix. Here we simply look at decisions about the choice of tactical e-tools. Do you recall the physical e-tools at your disposal? They include PCs and lap-tops, iDTV, i-radio, mobiles and hand-held devices, kiosks and miscellaneous devices discussed in Chapter 5. And then there are traffic tools such as banner ads, text messages, opt-in e-mail, viral marketing, search engine optimization – all discussed in Chapter 7.

Which of these tools are you going to use to implement the strategy? And will you be aware enough of the technology to adopt or abandon e-tools as and when necessary?

Now let's look at the e-marketing-specific tactical e-tools.

The web site

A web site could be pure brochureware, or a mechanism for creating and managing a dynamic dialogue with the customer, or a vehicle for generating sales. Don't denigrate brochureware that enhances the brochure. With appropriate use of Flash and similar products, and increasing installation of broadband, an online brochure can become a virtual experience. Imagine a cruise holiday web site that gives you video of the cabin you might be staying in or a property sale site where you can get a virtual tour of the house you might buy … properly-done brochureware needn't be as soporific as it normally is. Remember: good tactics will still need good execution!

Interactive advertising and sponsorship

Advertising your wares on other online media properties to promote your brand, create market awareness or bring traffic to your door. You can also sponsor a well-targeted portal; or if a market you want to reach is well covered by some other company running an opt-in e-mail newsletter, you could advertise on this.

Opt-in e-mail

We all receive e-mail from a variety of commercial sources; besides the pure junk you receive, there are a number of companies you deal with who offer opt-in email – 'Would you like to receive more information on our company and our products'? Used sensibly, as companies from Amazon to Symantec do, this is very effective. Amazon will e-mail you when a book you might like is published. Customers can receive e-mails to alert them when their favourite band is on tour, or when there's an unmissable holiday offer. With reasonable software at your end, opt-in e-mail is an extremely effective way to market. There are even opt-in e-mail products you could usefully use yourself (see Web links at the end of this chapter).

Customer relationship management tools

If you then provide benefits or added value information through the opt-in e-mail service … you can develop an integrated database of customers and prospects which can be exploited in further ways: send them gifts, invite them to enter contests, run a free draw for tickets to a sports or cultural event you sponsor … the trick is to use the connection with the customer to create ongoing relationships which give you regular access points where you can deliver a marketing message. CRM online presents one of the greatest challenges to the marketer particularly as 50 per cent of CRM projects fail (Gartner Group, 2004).

But before you choose your e-tools, you need to really understand what each can and cannot do; there is no short-cut to spending time on the web and on interactive TV and exploring other e-marketers' activities!

CONTROLLING TACTICS

Who has control of tactics and implementation is a big question and the e-marketer must win the ownership argument. Take the web site: is it controlled by marketing or by technical or some other function? Many web sites actually damage brands with their broken links, dead ends, cumbersome downloads, out-of-date content, impossible navigation and unanswered e-mails (see Sloppy e-marketing in Section 1.5). No e-marketer would let this happen. You can usually tell from a site whether the webmaster is a 'techie' or a marketer. Many sites skip the cardinal rule of asking customers what they would like on a web site. Then having put it up, they forget to check to see if they got it right. Regular reviews should not be devoted to reviewing the latest technology but rather, they should be focused on customer reviews. As an e-marketer, you'll want a site that is easy on the eye and clear to the reader and lightning fast to download. If that means dispensing with some of the techies' zanier ideas … well the customer will thank you for it!

E-MARKETING EXCELLENCE

Pepsi use a range of e-tools

The e-marketing strategy of Pepsi UK focuses on using push techniques (opt-in e-mail) to keep the customers in a dialogue and provide offers to stimulate sales. The tactical e-tools used are:

- Pepsi web site to gather customer e-mails.
- Sponsorship of other sites, e.g. Pepsi Chart.
- Regular opt-in e-mails, e.g. Pepsi Chart predictions.
- Opt-in e-mail promotions, e.g. Win a holiday.
- E-mail requests to participate in online survey.
- E-mail a friend a Christmas themed animation.

Offline communications are also used to capture e-mail addresses and provide information about the online services.

E-MARKETING INSIGHT

Willcocks and Plant on tactics to achieve differentiation

Willcocks and Plant (2000) describe two dimensions to 'sustain the e-advantage through differentiation' that can be considered as e-marketing tactics:

- Merchandise dimension – for a car this includes its characteristics such as performance, image and options. The web site can use content to differentiate by describing what the offer will do for the customer, or aura – what the offer will say about the customer.
- Support dimension – differentiating features which help them in choosing, obtaining and using the offering. For a car, examples include availability of information, ease of test drive, ordering a brochure and the purchase mechanism via the web site. Personalization and expertise available via the web site can help enhance the support dimension.

Tactics

Tactics are the details of strategy. Tactics list the events and e-tools that will be used over time. Now you have a tactical plan (Gantt chart) – now make it happen. The next section, 'Actions' shows you how.

10.6 Actions

Everything degenerates into work – strategies and tactics eventually cascade into actions which become work that has to be carried out and eventually checked for any mistakes. According to John Stubbs, former executive director of the Chartered Institute of Marketing, up to 40 per cent of marketing expenditure is wasted through poor execution.

As mentioned in Chapter 1, we are swimming in a sea of sloppy marketing and e-marketing. It is not surprising that Bossiddy and Charan (2004) suggest that 'execution is the missing key between aspirations and results'. So, the action stage, or execution, may be the weakest link in the planning process.

Tactics break down into actions. In fact a series of actions, for example to build a web-site or run an online advertising campaign. Each tactic becomes a mini project.

You need to produce a project action plan for each project, with key steps allocated to specific people with specific timescales. Good project management skills are essential. Apply more Gantt charts, or critical path analysis, flow charts or whatever project management approach is best. Most e-marketing plans would not necessarily go into this level of detail. These project action plans need to be drawn up at some stage, whether in the appendix or the main plan.

Each tactical e-tool requires careful planning and implementation. Whether building a web site, a banner ad, an interactive TV ad, a viral campaign or an opt-in campaign, good project management skills and diligent attention to detail is required.

It is at this stage that you build your web-site or commission the creatives to produce your banner ad campaign, devise the e-mail campaign or get the techies to design the database which will be populated by customer data generated by your feedback systems.

Think about the sort of actions you might be pursuing for achieving different web site objectives:

1 *Traffic building actions*. To generate visits and/or traffic to your web site, portal or iDTV channel – you will probably be using links or banners on other sites, sponsoring other

online activities, possibly using competitions or creative content ideas to generate interest. You'll need creative input and a budget to buy media space.

2 *Actions to achieve customer response.* To capture user enquiries – thus turning visitors into sales prospects, capturing data, using enquiry data to analyse customer needs, plan development – you'll need a response mechanism for customers to enter their data online and a database logging and processing the data as it comes in.

3 *Actions to gain sales.* For collecting sales orders: use iDTV or the web site to generate actual sales, handle money transactions, and initiate order processing systems.

4 *Fulfilment actions.* Efficient data transfer to warehouse to get product off shelf and into the box for despatch … Orders might be one-off products or subscription services. More software and hardware solution to implement here: ideally, dovetail into parents' existing systems used for mail order and phone order businesses – then you know that the processes that are invisible to the customer have been installed, tested and proven already.

5 *E-CRM actions.* To build better relationships by creating dialogue with customers … you might be running online polls, using rewards and competitions to secure commitment and response; you could also set up and moderate an online user group: in this way you empower customers by means of interactivity – feedback, listen to customer response and visibly act on it. Staff training and motivation (incentive systems) are crucial.

Success in all these actions requires good implementation. The best strategy in the world will achieve nothing if it is not implemented well. Good implementation only happens if you plan well and use your resources well. First of all you have to communicate to get the plan approved and supported from above and below. Among the activities are going to be: project management schedules, meeting deadlines, meetings, memos, phone calls, chasing people, careful preparation, constant checking and attention to vast volumes of details. Free lunches and tickets to Wimbledon come but rarely!

RISK MANAGEMENT

Action, or implementation, also requires an appreciation of what can go wrong from cyber libel to viruses, to mail bombs, hackers and hijackers to cyber squatting and much more … contingency planning is required. What happens when the server goes down or a virus comes to town? What happens if one of the e-tools is not working, or is not generating enough enquiries? Something has to be changed. **Risk management** involves:

- Brainstorming a list of all the things that could go wrong.
- Assessing their impact and likelihood.
- Creating contingency plans for the highest impact and most probable risks.
- Revising and refining according to lessons learnt.

This may seem obvious, but it takes time. Do you take the time?

E-MARKETING EXCELLENCE

An example Gantt chart

Company: Acme Widgets Ltd

Situation: Market grew 10% last year but we only grew sales by 2%: main competitor has started trading over the Internet and two of our top ten customers say they would prefer to do this too.

Objective: To recover market share and benefit from overall market growth by increasing sales.

Strategy: To achieve 5% of sales via trading online; combination of transferring existing customers and acquiring new ones.

Tactics: See tactics summarized in Figure 10.6.

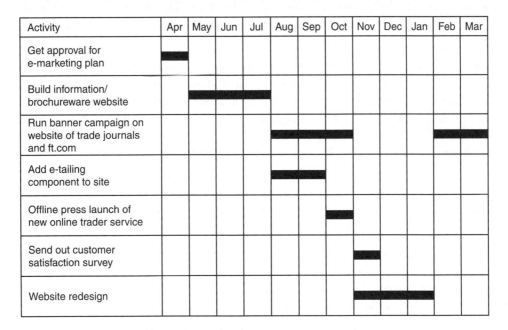

Activity	Apr	May	Jun	Jul	Aug	Sep	Oct	Nov	Dec	Jan	Feb	Mar
Get approval for e-marketing plan	▬											
Build information/ brochureware website		▬	▬	▬								
Run banner campaign on website of trade journals and ft.com					▬	▬	▬				▬	▬
Add e-tailing component to site					▬							
Offline press launch of new online trader service							▬					
Send out customer satisfaction survey								▬				
Website redesign								▬	▬	▬		

Figure 10.6 Example Gantt chart for Acme Widgets

SECTION SUMMARY 10.6

Actions

Good project management skills are essential during the implementation or action stage. You are now ready to control your destiny by building control mechanisms into your e-plan.

10.7 Control

Are you feeling lucky? Without control mechanisms, e-marketing depends on luck. It's a bit like playing darts in the dark. How do you know if you are hitting the target or are just shooting blindly and wildly? How do you know if you're targeting the right customers? Who are they? What do they like and not like? How many of them become repeat customers? Which e-tool works best? How much does each customer actually cost you? By the end of this section you'll be able to answer these questions and begin to take control of your destiny instead of spinning out of control. Control also includes monitoring your competitors – what they're doing; what they're repeating; what works for them; what they're stopping doing.

THE CONTROL PROCESS

Good marketers build in control systems to ensure they know what's working and what's not, early rather than late. Why wait until the end of the year? Why not have a system in place to keep track of key performance indicators?

You have done the work – implemented the tactics, performed the actions ... now, is the plan working? Have you achieved the objectives, is the strategy working, did you choose the right tactics ... have you spent the money and time wisely? To find out you must measure and review what you did – performance measurement. To do this, you need to determine what data you will look at each day, each week, each month, each quarter. This is the Control section of the e-marketing SOSTAC cycle. Remember we agreed in Section 10.2 that your objectives had to be SMART: Specific, Measurable, Achievable, Realistic and Time-related. Now we test whether they were!

Time has to be made for a regular review of what's working and what's not – performance diagnosis. Good marketers have control over their destinies. They do not leave it to chance and hope for the best. They reduce risk by finding what works and what doesn't. Then, your e-tactics, or even strategy, can be changed through corrective action if necessary.

And you don't want to wait for the year end to find out something isn't working. If something is wrong, you need to have control systems (reviews) in place so that you find out and correct the problems early rather than late. Equally, if something is working unbelievably well, you need to know so you can learn and perhaps accelerate the success.

Figure 10.7 summarizes key issues in the control process for e-marketing.

THE METRICS

Performance is measured against detailed targets based on the objectives and strategy.

So you need to measure the KPIs that were detailed in Section 10.2 Situation analysis and Section 10.3 Objectives. For example, for a web site they might be:

- Sales (number of and source of)
- **Online revenue contribution**
- Subscriptions (number of and source of)

Key questions

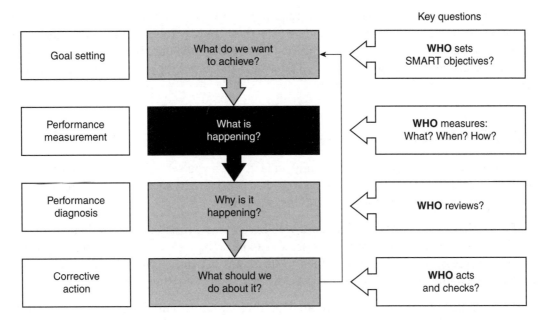

Figure 10.7 Summary of the control process for e-marketing planning

- **Conversion rates**
- Enquiries (number of and source of)
- Number of **unique visitors**
- Number of **repeat visitors**
- **Average duration** (proportion of active or engaged visitors)
- **Churn rates**
- **Termination rate** or **attrition rate**
- Awareness levels.

So where do you get this information? Many of the metrics concerning visitor behaviour are available from **web analytics**. Collection by other information systems or processes is required for key measures such as sales, subscriptions, conversion and attrition rates. Standard practice should ensure data from the different sources is compiled into a monthly or weekly report and is delivered *and* reviewed by the right people. Decide which metrics need to be reviewed daily, weekly or monthly, and by whom. The e-marketer must know which tools are working. That's why 'source of' sales or enquiries is useful – if a particular banner ad doesn't pull customers drop it and try another until you find one that does.

Remember all forms of measurement (or metrics) cost money – you'll have to factor in budgets and resources for the following mechanisms:

- Monitoring customer awareness
- Monitoring customer satisfaction
- Monitoring customer attitudes.

Other forms of control like sales analysis require only that you allocate quality time. So how do you know if things are going well? Some objectives are easy to state and easy to measure: existing recording systems in the organization will produce the data to answer the question: so if the objective is to grow sales ... well what was the target for growth and the timetable for achieving it ... and did you make it?

PERFORMANCE DIAGNOSIS

Some objectives require more careful study: in fact, when you set objectives and define strategy, you should already be thinking: what would be considered a successful outcome and how are we going to monitor performance and measure this?

So if the objective is to create a dominant web-based brand (first stage) and then to make a profit within 18 months on advertising sales and sponsorship ... well what criteria can you set to define success, and how will you then measure against these criteria? You may need to implement data recording systems and develop analysis tools within the action plan.

Similarly, if the objectives revolve around getting closer to customers – customer relationship management or CRM – your measurement tools must be carefully defined and implemented.

Consider how the motor industry has adapted to the Internet. Many manufacturers are dealing direct with consumers, not only in terms of information provision but even order-taking: some dealerships should be worried, the process of disintermediation is going to squeeze them out. But how should industry measure its success? By counting sales and sales leads directly generated by the Internet – that's the easy bit. And also: by measuring conversion rates for people who visit the web-site and choose your car when they subsequently go to a dealer. This is hard to measure so you need to be capturing customer feedback scientifically and measuring levels of customer satisfaction – that's the hard part.

CORRECTIVE ACTION

Corrective action is used to revise the strategies and tactics to ensure the objectives are achieved. Or perhaps the objectives need revising? To minimize the need for corrective action good marketers can monitor e-tools before they are rolled out through testing, testing and testing. E-marketers can reduce risk with relevant information so that their decisions are made upon fact instead of blind luck. This applies even to web site development – researching concepts and usability testing helps to ensure the design is right and you don't have high termination rates.

So which of the e-tools are giving the best return on investment? Why?

Good marketers also have contingency plans. What happens if Plan A doesn't work? Or worse still, what happens if competition cut prices? Or worse still, what happens if the server goes down and your network crashes? Do you have a second server? Good marketers think things through.

E-MARKETING EXCELLENCE

Dell controls e-mail marketing

Iconocast (2001) reported that Dell derives more than $1 million in revenue per week through e-mail marketing campaigns and its lead generation activities are up more than 60 per cent. This success is based on adjustment of its approach to e-mail marketing. Dell Computer's consumer group evaluated their approach to e-mail marketing which was based on a full-service bureau approach after analysing the rapidly multiplying cost of the outsourced model. Dell brought e-mail marketing in-house by purchasing Annunico Live as its stand-alone platform.

E-MARKETING INSIGHT

Chaffey on key areas of e-marketing metrics

Chaffey (2003) suggests that control should consider the effectiveness of e-marketing in five key areas shown in Figure 10.8. Each e-marketing channel such as web or interactive TV should be considered separately against traditional channels using this framework.

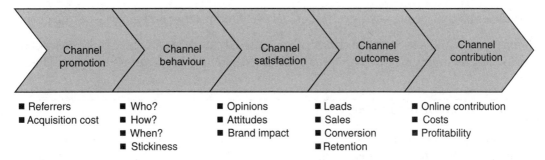

Channel promotion	Channel behaviour	Channel satisfaction	Channel outcomes	Channel contribution
■ Referrers ■ Acquisition cost	■ Who? ■ How? ■ When? ■ Stickiness	■ Opinions ■ Attitudes ■ Brand impact	■ Leads ■ Sales ■ Conversion ■ Retention	■ Online contribution ■ Costs ■ Profitability

Figure 10.8   Key metrics from the Chaffey (2003) framework for assessing e-marketing effectiveness

SECTION SUMMARY 10.7

Control

Control is about monitoring whether your objectives are being achieved and then modifying the tactics and actions to ensure they are.

10.8 Resources: men, money and minutes

Budgeting for the delicate balance of resources required to run an online operation is a science not yet fully understood by many. The late Professor Peter Doyle simplified this critical issue when he said: 'The resource allocation decision is the choice of which products and markets offer the best opportunities for investment'.

We are going to consider resource allocation among different products, markets and e-marketing tools by splitting the resource issue into three components – the 3Ms: men (and women, the human resource), money (budgets) and minutes (time scales and time horizons for production, delivery, service, etc.).

MEN (AND WOMEN)

How many bodies are required to deal with incoming e-mail enquiries and outgoing telephone calls triggered by the 'call back' facility on the web site? Or can it be automated and personalized? How much time to allow and notify customers of deliveries? How much time to set up a project and integrate with the existing (legacy) database systems, etc.? There are some key questions in the area of people resources. Even at times when many tech companies are shedding staff, really able people who know what they are doing in terms of web-site design, e-commerce delivery, e-business strategy, online media sales, etc. are not in huge supply. So you will have to call on a mixture of internal resources and external skills to deliver your plans.

It is often said that a company's greatest assets walk out the door each night – i.e. the people.

Human resource allocation can be critical: if you can find existing resources to fulfil some of the e-marketing requirements, then you keep costs down and that reduces pressure on revenues.

Outsourcing or insourcing

To outsource or not to outsource – that is the question. Outsourcing continues to grow in popularity both in major strategic aspects of e-marketing and also in shorter-term tactical aspects of e-marketing. In Chapter 3, we explained how value networks and their dependence on excellent outsourcing management skills are becoming increasingly popular. Here are a few specific outsourcing questions to consider.

So you need a web site – do you do it in-house or contract out to an agency? And what balance should you strike between resources allocated to building the site and those required to maintain it on a regular basis and leaving a pot aside for a complete review and upgrade in 3, 6 or 9 months? Do not forget traffic – resources are also required to build traffic. Remember out-of-date web sites can damage brands: who will trust your airline if the offers on the web site have expired? Resourcing for promoting the web site is reviewed in Section 7.10.

Other resources to consider are telesales: are additional staff required or can the in-house team do it? Who will do the e-marketing research? Who is going to analyse the data you get from the customer feedback, and who is going to produce the recommendations? Is it the existing team, or a new position? If customers show there is need to change procedures, do we have the people to react and respond?

Don't underestimate the ability of customers to consume your people resources: if you offer an e-mail response mechanism, who is going to answer the incoming e-mails? But if you don't answer them, or don't even offer an e-mail response … how will your customers view this? Pretty badly is the answer!

MONEY

Of course, to a large extent the people resources at your disposal will be a function of the money resources. So once you have calculated the people requirements for your e-marketing plan … you need to work out how to get them: you need to find the skills, and you need the budget to pay for them.

Marketing costs money; e-marketing is no different. Your e-marketing plan must include a budget covering the costs you will incur and a clear benefit statement – what will the return on the investment be?

Be aware that the very nature of e-marketing is that you may be expected to demonstrate a clear relationship between investment and return: if your budget is allocated in order to create an online service that generates sales, then you'll have to create a model showing the ratio of e-marketing cost to sales return.

And be realistic in your expectation: if revenues fall short of the plan, you should assume this will bring pressure on the money resources left at your disposal! You may have to trim costs on the web-site or reduce the online marketing spend.

Try therefore to get some sliding scale agreed, so that there is also an upside: develop plans for additional marketing activity if sales are going well so you can quickly up a gear and build on the success.

But with e-marketing you also have some opportunities to generate some income: can you get sponsors for your web site or sell some banner ads? Can you partner with suppliers of other products and get them to give you a cut of their income? If you can do any of these, you can then approach the budget-decision makers and negotiate to be able to spend some or all of the income you generate.

Also don't forget the obvious: work out what you could usefully do for free. You may find a complementary business prepared to exchange banners and links, you must certainly ensure you are well represented on search engines. Look around the web for opportunities to promote your sites and services or acquire names for your database which won't cost you a penny.

A specific warning too: don't underestimate the resources required to maintain a web site Too often, companies go out and spend vast sums getting designer-rich agencies to build flashy and complex sites and then find that when it comes to updating the content and answering the customers, there is no resource left to cover this.

MINUTES

Time is often the most tight of the resources: there seem to be not enough hours in the day or days in the week, and when you have the impetus of a plan to implement, there is always more that could be done.

Of course the e-marketing world is used to shorter timescales: you might need three months to prepare a TV campaign or twelve months to create a new pack; but you could build a new web site in a lot less time. The creatives required for an online banner campaign are generally less complex than those for a print campaign; and of course booking times are shorter: you can in theory plan, design and deliver an online campaign in a matter of days.

So get the balance right: recognize that e-marketing has an expectation of being able to think, plan, react, change and respond quickly; that's the fun and excitement, and also the power of e-marketing. But don't be bullied into skimping on the planning and research and design and development just because timescales have been made arbitrarily or are artificially short.

E-MARKETING INSIGHT

5:2:1 versus 1:2:5

It has been suggested that UK companies tend to adopt a ratio of 5:2:1 (design to service to traffic building), whereas the ratio tends to be 1:2:5 ratio in the US. The US approach makes sense as there's no point having a wonderful (expensive) web site if no customers or prospects bother to visit. In addition, as mentioned earlier, popular sites are frequently updated during maintenance (serviced) and quick to download (not too many lavish graphics or animations).

E-MARKETING INSIGHT

Gulati and Garino (2000) on restructuring to obtain resources

Gulati and Garino (2000) identify a continuum of strategic approaches from integration to separation. They describe the choices as:

1 *In-house division (integration)*. Example: RS Components Internet Trading Channel (www.rswww.com)
2 *Joint venture (mixed)*. The company creates an online presence in association with another player.
3 *Strategic partnership (mixed)*. This may also be achieved through purchase of existing dotcoms, for example, in the UK Great Universal Stores acquired e-tailer Jungle.com for its strength in selling technology products and strong brand while John Lewis purchased Buy.com's UK operations.

4 *Spin-off (separation)*. Example: Egg bank is a spin-off from the Prudential financial services company.

These authors give the advantages of the integration approach as being able to leverage existing brands, to be able to share information and achieve economies of scale (e.g. purchasing and distribution efficiencies). They say the spin-off approach gives better focus, more flexibility for innovation and the possibility of funding through flotation. For example Egg has been able to create a brand distinct from Prudential and has developed new revenue models such as retail sales commission. They say that separation is preferable in situations where:

- A different customer segment or product mix will be offered online
- Differential pricing is required between online and offline
- If there is a major channel conflict
- If the Internet threatens the current business model
- If additional funding or specialist staff need to be attracted.

SECTION SUMMARY 10.8

Resources: men, money and minutes

Your e-marketing plan must provide properly for the resources you will need to deliver:

- Men (and women) – You need to work out what people resources you will need and how to acquire these in a market where core skills are not abundant.
- Money – You need adequate budgets in order to achieve your plans; this will include a forecast for the return on investment and a plan to be able to adjust costs if sales figures are higher or lower than expected.
- Minutes – Your e-marketing plan must contain timescales, schedules and deadlines. And if you want it to work, your actions will stick to them!

CHAPTER SUMMARY

1 E-marketing plans must support and be integrated with corporate or business plans and marketing plans. SOSTAC® stands for: Situation, Objectives and Strategy, Tactics, Action and Control.
2 Situation analysis is the first part of the e-marketing plan. It explains 'where are we now? It reviews internal resources and e-marketing performance and external factors such as customer, competitor and intermediary activity. It also reviews the PEST factors – Political, Economic, Social and Technology.
3 SWOT analysis is used to summarize Strengths, Weaknesses, Opportunities and Threats.
4 Objectives are set to define the direction of the plan. Objectives can be constructed by reviewing the 5 Ss of Sell, Serve, Speak, Save and Sizzle. Objectives must be checked

to ensure they are they SMART: Specific, Measurable, Achievable, Realistic and Time-related.

5 Strategy summarizes how the objectives will be achieved. The key components are high-lighted by STOP and SIT (Segments (S), Target markets (T), Overall objectives (O), Positioning (P) and Sequence or Stages (S), Integration (I) and Tools (T).

6 Tactics define how the strategy will be achieved. It describes the e-tools used and how they will be sequenced through time.

7 Action equals implementation plans. Actions should be defined to build traffic, gain customer response, gain sales and fulfil them if appropriate and foster e-CRM. Risk management should be used.

8 Control gives a feedback loop starting with monitoring whether the objectives are achieved, assessing what the problems are and then revising the strategies, tactics and actions as appropriate.

9 Resources can be planned through the 3Ms of men (and women, the human resource), money (budgets) and minutes (time scales and time horizons for production, delivery, service, etc.).

 **References**

Bossiddy, L. and Charan, R. (2004) *Execution, the discipline of getting things done*. Crown Business.

Chaffey, D. (2004) *E-business and e-commerce management. Strategy, implementation and practice*. Pearson Education, Harlow, 2nd edition.

Chaffey, D., Mayer, R., Johnston, K. and Ellis-Chadwick, F. (2003) *Internet Marketing: Strategy, Implementation and Practice*. Prentice Hall/Financial Times, Harlow, 2nd edition.

Cutler, M. and Sterne, J. (2001) E-metrics. Business Metrics for the New Economy. Research report from NetGenesis (www.netgen.com).

Cummings, T. (2001) *Little e, big commerce – how to make a profit online*. Virgin Publishing, London.

Doyle, P. (1994) *Marketing Management and Strategy*. Prentice Hall, London.

Financial Times (2000) Hamleys: Where to buy a gold-plated model of James Bond's Aston Martin. *Financial Times*. http://www.ft.com/ftsurveys/spbf9a.htm.

Fisher, A. (2001) Sandvik – The challenge of becoming an e-business. *Financial Times*, 4 June.

Gartner Group (2004) CRM. *Marketing Business*, February.

Gulati, R. and Garino, J. (2000) Getting the Right Mix of Bricks and Clicks for your Company. *Harvard Business Review*, May–June, pp. 107–14.

Iconocast (2001) Upfront Market Reflects Ad Weakness, E-mail Strategy, Pt. I (12 July). www.iconocast.com.

Kumar, N. (1999) Internet distribution strategies: dilemmas for the incumbent. *Financial Times Special Issue on Mastering Information Management*, No. 7. Electronic Commerce.

Ohmae, K. (1999) *The Borderless World: Power and Strategy in the Interlinked Economy*. Harper Business, New York.

Quelch, J. and Klein, L. (1996) The Internet and international marketing. *Sloan Management Review*. Spring, 61–75.

Simons, M. (2000) Barclays gambles on web big bang, *Computer Weekly*, 13 July, p. 1.

SOSTAC® was created by P.R. Smith in 1993. SOSTAC® is a registered trademark of P.R. Smith. See www.PRSsmith.org for more.

Smith, P.R. and Taylor, J. (2004) *Marketing Communications – An Integrated Approach*. Kogan Page, 4th edition.

Willcocks, L. and Plant, R. (2000) Business Internet Strategy: Moving to the Net. In Willcocks, L., Sauer, C. (eds) *Moving to E-business*. Random House.

Wing, R.L. (1989) *The Art of Strategy* (translation of Sun Tzu, c. 480–221BC, *The Art of War*). Aquarian Press, Wellingborough, Northants.

Further reading

Chaffey, D., Mayer, R., Johnston, K. and Ellis-Chadwick, F. (2003) *Internet Marketing: Strategy, implementation and practice*. Financial Times/Prentice Hall, Harlow, 2nd edition. This book covers a structured approach to e-planning in detail, with Chapters 2 and 3 looking at situation analysis and Chapter 4 at Internet marketing strategy.

Web links

DaveChaffey.com (www.davechaffey.com). Articles about e-planning and other aspects of e-marketing.

E-consultancy (www.e-consultancy.com). Discussion and articles about e-planning.

Marketing Sherpa (www.marketingsherpa.com). Case studies and news about e-marketing.

New Media Age (www.nma.co.uk). A UK digital marketing trade weekly which is useful for reviewing new technology platforms and e-marketing approaches.

Revolution magazine (www.revolutionmagazine.com). Articles and interviews with e-planners are useful for reviewing different strategies.

Self-test

1 Summarize the relevance of the elements of a SOSTAC® e-plan for your organization.

2 What are the main factors of situation analysis that should be reviewed in the areas of internal and external review?

3 Summarize objectives for your organization for each one of the 5 Ss.

4 What are the elements of strategy summarized by STOP and SIT?

5 Write down each of the e-tools used as part of tactics that are most relevant to your organization.

6 Which specific actions are required for you to build traffic, gain customer response, gain sales and fulfil them if appropriate and foster e-CRM?

7 What are the key measures of the effectiveness of your online presence?

8 Specify the main resource types required to develop an online presence.

Glossary

3G   Third generation of mobile phone technology based on UMTS standard with high speed-data transfer enabling video calling and download.

Acceptance (of customer)   One of Hofacker's five stages of web site information processing. Does the customer accept (believe) the message?

Accessibility legislation   Legislation intended to protect users of web sites with disabilities including visual disability.

Acquisition, cost   Total promotional cost to gain a new customer.

Ad network   A collection of independent web sites of which each has an arrangement with a single advertising broker to place banner advertisements.

Aesthetics of site design   Graphics + Colour + Style + Layout + Typography.

Affiliate marketing   A commission-based arrangement where referring sites (publishers) receive a commission on sales or leads by merchants (retailers).

Affiliate networks   Brokers known also as affiliate managers who manage the form of links, tracking and payment between a merchant and a range of affiliates.

AIDA model   Attention, Interest, Desire, Action. A hierarchy of responses model to communications.

ALEA model   Attention, Learning, Emotional response and Acceptance. A hierarchy of responses model to communications.

Allowable customer acquisition cost (CPA)   The maximum acceptable cost for gaining a new customer typically based on consideration of the lifetime value for gaining that customer type.

Animated ads   A *GIF* file is used to present a sequence of several different images to the viewer.

Anti-aliasing   A technique to smooth the edges of curves or fonts in graphic images such as *GIF* or *JPEG*.

ATR model   Awareness, Trial and Reinforcement.

Attention   One of Hofacker's five stages of web site information processing. Can the site attract the customer's attention?

Attrition rates   Percentage of site visitors that are lost at each stage in making an online purchase.

Average order value (AOV)   The typical amount spent in a single visit to a retail site for a particular customer group.

Auctions   A buying model where traders make offers and bids to sell or buy under certain conditions.

Auditing   An independent body verifies the number of *page impressions* and *visitors* for a *web site*.

Autoresponders   Software tools or 'agents' running on a *web server* which automatically send a standard reply to the sender of an e-mail message.

Bandwidth   Bandwidth indicates the speed at which data is transferred using a particular network media. It is measured in bits-per-second (bps).

Banner adverts   A typically rectangular graphic displayed on a web page for purposes of brandbuilding or driving traffic to a site. It is normally possible to perform a *click-through* to access further information from another web site.

Banner adverts, animated   Early banner adverts only featured a single advert, but today they will typically involve several different images which are displayed in sequence to attract attention to the banner and build up a theme, often ending with a call to action to click on the banner.

Bid management software   Software for automating the process of managing *PPC marketing* for large PPC campaigns. Bids are adjusted automatically in line with bidding strategy parameters set by the user.

Blog   An online diary regularly updated by an individual or group with topical news and views.

Bluejacking   Sending a message from a mobile phone or transmitter to another mobile phone which is in close range via *Bluetooth* technology (without the user's permission).

Blueprints   Show the relationships between pages and other content components, and can be used to portray organization, navigation and labelling systems.

Bluetooth   A standard for wireless transmission of data between devices, e.g. a mobile phone and a *PDA*.

Breadcrumbs   An indication of position in site structure which also allow users to go up a level within the site.

Broadband   A term referring to methods of delivering information across the Internet at a higher rate by increasing *bandwidth*, e.g. fibre-optic cable access.

Brochureware   A web site in which a company has migrated their existing paper-based promotional literature onto the Internet without recognizing the differences required by this medium.

Browser safe palettes   A set of 216 standard colours designed to achieve colour consistency on different web browsers where the display colours are set to 256 colour.

Business cards (interactive)   A CD-ROM of a similar size to a business card containing company and product information.

Business models   A summary of how a company will generate revenue identifying its product offering, value-added services, revenue sources and target customers.

Business-to-business (B2B)   Commercial transactions between an organization and other organizations.

Business-to-business (B2B) exchanges   Virtual locations with facilities to enable trading between buyers and sellers.

Business-to-consumer (B2C)   Commercial transactions are between an organization and consumers.

Buy-side e-commerce   E-commerce transactions between a purchasing organization, its suppliers and partners.

Call-back   A direct response facility available on the web site for a company to contact a customer by phone at a later time as specified by the customer.

Cannibalization   Sales achieved via an e-commerce site replace sales traditionally via other channels.

Card sorting or web classification   The process of arranging a way of organizing objects on the web sites in a consistent manner.

Channel conflict   A significant threat arising from the introduction of an Internet channel is that while *disintermediation* gives the opportunity for a company to sell direct and increase profitability on products, it can also threaten existing distribution arrangements with existing partners.

Churn rate   The percentage rate at which customers stop/lapse in use of a service or product.

Clicks and mortar   A business combining an online and offline presence.

Clickstream   A record of the path a user takes through a web site. Clickstreams enable site designers to assess how their site is being used.

Click-through   A click-through (ad click) occurs each time a user clicks on *banner adverts* with the mouse to direct them to a *web page* with further information.

Click-through rates (CTR)   The click-through rate is expressed as a percentage of total ad impressions, and refers to the proportion of users viewing *banner adverts* who click on them. It is calculated as the number of *click-throughs* divided by the number of ad impressions.

Cloaking   Serving different pages to a visitor than those indexed by a search engine. This is unethical, but surprisingly common. One example is using hidden text on the site that can't be seen by visitors, another is serving different pages to the searchers to those served to search engine robots by identifying the type of visitor.

Co-branding   An arrangement between two or more companies where they agree jointly to display content and perform joint-promotion using brand logos or a *banner advert*. The aim is that the brands are strengthened if they are seen as complementary. This is a reciprocal arrangement which can occur without payment.

Co-browsing   Customers screen can be viewed by the call-centre operator in combination with *callback* or *realtime chat*.

Co-buying   Group buying enabling a reduction in price for a volume purchase.

Collaborative filtering   Profiling of customer interests coupled with delivery of specific information and offers, often based on the interests of groups of similar customers.

Commoditization   Products are selected primarily on price due to minimal differences between competitive products.

Comprehension   One of Hofacker's five stages of web site information processing. Does the customer understand the message as intended?

Contact strategy   The approach to achieve the desired pattern of customer contacts, e.g. principally e-mail, unresolved e-mail queries resolved by phone after two exchanges.

Content   Content is the design, text and graphical information which forms a *web page*. Good content is the key to attracting customers to a web site and retaining their interest or achieving repeat visits.

Content management system (CMS)   A software tool/web application for creating, editing and updating documents accessed by intranet, extranet, or Internet.

Content owners   Company staff, usually within the business who are responsible for updating content.

Continuous traffic building activities   Communications activities such as affiliate marketing, search engine marketing and online sponsorship intended to drive visitors to the site which tend not to occur in short burst campaigns, but across the year.

Convergence   A trend in which different hardware devices such as TVs, computers and phones merge and have similar functions.

Conversion rate   Percentage of site visitors that perform a particular action such as making a purchase.

Cookie   Small text files placed on an end-user's computer to enable web sites to identify the user. They enable a company to identify a previous visitor to a *web site*, and build up a profile of their behaviour.

Cost per acquisition (CPA)   The cost of acquiring a new customer. Typically limited to the communications cost and refers to cost per sale for new customers. May also refer to other outcomes such as cost per quote or enquiry.

Cost per click   The cost of each click from a referring site to a destination site, typically from a search engine in pay per click search marketing.

Cost per thousand (CPM)   Cost per 1000 *ad impressions* for a *banner advert*.

Countermediation   A response to *reintermediation* where an established organization creates or purchases a rival portal that is positioned as independent or part of an existing brand.

Customer lifetime value (LTV)   A modelled future value of customers over a set number of years based on future purchases and customer acquisition and management costs.

Customer orientation   Providing content, services and offers on a *web site* consistent with the different characteristics of the audience of the site.

Customer preferred channel   Customer prefers a particular channel for certain activities, e.g. phone to purchase, e-mail for support.

Customer-to-business (C2B)   Customer is proactive in making an offer to a business, e.g. the price they are prepared to pay for an airline ticket.

Customer-to-customer (C2C)   Interactions between customers on a web site, e.g. posting/reading of topics on an electronic bulletin board.

Customer scenarios   Alternative tasks or outcomes required by a visitor to a web site. Typically accomplished in a series of stages of different tasks involving different information needs or experiences.

Customer unions   The same as *co-buying*.

Data mining   Searching organizational databases in order to uncover hidden patterns or relationships in groups of data. Data mining software attempts to represent information in new ways so that previously unseen patterns or trends can be identified.

Data warehouse   Data warehouses are large database systems containing detailed company data on sales transactions which are analysed to assist in improving the marketing performance of companies.

Database driven marketing   The process of systematically collecting data about past, current and/or potential customers, maintaining the integrity of the data by continually monitoring customer purchases, by inquiring about changing status and using the data to formulate marketing tactics and foster personalized relationships with customers.

Destination site   Frequently used to refer to the site that is visited following a *click-through* on a banner advert. Could also apply to any site visited following a click on a *hyperlink*.

Digital audio broadcasting (DAB) radio   Digital radio with clear sound quality with the facility to transmit text, images and video.

Digital value   Offers or services that can only be accessed or delivered online.

Direct response   Usually achieved in an Internet marketing context by banner ads, *callback services* or *e-mail marketing*.

Directories   A directory provides a structured listing of registered web sites in different categories. They are similar to an electronic version of the *Yellow Pages*.

Disintermediation   The removal of intermediaries such as distributors or brokers that formerly linked a company to its customers. It enables a company to sell direct to the customer by 'cutting-out the middleman'.

Dithering   The browser renders the nearest match to a colour when the site designer has used a colour which is not in the *browser safe palette* and the user's monitor is set to 256 colours.

Doorway pages   Pages deliberately created which are optimized for particular key phrases or search engines in order to increase listings in SERPS which often re-direct to other pages in sites. Typically they are entry points that are not part of the main navigation. They are considered to be an unethical approach known as search engine spamming. Ethical search marketers instead create search entry pages that are part of the main site navigation which are themed around particular phrases customers are likely to use.

Dynamic ad targeting   Specific ads are served in real-time to visitor clusters according to their characteristics and behaviour assessed by content types viewed.

E-business   All electronically mediated information exchanges, both within an organization and with external stakeholders supporting the range of business processes.

E-commerce   All electronically mediated information exchanges between an organization and its external stakeholders. Can refer to purchase transactions only.

EDGE   Evolved Data for GSM Evolution. Intermediate mobile standard between *GSM* and *UMTS*.

E-mail   Push sending of messages or documents, such as news about a new product or sales promotion.

E-mail inbound   E-mails received by a company from customers and other stakeholders.

E-marketing   Achieving marketing objectives through use of electronic communications technology.

Enterprise application integration (EAI)   The middleware technology that is used to connect together different software applications and their underlying databases is now known as 'enterprise application integration (EAI)'.

Enterprise resource planning   Software providing integrated functions for major business functions such as production, distribution, sales, finance and human resources management.

Environment scanning   The process of continuously monitoring the environment and events, and responding accordingly.

E-procurement   The electronic integration and management of all procurement activities including purchase request, authorization, ordering, delivery and payment between a purchaser and a supplier.

Expert reviews   Often performed at the beginning of a redesign project as a way of identifying problems with a previous design.

Exposure   One of Hofacker's five stages of web site information processing. Does the customer see the message?

Extended enterprise   Functions of an organization *outsourced* as part of a *value network*.

Extranet Formed by extending the *intranet* beyond a company to customers, suppliers, collaborators or even competitors. This is password protected to prevent access by general *Internet* users.

Fast moving consumer goods (FMCG) The term says it all.

Firewall A specialized software application mounted on a server at the point the company is connected to the Internet. Its purpose is to prevent unauthorized access into the company from outsiders.

Focus groups Online these follow a bulletin board or discussion group form where different members of the focus group respond to prompts from the moderator and each other.

FRAC A data analysis technique based on assessing the Frequency, Recency Amount and Category of purchases by customers.

Frames A technique used to divide a *web page* into different parts such as a menu and separate content.

General Packet Radio Services (GPRS) A standard offering mobile data transfer and WAP access approximately five to ten times faster than traditional GSM access.

Geographical portal A *portal* limited to a single country, area or city.

GIF (Graphic Interlaced File) GIF is a graphic format used to display images within a *web page*. An interlaced GIF is displayed gradually on the screen building up an image in several passes.

Globalization The increase of international trading and shared social and cultural values.

Google dance A periodic change to the search engine algorithm weighting that affects rankings and so causing companies' positions in the SERPS to change, sometimes dramatically.

Graphics-intensive sites Sites in which white space or large images are mainly used to convey the message rather than text.

Group characterization Web site communications are based on grouping people's preferences as part of *mass customization*.

Hit A hit is recorded for each graphic or block of text requested from a *web server*. It is not a reliable measure for the number of people viewing a page.

Horizontal portal A *portal* with a wide audience or *reach* offering general services, e.g. Yahoo!, MSN.

HTML HTML (hypertext markup language) is a standard format used to define the text and layout of a *web page*. HTML files usually have the extension .HTML or .HTM.

Hubs Alternative term for *B2B exchange*.

Ideal customer Preferred customer who is targeted due to their potential for a profitable relationship.

I-MODE A successful mobile standard originating in Japan that enables transfer of colour images between phones.

Incidental advertising Offline advertising where the web address is incidental to the main aim and creative.

Indirect online contribution Assesses the influence of the web site in generating offline purchases.

Individualization   Tailoring of content or offer to individual preferences.

Infobots   Software tools that collect information from the web for their users according to predefined preferences.

Infomediaries   An *intermediary* business whose main source of revenue derives from capturing consumer information and developing detailed profiles of individual customers for use by third parties.

Information architecture   The combination of organization, labelling, and navigation schemes comprising an information system.

Information-intensive sites   Sites in which text is mainly used to convey the message rather than white space or large images.

Interactive banner ads   Banner ads where the user can type in information and receive a response, for example loan interest for a particular loan.

Interactive business cards   A CD-ROM of a similar size to a business card containing company and product information.

Interactive kiosks   Fixed site access to information about an organization and its services through a PC simplified through touch-screen access.

Interactive radio   Access to radio via a web site or digital radio.

Intermediary   Online sites that help bring different parties such as buyers and sellers together. Pay a similar role to traditional brokers or channel partners.

Internet   The physical network that links computers across the globe. It consists of the infrastructure of network servers and communications links between them that are used to hold and transport information between the clients and servers.

Internet value proposition   See **Online Value Proposition**.

Interstitial ads   Ads that appear between one page and the next.

Intranet   A network within a single company which enables access to company information using the familiar tools of the *Internet* such as *web browsers* and *e-mail*. Only staff within a company can access the intranet, which will be password protected.

IP address   The unique address of a computer accessing the Internet or a server used to host information (e.g. 207.68.156.58).

JPEG (Joint Photographics Experts Group)   A graphics file format and compression algorithm best used for photographs.

'Just-in-time'   An approach to operations management where inventory holding is minimized by manufacturing according to immediate demand.

Key performance indicators (KPIs)   Key measures collected to assess whether an organization's objectives are achieved.

Keyphrase   The combination of keywords typed into a search engine by a user.

Keyphrase analysis   A structured approach to identifying and selecting relevant combinations of keywords for *SEO marketing* and *PPC marketing*.

Keyphrase density   The percentage importance of a keyphrase in comparison with the total number of words within a title, meta tag or web page.

Knowledge management   Techniques and tools for disseminating knowledge within an organization. Knowledge is used to apply staff experience to problem solving.

Lean back medium   Used to describe traditional TV.

Lean forward medium   Used to describe interactive TV or web usage.

Legacy systems   Old IT systems on which an organization is reliant, but they do not meet the current organizational requirements.

Lifetime value (LTV)   The estimated value of a customer or group of customers integrated across their past, current and future revenue.

Link anchor text   The text used to form the blue underlined hyper link viewed in a web browser defined in the HTML source. For example: Visit Dave Chaffey's web log is created by the HTML code: <A HREF = "http://www.davechaffey.com">Visit Dave Chaffey's web log</A>

Link building   A structured activity to include good quality hyperlinks to your site from relevant sites with a good Page Rank.

Link farms   Interlinked sites set up to increase Page Rank. Considered to be *search engine spamming*.

Live chat sessions   A user asks questions of a company representative by typing into their browser. The representative replies in real-time.

Localization   Designing the content of the *web site* such that it is appropriate to different audiences in different countries.

Mass customization   Using technology to create tailored marketing messages or products for individual customers or a group of similar customers yet retain the economies of scale of mass marketing or production.

Measurement   A process that collects metrics to indicate the effectiveness of Internet marketing activities in meeting e-marketing objectives.

Meta tags   Text within an *HTML* (hypertext markup language) file summarizing the content of the site (content meta-tag) and relevant keywords (key-word meta-tag) that are matched against the keywords typed into search engines.

Meta-market switchboards   Third-parties that provide a single point of contact and deliver a range of services between customers and suppliers.

Microsite   Specialized *content* that is part of a media owner web site, e.g. ad specific content for a company on an independent portal.

Middleware   Software used to facilitate communications between business applications including data transfer and control.

Mixed-mode buying   The process by which customer switches between online and offline channels during the buying process.

Modems   Device used to connect to the Internet via phone lines. Converts signals from digital to analogue.

Natural or organic listings   The pages listing results from a search engine query which are displayed in a sequence according to relevance of match between the keyword phrase typed into a search engine and a web page according to a ranking algorithm used by the search engine.

Navigation   Navigation describes the methods of finding and moving between different information and pages on a web site. It is governed by menu arrangements, site structure and the layout of individual *Web pages*.

Negative working capital   Working capital refers to money tied up in stocks and debtors. If *Just-in-time* delivery occurs and customer payments are taken in advance of supplier payment, negative working capital can be created.

Offline promotion   Offline promotion uses traditional media such as TV or newspaper advertising and word of mouth to promote a company's *web site*.

One-to-one marketing   Communication and tailoring of offer at an individual level.

Online PR   Maximizing favourable mentions of your company, brands, products or web sites on third-party web sites that are likely to be visited by your target audience.

Online promotion   Online promotion uses communication via the *Internet* itself to raise awareness about a *web site* and drive traffic to it, e.g. *hyperlinks* from other *web sites, banner adverts* or targeted *electronic mail (e-mail)*.

Online reputation management   Controlling the reputation of an organization through monitoring and controlling messages placed about the organization.

Online revenue contribution   An assessment of the extent to which the *Internet* contributes to sales is a key measure of the importance of the Internet to a company.

Online surveys   Surveys on-site through pop-up questionnaires.

Online value proposition   Defines an organization's online offering distinct from offline or competitor offering.

Onsite search engine   Search engine specific to a single site to help users find content.

Opt-in e-mail   The customer is only contacted when they have explicitly asked for information to be sent to them (usually when filling in onscreen *forms*).

Opt-out   The customer is not contacted subsequently if they have explicitly stated they do not want to be contacted in future. Opt-out or *unsubscribe* options are usually available within the e-mail itself.

Outsourcing   Contracting an outside company to undertake e-marketing (or any) activities.

Page impressions   A *page impression* denotes one person viewing one web page.

Page template   A defined layout that is used throughout the site.

Page Rank   An index used to assessed the interconnections between web pages. A trademark of Google. Based on 'link popularity' or the number of inbound links and the Page Rank of the linking sites.

Paid for inclusion (PFI)   The advertiser specifies pages with specific URLs for incorporation into the search engine organic listings. There is a setup fee and/or annual fee and pay per click charge.

Panel   Members are recruited in order that their TV or web usage can be measured.

Panel data   Includes time and duration of access and content accessed for different geodemographics.

Partner relationship management   Management of marketing activities performed by downstream (or upstream) channel partners.

Pay per click (PPC) search marketing   Refers to when a company pays for text ads to be displayed on the search engine results pages when a specific key phrase is entered by the search users. It is so called since the marketer pays for each time the hypertext link in the ad is clicked on.

Permission-based marketing   Customers agree (*opt-in*) to be involved in an organization's marketing activities usually as a result of an incentive.

Personas   A summary of the characteristics, needs, motivations and environment of typical web site users.

Personal digital assistants (PDAs)   Digital organizers with a touch screen that can be used to access the Internet and personal productivity applications.

Personal video recorder (PVR) or digital video recorder (DVR)   Home consumer electronics device that records television shows to a hard disk in digital format.

Personalization   Delivering customized content for the individual either through *web pages*, *e-mail* or *push technology*.

Person-to-person (P2P)   *Intermediaries* such as Napster which enable individuals to share information or files, similar to *C2C*.

Plug-in   A program that must be downloaded to view particular content such as an animation.

Portals   A web site that acts as a gateway to the information on the Internet by providing search engines, directories and other services such as personalized news or free e-mail.

Price transparency   Prices can be readily compared by purchasers using the Internet, particularly through *shopping bots*.

Privacy   Concerns that affect an individual's or company's personal details.

Profiling   Determining the customer key characteristics to enable *segmentation*.

Promotion   *Online promotion* uses communication via the Internet itself to raise awareness about a site and drive traffic to it. This promotion may take the form of links from other sites, banner adverts or targeted e-mail messages. *Offline promotion* uses traditional media such as TV or newspaper advertising and word of mouth to promote a company's *web site*.

Prosumer   Typically 'proactive consumer', but see the range of definitions on pages 43–5.

Reach   The audience size of a web site as a percentage of total possible audience.

Really Simple Syndication (RSS)   An extension of blogging where a blog, news or any type of content is received by specialist RSS reader software such as RSS reader (www. rssreader.com). It offers a method of receiving news that uses a different broadcast method to e-mail, so is not subject to the same conflicts with SPAM or SPAM filters.

Realtime chat   A customer support operator in a call-centre can type responses to a site visitor's questions.

Reciprocal links   Two organizations agree to link to each other's sites.

Redirects   A temporary web page or address is used, often for measurement purposes, before the required page is served to the user.

Referrals   The number of links from other sites.

Referrers   A previously visited site from which the user followed links to reach the current site. Can also refer to offline referrers such as print ads.

Reintermediation   The creation of new intermediaries between customers and suppliers providing services such as supplier search and product evaluation.

Relationship building   Consistent application of up-to-date knowledge of individual customers to product and service design which is communicated interactively in order to develop a continuous and long-term relationship which is mutually beneficial.

Repeat visits   A *tagged* visitor is recorded as visiting a site again.

Representation   Defines all the locations on the Internet where an organization is referred to or purchases can be made. Includes own web site and intermediary sites.

Repurposing   Porting content from one digital platform to another, for example, web to interactive digital TV.

Return path   An interaction where the customer sends information to the provider using a phone line or cable.

Return on investment (ROI)   A measure of the value derived from a marketing campaign (or any business activity) compared to its costs. There are many forms of ROI equation, but they can be simplified to: Profit generated from activity divided by amount spent on activity (over a defined period of time).

Revenue models   Different options for generating revenue from an online presence including sale, affiliate, subscription and advertising.

Reverse auctions   The buyer places a request for tender or quotation (RFQ) and many suppliers compete, decreasing the price with the supplier with the lowest price winning the contract.

Rich media adverts   *Banner adverts* that are not static, but provide animation, sound or interactivity. An example of this would be a banner advert for a loan in which a customer can type in the amount of loan required, and the cost of the loan is calculated immediately.

Robots   A software tool employed by *search engines* to regularly index web pages of registered sites. Can also refer to any automated agent.

Scenarios   See *Customer scenarios*.

Scenario-based design   Site design and testing is based on common path or flow of events or activities performed by visitors.

Screen resolution   Number of pixels (dots) displayed, e.g. 800 across by 600 vertical.

Search bots   Software agents that search the web for information based on keywords.

Search engine   A specialized website that uses automatic tools known as *spiders* or *robots* to index web pages of registered sites. Users can search the index by typing in keywords to specify their interest.

Search engine optimization (SEO)   A structured approach used to increase the relative ranking position of a company or its products in search engine *natural* or *organic* results listings on *search engine results pages* for selected *keyphrases*.

Search engine results pages (SERPS)   The pages generated and displayed by a search engine after a search engine user types in their key phrase.

Search engine spamming   Unethical actions deliberately taken by marketers to mislead the search engines and give a higher ranking such as repeated use of *keyphrases* and use of *link farms*, *doorway pages* and *cloaking*. Search engines may penalize if they detect spamming.

Second layer selling   Product is sold via an intermediary.

Secure Electronic Transaction (SET)   A standard for public-key encryption intended to enable secure e-commerce transactions lead-developed by Mastercard and Visa.

Secure Sockets Layer (SSL)   A commonly used encryption technique for scrambling data as it is passed across the Internet from a customer's web browser to a merchant's web server.

Security   Security attributes include:

1 *Authentication* – are parties to the transaction who they claim to be? This is achieved through the use of digital certificates.

2 *Privacy* and *confidentiality* – is transaction data protected? The consumer may want to make an anonymous purchase. Are all non-essential traces of a transaction removed from the public network and all intermediary records eliminated?

3 *Integrity* – checks that the message sent is complete, i.e. that it isn't corrupted.

4 *Non-repudiability* – ensures the sender cannot deny sending the message.

5 *Availability* – how can threats to the continuity and performance of the system be eliminated?

Segmentation   Identification of different groups within a target market in order to develop different offerings for the groups.

Sell-side, e-commerce   E-commerce transactions between a supplier organization, intermediaries and its customers.

Share of wallet   Amount of customer income spent at a single organization as a proportion of all expenditure in a category, e.g. financial services.

Shopping bots   Software agents that find the lowest price for a specified product.

Short message service (SMS)   Also known as text messaging between mobiles.

SOSTAC®   SOSTAC® is a simple planning system covering Situation Analysis, Objectives, Strategy, Tactics, Action and Control. SOSTAC® was created by P.R. Smith in 1993. SOSTAC® is a registered trademark of PR Smith. See www.PRSmith.org for more.

SPAM   Unsolicited e-mail (usually bulk mailed and untargeted).

Spamming   Bulk sending of SPAM.

Specific advertising   Offline ads that specifically highlight the *online value proposition*.

Spiders   Automatic tools known as spiders or robots index registered sites. Users search by typing keywords and are presented with a list of pages.

Statement of origination   A message in an opt-in e-mail showing who has sent the message and why they have permission to send it.

Static ads   *Banner ads* that are not *animated*.

Stickiness   An indication of the duration of how long a visitor stays on a site.

Strategy, e-marketing   Definition of the future direction and actions of a company defined as approaches to achieve specific objectives.

SWOT   Internal strengths and weaknesses, external opportunities and threats.

Superstitials   Pop-up adverts that require interaction to remove them.

Tagging visitors   Tracking of origin of site visitors, their actions and spending.

Touch strategy   The sequence, frequency and content of outbound communications such as e-mail and direct mail.

Traffic building   The use of *online promotion* and *offline promotion* techniques to increase the audience of a site (both new and existing customers).

Unified message service   *Portal* offering combined access to mobile, landline and e-mail messaging, e.g. e-mails can be heard by phone.

Uniform resource locator (URL)   A unique web address in the format, for example, http://www.company.com.

Unique visitors   The number of individuals who visit a web site in a fixed time period.

UMTS   Universal Mobile Telecommunications System. The standard for *3G mobile access*.

URL strategy   A defined approach to how content is labelled through placing it in different directories/folders with distinct web addresses.

URL rewriting   A technique used to make complex web addresses for pages associated with dynamic content such as product catalogues or news articles visible to search engines.

Usability   An engineering approach to website design to ensure the user interface of the site is learnable, memorable, error free, efficient and gives user satisfaction. It incorporates testing and evaluation to ensure the best use of navigation and links to access information in the shortest possible time.

User testing   Representative users are observed performing representative tasks using a system.

Value chain   A model for analysis of how supply chain activities can add value to products and services delivered to the customer.

Value networks   The links between an organization and its strategic and non-strategic partners that form its external value chain.

Vertical integration   The extent to which supply chain activities are undertaken and controlled *within* the organization.

Vertical portal   A *portal* with specialized content, often for a vertical market.

Viral marketing   E-mail is used to transmit a promotional message to another potential customer. 'Online word of mouth'.

Virtual assistants   Different types of software agents such as shopping bots and infobots.

Virtual business   An organization which uses information and communications technology to allow it to operate without clearly defined physical boundaries between different functions. It provides customized services by outsourcing production and other functions to third parties.

Virtual communities   A customer-to-customer interaction delivered via e-mail groups, web-based discussion forums or chat.

Virtual integration   The majority of supply chain activities are undertaken and controlled *outside* the organization by third parties.

Visitor session   One visit by a single customer. Visit ends after no activity for 30 minutes. The number of unique visitors is always less than visitor sessions.

Visits, site   The number of visits to a web site in a fixed time period.

Voice portals   Portals that can be accessed by phone to hear information such as news or e-mails.

Web accessibility   Designing web sites so that they can be used by people with visual impairment or whatever browser/access platform they use.

Web analytics   Techniques used to assess and improve the contribution of e-marketing to a business including reviewing traffic volume, referrals, clickstreams, online reach data, customer satisfaction surveys, leads and sales.

Walled garden   Access is limited to a selection of online stores – characteristic of interactive digital TV.

Web browsers   Browsers such as Netscape Navigator or Microsoft Internet Explorer provide an easy method of accessing and viewing information stored as *HTML* (hypertext markup language) web documents on different *web servers*.

Web log file   A log file analyser is a software tool used to summarize the information on visitor activity in a log file which contains a line defining the page, access time and *IP address* of the visitor.

Web pages   A single page of a *web site*.

Web response ad campaign   An offline print or TV campaign where one of the main campaign objectives is to encourage ad viewers to visit the web site. For example, to request a sample, enter a competition, find further information or buy online.

Web servers   Used to store the *web pages* accessed by *web browsers*. It may also contain databases of customer or product information which can be queried and retrieved using a browser.

Webographics   The web access characteristics of users such as place of access, connection speed and experience.

Wi-Fi ('wireless fidelity')   A high-speed wireless local-area network enabling wireless access to the Internet for mobile, office and home users.

Wireframe   Also known as schematics, a way of illustrating the layout of an individual webpage.

Wireless application protocol (WAP)   Offers Internet browsing from mobile handsets. Mainly text-based sites developed in wireless markup language (WML).

World wide web   A medium for publishing information on the Internet. It is accessed through *web browsers* which display *web pages* and can now be used to run business applications. Company information is stored on *web servers* which are usually referred to as *web site*.

XML or eXtensible Markup Language   A standard for transferring structured data, unlike HTML which is purely presentational.

XMOS (cross-media optimization studies)   XMOS research is designed to help marketers and their agencies answer the question 'What is the optimal mix of advertising vehicles across different media, in terms of frequency, reach and budget allocation, for a given campaign to achieve its marketing goals?' The mix between online and offline spend is varied to maximize campaign metrics such as reach, brand awareness and purchase intent.

Yielding   One of Hofacker's five stages of web site information processing. Does the customer accept (believe) the message?

Index